STAT ONE

A NEW SYSTEM FOR RATING
BASEBALL'S ALL-TIME GREATEST PLAYERS

CRAIG MESSMER

New York   Chicago   San Francisco   Lisbon   London   Madrid   Mexico City
Milan   New Delhi   San Juan   Seoul   Singapore   Sydney   Toronto

The McGraw·Hill Companies

Library of Congress Cataloging-in-Publication Data

Messmer, Craig M.
    Stat one : a new system for rating baseball's all-time greatest players / Craig M.
    Messmer.
        p.   cm.
    ISBN-13: 978-0-07-149633-9 (alk. paper)
    ISBN-10: 0-07-149633-5 (alk. paper)
        1. Baseball—United States—History.   2. Baseball—United States—Statistics—
    History.   3. Baseball players—United States—History.   I. Title.

    GV863.A1M47   2008
    796.357—dc22   2007026339

Copyright © 2008 by Craig Messmer. All rights reserved. Printed in the United States of America. Except as permitted under the United States Copyright Act of 1976, no part of this publication may be reproduced or distributed in any form or by any means, or stored in a database or retrieval system, without the prior written permission of the publisher.

1 2 3 4 5 6 7 8 9 10 11 12 13 14 15 16 17 18 19 20   FGR/FGR   0 9 8 7

ISBN 978-0-07-149633-9
MHID   0-07-149633-5

Interior design by Rattray Design

McGraw-Hill books are available at special quantity discounts to use as premiums and sales promotions, or for use in corporate training programs. For more information, please write to the Director of Special Sales, Professional Publishing, McGraw-Hill, Two Penn Plaza, New York, NY 10121-2298. Or contact your local bookstore.

This book is printed on acid-free paper.

This book is dedicated to the memory of my grandfather, Thomas Bertram (who taught me virtually everything I know about baseball history), to my son, Ryan Bertram (may he one day crack the top 100), and to all those in the on-deck circle.

Contents

Foreword by Bill Madden   vii

Acknowledgments   ix

Introduction   xi

1   Methodology and Organization   1

2   Catcher   17

3   First Base   49

4   Second Base   87

5   Third Base   121

6   Shortstop   147

7   Left Field   179

8   Center Field   215

9   Right Field   247

10   Multiposition   291

11   Nineteenth-Century Stars   313

12   Negro League Stars   321

13   The Top 100   329

Conclusion   365

Appendix A: Career P/E Averages   367

Appendix B: Single-Season P/E Averages   369

Appendix C: Career MVP Shares   371

Appendix D: C5 P/E Calculations   373

Index   425

Foreword

Before I begin singing the praises here for Craig Messmer's terrific and thought-provoking *Stat One*, in the interest of full disclosure I have to say I hate what all these stat geeks are doing to baseball. It's like we've totally removed the human element from the game, reducing players to numbers and percentages. Almost every general manager in baseball now employs at least one and usually two or three stat geeks to run numbers on a player before a making a trade. Whatever happened to the days when GMs would gather information from their scouts—including perhaps the most important factor of all, the player's makeup—and then consummate deals on cocktail napkins over drinks in the hotel bar? I had to laugh at what a GM told me during the summer of 2007 about a relief pitcher in his minor league system who was striking out more than a batter per inning but was reputed to have only one out pitch—a changeup. When informed that scouts who had been watching this kid every day maintained he had a fastball that could reach the mid-90s, the GM confessed: "I have to tell you, we never actually saw him. We signed him off stats."

Anyway, that's my rant on stats—and it's kind of what I told Craig Messmer when he contacted me for advice as to how to get his own statistics project off the ground. "Would you just take a little time to look at it and tell me what you think?" he said. Reluctantly, I agreed, and a couple of days later this rather sizeable package arrived at my office at the *New York Daily News*.

Perhaps it was because Craig was so persistent, but my curiosity got the best of me, and I started wading through the material, astonished that I was actually understanding it. His formulas for evaluating players' performance—nothing about makeup, mind you—make sense, to the point where I asked myself, "Why hasn't anyone else ever come up with something like this?" For instance, Craig uses what he calls "complete bases" (as opposed to the longtime standard "total bases") as part of his offensive performance formula, in which he includes walks, hit-by-pitches, and stolen bases and subtracts caught-stealings. All these years, we just assumed total bases was all-inclusive.

While, again, I would never suggest GMs should use *Stat One* as a primary tool for evaluating players, it seems to me this is an invaluable resource for comparing players in all eras. I was glad, for example, that Craig's formulas determined the Red Sox's David Ortiz had a slightly better offensive season than Alex Rodriguez in 2006, as I would have voted for Ortiz for MVP despite the fact he was a DH. I just thought he was a more productive player than A-Rod, especially in the clutch, and that A-Rod didn't win any games with his glove.

Just as interesting, however, is Craig's analysis of players' Hall of Fame credentials. I usually vote for the same five or six players every year, but I will definitely consult with *Stat One* in the future for "on the bubble" guys. In that respect, Craig has won me over on Jim Rice, whose lifetime numbers belie the dominant slugger he was in the American League for 10 years. I also found interesting his reaffirmation of the Baseball Writers Association's conclusion that Gil Hodges, popular as he was in New York, fell short of Hall of Fame status as a player. On the other hand, I respectfully differ with his opinion that my all-time favorite player, Nellie Fox, was not a Hall-of-Famer.

What I think will be most impressive to the average fan is the thoroughness of Craig's research and analysis in rating the all-time best players and the Hall of Fame. He didn't just limit his ratings to the usual suspects. He included just about everybody's favorite player.

Bill Madden

Acknowledgments

So many people have been helpful and instrumental in this project that I hope I don't forget anyone. Bill Parcells has been a good friend to my mother and our family for decades. He is the one who got the ball rolling for me when this entire book was nothing more than an idea and a whole bunch of handwritten statistics and notes with no sense of where it might lead. He introduced me to my first real contact, and for that I'm thankful.

Bill Madden of the *Daily News* was that contact, and he bought into my idea and my new statistic right from the beginning. I'll never forget that sunny Friday morning when I first met Bill in the newsroom for a face-to-face meeting that took my project to the next level. He's a tremendous source of baseball knowledge. He's also a great guy.

I owe a tremendous amount of gratitude to my agent, Robert Wilson, of Wilson Media. Rob just happens to be Bill Madden's guy as well, and I couldn't have hoped for a better agent with whom to do business. While I typed and typed, Rob did all of the other legwork necessary to get this into the hands, minds, and eyes of publishers. This book would not have happened without his expertise.

McGraw-Hill agreed to take a chance on a first-time author, and I'm certainly glad they did. Throughout, everyone there has been extremely cooperative, knowledgeable, and creative regarding this project. Especially, I'd like to recognize the outstanding work of Ron Martirano, who was our first contact at McGraw-Hill. A fellow Mets fan, Ron has really been a driving force in getting this done. I'd like to also recognize the tireless work of Craig Bolt, Stacy Shands, and their respective staffs. Thank you for all you've done.

My friends have been very important to me. They have had my back and always encouraged me to be my best. Rory Camangian, also my business advisor, has helped spread the word about my book. Mike Shatzer, the funniest man I know, provided some very helpful feedback and was immediately enthusiastic about the concept. Thanks to them and all my other close friends.

Baseballreference.com is the best website I found in terms of anything related to baseball. I used it extensively throughout this book's formulation, and I am grateful that it is available. I would recommend it to anyone interested in the sport, its players, and their statistics.

Naturally, these Acknowledgments wouldn't be complete without thanking my family. They have always been there for me. Their encouragement, support, and love have meant more to me than they could ever possibly know. My brother, Don, has taught me so much about baseball. My mother has taught me so much about life.

I've saved the best for last. My wife, Megan, has invested almost as much as I have in this book. When I have needed countless hours on the computer, she has been there taking care of everything else. She does it without asking for anything in return, and I love her for that and for a million other things. I couldn't have completed this long journey without her, and I wouldn't even have wanted to try. She has my eternal respect and devotion.

Introduction

Baseball is a game ultimately defined by its history and its numbers: 755, .406, 56 in a row. These are some of the most recognizable statistics in all of sports, and they help provide baseball its identity and structure. They are eternal.

Growing up as a young baseball fan, I would often listen to my grandfather talk about these numbers and about the great players I never would have the chance to see play. Slowly, the statistics and the stories began to seep into my consciousness and take root. As I searched for a way to understand everything he was teaching me and to organize it into a form I could understand, I began to develop a love for statistical analysis. I also began to ask questions that I couldn't find plausible and consistent answers to regarding the game's immortal stars and what they accomplished. Who is the best shortstop ever? How does Mickey Mantle compare with Willie Mays? Did DiMaggio really deserve the MVP in 1941, or should it have gone to Ted Williams? Was Cobb better than Hornsby? Who is the greatest baseball player in history?

The idea behind this book was to search for a single measure of a baseball player's offensive effectiveness. The title, *Stat One*, is symbolic: it attempts to succinctly communicate the notion that a comprehensive statistic could be developed to analyze and compare baseball players across history with one another and to help answer those questions just posed and the countless others that remain unanswered. To my knowledge, no statistic like this currently exists, or has ever existed for that matter.

If you ask any baseball fan to give the one best statistic available to determine a player's offensive success, then you will probably get many different answers: Batting average. Runs batted in. Home-run percentage. OPS (on-base plus slugging). These statistics, while beneficial, are limited.

Measures of efficiency, such as batting average, on-base percentage, slugging percentage, OPS, walk-to-strikeout ratio, stolen bases, and so forth, do not take into account a player's run production. A player, for example, might have a high batting average and get on base a great deal, yet rarely score or drive in runs. Measures of production, runs scored and runs batted in, are often dependent on other players in a lineup. Unless he hits a home run, a player needs teammates to be on base in order to knock them in, and he needs to be driven home by those batting behind him. I have decided to fix this problem by combining traditional measures of production and efficiency into a single objective score that is easy to comprehend.

The goal of this book is twofold. First, it intends to introduce a new statistic never before formulated. That statistic is called Offensive Production and Efficiency Average, or P/E Average for short. Incorporating aspects of production and efficiency into one understandable number, P/E Average is a comprehensive measure of a player's overall offensive contribution, equitable in its design and applicable to every player who has ever played the game.

The second goal is to analyze, rate, and rank the greatest players in baseball history at each position. Objectively, I compare P/E Averages along with more traditional statistics, such as home runs, stolen bases, and slugging percentage. Subjectively, I study MVP performance, postseason success, defense, leadership, individual awards, and other measures of a player's overall contribution. I analyze a wide range of players, both past and present, rate them according to one of five categories, and then rank the 10 best players at each position. Finally, I offer my list of the 100 greatest players of all time. Again, these opinions are formed through analysis of both objective statistics and subjective measures of various types. I believe that is the best way to proceed.

Baseball will always be saturated with a hundred different statistics measuring everything from extra-base hits to intentional walks to grand slams. A big part of baseball's charm resides in the fact that it's fun to study all of these numbers and use them selectively in making the case for one player over another. My objective is not to replace what's out there. My objective is to enhance and clarify.

In examining various books and studies, charts and graphs, a vast array of mind-boggling formulas, and every type of all-time list imaginable, I have often come away feeling disappointed and more confused than when I began. My questions were not answered. In fact, the answers seemed to get more elusive because everything was scattered and random. There was no organization where there needed to be. In formulating Offensive Production and Efficiency Average and using it to review the game's all-time greats, I believe it to be the single best statistic available to measure a baseball player's offensive success and contribution. I hope you find my book to be informative, accurate, and enjoyable, and I hope it helps answer some of the questions you may have regarding the game's greatest players.

Please visit www.statonebaseball.com for more information about P/E Averages and baseball's greatest players.

Methodology and Organization

Methodology

Every time a batter steps to the plate, his level of success can be measured across two categories. First, effectiveness can be viewed in terms of production. Traditional statistics that measure production are runs batted in and runs scored. Second, a batter can be evaluated in terms of efficiency. I am defining efficiency as a player's ability to gain bases in relation to plate appearances. The more bases gained, the more efficient the player. Batting average, on-base percentage, slugging percentage, OPS (on-base plus slugging), stolen bases/caught stealing, and walks/strikeouts all measure efficiency. The problem with these traditional statistics is that they are limited and have inherent flaws. Let me elaborate on this notion of statistical limitations before I explain P/E Average and how it solves these problems.

Production

The ultimate goal of an offensive baseball player is to produce as many runs as possible for his team in order to maximize its chances of winning. The team with more runs is victorious, so producing runs is of ultimate importance. Looking at a player's statistics in terms of runs scored and runs batted in provides an accurate measure of how productive that player is. Production statistics have a direct relationship to winning and losing; the more runs produced, the higher the likelihood of victory.

Measures of production are limited, however, because they are often dependent on other players on a team. Unless a player hits a home run or steals his way around the bases after a base hit or walk, he needs his teammates' help to produce runs. He needs those in front of him to be on base to accumulate RBI, and he needs those behind him in the order to drive him home to score runs. A player fortunate enough to be on a talented team of All-Stars and Hall of Famers will likely have better production statistics in comparison with someone laboring on a team lacking offensive threats.

Efficiency

The majority of baseball statistics, such as batting average, slugging percentage, stolen bases, walks, and so on, measure efficiency. By efficiency I mean how many bases a player is able to gain in relation to plate appearances. A batter who has a .323 batting average is relatively efficient in comparison with the other players in a league where a .265 average is the norm. Furthermore, players who are on base often, have high slugging percentages, walk a lot, and are able to steal bases without being caught can be considered efficient. The benefit of analyzing efficiency statistics is that they are independent of teammates and, therefore, the fairest way to judge individual players. A player can have a high average, steal bases, and walk more than he strikes out even if he is on a poor team. A player can win the league batting title on a last-place team that doesn't score many runs. On the '96 Giants, a team that lost 94 games and scored only 752 runs, Barry Bonds was able to post high on-base (.461) and slugging (.615) percentages. Even though his teammates, who batted a combined .247, were not very efficient that year, Bonds was.

Although efficiency measures are a fair way to evaluate individual players, those same measures are ultimately flawed because teams don't win or lose based on efficiency. They win or lose based on run production. In 1993 Tony Gwynn hit .358, which was the second best average in the National League. However, he scored just 70 runs and drove in only 59. The Padres lost 101 games during that forgettable campaign. It can be argued that Gwynn's lack of production was the result of him being on a poor team. But it can also be argued that the Padres had a disappointing season because Gwynn failed to be productive in clutch situations.

The Confusion

Production statistics are tied to a team's ability to score runs. Therefore, they correlate directly with wins and losses, which are ultimately what matters. However, run production is often dependent on other players on a team, which creates an unequal playing field when comparing players on talented teams with those on poor offensive teams. Measures of efficiency, although fair and independent of teammates, have no direct result on scoring runs and winning games. Theoretically, a player can have high efficiency averages while rarely producing runs for his team's scoreboard. When analyzed separately, these statistics are limited and fail to present a definitive account of a player's overall offensive effectiveness.

The Solution

The new statistic I have developed, Offensive Production and Efficiency Average, incorporates measures of production and efficiency into a single, comprehensive score to gauge offensive performance. It is not meant as a replacement for conventional statistics. Rather, its purpose is to enhance and streamline statistical analysis by combining measures of production and efficiency, which has never been done. In devising and formulating P/E Average, my goal has been to create a fair, comprehensive, objective value so that players throughout baseball history can be compared, rated, and ranked in a more thorough manner than ever before.

The Statistic

Offensive Production and Efficiency Average assigns a point value for each plate appearance. A player accumulates points for generating runs and gaining bases through hits, walks, hit by pitch, and steals. This point accumulation is then divided by total plate appearances. The result, rounded off to the nearest thousandth, is a single, easy-to-understand score of offensive effectiveness.

Before I explain the specifics of how P/E Average is formulated, however, it is first necessary to define two terms, *net runs* and *complete bases*. In calculating P/E Averages, the production component comes from net runs and the efficiency component from complete bases. A thorough explanation with relevant examples is provided for each term.

Net Runs (Runs Scored + Runs Batted In − Home Runs). Net runs refers to the total number of team runs a player is directly responsible for providing. It is his individual contribution to his team's scoreboard. Net runs are calculated by adding runs scored and runs batted in and then subtracting home runs. For example, Willie Mays scored 123 runs, drove in 127, and hit 51 home runs for the Giants in 1955. By adding runs (123) plus RBI (127) and then subtracting home runs (51) we get Mays's net runs (199). For the 1955 season, Willie Mays was directly responsible for supplying 199 runs to his team's scoreboard over 152 games, which averages to 1.31 net runs per contest.

It is important to understand why home runs are subtracted when calculating this statistic. Let's pretend that Willie Mays came to bat in the third inning of a scoreless game. With men on first and third, Mays, as he did 660 times during his career, hits a home run. The Giants take a 3–0 lead. In our example, Mays registered one run scored and three runs batted in for a total of four. However, his team only has three runs on the scoreboard. If we simply add runs scored plus runs batted in, then we get an inaccurate measure. Therefore, to accurately define run production, it is necessary to add runs scored plus runs batted in and then subtract home runs. This total, which I call net runs, specifically delineates a player's contribution to his team's scoreboard.

Complete Bases (Total Bases + BB + Hit by Pitch + Stolen Bases − Caught Stealing). This statistic measures how many bases a player gains through a variety of means. A player who gets a double is essentially as efficient as a player who singles and steals second or a player who walks and steals. Furthermore, getting to first base through a base on balls has the same result as getting there by being hit by a pitch. Walk and HBP statistics are recorded separately from one another. Intentional walks, conversely, are already factored into walk totals and, therefore, do not get separate consideration when calculating complete bases.

I like the term *complete bases* because of the connotation that it is an all-encompassing measure of the number of bases a player gains. Analyzing only total bases as a sole efficiency statistic, which is how slugging percentage is determined, fails to take into account other ways players reach base and gain additional bases. By adding walks and hit-by-pitch totals, we get a more complete picture of how batters get on base. Furthermore, adding stolen bases accounts for players such as Ty Cobb and Rickey Henderson, who used their base-running expertise to move around the diamond without help from teammates. Stolen bases are then balanced by subtracting caught-stealing totals. While Henderson did steal 130 bags in 1982, he was also caught 42 times. It would favor base stealers unfairly if stolen bases were added without also subtracting the number of times they were unsuccessful.

In analyzing players from the early to mid-1900s, an unexpected problem became apparent. Although stolen-base statistics are complete, caught-stealing totals often are not. Henderson, who began his career in 1979, has complete totals. He swiped 1,406 bags and was caught 335 times during his career. In calculating his complete bases, one would take his total bases plus walks plus hit-by-pitch numbers, add 1,406, and subtract 335. Ty Cobb, on the other hand, played from 1905 through 1928 and had incomplete statistics. From 1905 to 1913 and 1917 to 1919, Cobb had 566 steals. However, baseball does not have any caught-stealing information over those 12 years. Common sense dictates that it would be all but impossible for him to steal 566 times without ever being caught; caught-stealing statistics simply were not recorded during those years. It would be unfair to give Cobb credit for all of those stolen bases without also subtracting for the times he was unsuccessful.

To solve this problem I have devised the following system for any player with missing caught-stealing statistics. I calculated the ratio of stolen bases to caught stealing in the years when complete statistics were made available. For example, Cobb had complete statistics from 1914 to 1916 and 1920 to 1928. During that time, his ratio, rounded off to the nearest hundredth, was 1.83 steals for every time he was caught stealing. I then applied that ratio to the years with incomplete statistics and to his career numbers. By dividing 892 (Cobb's career stolen bases) by 1.83 (his known ratio), I arrived at an estimated total, rounded off to the nearest whole number, of 487 times caught stealing for his career. For players with no information, I used a standard ratio of 2 steals per 1 time caught stealing.

P/E Average

Now that the calculation of net runs and complete bases is clear, we can progress to the formulation of P/E Average. P/E Average is calculated like this:

(net runs + net runs + complete bases) ÷ plate appearances

As stated earlier, P/E Average incorporates both production and efficiency measures into one score. The production aspect comes from net runs. Efficiency is determined by complete bases. The value that divides them both is plate appearances.

Why do net runs get counted twice? The answer is simple. The goal is to combine production and efficiency as equally as possible so that the individual statistical limitations discussed earlier can be eliminated, like a system of checks and balances. To approach a perfect 50/50 split, it is necessary to double net runs. Over the course of a season, a player will normally have about twice the number of complete bases as net runs. By doubling net runs, an equitable contribution is made from both production and efficiency. Consider the following example of Tony Perez's statistics during the 1976 season:

$$91 \text{ RBI} + 77 \text{ runs} - 19 \text{ HR} = 149 \text{ net runs (production)}$$
$$238 \text{ total bases} + 50 \text{ BB} + 5 \text{ HBP} + 10 \text{ SB} - 5 \text{ CS} =$$
$$298 \text{ complete bases (efficiency)}$$

By doubling the production side (net runs), we obtain a perfect 50/50 split. In 1976 Perez obtained 298 points of production (149 net runs + 149 net runs) and 298 points of efficiency (298 complete bases) for a total of 596 points over 586 plate appearances. Dividing 596 by 586 gives a P/E Average of 1.017 for Perez in '76. Of course, it doesn't normally work out this neatly. In 1974, for example, the Cincinnati slugger had 154 net runs and 335 complete bases. In 1975 he had 163 net runs and 294 complete bases. In 1974 Perez was more efficient. In 1975 he was more productive. In 1976 a perfect balance of 50 percent production and 50 percent efficiency was obtained. The goal is to combine equal parts of production and efficiency into a single comprehensive point value. This is best accomplished by doubling net runs.

Some players, such as Orlando Cepeda, got a majority of their points (52.7 percent for Cepeda) from efficiency. Some, such as Bill Terry, got a majority of their points (51.9 percent for Terry) from production. And others, such as Lou Gehrig (50.6 percent production, 49.4 percent efficiency) and Jimmie Foxx (49.4 percent production, 50.6 percent efficiency), hovered just around a 50/50 split for their careers. A player with a majority of his points from production is not necessarily productive in comparison with other players. It just means that he is more productive than efficient in comparison with himself.

P/E Averages should be viewed as a tool to help rate, rank, and compare players; however, subjective considerations to defense, leadership, individual awards, team performance, postseason success, and other intangibles are also extremely important. This balancing of objective statistical analysis and various subjective measures when evaluating players is employed throughout this book; I feel that it's the best way to rate, rank, and compare players.

Organization

Beginning with the catchers in Chapter 2, each position is analyzed in the same numbered order they follow on the baseball diamond. Each chapter begins with an introduction followed by a career P/E Average list of a variety of players. The list is comprehensive only in terms of scope, intended to provide a representative sample of players from various eras. Many of the players selected are well-known names with histories and accomplishments that were noteworthy. Within each chapter, a selection of players from the list will be highlighted, and narrative summaries of players' careers will be provided.

I have grouped the players into five categories based on their career numbers and accomplishments; the standards for each category are detailed in the next section. Category 1, 2, and 3 players have short summaries, while Category 4 stars are given more in-depth narratives. The immortal Category 5 players are analyzed to the greatest degree.

After all Category 4 and 5 players have been presented, I set forth my top-10 list for each position with explanations as to why one player ranks ahead of another. Finally, I put forth individual cases for each of the top three players to be considered number one before completing the list. For those players who failed to play 60 percent of their games at a single position, Chapter 10 focuses on designated hitters and multiposition players.

Chapter 11 includes athletes who played the majority of their careers in the 1800s, and Chapter 12 documents the careers of famous Negro League stars. Because of the unique nature of the era and leagues in which these men played, I provide only brief narrative summaries of their careers and accomplishments. I refrain from rating them according to a specific category or ranking them against one another.

Chapter 13 serves as an all-important culminating piece to this work. I provide my list of the 100 greatest baseball players in history. Along the way, reasons and rationales are provided to support my argument for each ranking. As always, objective examination of P/E Averages and other statistics are balanced with subjective analysis of various measures, such as MVP balloting, postseason performance, and defense.

Finally, Appendices A through D provide a multitude of statistical information to help you create your own ratings, rankings, and all-time lists. Please use this book as a handy reference tool and as a medium for generating conversations about your favorite players and teams from baseball history.

Throughout this book, I will often refer to specific terminology, which I feel needs to be explained before proceeding. Some of this terminology is of my own creation. Some of it is already widely used in baseball but needs elaboration and examples to make it understandable for the casual fan. You may want to refer to these descriptions as you read along.

Categories of Baseball Players

I have developed my own system for rating players. This system is used throughout the book to place players into one of five categories based on their playing careers. The system, a balance of objective statistics and subjective analysis, follows:

- **Category 5:** A player in this category is one of the 50 best players ever and one of the top players at his position in history. Each position has from four to eight C5 players. Dominant statistical performances, multiple MVPs, defensive mastery, and post-season success are often characteristic of these legends. Above all else, these players clearly distinguished themselves from their peers.
- **Category 4:** These players had Hall of Fame careers, in my opinion, but not quite on the same level as a Category 5 player in terms of statistics, individual awards, impact, uniqueness, or postseason success.
- **Category 3:** These players had solid careers. Occasional outstanding seasons are offset by mediocre ones or a lack of sustainability over the long term. In my opinion, Category 3 players are not Hall of Famers. However, some players rated as Category 3 in this book have already been enshrined in Cooperstown or may one day gain induction.
- **Category 2:** These players had occasional success but lack the overall statistics and accomplishments of Category 3 players. A

rating of Category 2 means virtually no chance of Hall of Fame induction.

- **Category 1:** Category 1 players normally had brief careers that lacked statistical success and individual notoriety. However, I felt it would be worthwhile to analyze their statistics and accomplishments to better appreciate the overall rating system I have formulated.

Hall of Fame Status

Going along with the five categories of players is my system for specifying Hall of Fame status. Based on career statistics, individual awards, postseason success, defensive ability, and leadership, players will be evaluated in terms of their chances for Cooperstown. For those already inducted, that will be noted. For those not already inducted, the following terms will apply:

- **Imminent:** These players await certain induction at retirement.
- **Probable:** Although not yet in the Hall of Fame, these players have had outstanding careers and are likely to be enshrined one day.
- **Possible:** These players are tough calls. They are most likely rated as Category 3 or 4. They have had successful careers, but they also have substantial reasons counting against Hall of Fame consideration.
- **Doubtful:** Unless a small miracle occurs, these players will not be inducted. Sometimes, however, the Veteran's Committee grants access for the most unexpected of players.
- **No Chance:** Unfortunately, some players have no chance of ever making it to Cooperstown. All Category 1 players, and the vast majority of Category 2 players, fit this description.

The recent steroid controversy rears its ugly head at this time. Some players have established successful and even legendary careers but have also been associated with steroids. Barry Bonds, for example, falls into the "imminent" description in terms of his future Hall of Fame status, but he could be derailed one day if the federal government continues to force baseball's hand. Although I doubt they will ever go so far as to deny induction into Cooperstown based solely on steroid allegations, I do think there is a possibility that changes may occur. Nevertheless, these players have been included in the book because I can't specifically determine who took what, what effect it had on their performance, how long they took a substance, or what their competition was or wasn't taking. Their careers have been analyzed strictly based on statistics and accomplishments. I have tried to set personal opinions aside when rating and ranking them.

MVP Shares

In rating and ranking the all-time great players, I have also relied heavily on Most Valuable Player awards and career shares. Let me provide an example to explain how MVP shares work. Over his illustrious career, Mickey Mantle won the American League MVP three times. He also finished second three times, third once, and fifth twice. In five other seasons, Mantle received votes but did not finish near the top of the balloting. For his career, Mantle totaled 5.79 MVP shares, which is a considerable number. Let's see how these shares were accumulated.

In 1956 Mantle received all 24 first-place votes. As the unanimous selection, he registered 336 points out of a possible 336, which resulted in 1.00 shares. In 1957 he again won the award. This time, however, he received only six first-place votes and 233 points out of a possible 336, which amounts to 69 percent, or .69 shares. From 1956 to 1957, therefore, the Mick accumulated 1.69 combined MVP shares. In each year in which he received votes, Mantle continued to add to his total. In 1958 he finished fifth in the balloting but still managed to gain .38 shares. Throughout his career, the Yankees legend received MVP consideration in 14 seasons, which resulted in a total of 5.79 career shares.*

162-Game Averages

As you read this book, you will notice that every Category 4 and Category 5 player has a section in which his 162-game averages are displayed. These are helpful statistics in comparing players who may have had vastly different careers in terms of games played per season. These averages are calculated by first dividing career games played by 162 and then dividing the other career totals by that factor. Batting average, on-base percentage, and slugging percentage remain the same, but all of the other career statistics are condensed into one season of 162 games.

P/E Averages and SAT Scores

An easy way to think about P/E Averages is by relating them to the old system of calculating Scholastic Aptitude Test scores from high school. SAT scores were generally considered to be good around the 1,000-point mark. A student scoring in the 1,100s or 1,200s would be seen as very bright, and those in the range of 1,300–1,400 would have their pick of almost any college. A pupil scoring in the 1,500 range was

---

*All MVP as well as Gold Glove and Silver Slugger information in Stat One *is accurate through the 2006 season.*

probably en route to an Ivy League school, and a score of 1,600 was perfect. Similarly, P/E Averages of 1.000 and above indicate solid performance by an offensive player. Averages of 1.100 or 1.200 indicate an outstanding season. Players scoring in the 1.300–1.400 range have had a career season or are destined for the Hall of Fame if those averages are attained year in and year out. Only a handful of players have ever attained a P/E Average of 1.500 for a single season, and no player has been able to maintain it for a career, although one did come close. Finally, a single-season score above 1.600 has only happened three times in the history of baseball.

Obviously, this book is saturated with statistics and number-crunching analysis of the game's most memorable players. Don't be overwhelmed. Even if you are not a statistician, mathematician, or sabermetrician, you can still enjoy this book and use it to suit your needs. Offensive Production and Efficiency Average is meant to streamline statistical analysis, not confuse it even more. The formula to determine P/E Average is fairly simple and can be computed for any player as long as traditional statistics of production and efficiency are available. Of course, a calculator helps, too. Once again, here is the formula for P/E Average that has been the catalyst for this book:

$$P/E = (\text{net runs} + \text{net runs} + \text{complete bases}) \div \text{plate appearances}$$

It's time to get started. I hope you enjoy analyzing baseball's greatest players as much as I have.

Catcher

With their backs to the backstop as the only defensive player to have a view of the whole field, catchers are a rare breed. They are their squad's field generals and, in my opinion, the most important defensive player on the team. They are involved in every play, from signaling to the pitcher what to throw to framing the received pitch so that balls look like strikes. Catchers are invaluable and often overlooked.

Not by coincidence, some of the greatest teams in history were led by outstanding men behind the mask. The New York Yankees, the most successful franchise in the history of baseball, have always been blessed at this critical position. From Dickey to Berra to Howard to Munson to Posada, Yankees catchers have won five Most Valuable Player awards and finished in the voting's top three on 11 different occasions.

The great catchers are tough, natural leaders, skilled with the glove, and incredibly clutch. Johnny Bench, Yogi Berra, and Mickey Cochrane each fit that description, and they round out my top three catchers of all time. These three legendary players combined for seven MVPs and 15 championships.

It takes a special individual to be a catcher. They get beat up badly and blamed often. Years of foul tips and home-plate collisions leave these heroes of the diamond with battle scars and wounds that sometimes last a lifetime. In the end, however, they take great pride in the fact that they wore the equipment, endured the pain, squatted pitch after pitch, and were essential contributors to the teams that they loved.

Catcher: Career P/E Averages

Mickey Cochrane, 1.109; Mike Piazza, 1.093; Bill Dickey, 1.084; Roy Campanella, 1.069; Yogi Berra, 1.064; Jorge Posada, 1.040; Gabby Hartnett, 1.030; Johnny Bench, 1.008; Ivan Rodriguez, .986; Carlton Fisk, .966; Javy Lopez, .963; Ernie Lombardi, .942; Ted Simmons, .940; Roger Bresnahan, .934; Wally Schang, .929; Darrell Porter, .917; Gary Carter, .916; Lance Parrish, .892; Thurman Munson, .887; Sherm Lollar, .885; Elston Howard, .875; Bill Freehan, .837; Benito Santiago, .837; Rick Ferrell, .836; Earl Battey, .826; Del Crandall, .824; Ray Schalk, .767; Tony Pena, .762; Al Lopez, .755; Jim Sundberg, .739; Bob Boone, .734; Bob Uecker, .660

Category 1–3 Catchers

Roger Bresnahan

Career P/E: .934; Postseason P/E: 1.000

Notable seasons (P/E): 1903 (1.179); 1904 (.976); 1905 (1.008)

Roger Philip Bresnahan began his career before the turn of the century as a catcher with the Washington Senators in 1897. The Duke of Tralee hit .312 and was on base in 11 of his 22 plate appearances in the 1905 World Series, which his Giants won in five games against the Athletics. Bresnahan was behind the plate as three Giants' pitchers, including the great Christy Mathewson, combined to throw 45 innings without allowing an earned run.

Statistically, Bresnahan's career does not compare with other Hall of Fame catchers. He hit just 26 home runs over 17 seasons and had more than 50 runs batted in only three times, peaking at 56 in 1902. His career slugging percentage, .377, is actually lower than his career on-base percentage, .386.

Roger Bresnahan was inducted into baseball's Hall of Fame in 1945, 30 years after his retirement. In my book, Bresnahan ranks only as high as Category 3 despite his Hall of Fame status. I think of him as a poor man's Mickey Cochrane; that's not too bad.

Bill Freehan

Career P/E: .837; Postseason P/E: .634

Notable seasons (P/E): 1964 (.962); 1967 (.911); 1968 (.940); 1971
    (.874); 1974 (.920)

Born in Detroit and educated at the University of Michigan, Bill Freehan was a hometown prospect who played his entire career with the Tigers. Freehan made the All-Star team every season from 1964 to 1975, excluding 1974. Over that stretch, he also won five straight Gold Gloves and finished in the top seven of MVP balloting three times, finishing third in 1967 and second in 1968.

Although Detroit was victorious in the '68 Series versus St. Louis, the Tigers backstop never had much individual success in the play-offs. In 36 postseason at-bats, Freehan managed just five hits and two runs scored while striking out nine times and slugging only .278. He also managed to drive in 80 runs in a season only twice.

William Ashley Freehan was a solid signal caller for the Detroit Tigers in the 1960s and 1970s. In 1961, playing in his final season with the Michigan Wolverines, Freehan set an all-time Big Ten Conference record by batting .585. Although his major league statistics were not as gaudy, he regularly received league notoriety, Gold Gloves, All-Star selections, and MVP consideration. Therefore, I rank him as Category 3.

Al Lopez

Career P/E: .755; Postseason P/E: never in the postseason
Notable seasons (P/E): 1930 (.929); 1934 (.851); 1936 (.781)

Alfonso Ramon Lopez caught more than 1,900 games in the majors for four different teams. He began his career in 1928 with Brooklyn and enjoyed his finest individual season with the Dodgers in 1930, when he hit .309. Lopez was a much more successful manager than player. From '49 to '64, the Yankees won the pennant every season except two. In those two years, 1954 and 1959, Lopez was the pennant-winning skipper.

Al Lopez's career statistics are not good. He never came very close to 200 total bases in any season, and his best home-run effort occurred in 1939 when he hit eight for Boston's National League squad. Although he led the '54 Indians and the '59 White Sox to the World Series, he never tasted the playoffs during his playing days.

Lopez, a Category 2 ballplayer, should best be remembered as the man who guided the '54 Indians to 111 regular-season victories and a winning percentage of .721.

Thurman Munson

Career P/E: .887; Postseason P/E: 1.074
Notable seasons (P/E): 1973 (.991); 1975 (.989); 1976 (.964); 1977 (1.017)

Thurman Munson was a Yankees captain and recipient of the American League's MVP award in 1976. The American League Rookie of the Year for 1970, Munson led his Yankees squad to three pennants and two World Series crowns. He was often at his best in the playoffs, batting .357 for his postseason career. Munson had eight hits and 12 net runs when the Yankees defeated the Dodgers in the '78 Fall Classic.

Munson's life was tragically cut short when he perished in a plane crash on August 2, 1979. Munson finished his career with 113 home runs, 701 runs batted in, and 696 runs scored. Needless to say, these career marks would have been much more impressive had Munson never gotten on that plane.

I consider Munson to be Category 3. I believe he has a doubtful chance for Cooperstown, but it's possible for the Veteran's Committee to give him the nod one day in the future.

Tony Pena

Career P/E: .762; Postseason P/E: .833

Notable seasons (P/E): 1982 (.849); 1983 (.824); 1984 (.939); 1985
   (.739); 1986 (.807)

Tony had his best years with the Pirates, going to four All-Star
Games and winning three Gold Gloves. From 1982 to 1986, Pena averaged 217 total bases and 150 hits per season while batting over .285
four times. After Gary Carter and Lance Parrish, Tony was generally
considered the third best catcher in baseball in the early to mid-1980s.

Pena never had that one breakout season. His power was negligible. He never scored or drove in 80 runs in a season, and he hit over
.300 only once, when he hit .301 playing for Pittsburgh. This catcher
received MVP consideration only twice.

Pena was very good defensively but very ordinary with the bat.
While he has no chance to enter Cooperstown, he did have a good run
of success in the mid-'80s and again in the early '90s with Boston. I
rate him as a Category 2 player for his career.

Bob Uecker

Career P/E: .660; Postseason P/E: never in the postseason

Notable seasons (P/E): 1966 (.709); 1967 (.602)

Robert George Uecker spent six forgettable seasons behind the
plate in the National League during the mid-'60s. Ever since, however,
Uecker has been a household name with baseball fans throughout the
country thanks to an engaging sense of humor and many years behind
the microphone and in front of the camera. He played his final game
in 1967, just in time to preserve a career batting average of exactly
.200.

Uecker hit just 14 home runs during his brief career. He caught only 271 games, and he finished with 74 runs batted in and 65 runs scored. His career slugging percentage, .287, is even lower than his career on-base percentage, .293, itself extremely poor.

Uecker went from unknown during his playing career to well known after it. He has written two books and appeared in a variety of movies, commercials, and television specials. Mr. Baseball has been broadcasting games for the Milwaukee Brewers since 1970. He earns further notoriety as this chapter's sole Category 1 catcher. Cooperstown may someday await Uecker as a broadcaster. Otherwise, he will have to buy a ticket like everyone else if he wants to get in.

The Best Catchers

162-Game Averages

Player	BA	OBP	SLP	HR	TB	R	RBI	H	XBH	BB	K	SB
Bench	.267	.342	.476	29	274	82	103	154	60	67	96	5
Berra	.285	.348	.482	27	278	90	109	164	56	54	32	2
Campanella	.276	.360	.500	32	280	84	114	155	58	71	67	3
Carter	.262	.335	.439	23	247	72	86	148	51	60	70	3
Cochrane	.320	.419	.478	13	270	114	91	181	56	94	24	7
Dickey	.313	.382	.486	18	277	84	109	178	56	61	26	3
Fisk	.269	.341	.457	24	259	83	86	153	54	55	90	8
Hartnett	.297	.370	.489	19	256	71	96	156	56	57	57	2
Piazza	.308	.377	.545	36	319	89	113	180	66	64	94	1
Rodriguez	.303	.340	.479	22	298	91	89	188	63	34	92	9
Simmons	.285	.348	.437	16	250	71	92	163	51	56	46	1

Category 4 Catchers

Gary Carter

Career P/E: .916; Postseason P/E: .922
MVP: never won; 1.93 career shares
Hall of Fame: inducted in 2003

Gary Edmund Carter was widely considered to be the best catcher in baseball in the years between Johnny Bench and Ivan Rodriguez. In 1986 he led the Mets to the World Series with his leadership and clutch hitting. What Carter lacked in athletic ability he made up for in terms of hustle, toughness, and smarts. From 1980 through 1986, Carter finished in the top six in MVP voting four times. He also won three Gold Gloves and five Silver Slugger awards during that stretch. An 11-time All-Star, Carter was twice named MVP of the midsummer clash (1981 and 1984).

Carter's career P/E Average of .916 ranks behind every other catcher in my top 10. He never scored 100 runs, never hit .300, and never won the MVP. In the late '80s and early '90s, his career production trailed off dramatically. Hitting only 33 home runs over his last five seasons, Carter never was able to return to his glory days.

Carter's leadership, toughness, consistency, and run-producing ability for the better part of his career outweigh the decline he suffered toward the end. The argument can be made that he was the best catcher in baseball for a decade. As the cleanup hitter on the 1986 Mets championship team, Carter often provided the clutch hit at the perfect time. I rate him as a Category 4 player.

Year	RBI	R	HR	NR	TB	BB	HBP	SB	CS	CB	PTS	PA	P/E
1982	97	91	29	159	284	78	6	2	5	365	683	653	1.046
1985	100	83	32	151	271	69	6	1	1	346	648	633	1.024
1986	105	81	24	162	215	62	6	1	0	284	608	573	1.061
Career	1,225	1,025	324	1,926	3,497	848	68	39	42	4,410	8,262	9,019	.916

Carlton Fisk

Career P/E: .966; Postseason P/E: .952

MVP: never won; 1.27 career shares

Hall of Fame: inducted in 2000

Carlton Fisk won the American League Rookie of the Year and Gold Glove awards in 1972 and went on to play 2,226 games behind the plate. The 11-time All-Star selection is best known for his home run in Game 6 of the 1975 World Series against Cincinnati. Hopping down the first-base line, thrusting both arms through the air, virtually willing the ball to stay fair, Fisk will always be remembered in baseball history for forcing a seventh game against the Reds. Fisk had consistent, if not great, home-run power. He hit at least 20 round-trippers eight times, topping out at 37 for the '85 White Sox. Except for the shortened '81 season, Pudge posted double-digit home-run totals every year from 1972 through 1991.

Fisk's impressive career numbers are more the result of sustained productivity than concentrated excellence. Exceeding 100 runs batted in only twice, Fisk often had marginal years in terms of run production. In fact, he batted in more than 80 runs in a season just four times. He never finished better than third in MVP balloting.

Carlton Fisk makes it into the top-10 catchers of all time. He comes in as a Category 4 ballplayer, but he's on the lower end of the scale, much closer to Category 3 than 5. Fisk compiled impressive numbers over an extensive career.

Year	RBI	R	HR	NR	TB	BB	HBP	SB	CS	CB	PTS	PA	P/E
1977	102	106	26	182	279	75	9	7	6	364	728	632	1.152
1983	86	85	26	145	253	46	6	9	6	308	598	545	1.097
1985	107	85	37	155	265	52	17	17	9	342	652	620	1.052
Career	1,330	1,276	376	2,230	3,999	849	143	128	58	5,061	9,521	9,853	.966

Gabby Hartnett

Career P/E: 1.030; Postseason P/E: .571
MVP: National League MVP in 1935; 2.52 career shares
Hall of Fame: inducted in 1955

Charles Leo Hartnett caught between 85 and 141 games with the Chicago Cubs every year but one from 1923 until 1939. He won the National League MVP in 1935 when he batted .344, leading the Cubs to the pennant. That season, he also led National League catchers in assists, double plays, and fielding average. In 1937, he was runner-up to Joe Medwick. In all, Hartnett finished in the top 10 of the balloting four times, and eight times he finished in the top 15. Upon his retirement, he was regarded as the best catcher ever in the National League.

Unfortunately for him, the Cubs, and the city of Chicago, Hartnett was not very productive in the World Series. His .241 career postseason batting average is relatively poor, but not as poor as his .571 P/E mark. In 16 World Series games, Hartnett managed just four net runs and an on-base percentage of .255. His teams needed him to be better. In the four World Series in which he appeared, the Cubs lost all four.

Hartnett cracks the top 10. He is a C4 player based on his MVP success and Hall of Fame status. While contemporary backstops have proven to be better, it should not be forgotten that Hartnett was once considered his league's best catcher.

Year	RBI	R	HR	NR	TB	BB	HBP	SB	CS	CB	PTS	PA	P/E
1930	122	84	37	169	320	55	1	0	0*	376	714	578	1.235
1934	90	58	22	126	220	37	3	0	0*	260	512	487	1.051
1935	91	67	13	145	225	41	1	1	0*	268	558	461	1.210
Career	1,179	867	236	1,810	3,144	703	35	28	12*	3,898	7,518	7,297	1.030

* CS totals estimated based on known statistics

Mike Piazza

Career P/E: 1.093; Postseason P/E: .835
MVP: never won; 3.15 career shares (through '06 voting)
Hall of Fame: imminent

Michael Joseph Piazza won the NL Rookie of the Year award in 1993 and has been hitting his way to the Hall of Fame ever since. Already with the most career home runs at the position, Piazza is often regarded as the greatest offensive catcher in history. One has only to look at his 1997 campaign for justification. He batted .362, belted 40 homers, drove in 124 runs, and topped 200 hits, a rare feat for a catcher (career-best P/E Average of 1.275). He hit at least 30 home runs every year from 1993 until 2002, excluding the strike-shortened '94 season. Over the same period, Piazza had P/E Averages exceeding 1.000 every year, often by wide margins.

Defensively, he was not good. Piazza lacked soft hands behind the plate. He would often lose strikes for his pitchers and, therefore, extend at-bats and innings by failing to frame pitches and receive the baseball in a fluid manner. Most fans don't notice that. Most umpires do.

Mike Piazza overcame his defensive shortcomings by hitting better and more consistently than any catcher in baseball history. However, catcher is the single most important defensive position on the field in my opinion. Had he been good or even average behind the plate, I would rank him much higher, but he's still a C4.

Year	RBI	R	HR	NR	TB	BB	HBP	SB	CS	CB	PTS	PA	P/E
1997	124	104	40	188	355	69	3	5	1	431	807	633	1.275
1999	124	100	40	184	307	51	1	2	2	359	727	593	1.226
2000	113	90	38	165	296	58	3	4	2	359	689	545	1.264
Career	1,335	1,048	427	1,956	3,768	759	30	17	20	4,554	8,466	7,745	1.093

Ted Simmons

Career P/E: .940; Postseason P/E: .750

MVP: never won; .68 career shares

Hall of Fame: possible

Ted Simmons's best years were from 1972 through 1983. Excluding the strike-shortened season of 1981, Ted averaged 148 games played and 94 RBI per year. In 6 of those 11 seasons, he also batted over .300, with a high of .332 in 1975. Five times Simmons had season P/E scores above 1.000. His highest average came in his last year in St. Louis, 1980, when he produced 161 net runs and attained a terrific 1.128 P/E. Impressively, he finished his career with more walks (855) than strikeouts (694).

One of the major knocks against him was his defense. As with Piazza, Simmons would rate much higher on my list if he were better with the glove. Ted is not in the Hall of Fame, and he may never be inducted. Poor defense, unproductive postseasons, several years spent as a designated hitter, and the lack of any substantial MVP voting (he never finished better than sixth) are the reasons for his exclusion from the hallowed halls of Cooperstown.

On my list, Simmons just misses inclusion into the top 10. However, I still rate him as a Category 4 player, and I believe that his career is worthy of induction into the Hall of Fame. In my opinion, his poor defense and lack of postseason success are offset by his consistent, sometimes outstanding, production in the 1970s and 1980s.

Year	RBI	R	HR	NR	TB	BB	HBP	SB	CS	CB	PTS	PA	P/E
1975	100	80	18	162	285	63	1	1	3	347	671	649	1.034
1980	98	84	21	161	250	59	2	1	0	312	634	562	1.128
1983	108	76	13	171	269	41	2	4	2	314	656	650	1.009
Career	1,389	1,074	248	2,215	3,793	855	39	21	33	4,675	9,105	9,685	.940

Category 5 Catchers

Johnny Bench

Height: 6'1"; Weight: 208; Bats: right; Throws: right

First game: August 28, 1967; Final game: September 29, 1983

Team(s): Cincinnati Reds (1967–1983)

MVP: National League MVP in 1970, 1972; 2.77 career shares

Hall of Fame: inducted in 1989

162-game avg.: .267 batting, .342 on-base, .476 slugging, 29 home
runs, 274 total bases, 82 runs scored, 103 runs batted in, 154 hits,
60 extra-base hits, 67 BB, 96 K, 5 SB

Career P/E: 1.008; Postseason P/E: .989

The Good. Johnny Lee Bench is considered by many to be the greatest catcher of all time and the pure embodiment of what a catcher should be. Bench was twice named Most Valuable Player; he finished in the top 10 of the league's voting for the award five times.

Playing his entire career with the Cincinnati Reds, Bench had few flaws. Defensively, he was without peer. In 1968 he was named National League Rookie of the Year, winning the first of his 10 consecutive Gold Glove awards and being named to his first All-Star Game. He would play in a total of 14 All-Star Games throughout his illustrious career.

Offensively, he was at the center of the Big Red Machine of the 1970s, which won four pennants and two World Series. Bench was a great run producer; he topped 100 runs batted in six times, including the 1970 campaign when he knocked in 148 runs while hitting 45 homers. That year also marked Bench's best individual season in terms of P/E Average: 1.210. Bench eclipsed a 1.000 P/E Average eight seasons. He retired with 389 career home runs and 1,376 runs batted in.

The Bad. Not much. Bench was a complete player and put up some of the great individual seasons any catcher has ever had. However, he did have holes in his career. In 1971, the season after his breakout MVP year, Bench knocked in only 61 runs and produced a very pedestrian P/E Average of .842. Again in 1976, Bench failed to be a consistent run producer for the Reds, driving in 74 runs and hitting just 16 home runs (P/E Average: .937).

Bench was never a high-average hitter, topping out at .267 for his career and never reaching the .300 plateau except for the strike-shortened 1981 season when he hit .309 in only 52 games. A substantial knock against Bench can also be made in terms of strikeouts. From 1968 through 1978, he struck out more than 80 times every season, twice topping 100. For his career, the Little General struck out almost 1,300 times while drawing fewer than 900 bases on balls. Picky, I know, but perfection in baseball is saved for pitchers, and there it's usually across nine innings.

The Verdict. Johnny Bench is a Category 5 player and one of the three greatest catchers in the history of the game. It is hard to argue against Bench as the best ever. Indeed, his 1970 season may be the greatest of all time behind the plate. Most impressive statistically is the fact that Bench reached 200 net runs in two different seasons, a feat only equaled by one other catcher, Mickey Cochrane.

Yogi Berra

Height: 5′8″; Weight: 194; Bats: left; Throws: right

First game: September 22, 1946; Final game: May 9, 1965

Team(s): New York Yankees (1946–1963); New York Mets (1965)

MVP: American League MVP in 1951, 1954, 1955; 3.98 career shares

Hall of Fame: inducted in 1972

162-game avg.: .285 batting, .348 on-base, .482 slugging, 27 home runs, 278 total bases, 90 runs scored, 109 runs batted in, 164 hits, 56 extra-base hits, 54 BB, 32 K, 2 SB

Career P/E: 1.064; Postseason P/E: .969

The Good. Lawrence Peter Berra was an integral cog in the Yankees dynasties of the '40s, '50s, and '60s. Berra played in 14 Fall Classics, winning 10. A three-time Most Valuable Player, Berra symbolized everything a catcher is supposed to be: tough, dependable, productive, and, most important, a leader. Berra's best years came in the 1950s, when he finished in the top four of the American League's MVP voting for seven straight years.

Berra was a tremendously productive ballplayer. Averaging 1.06 net runs per game for his career, he knocked in at least 100 in five seasons. From 1948 through 1958, Yogi averaged more than 101 runs batted in per season. An All-Star selection every year from 1948 to 1962, Berra was at his best in the '56 World Series. In seven games, he led the Yankees to the World Series title over the rival Brooklyn Dodgers by batting .360 with three home runs and 10 runs batted in. He also caught Don Larsen's perfect game, the only one in Series history.

Berra's best individual season statistically was 1950, when he produced 212 net runs and had a P/E Average of 1.224. Despite these gaudy numbers, Berra finished third in the MVP balloting; teammate Phil Rizzuto won the award that year.

The Bad. As with Bench, not much. However, the most ardent skeptic can find flaws with the best. Berra had seasons that were less than spectacular. After 1958, his production fell off dramatically, obviously the result of years behind the plate. Yogi had good, but not great, power. Twice he slugged 30 home runs in a season, but he was never considered a home-run threat like other players of his day and age. Defensively, Berra was also considered good but not great. One of the enduring moments in baseball history took place in the 1955 World Series when Jackie Robinson stole home under his tag. To this day, Berra insists Robinson was out.

Yogi Berra retired after playing just four games during the 1965 campaign. Notably, those games were played as a member of the New York Mets, the team he managed to the 1973 National League pennant.

The Verdict. A Category 5 player and one of the three greatest catchers of all time, Berra was the centerpiece in the greatest run of success in baseball history. He played in 75 World Series games, by far a record. Incredibly clutch and always a great quote, Berra finished his career with 358 home runs, 10 championships, and an indelible mark left on the game.

Roy Campanella

Height: 5′8″; Weight: 200; Bats: right; Throws: right

First game: April 20, 1948; Final game: September 29, 1957

Team(s): Brooklyn Dodgers (1948–1957)

MVP: National League MVP in 1951, 1953, 1955; 2.52 career shares

Hall of Fame: inducted in 1969

162-game avg.: .276 batting, .360 on-base, .500 slugging, 32 home
   runs, 280 total bases, 84 runs scored, 114 runs batted in, 155 hits,
   58 extra-base hits, 71 BB, 67 K, 3 SB

Career P/E: 1.069; Postseason P/E: .762

The Good. Despite playing only 10 seasons, Roy Campanella won three MVPs in the early to mid-1950s. In 1955 the Brooklyn Dodgers shocked the world by finally overcoming the rival Yankees in the World Series. Campy had two home runs, four runs batted in, and four runs scored in the seven-game series.

The 1953 season was a tremendous individual season for Roy—he exceeded 300 total bases and 200 net runs for the only time in his career. His 1.353 P/E that season ranks as one of the highest single-season averages ever for a catcher. In total, Campanella had six seasons out of seven from 1949 through 1955 when his P/E Average eclipsed 1.000, often going well above that plateau.

Statistically, his 1.02 net runs per game are extremely productive and place him only slightly behind Berra (1.06) and ahead of Bench (.96) for their careers. Roy Campanella played in the All-Star Game every year from 1949 through 1956.

The Bad. While Campanella was a tremendous player, he didn't do it long enough to be considered in the same class as Bench, Berra, and Cochrane. For his career, Campy compiled only 856 runs batted in and 627 runs scored, which pale in comparison with other Hall of Fame catchers.

The years in between his MVP seasons were far below his best performances. In 1952, he hit only .269. Campy had a terrible year in 1954. He hit .207 and had a .285 on-base percentage while managing only 75 net runs. His P/E Average for 1954 was a paltry .785. In each season, he struck out more than he walked.

Most notable, however, was Campanella's ineffectiveness in World Series play. Although he was somewhat productive in the '53 Series, he was anything but dangerous against the Yankees in 1952 and again in 1956, when he combined to go 10 for 50 with only two runs scored in 14 games. His career postseason P/E number (.762) reminds us why 1955 was truly a magical, once-in-a-lifetime moment for Brooklyn fans to hold onto forever.

The Verdict. I have Roy Campanella ranked as one of the five best catchers ever. Certainly, his career numbers don't warrant that high of a ranking. However, he did win three MVP awards, and MVP voting is a critical measure in determining a player's overall value. Had he won only one or two, or if the Dodgers had lost as usual to the Yankees in 1955, I would have a much different opinion of Campanella. But that's not the case. He's a Category 5 player in my book.

Mickey Cochrane

Height: 5′10″; Weight: 180; Bats: left; Throws: right

First game: April 14, 1925; Final game: May 25, 1937

Team(s): Philadelphia Athletics (1925–1933); Detroit Tigers
(1934–1937)

MVP: American League MVP in 1928, 1934; 2.69 career shares

Hall of Fame: inducted in 1947

162-game avg.: .320 batting, .419 on-base, .478 slugging, 13 home
runs, 270 total bases, 114 runs scored, 91 runs batted in, 181 hits,
56 extra-base hits, 94 BB, 24 K, 7 SB

Career P/E: 1.109; Postseason P/E: .766

The Good. Gordon Stanley Cochrane, also known as Black Mike, was
a two-time MVP, a three-time World Series winner, and considered
to be the greatest catcher and leader of his day. Cochrane finished in
the top five of MVP balloting three times, and six times he finished in
the top 10.

Cochrane batted over .300 eight times, hitting as high as .357 in
1930. Even more impressive was Cochrane's on-base percentages.
From 1925 through 1937, he topped .400 every year but three. In those
three seasons, his on-base percentages were .397, .369, and .395. For
his career, Cochrane batted .320 with an outstanding on-base percentage of .419.

In terms of P/E Averages, Black Mike's best years came in the early
1930s, when he topped 1.200 three straight years. His best individual
season may have been 1932 (P/E: 1.250), when he contributed 207 net
runs to his team's scoreboard and batted a career-best 23 homers.
Ironically, that was one of the rare seasons when he failed to hit .300.

Cochrane was almost impossible to strike out. In 1927 and 1929 combined, he struck out just 15 times in 261 games! At the same time, Mickey was getting on base consistently through bases on balls. For his career, Cochrane walked 857 times while striking out only 217.

The Bad. The most glaring weakness in Cochrane's game was in the power department. Despite six seasons of double-digit home-run totals, Cochrane's career slugging percentage is .478, only 59 points higher than his on-base percentage. Because of this relative lack of power, Cochrane knocked in 100 runs only once in his career.

Surprisingly, Cochrane was less than spectacular in the postseason. Although he won three championships behind the plate, his career batting average in the Fall Classic was only .245, and his slugging percentage in five postseason series was a dreadful .336. While Cochrane was great in the 1929 Series against the Cubs (.400 batting average, .591 on-base percentage, five runs, seven walks, and no strikeouts in five games), he failed to reach those lofty heights again in the 1930s championship games. A postseason P/E Average of only .766 falls far below the expectations associated with a player as great as Cochrane.

The Verdict. Cochrane's illustrious career marks him as a Category 5 player and one of the three greatest catchers of all time. In today's game, Cochrane would be a perfect fit as a number two hitter in a lineup. Smart, tough, and a great leader, Cochrane was the reason Mr. Mantle named one of his sons Mickey.

Bill Dickey

Height: 6′2″; Weight: 185; Bats: left; Throws: right

First game: August 15, 1928; Final game: September 8, 1946

Team(s): New York Yankees (1928–1943, 1946)

MVP: never won; 2.02 career shares

Hall of Fame: inducted in 1954

162-game avg.: .313 batting, .382 on-base, .486 slugging, 18 home runs, 277 total bases, 84 runs scored, 109 runs batted in, 178 hits, 56 extra-base hits, 61 BB, 26 K, 3 SB

Career P/E: 1.084; Postseason P/E: .913

The Good. Dickey was a part of eight pennant-winning teams, going 7–1 in the World Series. An 11-time All-Star, he played with Ruth, Gehrig, and DiMaggio. Although he never won an MVP, he finished in the top five three times and in the top 10 five times. From 1929 to 1939, Dickey hit over .300 10 out of 11 seasons, topping out at .362 in 1936.

Bill Dickey had five outstanding seasons and a few very good ones as a member of the Yankees. The first one came in 1933 when he hit .318 and drove in 97 runs. When Joe DiMaggio was a rookie in 1936, Dickey was at his best. From 1936 through 1939, the catcher hit over .300 and knocked in more than 100 runs every season. His P/E Averages for those four years are outstanding (1.432, 1.253, 1.282, and 1.221).

In a four-game sweep of the Cubs in the '32 Series, Dickey had seven hits, four RBI, and a .438 batting average. A .313 career batter, Bill Dickey was very difficult to strike out. Only twice did he have more than 30 Ks in a season, and his career ratio of 678 to 289 strikeouts demonstrates the outstanding plate discipline he displayed throughout his career.

The Bad. The most glaring knock against Dickey's Hall of Fame career is the fact that he never won an MVP. One could argue that immortal players such as Ruth, Gehrig, and DiMaggio overshadowed Dickey's accomplishments. Yet Berra, Campanella, Cochrane, and Bench all won MVP awards on outstanding teams loaded with stars. The fact remains, however, that Dickey finished better than fifth in the voting only once as runner-up to Jimmie Foxx in '38.

Aside from 1933 and 1936–1939, Dickey was never a great run producer. His totals for runs scored and runs batted in were average to good during the other dozen years of his career. A career .255 hitter in World Series play, Dickey was often disappointing in the postseason. In 10 games in the 1941 and 1942 World Series, he combined to go 8 for 37 with only one RBI.

The Verdict. I rate Bill Dickey as a Category 5 player based on his team's postseason success and his impressive statistics. He was a member of seven championship teams, and his 1936 P/E Average of 1.432 is the highest single-season mark ever for a catcher. His No. 8 was retired by the Yankees in honor of him and Yogi Berra, his protégé who would later wear that same number. In 1999, *Sporting News* published its "100 Greatest Baseball Players" list. Bill Dickey came in at number 57. I believe he is one of the 10 greatest catchers of all time.

Ivan Rodriguez

Height: 5'9"; Weight: 205; Bats: right; Throws: right

First game: June 20, 1991; Final game: still active

Team(s): Texas Rangers (1991–2002); Florida Marlins (2003);
   Detroit Tigers (2004–present)

MVP: American League MVP in 1999; 1.04 career
   shares (through '06 voting)

Hall of Fame: probable

162-game avg.: .303 batting, .340 on-base, .479 slugging, 22 home
   runs, 298 total bases, 91 runs scored, 89 runs batted in, 188 hits,
   63 extra-base hits, 34 BB, 92 K, 9 SB

Career P/E: .986; Postseason P/E: .888

The Good. Ivan Rodriguez is a 13-time All-Star and winner of seven Silver Slugger awards and 12 Gold Gloves. Generally regarded as the best defensive catcher of his era, and one of the best of all time, Pudge was once described by a *Sports Illustrated* cover as "The Game's Most Indispensable Player."

He was at his best in the 2003 National League playoffs. After upsetting the San Francisco Giants in the first round with six runs batted in and a .353 batting average, Rodriguez was even better against the Cubs in the NLCS. Over seven games, the catcher pounded out nine hits, including two home runs. He scored five times and knocked in another 10 runs, earning NLCS MVP honors. The Marlins went on to beat the Yankees in six games in the World Series.

Ivan's career P/E Average of .986 lags behind the likes of Berra, Cochrane, and Campanella, but it is just shy of Bench's 1.008. In 1997 Pudge finished his year with Texas with a P/E Average nearly identical to his career mark. Even his batting average, on-base percentage, and slugging percentage for that season closely mirror his career numbers. Following up his MVP campaign of 1999, Rodriguez was posting monster numbers in 2000 before succumbing to injury. He played only 91 games but still managed 83 RBI and a P/E Average of 1.301.

The Bad. As with Berra, Rodriguez has good, but not great, power. He knocked in 100 or more runs only once, although he was certainly on pace to do it again in 2000. Despite his outstanding 2003 postseason, his P/E Average for the playoffs, .888, is less than spectacular. In the 1998 ALDS against the Yankees, Rodriguez went 1 for 10 with five strikeouts in a three-game sweep by the eventual champs.

One significant argument against Ivan Rodriguez can be made in terms of strikeouts. In 11 seasons he has struck out at least 70 times, and his 1,221 career Ks overwhelms only 446 career walks. He has 32 strikeouts in 40 postseason games. In recent years, his name has also been associated on a casual basis with the steroid controversy. He is noticeably leaner than in the past, and his home-run totals have dropped every season but one since 1999.

The Verdict. I rate Rodriguez as a Category 5 catcher with a probable, almost imminent, Hall of Fame induction awaiting him on retirement. His résumé is loaded with Gold Gloves and MVP consideration. I-Rod is one of the game's five best catchers.

Catcher: The Top 10

How do the 10 greatest catchers rank in relation to one another? As I mentioned in this chapter's introduction, mere statistical analysis by itself is insufficient, especially for a position such as this that demands defense, leadership, toughness, and other intangible qualities, which P/E scores cannot quantify. In the following list, I provide brief rationales for each player's ranking, which places him higher than the signal caller he precedes. The top three are then discussed in more detail, with an argument formulated for each. As I see it, these are the top 10 catchers in history.

10. Carlton Fisk

One of the most difficult decisions was choosing between Fisk and Ted Simmons for this spot. The original Pudge gets the nod based on better postseason play, more home runs, and his career MVP shares, which almost double those of Simmons. If I had to choose one of the two to have for an entire season, I'd take Simmons. But if I had one game I needed to win, Carlton Fisk would be my choice. Fisk wins by a nose.

9. Gabby Hartnett

In ranking Hartnett in front of Fisk, I gave way to trusting everything I read about him and listening to people who have watched baseball much longer than I have. Hartnett won an MVP and finished in the top 10 four times. That alone distances him quite considerably from Fisk. Add in the fact that his career P/E is better, and the choice becomes quite clear. I'll take Hartnett over Fisk by a wide margin.

8. Mike Piazza

Mike Piazza registers the second-highest career P/E Average for catchers in history, slightly behind Mickey Cochrane for the top spot. He combined the tools to hit for power and average better than any player at the position. However, his defense was subpar, he never won an MVP (although he certainly could have in 1997), and his teams never won a championship. Still, his 1.093 career mark is terrific and warrants him narrowly edging Gabby for eighth place.

7. Gary Carter

If Mike Piazza was hurt by the fact that I saw him play in so many games, then Gary Carter is helped by that same fact. Carter was a tremendous leader and a winning ballplayer. As a Mets fan, if I had to choose one or the other to backstop my team, I'd take Carter. He was clutch when it mattered most, and he was arguably the best catcher in baseball for a decade. His .916 career P/E mark pales in comparison with the others in my top 10, but he certainly doesn't. He's a great example of the need to look beyond the numbers in determining a catcher's overall value and significance.

6. Bill Dickey

Bill Dickey comes in ahead of Gary Carter based on better offensive statistics. It's as simple as that. With a 168-point advantage in Production and Efficiency Average, Dickey was clearly the better hitter. I think both players were probably great in terms of their overall defense, toughness, and leadership ability. Therefore, Dickey takes over spot number 6 based on his magnificent work with the lumber.

5. Ivan Rodriguez

I went back and forth several times deciding whom to put in this spot. I finally chose I-Rod over Dickey for two reasons. First, Rodriguez won an MVP, and I consider that a valid indicator of a player's value. Second, I-Rod's Gold Glove history is too impressive to overlook. Of course, Dickey never had the opportunity to win the award. Nevertheless, I don't think he would have fared quite as well as Pudge even if given the opportunity. I like Ivan Rodriguez for spot number 5 on this list of all-time backstops.

4. Roy Campanella

Three to one. At some point, I had to decide where Campy fits into this list, and I think this is the right spot. He won three MVPs to Rodriguez's one. That's convincing enough for me. Certainly, Campy's career lacks the overall numbers, but I simply can't ignore a player winning the Most Valuable Player over and over at such a critical position. It's too much of an advantage over Pudge, and it's the reason the Brooklyn Dodgers legend earns my vote for fourth place in my top 10.

The Top Three

Johnny Bench, Yogi Berra, and Mickey Cochrane are the three best catchers of all time, and I state that with unquestioned certainty. Intending no disrespect to Campanella, Dickey, Rodriguez, and the other members of the top 10, there is a wide margin between them and these three immortals. They each won multiple MVP awards and multiple championships. Each had outstanding statistical seasons and numerous reasons for them to earn the top spot. But it can only go to one man.

The Case for Bench

10 consecutive Gold Gloves

His 1970 season, perhaps the greatest ever (P/E: 1.210)

389 home runs

Three seasons with 125 or more runs batted in

Two MVPs, five times in the top 10, and 2.77 career shares

The Case for Berra

Three MVPs and 3.98 career shares

14 pennants and 10 championships

11 seasons with P/E scores above 1.000

1,430 career runs batted in

358 career home runs and only 414 strikeouts

The Case for Cochrane

Highest P/E Average of the three

1.18 net runs per game

Six top-10 finishes in MVP balloting

.320 lifetime batting average and eight seasons over .300

.419 career on-base percentage with only 217 strikeouts

3. Mickey Cochrane

There is no shame in finishing third in this race. While Cochrane statistically outranks Berra and Bench, he did also play during a time when offensive numbers were extremely high. Even so, he did not hit well in 14 combined World Series games in 1931 and 1934, watching his team fall short both times. In fact, 1930 was the only time Black Mike ever drove in more than one run in five championship appearances. Nevertheless, he ranks ahead of Roy Campanella by a fairly wide margin. He falls short of the top two catchers of all time, however, failing to match their power and overall excellence, but only slightly. Mickey Cochrane finishes third, but a bronze medal in this field is an outstanding accomplishment.

2. Johnny Bench

Blasphemy! Johnny Bench is not the greatest catcher of all time? Not on my list at least. The toughest part about selecting Bench for the silver is that it goes against every commonsense notion I have as a baseball fan. His name is almost synonymous with the position he played so expertly. I rank him ahead of Cochrane because of these commonsense notions and because he may be the greatest defensive catcher ever. I think his 1970 MVP season, in which he amassed 355 total bases, is probably the best ever for a catcher. In terms of peak value, he is number one. Unfortunately for Reds fans everywhere, he's only second on my list.

1. Yogi Berra

Only after endless hours of careful scrutiny and analysis did I surmise that Yogi Berra is the greatest catcher of all time, beating Bench in a photo finish. In terms of the numbers, Yogi's career P/E score and individual season scores are better than Johnny's. The 10 best single-season P/E Averages for these two catchers favor six for Berra and four for Bench. Furthermore, Yogi owns the highest single mark and two of the top three:

1. Berra, '50—1.224
2. Bench, '70—1.210
3. Berra, '56—1.147
4. Bench, '74, Berra '53—1.140 (tie)
6. Berra, '48—1.133
7. Bench, '72—1.130
8. Bench, '75—1.129
9. Berra, '54—1.113
10. Berra, '49—1.102

The factor that finally tipped the scales in Berra's favor, for me, rested with MVP performance. Bench won two, finished fourth twice, and was in the top 10 one other time. In 1971, however, he struggled. Again in '76, he failed to produce a typical Bench masterpiece. Berra did not suffer these lapses. From 1950 through 1956, the Yankees catcher won three MVP awards and finished fourth once, second twice, and third in arguably his best season, 1950. During that stretch, the New York Yankees won six pennants and five World Series titles. It was the greatest individual run in history for any catcher at any time, and it's the reason Yogi Berra is number one in my book.

Twins?

They say that everyone has a twin somewhere in the world. Does the same hold true for catchers? In analyzing this position, I discovered two sets of signal callers with striking resemblances. Rick Ferrell and Roger Bresnahan could have been separated at baseball birth in the early half of the twentieth century while Bob Boone and Benito Santiago mirrored one another more recently. Enjoy the comparisons!

Rick Ferrell

.281 career batting average

.378 career on-base percentage

.363 career slugging percentage

28 lifetime home runs

47.1% production and
    52.9% efficiency

Waited 37 years for Hall of
    Fame induction

687 runs scored

Roger Bresnahan

.279 career batting average

.386 career on-base percentage

.377 career slugging percentage

26 lifetime home runs

47.2% production and
    52.8% efficiency

Waited 30 years for Hall of
    Fame induction

682 runs scored

Benito Santiago

115 postseason plate appearances

48 complete bases in the playoffs

23 net runs in the postseason

.817 postseason P/E

5 All-Star appearances

.01 career MVP shares

Finished twentieth and
    twenty-third in MVP voting

.263 career batting average

.307 career on-base percentage

Bob Boone

121 postseason plate appearances

48 complete bases in the
    playoffs

23 net runs in the postseason

.777 postseason P/E

4 All-Star appearances

.03 career MVP shares

Finished sixteenth and
    twenty-third in MVP voting

.254 career batting average

.315 career on-base percentage

First Base

Traditionally, first base has always been a power position in a team's lineup. While defensive prowess is an asset, first basemen are usually more valued for their bat than their glove. Sluggers at the heart of the batting order, the best players combine an ability to hit home runs with high marks in terms of production and efficiency. Not surprisingly, the top players at this position have some of the highest single-season and career P/E Averages in history.

Jimmie Foxx, Lou Gehrig, and Hank Greenberg, who played against one another in the American League during the 1930s, make up my top three of all time. These immortals combined to drive in at least 150 runs in a season 14 times over their Hall of Fame careers. They also hit for high averages and won multiple championships and multiple MVP awards.

Along with left field and right field, first base is a position where I put more emphasis on objective statistics. Most important, of course, P/E Averages for these players weigh heavily when rating, ranking, and comparing them with one another. Foxx, Gehrig, and Greenberg set the bar extremely high. For others to gain entrance into my top 10, they needed to separate themselves from the pack. The best way to do that is with impressive offensive numbers.

Production and efficiency rolled into one, these first basemen set the standard with some of baseball's most dominant statistics. But who will emerge as the best ever? Who deserves a place in Cooperstown, and who falls just shy of the honor? Let's find out.

First Base: Career P/E Averages

Lou Gehrig, 1.387; Hank Greenberg, 1.318; Jimmie Foxx, 1.315; Albert Pujols, 1.271; Todd Helton, 1.202; Johnny Mize, 1.185; Mark McGwire, 1.179; Jeff Bagwell, 1.173; Carlos Delgado, 1.139; Jason Giambi, 1.131; Hal Trosky, 1.130; Bill Terry, 1.107; Jim Bottomley, 1.102; Rudy York, 1.066; Will Clark, 1.061; Rafael Palmeiro, 1.058; Willie McCovey, 1.049; Fred McGriff, 1.047; Frank Chance, 1.045; Andres Galarraga, 1.042; Gil Hodges, 1.039; Ted Kluszewski, 1.030; George Sisler 1.030; Orlando Cepeda, 1.029; Cecil Fielder, 1.024; Kent Hrbek, 1.015; Norm Cash, 1.007; Eddie Murray, 1.006; John Olerud, 1.006; Tino Martinez, 1.004; Don Mattingly, .995; George Kelly, .992; Keith Hernandez, .984; Tony Perez, .977; Cecil Cooper, .973; Boog Powell, .972; Mark Grace, .969; Joe Adcock, .962; Mickey Vernon, .962; Bill White, .958; Joe Judge, .948; Moose Skowron, .943; Lee May, .941; Steve Garvey, .933; Wally Pipp, .924; George Scott, .903; Joe Pepitone, .868; Bill Buckner, .863; Marv Throneberry, .859; Wes Parker, .838; Vic Power, .833

Category 1–3 First Basemen

Steve Garvey

Career P/E: .933; Postseason P/E: 1.009

Notable seasons (P/E): 1974 (1.031); 1977 (1.020); 1978 (1.055); 1979 (1.013)

Steve Garvey won the 1974 National League MVP, finished second to Dave Parker in '78, and was in the top 10 of the vote five times. He played his entire career in Southern California with the Dodgers and the Padres. Garvey won four Gold Gloves and was named NLCS MVP with Los Angeles in '78 and again with San Diego in '84.

Garvey never displayed the type of power managers usually like to see at first base. The 185 net runs he produced in '74 was his career high, and he retired with fewer than 300 homers and a slugging percentage below .450. In the '78 Fall Classic, Garvey managed just one net run while striking out seven times over six games.

Garvey is Category 3. He had at least 200 hits in a season six times, and he owns 2.46 career MVP shares. His homer off Lee Smith saved the NLCS for the Padres in '84. It is doubtful Steve Garvey will ever make it to Cooperstown, but he did achieve a significant amount of success during his playing career.

Gil Hodges

Career P/E: 1.039; Postseason P/E: .881

Notable seasons (P/E): 1951 (1.129); 1953 (1.120); 1954 (1.177)

Gil Hodges was signed by Brooklyn in 1943 and played the majority of his career in Dodger blue. Hodges was considered an outstanding defensive player; he won the first three Gold Gloves awarded in the National League. Had the award been around longer, he no doubt would have won more. Hodges was an eight-time All-Star and averaged 112 runs batted in from 1949 through 1955.

Hodges never finished better than seventh in MVP balloting, and he owns only .65 shares for his career. He never slugged .600 and never reached a .400 on-base percentage. His 1.039 P/E mark only falls into the middle of the pack compared with the other first basemen on my list. His .881 postseason P/E is largely the result of going 4 for 39 during his first three World Series appearances.

Hodges is Category 3, very close to Category 4. I understand the arguments in favor of his enshrinement, but I don't think his career was quite good enough. He needed a few more solid years or that one breakout season, but I will rate his chances as possible.

Don Mattingly

Career P/E: .995; Postseason P/E: 1.360

Notable seasons (P/E): 1984 (1.091); 1985 (1.186); 1986 (1.132); 1987 (1.149)

In his prime, Donnie Baseball was arguably the best player in the game. From 1984 to 1989, Mattingly hit over .300 each year, batting as high as .352. In 1985 he won the American League MVP, easily beating out George Brett and teammate Rickey Henderson for the award. During that memorable season, Mattingly drove in 145 runs and won the first of his nine Gold Glove awards.

Longevity is the key argument against Mattingly's career. Back problems prevented this skilled player from sustaining his excellence. If he had been able to hang on a little bit longer, then I would consider him a Hall of Famer. At his best, he played like a Category 5 first baseman. Sadly, he wasn't able to maintain his dominance quite long enough.

Wally Pipp

Career P/E: .924; Postseason P/E: .571

Notable seasons (P/E): 1921 (1.010); 1922 (1.021); 1923 (.983); 1924 (1.075)

Often credited with having the most famous headache in the history of sports, Walter Clement Pipp was the man who gave way to Lou Gehrig in 1925. Although his alleged ailment is probably fiction, it is absolute fact that Pipp, and not Babe Ruth, was the first Yankee to lead the league in home runs. He hit 12, his career best, in 1916 before Ruth ushered in the era of the long ball in earnest.

After clearing the way for Gehrig, who was actually scouted by Pipp while at Columbia, Wally moved on to the Reds. For his career, he just missed some prominent offensive milestones, retiring with 90 homers, 997 RBI, 974 runs scored, and 1,941 hits.

Pipp will always be linked to Gehrig. Ironically, Gehrig's consecutive-game streak actually began as a pinch-hitter the day before he took Wally's place in the lineup for good. In his own right, Pipp was a good ballplayer for a number of years. Had he been able to sustain his success, I might rate him higher than the Category 2 nod he earns here.

Moose Skowron

Career P/E: .943; Postseason P/E: 1.106

Notable seasons (P/E): 1956 (1.130); 1960 (.991); 1961 (.959); 1962 (.966)

Skowron won four World Series with the Yankees and one against them as a member of the '63 Dodgers. Moose was often at his best in October. His P/E Average in the playoffs is more than 160 points higher than in the regular season. He boasts eight Series homers and, even more important, 40 net runs in 39 games. Although he never won a Gold Glove, he did finish his career with a .992 fielding percentage.

Skowron was tremendously productive in the postseason, but he was not a great run producer from April to September. He never scored 80 runs, and he drove in at least 90 only twice. His career mark of .82 net runs per game is low for a first baseman. Despite playing on teams that frequently won the pennant, Moose collected only .18 MVP shares and never finished better than ninth in the voting.

William Joseph Skowron Jr. rates as Category 2 for his career. Skowron was the kind of ballplayer who fit well when surrounded with talent, but he wasn't able to carry a team by himself. Playing with the likes of Berra, Mantle, and Koufax, Skowron produced when it mattered most, but he will not join his former teammates in the Hall of Fame.

Marv Throneberry

Career P/E: .859; Postseason P/E: .000
Notable seasons (P/E): 1960 (.946); 1962 (.675)

Marvin Eugene Throneberry was always more recognizable by his nickname, Marvelous Marv. Originally signed by the Yankees in 1952, Marv was probably best known for his time spent with the Mets. In terms of P/E Average, his best season came in 1960 as a member of the Kansas City Athletics.

In 1962 the Mets lost 120 games in their inaugural season, and Throneberry finished with more errors, 17, than home runs, 16. He epitomized the failure of this new franchise, and he was the player Casey Stengel had in mind when he uttered his famous question, "Can't anybody here play this game?"

Throneberry earns the distinction of this chapter's lone Category 1 entry. He played fewer than 500 career games and did not match the fielding prowess of Vic Power and Wes Parker, the men who trail him on the chapter's all-time P/E list.

The Best First Basemen

162-Game Averages

Player	BA	OBP	SLP	HR	TB	R	RBI	H	XBH	BB	K	SB
Bagwell	.297	.408	.540	34	317	114	115	174	73	106	117	15
Bottomley	.310	.369	.500	18	304	96	116	188	68	54	48	5
Cepeda	.297	.350	.499	29	302	86	104	179	63	45	89	11
Foxx	.325	.428	.609	37	347	122	134	185	76	102	92	6
Gehrig	.340	.447	.632	37	379	141	149	204	89	113	59	8
Greenberg	.313	.412	.605	38	365	122	148	189	90	99	98	7
McCovey	.270	.374	.515	33	264	77	97	138	58	84	97	2
McGriff	.284	.377	.509	32	294	89	102	164	63	86	124	5
McGwire	.263	.394	.588	50	315	101	122	141	73	114	138	1
Mize	.312	.397	.562	31	311	96	115	173	70	74	45	2
Murray	.287	.359	.476	27	289	87	103	174	59	71	81	6
Palmeiro	.288	.371	.515	33	308	95	105	173	68	77	77	6
Perez	.279	.341	.463	22	264	74	96	159	56	54	109	3
Pujols	.332	.420	.620	42	373	126	128	200	88	88	67s	6
Sisler	.340	.379	.468	8	305	101	93	222	55	37	26	30
Terry	.341	.393	.506	14	306	105	101	206	60	51	42	5

Category 4 First Basemen

Jim Bottomley

Career P/E: 1.102; Postseason P/E: .694

MVP: National League MVP in 1928; 1.61 career shares

Hall of Fame: inducted in 1974

Jim Bottomley played his rookie season with Rogers Hornsby, and something must have rubbed off. In 1923 he batted .371, and he hit .367 two years later. In all, he topped .300 in eight different seasons. In 1928 Bottomley won the NL Most Valuable Player award, due in large part to his career-best total of 228 net runs. He slugged .628 that year, also his best ever. Productive throughout much of his career, Bottomley finished with an average of 1.20 net runs per game and more than 1,400 RBI.

Jim hit 60 homers in 1928 and 1929 combined, but he never reached 20 in any other season. His career slugging percentage, .500, is good but not great, especially in comparison with other Hall of Fame players at his position. In the 1930s, his production and efficiency trailed off. He hit less than .260 in three of his last five seasons and never reached either 100 runs scored or 100 runs driven in after 1929. Aside from his first World Series, Bottomley went just 8 for 61 in the postseason.

I rank Sunny Jim in the top 10 at this position. He had tremendous seasons in the 1920s but then failed to sustain those high levels into the next decade. He had one outstanding World Series and three bad ones.

Year	RBI	R	HR	NR	TB	BB	HBP	SB	CS	CB	PTS	PA	P/E
1927	124	95	19	200	292	74	5	8	7*	372	772	679	1.137
1928	136	123	31	228	362	71	3	10	9*	437	893	667	1.339
1929	137	108	29	216	318	70	1	3	3*	389	821	648	1.267
Career	1,422	1,177	219	2,380	3,737	664	43	58	54*	4,448	9,208	8,355	1.102

* CS totals estimated based on known statistics

Orlando Cepeda

Career P/E: 1.029; Postseason P/E: .714
MVP: National League MVP in 1967; 1.87 career shares
Hall of Fame: inducted in 1999

Cepeda began his career with a tremendous start. He was selected National League Rookie of the Year in 1958, a year in which he also finished in the top 10 of MVP balloting. From his rookie season through 1964, Cepeda averaged 107 runs batted in and 32 homers and hit between .297 and .316 each year. When he reached 122 home runs by the end of just his fourth season, it looked as if the Baby Bull was on his way to immortality. Orlando's best statistical season was 1961, when he finished second to Frank Robinson for the MVP. He slugged .609 and produced 201 net runs for the Giants.

When you consider the start Cepeda enjoyed in his first seven seasons, his career as a whole can be considered somewhat disappointing. He was great in 1967 and again in 1970, but his numbers generally declined after leaving the Giants. He slugged .600 just one time and finished with a career percentage below .500. Cepeda was also not good in World Series play. He appeared in the Fall Classic in '62 and again in '67 and combined to go 6 for 48 with three RBI. For his career, he posted a batting average of .207 in October ball.

He is deserving of his Hall of Fame status, but he fails to make my top 10 for this position. He showed flashes of brilliance but failed to sustain his greatness. The Baby Bull comes in as a solid selection for Category 4.

Year	RBI	R	HR	NR	TB	BB	HBP	SB	CS	CB	PTS	PA	P/E
1958	96	88	25	159	309	29	3	15	11	345	663	644	1.030
1961	142	105	46	201	356	39	9	12	8	408	810	636	1.274
1962	114	105	35	184	324	37	6	10	4	373	741	676	1.096
Career	1,365	1,131	379	2,117	3,959	588	102	142	80	4,711	8,945	8,695	1.029

Willie McCovey

Career P/E: 1.049; Postseason P/E: 1.206
MVP: National League MVP in 1969; 1.63 career shares
Hall of Fame: inducted in 1986

Willie McCovey hit 521 home runs and had 1,555 runs batted in over a career that spanned four decades. Platooned with Orlando Cepeda early in his career, McCovey emerged as a legitimate star in the mid-1960s and enjoyed his best seasons through the early 1970s. He hit more than 35 homers six times and won the Rookie of the Year award in '59 with the Giants. Willie's best years came back-to-back in 1969 and 1970. He knocked in 126 each year and averaged 42 homers and 100 runs scored. His combined P/E Average for the two campaigns was 1.288, a very high mark.

In many ways, McCovey is the opposite of Hank Greenberg. Stretch posted significantly higher career totals but never approached Greenberg's excellence in terms of run production. For his career, the lefty slugger averaged a modest .87 net runs per game, a mark far below the other Hall of Famers at his position. At .92, Tony Perez is the only other first baseman rated above Category 3 who falls below .95 in this crucial statistic of production.

Willie Lee McCovey is Category 4. He compiled some impressive career numbers but was only dominant for a few seasons. He had fewer than 90 RBI 15 times in 22 years. His team never won a postseason series, and he tallied only 1.63 MVP shares.

Year	RBI	R	HR	NR	TB	BB	HBP	SB	CS	CB	PTS	PA	P/E
1963	102	103	44	161	319	50	11	1	1	380	702	627	1.120
1969	126	101	45	182	322	121	4	0	0	447	811	623	1.302
1970	126	98	39	185	303	137	3	0	0	443	813	638	1.274
Career	1,555	1,229	521	2,263	4,219	1,345	69	26	22	5,637	10,163	9,686	1.049

Fred McGriff

Career P/E: 1.047; Postseason P/E: 1.161
MVP: never won; 1.41 career shares
Hall of Fame: possible

Fred McGriff hit 493 major league home runs and knocked in 1,550 runs over his 19-year career. McGriff was the model of consistency throughout his tenure. He topped 90 RBI 12 times, spanning from 92 to 107, and he eclipsed the century mark eight times. He never hit 40 homers, but he did smack at least 30 ten times. He was on his way to probably his best season in 1994 when the strike occurred. Playing 113 games for Atlanta that year, McGriff posted his highest single-season P/E mark, 1.257. He was hitting .318 and had 34 homers and 94 RBI when the season ended.

Although he may have been on his way to a tremendous finish in '94, McGriff never had that one breakout season like many other Hall of Fame first sackers. He was in the top 10 of the MVP vote six times, but he never finished better than fourth, which he achieved in 1993, his first year with the Braves. Even more telling, Frederick Stanley McGriff never earned a single first-place vote in MVP balloting over his entire career.

Fred McGriff is not in the Hall of Fame, but I believe he should be. He topped 1,500 RBI and approached 500 homers and 2,500 hits. He was never dominant, but he was extremely consistent, and he was great in the postseason. He is Category 4, closer to 3 than 5, and a borderline call for induction. I think Crime Dog will be there one day.

Year	RBI	R	HR	NR	TB	BB	HBP	SB	CS	CB	PTS	PA	P/E
1992	104	79	35	148	295	96	1	8	6	394	690	632	1.092
1993	101	111	37	175	306	76	2	5	3	386	736	640	1.150
1994	94	81	34	141	264	50	1	7	3	319	601	478	1.257
Career	1,550	1,349	493	2,406	4,458	1,305	39	72	38	5,836	10,648	10,174	1.047

Johnny Mize

Career P/E: 1.185; Postseason P/E: 1.064

MVP: never won; 2.46 career shares

Hall of Fame: inducted in 1981

John Robert Mize was known as Big Cat, and he lived up to that nickname by walloping 359 career homers despite missing three full seasons during the 1940s. Had he not missed that time, Mize might have accumulated upwards of 1,600–1,700 runs batted in and close to 500 home runs. The years he missed were during his peak. Mize was perfect in the World Series, going 5–0 with the Yankees during the last five seasons in his career. He was at his best in the '52 classic against the rival Dodgers. He batted .400 and had a P/E mark of 1.722 against Brooklyn over the five games he played.

Mize just made it to 2,000 hits for his career. His career runs scored total is 1,118, a tally that does not measure up to many other Hall of Famers. Of course, these totals are low because of the years he missed in the war effort. More important, the case can be made against Mize's selection for Category 5 based on his lack of winning an MVP. He had two second-place finishes, but he was never close to winning the award in either year.

In his prime, Big Cat was a tremendous offensive weapon. Mize was a lot like Hank Greenberg, although he was not quite as dominant. Both men missed extensive time in the 1940s and, therefore, have career numbers that don't reflect their greatness.

Year	RBI	R	HR	NR	TB	BB	HBP	SB	CS	CB	PTS	PA	P/E
1940	137	111	43	205	368	82	5	7	4*	458	868	666	1.303
1947	138	137	51	224	360	74	4	2	1*	439	887	664	1.336
1948	125	110	40	195	316	94	4	4	2*	416	806	658	1.225
Career	1,337	1,118	359	2,096	3,621	856	52	28	14*	4,543	8,735	7,371	1.185

* CS totals estimated based on known statistics

Eddie Murray

Career P/E: 1.006; Postseason P/E: .946

MVP: never won; 3.33 career shares

Hall of Fame: inducted in 2003

Steady Eddie was just that over his 21 seasons in the majors. An RBI machine, Murray drove in 1,917 runs for his career. Excluding the strike-shortened season of 1981, Eddie averaged 99 RBI per season from 1977 until 1993, a tremendous level of sustained production. Murray began his career with a bang by winning the Rookie of the Year award with Baltimore in '77. He went on to make eight visits to the All-Star Game and won three Gold Gloves and three Silver Sluggers. He never won the MVP, but he did total 3.33 career shares, a fairly substantial number.

While he was steady, he was never as dominant as some of the others in this section. He never reached 125 runs batted in for a season, and he never hit more than 33 home runs. He never slugged .550, and he reached a .400 on-base percentage only twice. Murray's highest single-season P/E score was 1.185 set in 1985. He had 11 full seasons (at least 100 games played) in which he posted a P/E Average below 1.000.

Obviously, Murray deserves to be in Cooperstown. He was a tremendous run producer for more than a decade and a half. He reached the 500-home-run plateau, batted .300 or better seven times, and drove in more than 1,900 runs. He is not on the level of Gehrig and Foxx, but he is in my top 10 for this position. Steady Eddie is Category 4.

Year	RBI	R	HR	NR	TB	BB	HBP	SB	CS	CB	PTS	PA	P/E
1980	116	100	32	184	322	54	2	7	2	383	751	683	1.100
1983	111	115	33	193	313	86	3	5	1	406	792	680	1.165
1985	124	111	31	204	305	84	2	5	2	394	802	677	1.185
Career	1,917	1,627	504	3,040	5,397	1,333	18	110	43	6,815	12,895	12,817	1.006

Rafael Palmeiro

Career P/E: 1.058; Postseason P/E: .868
MVP: never won; 1.20 career shares
Hall of Fame: possible

Over the course of a long career, Rafael Palmeiro compiled 569 home runs, 1,663 runs scored, and 1,835 runs batted in. Those are Hall of Fame numbers. In 1996 he knocked in 142 and generated 213 net runs of offense for Baltimore. His highest P/E score came in '99 with Texas. Rafael recorded career bests in all three efficiency averages: .324 batting, .420 on-base, and .630 slugging. Palmeiro won three Gold Gloves and made four All-Star appearances.

Like McGwire's, Rafael's career has had a dark shadow cast over it by the steroid controversy. He adamantly waved his finger at Congress and declared, in no uncertain terms, that he never took steroids. During the 2005 season, however, it was revealed that he had failed a drug test, and the public outcry against him was substantial. Palmeiro's dominant seasons occurred during the height of the steroid era. From '98 to '01, he hit 176 homers and drove in more than 500 runs as his career numbers went from very good to tremendous.

Palmeiro's career power numbers point to a Category 5 career, but his 1.058 P/E mark tells otherwise. I rate him as Category 4, missing the top 10 list that follows shortly. He's similar to Murray, except that Palmeiro carries the weight and shame of serious steroid allegations.

Year	RBI	R	HR	NR	TB	BB	HBP	SB	CS	CB	PTS	PA	P/E
1996	142	110	39	213	342	95	3	8	0	448	874	732	1.194
1999	148	96	47	197	356	97	3	2	4	454	848	674	1.258
2000	120	102	39	183	315	103	3	2	1	422	788	678	1.162
Career	1,835	1,663	569	2,929	5,388	1,353	87	97	40	6,885	12,743	12,046	1.058

Tony Perez

Career P/E: .977; Postseason P/E: .788

MVP: never won; .93 career shares

Hall of Fame: inducted in 2000

Tony Perez was an integral part of Cincinnati's Big Red Machine of the 1970s, helping the team win back-to-back titles in '75 and '76. Like Murray, Palmeiro, and McGriff, he was a consistent, and at times outstanding, run producer in the middle of his team's lineup. He made seven visits to the All-Star Game and won the MVP honors for the midsummer showdown in 1967. Tony had a resurgence when he went to Boston in 1980. In his first year in the AL, he hit 25 homers and drove in 105 for the Sox. When he finally hung up his spikes for the last time, he had amassed 1,652 runs batted in.

Tony Perez finished with a P/E Average well below 1.000 for his career. He surpassed 1.100 only once, when he posted an outstanding mark of 1.219 in 1970. He was often below 1.000, and his net runs per game average of .92 is better than only one player in this section. Perez was never a threat to win the MVP award, finishing with just .93 shares. He was in the top 10 four times, but he was never able to win the honor.

Tony Perez deserves to be in the Hall of Fame based on his years of production and the dominance he displayed over back-to-back seasons in '69 and '70. That being said, I would probably rank him either last or next to last out of all the C4 first basemen. His totals were amassed over an extensively long career, and his P/E Averages are low.

Year	RBI	R	HR	NR	TB	BB	HBP	SB	CS	CB	PTS	PA	P/E
1969	122	103	37	188	331	63	2	4	2	398	774	704	1.099
1970	129	107	40	196	346	83	4	8	3	438	830	681	1.219
1975	109	74	20	163	238	54	3	1	2	294	620	574	1.080
Career	1,652	1,272	379	2,545	4,532	925	43	49	33	5,516	10,606	10,861	.977

George Sisler

Career P/E: 1.030; Postseason P/E: never in the postseason
MVP: American League MVP in 1922; .92 career shares
Hall of Fame: inducted in 1939

George Harold Sisler batted .340 for his career and was one of the great batsmen in baseball history. When he won the 1922 MVP honor, it was largely the result of his .420 batting average and 246 hits. Two years prior, Sisler was as good, if not better. For the 1920 St. Louis Browns, Gorgeous George totaled 257 hits and a .407 average. He also slugged .632 that year, the highest of his career. Amazingly, Sisler went over the .300 plateau 13 times, and five times he hit better than .350. From 1920 to 1922, George averaged almost 230 net runs per season, posting P/E scores of 1.376, 1.296, and 1.367.

After 1925, Sisler's production fell off quite dramatically. He drove in more than 80 runs only once in his last five seasons and failed to score more than 87 runs over that period. His lack of power prevented him from posting consistently high P/E Averages, aside from '20–'22. His career P/E Average is only slightly better than those of Orlando Cepeda and Cecil Fielder.

It is hard to discount a career that includes multiple seasons hitting above .400. He had negligible power, however, and that prevents him from placing in the top five for this position. He does make the top 10, though.

Year	RBI	R	HR	NR	TB	BB	HBP	SB	CS	CB	PTS	PA	P/E
1920	122	137	19	240	399	46	2	42	17	472	952	692	1.376
1921	104	125	12	217	326	34	5	35	11	389	823	635	1.296
1922	105	134	8	231	348	49	3	51	19	432	894	654	1.367
Career	1,175	1,284	102	2,357	3,871	472	48	375	197*	4,569	9,283	9,013	1.030

* *CS totals estimated based on known statistics*

Bill Terry

Career P/E: 1.107; Postseason P/E: .833

MVP: never won; 2.72 career shares

Hall of Fame: inducted in 1954

William Harold Terry, born in Atlanta, played his entire Hall of Fame career with the New York Giants. He had his best season in 1930, a year in which no MVP was given. Terry batted .401, scored 139 times, and drove home 129 runs. His total of 245 net runs that year was the highest mark of his career and one of five times he surpassed 200 for a season. For his career, he amassed 2.72 career shares. Terry had six hits in each of his October appearances on the big stage, although his .833 P/E postseason score is modest, especially for a player of his stature.

Other than his stretch of excellence from '27 through '32, Terry's statistics are not overly impressive. He usually had fewer than 70 RBI, and he hit fewer than 10 home runs every year but one during the early and late stages of his career. He retired with fewer than 1,100 RBI and just over 150 home runs. His postseason batting average, .295, is 46 points below his career mark, a sign that he wasn't at his best when it mattered most.

Memphis Bill is Category 4 and cracks my top 10. He averaged 1.19 net runs per game for his career, a substantial level of production. However, he failed to maintain that level beyond the six-year period in the middle of his career when his statistics were high.

Year	RBI	R	HR	NR	TB	BB	HBP	SB	CS	CB	PTS	PA	P/E
1930	129	139	23	245	392	57	1	8	10*	448	938	710	1.321
1931	112	121	9	224	323	47	2	8	9*	371	819	662	1.237
1932	117	124	28	213	373	32	1	4	5*	405	831	677	1.227
Career	1,078	1,120	154	2,044	3,252	537	9	56	67*	3,787	7,875	7,111	1.107

* CS totals estimated based on known statistics

Category 5 First Basemen

Jeff Bagwell

Height: 6′0″; Weight: 195; Bats: right; Throws: right

First game: April 8, 1991; Final game: 2005

Team(s): Houston Astros (1991–2005)

MVP: National League MVP in 1994; 2.89 career shares

Hall of Fame: probable

162-game avg.: .297 batting, .408 on-base, .540 slugging, 34 home
  runs, 317 total bases, 114 runs scored, 115 runs batted in, 174
  hits, 73 extra-base hits, 106 BB, 117 K, 15 SB

Career P/E: 1.173; Postseason P/E: .772

The Good. Jeff Bagwell was the 1991 National League Rookie of the
Year and won the MVP, Gold Glove, and Player of the Year honors in
his best season, 1994. During that strike-shortened campaign, Bagwell was on his way to one of the great seasons ever. In only 110
games, Bagwell drove in 116 runs, scored 104, and accumulated 300
total bases. His efficiency averages were outstanding: .368 batting, .451
on-base, and .750 slugging. He finished the season with a P/E Average of 1.549, one of the highest marks in baseball history.

While '94 was Bagwell's best season, it certainly was no aberration.
From 1996 to 2001, the Houston slugger had P/E averages above 1.200
and produced at least 200 net runs for the Astros every season, including 237 in 2000, when he slugged .615 and knocked in 152 runs. His
1.338 mark that season was the second highest of his career.

Bagwell had more than 1,500 runs scored and 1,500 driven in for
his career. He hit better than .300 six times and eclipsed a .400 on-base

percentage seven times. In 1997 he finished third in MVP balloting, and he was runner-up to Chipper Jones in '99. For his career, Bagwell owns an impressive total of 2.89 shares, finishing in the top 10 on six different occasions.

The Bad. Most notable has been Bagwell's lack of postseason success. In the '98 and '99 NLDS, he combined to manage only four singles while striking out 10 times over Houston's eight games. The Astros lost both series. Excluding the 2005 playoffs, when Jeff came to bat just 11 times, Houston went 1–5 in postseason series. For his career, the first bagger has hit .226 and slugged .321 in October games.

Statistically, Bagwell's regular-season numbers are outstanding. He does however, have a significant number of strikeouts, 1,558, for his career. He fanned more than 100 times in 10 seasons and at least 90 times during two others. That fact needs to be given some consideration.

The Verdict. Jeffrey Robert Bagwell, C5, should one day make it into the Hall of Fame. His mark of 1.21 net runs per game indicates how productive he was throughout his career. In 2004 he was able to redeem himself somewhat in the postseason when he hit .318 and slugged .682 while driving in five runs against the Braves. His Astros ultimately lost to St. Louis in the NLCS in seven games. The only way Jeff will not be enshrined is if voters view him as a beneficiary of the offensive explosion that surfaced after the strike in '94. I rank him in my top five first basemen, and I think Cooperstown should save a space for him in the near future.

Jimmie Foxx

Height: 6'0"; Weight: 195; Bats: right; Throws: right

First game: May 1, 1925; Final game: September 23, 1945

Team(s): Philadelphia Athletics (1925–1935); Boston Red Sox
(1936–1942); Chicago Cubs (1942, 1944); Philadelphia Phillies
(1945)

MVP: American League MVP in 1932, 1933, 1938; 4.21 career
shares

Hall of Fame: inducted in 1951

162-game avg.: .325 batting, .428 on-base, .609 slugging, 37 home
runs, 347 total bases, 122 runs scored, 134 runs batted in, 185
hits, 76 extra-base hits, 102 BB, 92 K, 6 SB

Career P/E: 1.315; Postseason P/E: 1.151

The Good. Jimmie Foxx won three MVPs and came close to winning
a fourth, finishing second to DiMaggio in '39. In 1933 Jimmie won
the Triple Crown, batting .356 with 48 homers and 163 driven in. His
RBI total for that season was only the third highest posted during his
illustrious career. The year before, 1932, he knocked in 169, and he set
a career best in 1938 when he drove home 175 runs for Boston. Upon
retirement, he had surpassed 1,900 RBI and 1,750 runs. He finished
with 534 career homers.

Foxx was a rare combination of production and efficiency rolled
into one and maintained over a long period of time. From 1929
through 1941, Foxx smacked 503 round-trippers while hitting above
.333 nine times. Over that period, Double X averaged 134 RBI and
120 runs scored per season. He also slugged better than .700 three
times and routinely surpassed 200 net runs for his teams. He is one

of only three players ever to have a single-season P/E Average above 1.500 more than once, and he is the only right-handed batter ever to accomplish that feat. He reached the 1.200 plateau in 15 of his 20 big-league seasons, and his career score of 1.315 places him in the top five all-time in terms of P/E Average.

In the World Series, Foxx was extremely consistent. In each of his three Series appearances, Double X scored between three and five runs, drove in between three and five, had seven or eight hits, and batted .350, .333, and .348. His teams were triumphant twice in three straight visits from '29 to '31.

The Bad. There's not much to complain about. Foxx was never great on the base paths, although he certainly couldn't be considered a liability either. He committed 192 errors in the field but did post a career fielding percentage of .992, very strong and above his league's average. The first few years at the beginning and end of his career lacked substantial statistical performances, but they were more than compensated for from 1929 to 1941. One could make the argument that Foxx's Philadelphia teams should have won more pennants or take shots at the fact that he failed to get the Red Sox into October. Other than that, it's hard to find many flaws.

The Verdict. Foxx is a no-doubt Category 5 player. I believe he's one of the three greatest first basemen ever, and I make the case for him being number one later in this chapter. Along with Aaron, Mays, DiMaggio, and Hornsby, he has to be considered one of the greatest hitters ever from the right side of the plate. More important, I feel he is one of the 10 best players in history.

Lou Gehrig

Height: 6'0"; Weight: 200; Bats: left; Throws: left

First game: June 15, 1923; Final game: April 30, 1939

Team(s): New York Yankees (1923–1939)

MVP: American League MVP in 1927, 1936; 5.44 career shares

Hall of Fame: inducted in 1939

162-game avg.: .340 batting, .447 on-base, .632 slugging, 37 home
runs, 379 total bases, 141 runs scored, 149 runs batted in, 204
hits, 89 extra-base hits, 113 BB, 59 K, 8 SB

Career P/E: 1.387; Postseason P/E: 1.493

The Good. Where shall we begin? Trying to condense Gehrig's statistics and accomplishments into a few short paragraphs is like shoving an elephant into a phone booth. His numbers are mind-boggling. From 1926 to 1938, Gehrig played every single game for the New York Yankees. Over that stretch, he *averaged* 250 net runs per season! The level of production that many Hall of Famers achieve only once or twice was matched, and often far exceeded, by Gehrig for 13 consecutive seasons without ever taking a day off. In 1931 the Iron Horse scored 163 times, drove in 184, and knocked 46 balls out of the park. Adding 163 to 184 and then subtracting 46 gives a net run total of 301, the highest mark ever in baseball history. Over 155 games that computes to an average of 1.94 runs produced by a single player every game.

In the postseason, Gehrig was even better than in the regular season. His 1.493 P/E Average in World Series play is remarkable, especially considering the fact that it was accumulated over 34 games. For his career, Gehrig posted extremely efficient averages in the World

Series: .361 batting, .477 on-base, and .731 slugging. His Yankees won six of the seven Series he played in, losing only the first in 1926.

Gehrig has the second highest P/E Average in history, and his career contribution of 1.57 net runs per game is number one and makes a strong argument that he is the most productive player of all time. He hit better than .350 six times and walked almost twice as much as he struck out. Twice, the Iron Horse had more home runs than strikeouts for an entire season.

The Bad. Lou never batted .400, and he never hit 50 homers in one season. He stole 102 bases but was caught 101 times. He also made 196 errors, although his fielding percentage, .991, is better than the league average. In the '38 World Series he was human, batting .286 as the Yankees swept the title in four games. He hit .295 twice in his career, his lowest average aside from the .143 mark he suffered over eight games in 1939 as he was fighting for his life. He died in 1941.

The Verdict. I believe that Lou Gehrig is one of the more underrated players ever. His statistics are out of this world, he repeatedly led his team to victory, and he showed up to work every day for 15 years. Obviously, he is Category 5, and he will be analyzed further when comparing the top three first basemen in history at the end of this section. One can only imagine how much more impressive his career totals would have been had he replaced Wally Pipp sooner or had he remained healthy and been able to play first base in Yankee Stadium for a few more years.

Hank Greenberg

Height: 6′3″; Weight: 210; Bats: right; Throws: right

First game: September 14, 1930; Final game: September 18, 1947

Team(s): Detroit Tigers (1930, 1933–1941, 1945–1946); Pittsburgh
  Pirates (1947)

MVP: American League MVP in 1935, 1940; 3.69 career shares

Hall of Fame: inducted in 1956

162-game avg.: .313 batting, .412 on-base, .605 slugging, 38 home
  runs, 365 total bases, 122 runs scored, 148 runs batted in, 189
  hits, 90 extra-base hits, 99 BB, 98 K, 7 SB

Career P/E: 1.318; Postseason P/E: 1.356

The Good. Hank Greenberg registers the fourth highest P/E Average
in history and the highest among right-handed hitters. Although he
finished his career in Pittsburgh, Hammerin' Hank will always be
remembered as a Tiger. In 1935, he led Detroit to the World Series
title, earning himself a unanimous MVP selection along the way. That
year, Greenberg hit .328, smacked 98 extra-base hits, and drove in 170
runs. In 1937 he was even more productive, collecting 183 RBI in one
of the great seasons of all time, substantiated by a remarkable P/E
Average of 1.522.

In 1940, Hank won his second MVP, this time as an outfielder.
Again Detroit won the pennant before falling short in the World
Series. Because of World War II, 1940 was the slugger's last full season
until 1946. Greenberg missed three entire seasons, and parts of two
others, while defending his country. Therefore, his career statistics
don't seem as impressive as they should. If he hadn't missed those seasons in the 1940s, Greenberg might have another 400 runs batted in

and 100 home runs on his résumé, and those are probably conservative estimates. From 1934 to 1940, Hammerin' Hank posted season P/E Averages of at least 1.310 each year. He often went well above 200 net runs produced, and his batting averages never came close to falling under .300. He hit .318 in World Series play and managed to post higher on-base and slugging percentages in October than during his regular-season career.

The Bad. As I stated before, Hank's career numbers are not spectacular. He finished with 1,276 RBI, 1,051 runs, and 331 home runs. He never had 400 total bases, although he did manage at least 380 four times. When he won the MVP in 1940, Greenberg made 15 errors and posted a poor fielding percentage of .954 for the season. He never stole 10 bases in any year, and he had only one hit in the '35 Series.

The Verdict. Hank Greenberg is a great example to illustrate how P/E Averages can be used to accurately gauge a player's offensive contribution and success. If one were to look solely at Greenberg's final statistics, he or she might come to the conclusion that Greenberg was just a solid player. That would be an injustice. When healthy and not off at war, Greenberg was a ferocious run producer. He had three seasons of at least 200 hits and walked more than he struck out for his career. His statistics lag behind some other first basemen simply because he played only nine full seasons. His P/E Averages, however, tell a far different and far more accurate story. Hammerin' Hank is Category 5 and one of the top three at his position.

Mark McGwire

Height: 6'5"; Weight: 225; Bats: right; Throws: right

First game: August 22, 1986; Final game: October 7, 2001

Team(s): Oakland Athletics (1986–1997); St. Louis Cardinals
    (1997–2001)

MVP: never won; 1.94 career shares

Hall of Fame: probable

162-game avg.: .263 batting, .394 on-base, .588 slugging, 50 home
    runs, 315 total bases, 101 runs scored, 122 runs batted in, 141
    hits, 73 extra-base hits, 114 BB, 138 K, 1 SB

Career P/E: 1.179; Postseason P/E: .722

The Good. What Roger Maris did in one glorious season Mark
McGwire maintained over four. From 1996 to 1999 Big Mac averaged
61 home runs per season. In 1998 he broke the major league single-
season home-run record when he outlasted Sammy Sosa to hit 70. He
followed that magical campaign with 65 the next year. In both years,
McGwire drove in 147 runs.

Some of McGwire's P/E Averages are simply outstanding. In his
best season, '98, he posted a 1.419 mark, which was actually bettered
by his 1.439 average in 2000, but that occurred in only 89 games. In
three other full seasons, Big Mac surpassed 1.300, often by a wide margin. He produced at least 200 net runs back-to-back with the Cardinals, and he surpassed 150 five other times. Mark McGwire won the
1987 Rookie of the Year award in the American League when he
smacked 49 homers, scored 97 runs, and drove home 118. That season, in which he posted a 1.173 P/E, comes the closest to matching his
career figure of 1.179.

Big Mac hit 583 homers, made 12 All-Star Games, and won three Silver Sluggers. In 1990 he was awarded the Gold Glove, and he was always considered to be good defensively. He finished second to Sosa for the '98 MVP, but he could have just as easily won; his statistics that year were tremendous. He finished in the top five three times and in the top 10 five times.

The Bad. McGwire's career and his accomplishments may forever remain tarnished because of steroid allegations. When he appeared before Congress, the slugger appeared nervous and guilty in my opinion. The court of public opinion may believe that he, along with Bonds, Giambi, and many other players from the past 10 years, in some way took supplements that helped his performance.

McGwire never won an MVP, and he was never dominant in October. He never hit more than one home run in any playoff series, and he managed just one net run and one extra-base hit when his Oakland squad swept the Giants in '89. In 42 postseason games, McGwire slugged just .349 and struck out 33 times. He was always susceptible to whiffing. He fanned more than 100 times in 10 seasons and struck out almost 1,600 times in his career. From 1997 to 1999, the slugger struck out 455 times, an average of more than 150 times per season.

The Verdict. McGwire is Category 5 for one simple reason. He has the best rate of at-bats per home run in history, better than Aaron, Bonds, and even Ruth. He is not, however, in my top three. He appears in the top 10, and I will leave it up to you to decide his fate with regard to steroids.

Albert Pujols

Height: 6'3"; Weight: 210; Bats: right; Throws: right

First game: April 2, 2001; Final game: still active

Team(s): St. Louis Cardinals (2001–present)

MVP: National League MVP in 2005; 3.96 career shares (through '06 voting)

Hall of Fame: imminent

162-game avg.: .332 batting, .420 on-base, .620 slugging, 42 home runs, 373 total bases, 126 runs scored, 128 runs batted in, 200 hits, 88 extra-base hits, 88 BB, 67 K, 6 SB

Career P/E: 1.271; Postseason P/E: 1.191

The Good. Few players in the history of baseball have gotten off to starts as good as Albert Pujols. Beginning in 2001 the Cardinals first baseman has been tremendously efficient, productive, and consistent, and his 1.271 lifetime P/E is evidence of that. A career .332 batter, Albert has hit between .314 and .359 each season. Although he's never reached 400 total bases, he has finished a year with as many as 394, and his lowest total was 321.

Pujols combines great bat control with power and a very good eye at the plate. In short, he is an absolute nightmare for opposing pitchers. At 1.31 net runs per game, he is more productive than almost every other player mentioned in this book, except for a handful of legends. He has topped 200 net runs every season but one, remaining healthy and in the lineup consistently. Until 2006 Pujols never played fewer than 154 games. From '01 through '05, he had 590–592 at-bats each season.

In the playoffs, Pujols has been nearly as lethal as in the regular season. In 11 postseason series, Albert has hit .300 or better in eight of them. Against the Astros in the 2004 NLCS, the righty slugger torched Houston pitching to the tune of a .500 batting average and 1.000 slugging percentage. He also scored 10 and drove in 9 (P/E: 1.938). Pujols's excellence has been recognized by finishing in the top four of the MVP vote each year from '01 through '06, including three runner-up finishes ('02, '03, and '06) to go along with his first-place honor in 2005.

The Bad. Albert began his career at third and in the outfield before finally finding a home at first base. He struggled at the hot corner and failed to distinguish himself in the outfield. At the plate, it's virtually impossible to find a flaw. He reaches base often, walks more than he strikes out, hits to all fields, and can steal a base if needed.

In the '06 World Series, Pujols hit .200, producing only four net runs against the Tigers. He did connect for one homer but failed to dominate the way he has usually done in the past.

The Verdict. Pujols added to his overall value by winning his first Gold Glove in '06. There is no telling exactly where his career will wind up, but I believe we're looking at one of the truly great players in history. My guess is that he will be considered one of the top dozen players of all time, if not better, in 8–10 years. According to my analysis, he rates as Category 5 and has already vaulted himself into this position's top five. That's pretty good for someone who won't turn 30 years old until January 16, 2010.

First Base: The Top 10

When it comes to ranking the 10 greatest first basemen in history, there is difficulty in choosing from a very strong group of current and potential Hall of Famers. This position is loaded with players who accumulated tremendous statistics. My rankings rely on statistical measures and P/E Averages more heavily than at any other infield position. After careful analysis, my top 10 goes like this.

10. Jim Bottomley

Jim Bottomley averaged more than 200 net runs per season for six straight years. His career average of 1.20 net runs per game edges out Sisler. Most important, Jim earns spot number 10 over Gorgeous George based on a much higher P/E Average, 1.102 to 1.030. Both men won an MVP, and both were tremendous hitters. Bottomley, however, played great in the '26 World Series while Sisler's teams never won a pennant. Bottomley wins this contest fairly easily.

9. Bill Terry

Bill Terry and Jim Bottomley share almost the exact same career P/E Averages, 1.107 and 1.102, respectively, so I need to look at other information to substantiate my ranking. Looking to MVP shares, even though Bottomley won the award in '28, he trails Terry in career shares quite substantially, by a count of 2.72 to 1.61. If the award had been given in 1930, I think it is safe to say that Terry would have finished at least third and, therefore, added even more to his total, probably coming close to doubling Bottomley's for their careers. Finally, I think the lifetime Giant was the better fielder.

8. Eddie Murray

The MVP résumés of Eddie Murray and Bill Terry are very similar. Neither man won the award, but they both received considerable recognition over several years. Murray, 3.33 shares, was in the top five six times. Terry, 2.72 shares, was in the top seven six times and hit .401 for the 1930 season, when no award was given. The steady one edges him out because of sustained run production and power. Murray drove in 839 more runs than Terry, and that is significant enough for me to overlook the fact that Terry's P/E Average is more than 100 points higher. Murray also hit more than 500 career homers while Terry retired with 154. That's a respectable total, but it trails Murray's by 350.

7. Johnny Mize

In my opinion, Mize was a better player than Murray. He was more productive (1.11 net runs per game to Eddie's average of 1.00) despite missing three full seasons in the mid-'40s. Johnny also has a 179-point P/E advantage in the regular season and a 118-point lead in postseason play, where his teams went 5–0 in the World Series.

6. Mark McGwire

Mark McGwire is the lowest ranked of the Category 5 first basemen, but there is no shame in that. Johnny Mize had a slightly higher career P/E Average (1.185 versus 1.179), and he was better in terms of net run production. McGwire earns this spot over Mize, however, because of the long ball. I cannot overlook the fact that Big Red smacked 224 more home runs than the Big Cat. Furthermore, McGwire's rate of one home run per 10.61 at-bats is the best in history, and that is quite significant.

5. Jeff Bagwell

Jeff Bagwell comes in ahead of Big Mac, and that may be surprising to some people. For me, I prefer Bagwell's production over McGwire's homers. McGwire reached 200 net runs in a season twice, something his rival accomplished six times, and that's not counting Bagwell's '94 strike-shortened season (181 scoreboard runs), when he was well on his way to 200 again. While they share nearly identical P/E scores and both won Rookie of the Year honors and one Gold Glove, Bagwell has an MVP trophy to his credit. McGwire hit balls over the fence more consistently, but Bagwell was the better player.

4. Albert Pujols

Albert has already put up numbers that few others have in the history of the sport. Beginning in '01, Pujols has produced more than 200 net runs for the Cardinals every year but one. Production like that hearkens back to DiMaggio and Williams, two immortal stars. Like Bagwell, Pujols has won an MVP. In fact, he's been in the top four every season through 2006. I don't see any reason why he'll slow down.

The Top Three

In his 1985 work, *The Bill James Historical Baseball Abstract*, James described the amazing confluence of talent that occurred in the AL in the 1930s at first base. Referring to Foxx, Gehrig, and Greenberg, the author offered the following: "That is probably the most remarkable concentration of talent at one position in one league that there has ever been." I couldn't agree more. These three immortals each accumulated unimaginable statistics while repeatedly playing against each other.

The Case for Foxx

Sustained performance: 1929–1941

Three MVPs (two with Philadelphia, one with Boston)

534 career home runs

150 homers from 1932 to 1934

Two seasons with more than 50 round-trippers

The Case for Gehrig

Sustained performance: 1926–1938

High career P/E Average, postseason P/E Average, and career net runs per game

5.44 MVP shares

Four seasons above 1.500 P/E

6–1 in World Series play

The Case for Greenberg

Two MVPs (one unanimous and one as an outfielder)

1.318 career P/E Average and 1.356 postseason P/E Average

1.43 net runs per game

Two seasons with at least 170 runs batted in

Three full seasons lost to World War II

3. Hank Greenberg

Although he was a tremendous player, Greenberg simply cannot match statistics with the other two. If he had not served in World War II, it might be a different story, but I think he would probably still be number 3. At this time, however, I still rank him ahead of Pujols. Two or three years down the road, that could change. For now, Hammerin' Hank gets the third spot on the strength of his multiple MVPs, his slightly better per-game run production, and the fact that he missed so much time to the war effort in the 1940s.

2. Jimmie Foxx

I think Hank Greenberg and Jimmie Foxx were extremely similar players. Their P/E scores, 1.318 and 1.315, are almost identical. Both were ferocious RBI machines from the right side of the plate, and both won multiple MVPs. Foxx earns the silver, however, because he simply did it longer. He finished with 646 more RBI, 700 more runs scored, and 203 more home runs. Also, Foxx slugged over .700 three times, and Greenberg never reached that mark.

1. Lou Gehrig

Lou Gehrig is unquestionably the greatest first baseman of all time. What Foxx was able to accomplish, Gehrig surpassed. Except in terms of home runs, the Iron Horse comes out ahead in virtually every offensive category. True, Foxx did win three MVPs to Gehrig's two, but the lifetime Yankee outdistances him in career shares (5.44 to 4.21).

Over their careers, each man came to the plate almost the exact same number of times, 9,670 for Foxx and 9,660 for Gehrig. Therefore, it is very convenient to compare their overall totals. I found an even better way to determine the winner, though, and I call it the Baker's Dozen Argument. Both players had stretches of exactly 13 years in which they compiled the vast majority of their statistics and accomplishments. I compared these stretches to see which player came out on top. I think you'll agree with my contention.

	Jimmie Foxx	Lou Gehrig
13-Year Span	1929–1941	1926–1938
Runs Batted In	1,745	1,912
Runs Scored	1,560	1,805
Home Runs	503	472
Net Runs	2,802	3,245
200-Hit Seasons	2	8
Seasons of .350 Batting	4	6
Seasons of .450 On-Base	5	8
Seasons of .700 Slugging	3	3
400 Total Bases	Two times	Five times
Combined P/E Average	1.358	1.406

Octobers of 2.000

In theory, a perfect P/E score is 12.000, but that can only be obtained by hitting a grand slam every time at the plate. Obviously, this has never been achieved. There have, however, been instances of extreme production and efficiency throughout the postseason by some of the first basemen cited in this chapter. They each had unbelievable individual success, although their teams didn't always prevail. Once, they even played against each other.

In the 1970 World Series, Cincinnati first baseman Lee May put on quite a show of offensive talent against Baltimore. Over five games, May hit .389 and slugged .833 while reaching safely 45 percent of the time. He had two homers and eight RBI en route to 12 net runs in 20 plate appearances. In spite of May's heroics, the Reds lost.

May's 1970 World Series P/E Average: 2.050

The '89 NLCS featured a matchup of two of the game's top first basemen, Mark Grace and Will Clark. Grace paced the Cubs with 11 hits, 5 of which went for extra bases. He walked four times and only struck out once as he posted tremendous efficiency averages: .647 batting, .682 on-base, and 1.118 slugging. He knocked in eight runs in five games. Unfortunately for the Windy City, Grace's counterpart was even better. Clark batted .650 and slugged 1.200 in leading the Giants to the World Series. He had 13 hits, 6 of which went for extra bases, in addition to 8 runs scored and 8 driven in. For his efforts, Clark walked away with the NLCS MVP.

Grace's 1989 NLCS P/E Average: 2.000

Clark's 1989 NLCS P/E Average: 2.455

The award for the best postseason series by a first baseman goes, not surprisingly, to Lou Gehrig, who demolished St. Louis pitching in the '28 World Series. In a four-game sweep of the Cardinals, Gehrig gained 25 complete bases and contributed 10 net runs to the Yankees' scoreboard. His efficiency averages were off the charts: .545 batting, .706 on-base, and 1.727 slugging. He hit four homers, knocked in nine, and walked six times without striking out. Needless to say, it was his greatest postseason performance.

Gehrig's 1928 World Series P/E Average: 2.647

Second Base

The fourth position on the diamond is second base. Players at this spot have traditionally been valued for their gloves and their ability to turn two. Whether taking the throw from shortstop or third, second basemen are involved in almost every double play. They have to be able to stand their ground and make strong relays to first as base runners are bearing down on them with their cleats up. Bill Mazeroski, Frank White, Roberto Alomar, and Ryne Sandberg were all virtuosos with the leather, winning 35 combined Gold Gloves over their illustrious careers.

Second basemen have also been dependable, and sometimes deadly, at the plate. Rogers Hornsby, Jeff Kent, and Alfonso Soriano all have broken the mold of a typical second baseman by hitting for power and knocking balls over the fence while being tremendous run producers. Not surprisingly, multiple MVPs have been granted to second basemen throughout history. These occurrences are listed in detail at the end of this chapter in the section called "Second to None."

I found second base to be one of the most difficult positions to rank. P/E Averages and other individual measures of offensive performance have been analyzed carefully and stringently. In addition, I have included a new statistic, assist-to-error ratio, which I have employed when ranking players at second, third, and shortstop. Just as point guards in basketball are evaluated in terms of assists to turnovers, players at these three infield positions can be fairly judged according to their ability to make defensive plays.

Defensive considerations, always important at second base, must be balanced with offensive statistics. Ranking the top 10, and especially the top three, was difficult for me, but I think I got it right, although there will certainly be those who disagree.

Second Base: Career P/E Averages

Rogers Hornsby, 1.214; Charlie Gehringer, 1.135; Tony Lazzeri, 1.081; Jeff Kent, 1.074; Nap Lajoie, 1.072; Alfonso Soriano, 1.037; Bobby Doerr, 1.036; Joe Gordon, 1.032; Eddie Collins, 1.025; Frankie Frisch, 1.019; Joe Morgan, 1.008; Roberto Alomar, .993; Ryne Sandberg, .971; Chuck Knoblauch, .963; Craig Biggio, .952; Lou Whitaker, .942; Jose Vidro, .936; Carlos Baerga, .923; Juan Samuel, .923; Davey Lopes, .918; Larry Doyle, .914; Billy Herman, .908; Bobby Grich, .907; Bobby Avila, .864; Willie Randolph, .848; Davey Johnson, .845; Red Schoendienst, .840; Tommy Herr, .832; Frank White, .806; Steve Sax .805; Nellie Fox, .799; Johnny Evers, .792; Harold Reynolds, .777; Bill Mazeroski, .750; Bobby Richardson, .708; Bobby Knoop, .688; Sparky Anderson, .590

Category 1–3 Second Basemen

Sparky Anderson

Career P/E: .590; Postseason P/E: never in the postseason
Notable season (P/E): 1959 (.590)

George Lee Anderson was inducted into baseball's Hall of Fame in 2000 for his outstanding managerial career with the Reds and the Tigers. His playing career, however, lasted only one season and was less than spectacular. Sparky was the second baseman on the '59 Phillies, a team that lost 90 games and finished in eighth place in the National League. Anderson made the most of his only season, though, playing in 152 games.

While Anderson was solid in the field, he was quite inept at the plate. He failed to hit a home run in his only season in the majors, and he accounted for exactly .50 net runs per game for Philadelphia. His .590 P/E Average is the lowest by far among the second basemen listed in this chapter. The righty second bagger had extremely poor efficiency averages as well: .218 batting, .282 on-base, and .249 slugging.

Anderson, originally drafted by Brooklyn, had an extremely short and forgettable playing career. As a manager, conversely, he was extraordinary. He won three World Series and five pennants and led four 100-win seasons over his tenure. As a skipper, I'd rate him Category 5, but as a second baseman, it's Category 1.

Carlos Baerga

Career P/E: .923; Postseason P/E: .814
Notable seasons (P/E): 1992 (.990); 1993 (1.103); 1994 (1.147);
   1995 (1.038)

Carlos Baerga was a very good offensive threat for Cleveland for several years. In '92 and again in '93, Baerga posted back-to-back 200-hit seasons. He scored 197 runs and drove in 219 over the two years while averaging more than 300 total bases per season. He finished eleventh in MVP balloting in '92 and tenth in '93.

Baerga had only four seasons with Cleveland that stand out as anything special. Defensively, Baerga was not good. He had five straight seasons in which he committed at least 15 errors at second base, and his career fielding percentage, .976, trails the league average, .981, by five points over the same period. After performing great in the '95 ALCS, he was an easy out (.192 batting average) for Atlanta in the Fall Classic.

Carlos Baerga, for a short time, was one of the better second basemen in the game. He teamed with Lofton, Belle, Ramirez, and Thome to form a potent lineup in 1995, the year Cleveland won the Central by 30 games. He failed to match that success after that memorable season, though. He is Category 2 with no chance for induction.

Joe Gordon

Career P/E: 1.032; Postseason P/E: .922
Notable seasons (P/E): 1939 (1.103); 1940 (1.108); 1942 (1.114);
    1948 (1.166)

Joe Gordon played on some of the great Yankees teams of the late '30s through the mid-'40s and won the American League MVP in 1942. He was in the top 10 five times and ended up with 1.57 career shares and nine All-Star nominations. In '42 Gordon hit .322 and reached base more than 40 percent of the time.

Gordon appeared in six World Series, but he was disappointing in four of them, batting .235 or less and failing to generate much offense.

In 1942 he managed just a single and a double in 21 trips to the plate while striking out seven times against St. Louis.

Joe Gordon is the best player in this section. I went back and forth on his rating many times before deciding on C3. He had some tremendous offensive seasons and was often on MVP ballots, but his career statistics leave him just shy of HOF status in my eyes. Had he not missed two seasons in the mid-'40s, I might view him differently.

Davey Lopes

Career P/E: .918; Postseason P/E: .966

Notable seasons (P/E): 1974 (.904); 1975 (.912); 1977 (.964); 1978 (.943); 1979 (1.039)

Davey Lopes stole more than 40 bags seven times, and he led the National League in '75 and again in '76. He was at his best when hitting at the top of the lineup, getting on base, and making things happen with his legs. He scored more than 100 runs twice, and he had at least 85 runs scored five times. In the '81 playoffs, Davey had 14 hits and 10 stolen bases without being caught as the Dodgers won all three of their postseason series.

Lopes was better offensively than defensively. His career fielding percentage, .977, is lower than the league average. When he won the Gold Glove in 1978, he did so after committing 20 errors and, again, having a lower than average fielding mark. Although he was a four-time All-Star, Lopes never received any serious MVP consideration. He retired with .04 lifetime shares, receiving votes only once (1978).

The Dodgers' second baseman comes in as Category 3. At his best, he was a multidimensional offensive weapon; he was a tremendous base runner. Defensively, he was average, and that prevents him from rating higher.

Steve Sax

Career P/E: .805; Postseason P/E: .726

Notable seasons (P/E): 1982 (.818); 1986 (.918); 1989 (.869)

Like so many other Dodgers players, Steve Sax won the Rookie of the Year, beating out fellow second basemen Johnny Ray and Ryne Sandberg for the award in 1982. He was a five-time All-Star, and he hit .332 in 1986, finishing second to Tim Raines for the batting title. From '82 to '92 Steve averaged 39 steals per season. He swiped five bags in the '88 NLCS, scoring seven times in leading L.A. to victory over the Mets.

Steve Sax suffered through throwing problems in Los Angeles. He made 73 combined errors from 1983 to 1985, but his defense rebounded somewhat in the latter half of his career. He had very little power, finishing with 54 homers and a slugging percentage of .358. His P/E score, .805, trails the likes of Bobby Grich, Billy Herman, and Davey Lopes by more than 100 points each.

Stephen Louis Sax is Category 2, but I think he is at least close to C3. He hit better than .300 three times but retired with a .281 average. He just missed reaching 2,000 hits, 1,000 runs scored, and 500 steals, numbers that might warrant pushing him up a notch.

Lou Whitaker

Career P/E: .942; Postseason P/E: .869

Notable seasons (P/E): 1978 (.859); 1983 (.939); 1985 (.956); 1986 (.951); 1987 (.942)

In 1978 Sweet Lou beat out Paul Molitor and teammate Alan Trammel to win the AL Rookie of the Year after hitting .285. He won three consecutive Gold Gloves in the mid-'80s and was always known for his work with the leather. His assist-to-error ratio of 35.2:1 is outstanding and ranks as one of the best marks in this chapter.

Whitaker hit better than .300 in only one full season, 1983. He had some years when his bat was quiet. In 1980, for example, he hit just .233, and in 1990 he batted .237. He never slugged .500 in a full season, and the 85 runs he drove home in '89 were a career high. In the '87 ALCS, Whitaker hit just .176. Detroit lost that series to the Twins.

Whitaker is Category 3. His career looks a lot like that of Red Schoendienst. Lou was a fixture at second base in Detroit from 1977 to 1995. He was consistent and steady, making five straight All-Star teams in the mid-'80s. He is a doubtful choice for enshrinement, but lesser players at this position have already been inducted.

The Best Second Basemen

162-Game Averages

Player	BA	OBP	SLP	HR	TB	R	RBI	H	XBH	BB	K	SB
Alomar	.300	.371	.443	14	274	103	77	185	53	70	78	32
Biggio	.281	.363	.433	17	268	105	67	174	58	66	100	24
Collins	.333	.424	.429	3	245	104	75	190	39	86	20*	43
Doerr	.288	.362	.461	19	284	95	108	177	60	70	53	5
Frisch	.316	.369	.432	7	276	107	87	202	50	51	19	29
Gehringer	.320	.404	.480	13	297	124	100	198	63	83	26	13
Hornsby	.358	.434	.577	22	338	113	114	210	73	74	49	10
Kent	.290	.357	.504	27	302	95	109	174	70	58	109	7
Lajoie	.338	.380	.467	5	292	98	104	212	59	34	32*	25
Lazzeri	.292	.380	.467	17	274	92	111	171	59	81	80	14
Morgan	.271	.392	.427	16	242	101	69	154	49	114	62	42
Sandberg	.285	.344	.452	21	284	99	79	179	57	57	94	26

* Estimated total for strikeouts based on statistics from known seasons

Category 4 Second Basemen

Craig Biggio

Career P/E: .952; Postseason P/E: .724

MVP: never won; 1.02 career shares (through '06 voting)

Hall of Fame: imminent

Craig Allan Biggio is the rarest of modern-day ballplayers. He has spent his entire career with one team, the Houston Astros. Houston used the twenty-second pick of the 1987 amateur draft to select Biggio out of Seton Hall University, where he had starred with Mo Vaughn. When he broke into the big leagues in '88, it was behind the plate, and he even won a Silver Slugger as a catcher. He moved to second base, however, and the rest is Astros history. Biggio has always been a hardnosed player who hustles. He is at his best at the top of the lineup, getting on and getting in. From 1995 to 1999, he averaged more than 125 runs scored per season.

Craig has been most disappointing in the playoffs, although he has fared much better in the postseason in the latter stages of his career. From 1997 to 2001, the Astros made it into October four times and failed to advance beyond the first round each time. Over 14 games, Biggio scored four runs and managed just one RBI. His batting averages were .083, .182, .105, and .167.

Biggio is Category 4. I believe he should be in Cooperstown when all is said and done. He has already reached 3,000 hits, which should ensure his nomination.

Year	RBI	R	HR	NR	TB	BB	HBP	SB	CS	CB	PTS	PA	P/E
1995	77	123	22	178	267	80	22	33	8	394	750	673	1.114
1997	81	146	22	205	310	84	34	47	10	465	875	744	1.176
1998	88	123	20	191	325	64	23	50	8	454	836	738	1.133
Career	1,175	1,884	291	2,728	4,711	1,160	285	414	124	6,446	11,902	12,503	.952

Bobby Doerr

Career P/E: 1.036; Postseason P/E: .875

MVP: never won; .93 career shares

Hall of Fame: inducted in 1986

Robert Pershing Doerr debuted on April 20, 1937, with the Boston Red Sox, the only team he ever played for over the course of 14 big-league seasons. For his career, he averaged 1.14 net runs per game, a mark that tops those of Alomar, Collins, and Sandberg. Year after year, Doerr posted P/E scores above 1.000, setting his career-best mark of 1.175 in 1944. That year, Bobby also set career bests in each of the three main efficiency averages: .325 batting, .399 on-base, and .528 slugging. In the field, he was great. His ratio of 26.7 assists for every error is very good. Doerr's solid combination of offensive production and defensive dependability made him a deserving Hall of Famer.

As with Ted Williams and his other Boston teammates, probably the most convincing argument against Doerr rests with his inability to secure a World Series title. The Red Sox sported talented teams in the '40s and '50s. In '46 they won 104 games but lost the Series in seven games to the Cardinals. Doerr was good, hitting .409 with nine Series hits, but he wasn't able to deliver a championship to the faithful fans of Fenway.

I think Doerr was an excellent second baseman. He topped 100 RBI in a season six times and retired with more than 2,000 hits. He is Category 4, which means that I agree with his Hall of Fame status. Teddy Ballgame loved him as a teammate.

Year	RBI	R	HR	NR	TB	BB	HBP	SB	CS	CB	PTS	PA	P/E
1948	111	94	27	178	266	83	4	3	2	354	710	618	1.149
1949	109	91	18	182	269	75	0	2	2	344	708	623	1.136
1950	120	103	27	196	304	67	1	3	4	371	763	663	1.151
Career	1,247	1,094	223	2,118	3,270	809	11	54	64	4,080	8,316	8,028	1.036

Frankie Frisch

Career P/E: 1.019; Postseason P/E: .671

MVP: National League MVP in 1931; 2.58 career shares

Hall of Fame: inducted in 1947

Born in the Bronx in 1898, Frankie Frisch (also known as the Fordham Flash) played 19 seasons in the NL for the Giants and the Cardinals. In 1931, he beat out Chuck Klein and Bill Terry to win the MVP. He also finished second in '27, third in '24, and in the top 10 four times to earn 2.58 career shares, an impressive number. Frisch walked 728 times while striking out only 272, and he never fanned 30 times in a single season. He topped 200 hits on three occasions and often was above .380 in terms of on-base percentage. His best season may have been 1930, when no MVP was awarded. He hit .346 and posted his career-best efficiency averages in on-base (.407) and slugging (.520).

The Fordham Flash appeared in eight World Series, winning four and losing four. He hit .363 over the first four but only .221 over the last four. His P/E postseason mark, .671, is low because Frisch generated just 26 net runs over 50 contests, an average of .52 per game. He never hit more than 12 homers in a season, winding up with 105 in more than 10,000 plate appearances.

This career National Leaguer is rated as C4. If he had more power, I would move him up to the top grouping. He falls just shy. He does make the top 10, however.

Year	RBI	R	HR	NR	TB	BB	HBP	SB	CS	CB	PTS	PA	P/E
1921	100	121	8	213	300	42	1	49	13	379	805	687	1.172
1923	111	116	12	215	311	46	4	29	12	378	808	702	1.151
1930	114	121	10	225	281	55	0	15	6*	345	795	611	1.301
Career	1,244	1,532	105	2,671	3,937	728	31	419	167*	4,948	10,290	10,100	1.019

* CS totals estimated based on known statistics

Jeff Kent

Career P/E: 1.074; Postseason P/E: 1.006

MVP: National League MVP in 2000; 1.58 career shares (through
'06 voting

Hall of Fame: possible

When the San Francisco Giants acquired Jeff Kent after the '96 season, it proved one of the smartest baseball moves of the decade. Kent was just coming into his own as a hitter, and the Giants struck at just the right time. Kent paid immediate dividends, knocking in 121 runs and posting a P/E Average of 1.086. During his six seasons in San Francisco, he posted P/E scores between 1.036 and 1.243 every year. In 2000 he beat out teammate Barry Bonds for the National League MVP, due in large part to 206 net runs produced and a batting average of .334. He has eight seasons of triple-digit RBI totals, and he has won four Silver Sluggers. Kent has been good in the playoffs also, hitting .615 against the Mets in defeat in the first round in '06.

Kent may need a few more seasons of good production to gain entrance into the Hall. He has never been known for his work in the field, so it will be his offensive statistics that ultimately decide his fate. He should be able to reach 400 career home runs, but 500 is improbable.

I believe Jeff Kent is a Hall of Famer. He has solidified himself as a dangerous hitter by consistently posting high RBI numbers. I have also ranked him in my top 10.

Year	RBI	R	HR	NR	TB	BB	HBP	SB	CS	CB	PTS	PA	P/E
1997	121	90	29	182	274	48	13	11	3	343	707	651	1.086
1998	128	94	31	191	292	48	9	9	4	354	736	594	1.239
2000	125	114	33	206	350	90	9	12	9	452	864	695	1.243
Career	1,459	1,278	365	2,372	4,062	776	118	94	59	4,991	9,735	9,063	1.074

Nap Lajoie

Career P/E: 1.072; Postseason P/E: never in the postseason
MVP: never won; .19 career shares
Hall of Fame: inducted in 1937

Napoleon Lajoie began his major league career before the turn of the nineteenth century and played for 21 seasons in both leagues. When he joined the upstart American League in its inaugural year of 1901, Lajoie put on a show for everyone to enjoy. Against weaker competition, Lajoie hit .426, smacked 14 homers, scored 145 times, and had 125 RBI while posting the highest P/E mark of his career, 1.550. He led the junior circuit in batting that year as well as in 1902, 1903, 1904, and 1910. He amassed 3,242 hits and surpassed 1,500 runs both scored and driven home. His average of 1.22 net runs per game is outstanding and points to a career that was extremely productive.

Lajoie failed to get his teams into the postseason every year. He never played on the big stage of the World Series. His teams were consistently in the middle to the back of the pack in league standings.

It is hard to get an accurate handle on Lajoie's career. His best season, 1901, came against significantly weaker competition in the upstart American League, but his numbers are outstanding nonetheless. He made a ton of errors, but he fielded much higher than his peers. He also played the majority of his career in the days before MVP voting.

Year	RBI	R	HR	NR	TB	BB	HBP	SB	CS	CB	PTS	PA	P/E
1898	127	113	6	234	280	21	7	25	22*	311	779	641	1.215
1901	125	145	14	256	350	24	13	27	24*	390	902	582	1.550
1904	102	92	6	188	305	27	8	29	25*	344	720	594	1.212
Career	1,599	1,504	83	3,020	4,474	516	134	380	333*	5,171	11,211	10,460	1.072

* CS totals estimated based on known statistics

Tony Lazzeri

Career P/E: 1.081; Postseason P/E: .968

MVP: never won; .99 career shares

Hall of Fame: inducted in 1991

Tony Lazzeri joined Babe Ruth, Lou Gehrig, and Bob Meusel to form the infamous Murderer's Row on the New York Yankees in the 1920s. When he debuted in 1926, Tony was an instant success. He drove in 114 runs in his rookie season and posted a P/E score of 1.033. That season marked the first of seven when Lazzeri would reach the century mark for runs batted in. In 1927 the Yankees fielded a team that may have been the greatest in baseball history. Gehrig won the MVP, the Yankees won 110 games, and they swept the Pirates in the Series. Lazzeri hit .309 that year and again topped 100 RBI.

Poosh 'Em Up Tony, as he was often called, had a career that started fast but ended unspectacularly. He had 10 seasons that ranged from good to excellent to go along with a handful that were forgettable. Six times he hit .275 or less, including his last season in the Bronx when he hit .244. His .292 career batting average is very good but would have looked even better had it been a few points higher.

Tony is Category 4. I support his status as a Hall of Famer. He was a great run producer, and he overcame mediocre defensive statistics by piling up just enough numbers at the plate. Nevertheless, Lazzeri fails to gain entrance into my top 10.

Year	RBI	R	HR	NR	TB	BB	HBP	SB	CS	CB	PTS	PA	P/E
1929	106	101	18	189	306	68	4	9	10	377	755	635	1.189
1930	121	109	9	221	264	60	3	4	4	327	769	650	1.183
1933	104	94	18	180	254	73	2	15	7	337	697	602	1.158
Career	1,191	986	178	1,999	2,938	869	21	148	79*	3,897	7,895	7,303	1.081

* CS totals estimated based on known statistics

Category 5 Second Basemen

Roberto Alomar

Height: 6'0"; Weight: 185; Bats: both; Throws: right

First game: April 22, 1988; Final game: 2004

Team(s): San Diego Padres (1988–1990); Toronto Blue Jays
    (1991–1995); Baltimore Orioles (1996–1998); Cleveland Indians
    (1999–2001); New York Mets (2002–2003); Chicago White Sox
    (2003–2004); Arizona Diamondbacks (2004)

MVP: never won; 1.91 career shares

Hall of Fame: probable

162-game avg.: .300 batting, .371 on-base, .443 slugging, 14 home
    runs, 274 total bases, 103 runs scored, 77 runs batted in, 185 hits,
    53 extra-base hits, 70 BB, 78 K, 32 SB

Career P/E: .993; Postseason P/E: 1.027

The Good. The player with the most Gold Gloves at the second base
position is Roberto Alomar. He won a total of 10, all in the American
League, from 1991 through 2001, failing to secure the award only in
1997 during that stretch. He was always a smooth-fielding, effortless
player who seemed to do everything well on the diamond. He averaged 36.0 assists for every error and retired with a career fielding percentage of .984.

Alomar was certainly no slouch at the plate either. He hit .300 or
better nine times and slugged at least .500 four times. His best season
may have been 1999 with Cleveland. The switch-hitter batted .323 and
produced 234 net runs for the Indians. He also recorded his best on-
base percentage that year, .422, while scoring 138 runs and driving

home 120. He finished third in the MVP vote that year, which was the best of his career.

Perhaps most impressive about Alomar was his work in the postseason. A career .313 hitter in the playoffs, Roberto was named ALCS MVP in 1992 after stroking 11 hits and stealing five bags as Toronto beat Oakland and advanced to the World Series, which they also won. When they repeated as champions in '93, Alomar was a big reason why. He hit .480 with 12 hits and six RBI, all postseason bests, against Philadelphia.

The Bad. Many people will always remember Alomar for spitting on umpire John Hirschbeck while wearing a Baltimore uniform in '96. That single incident did a lot to mar an otherwise stellar career. Alomar defended himself by reporting that he had been called a racial slur.

Alomar's last three seasons were forgettable to say the least. After leaving the Indians, Roberto played for the Mets, White Sox, and Diamondbacks, but he didn't play very well. He hit no better than .266 by the end of each season and seemed to be a shell of the once great player he was in Toronto, Baltimore, and Cleveland.

The Verdict. Roberto Alomar is Category 5 despite never winning an MVP. He's also a top-10 selection at second base according to my analysis. He is not eligible for Cooperstown yet, but he should become a Hall of Famer once his turn comes. He was outstanding defensively, multitalented on offense, and often at his best in big games. Aside from his incident with Hirschbeck, Alomar had a remarkable career, one of the best in baseball history at the position.

Eddie Collins

Height: 5'9"; Weight: 175; Bats: left; Throws: right

First game: September 17, 1906; Final game: August 2, 1930

Team(s): Philadelphia Athletics (1906–1914, 1927–1930); Chicago
   White Sox (1915–1926)

MVP: American League MVP in 1914; 3.86 career shares

Hall of Fame: inducted in 1939

162-game avg.: .333 batting, .424 on-base, .429 slugging, 3 home
   runs, 245 total bases, 104 runs scored, 75 runs batted in, 190 hits,
   39 extra-base hits, 86 BB, 22 K, 43 SB

Career P/E: 1.025; Postseason P/E: .938

The Good. Inducted into Cooperstown in 1939, Eddie Collins was one
of the great second basemen of all time. He batted .333 for his career,
going over .300 in 16 full seasons. He finished with 3,315 hits and an
on-base percentage of .424. Collins played 25 seasons in the American League for the Athletics and the White Sox. In 1914 he was named
AL MVP after batting .344 and producing 205 net runs. Two years earlier, Eddie also surpassed 200 net runs for the season.

The year after his 1919 White Sox became infamously known as the
Black Sox in reference to several players throwing the World Series,
Collins had arguably his best season. He hit .372 and racked up 224
hits, both career bests. His P/E Average that year, 1.076, marked one
of 11 seasons when he exceeded 1.000.

Collins was frequently in the World Series, and he usually played
well. He batted over .400 in three different Series and hit .328 for his
postseason career. When his teams won the title in 1910, 1911, 1913,
and 1917, Collins combined to record 32 hits, 18 runs scored, and 12
steals.

Edward Trowbridge Collins Sr. earned 3.86 career MVP shares, the highest total ever for a second baseman. He won only once, but he finished second twice—he was runner-up to Ruth in '23 and to Walter Johnson in '24. In all, he finished in the top three a remarkable five times.

The Bad. The only significant knock against Collins offensively was his lack of power. He retired with only 47 home runs and a slugging percentage, .429, only five points higher than his on-base average. Except for Joe Morgan, that mark is also lower than every other second baseman in this section. He never slugged .500 in a season and never hit more than six homers. Therefore, he never reached a 1.200 P/E in any full season, topping out at 1.186 in his MVP campaign of 1914.

Collins's defensive statistics are a little ambiguous. His fielding percentage, .970, was much higher than the league average, .958, over the course of his career. However, he did have 15 seasons in which he committed at least 20 errors. In 1912 the second baseman goofed 38 times. His assist-to-error ratio of 17.5:1 trails many of the other players in this section, but I do think he was still pretty solid defensively.

The Verdict. Eddie Collins had a top-five career and is an easy mark for C5. He produced more than 3,000 career net runs and averaged 1.09 per game. Collins, who later worked as general manager of the Red Sox and was instrumental in signing a young prospect named Ted Williams, was a tremendous star but not quite as good as my top three.

Charlie Gehringer

Height: 5'11"; Weight: 180; Bats: left; Throws: right

First game: September 22, 1924; Final game: September 27, 1942

Team(s): Detroit Tigers (1924–1942)

MVP: American League MVP in 1937; 3.55 career shares

Hall of Fame: inducted in 1949

162-game avg.: .320 batting, .404 on-base, .480 slugging, 13 home
   runs, 297 total bases, 124 runs scored, 100 runs batted in, 198
   hits, 63 extra-base hits, 83 BB, 26 K, 13 SB

Career P/E: 1.135; Postseason P/E: .867

The Good. Charles Leonard Gehringer was a Michigan man through and through. Born in Fowlerville, he died in Bloomfield Hills and attended the University of Michigan along the way. He played 19 seasons with the Detroit Tigers and became a Hall of Famer in 1949. Gehringer was a tremendous talent, anchoring the Tigers at second base. He hit over .300 13 times and at least .330 half a dozen seasons. He was a great example of sustained excellence. Gehringer routinely scored 100 runs, drove in 100 runs, and exceeded 200 hits. His career mark of 1.30 net runs per game is the best ever for a second baseman.

In '37 Gehringer's accomplishments were recognized by being awarded the American League MVP. He hit .371, reached safely more than 45 percent, and scored 133 runs. His P/E of 1.244 that season was one of seven times he bettered 1.200. His career mark of 1.135 trails only the great Rogers Hornsby at this spot on the diamond.

Gehringer produced at least 200 net runs eight times. In 1934 he was responsible for 250 runs for the Tigers scoreboard, a remarkable total for a middle infielder. Two years later, he was nearly as productive. He scored 144 runs and drove home 116 with only 15 homers in 1936, a year that saw Charlie smack 60 doubles and slug .555 for the season.

The lifelong member of the Tigers had a tremendous eye at the plate as well. From 1929 to 1930, he struck out 36 times in 309 games. Later in his career he was even better, striking out only 29 times in 304 games over the '35 and '36 campaigns. He retired with an outstanding ratio of 1,186 bases on balls to 372 strikeouts.

The Bad. Gehringer was not good in the '40 Series in which the Tigers lost to the Reds in seven games. Charlie managed six singles and only one RBI in defeat. He hit .321 in postseason play, but that was often accompanied by a lack of power. He slugged only .407 in World Series games. Gehringer was solid defensively, but he did commit 85 errors over three seasons from 1927 to 1929. He had more than 20 errors six times but finished with a .976 fielding mark. Other than that, it's hard to find fault with the man's career.

The Verdict. Gehringer is one of the most underrated players ever. He might be the least known superstar the game has produced. Year after year, Gehringer manned his second-base position, provided leadership in his clubhouse, and put up tremendous statistics. He is Category 5, and I believe he is one of the three greatest second basemen to ever lace up his spikes.

Rogers Hornsby

Height: 5'11"; Weight: 175; Bats: right; Throws: right

First game: September 10, 1915; Final game: July 20, 1937

Team(s): St. Louis Cardinals (1915–1926, 1933); New York Giants (1927); Boston Braves (1928); Chicago Cubs (1929–1932); St. Louis Browns (1933–1937)

MVP: National League MVP in 1925, 1929; 3.33 career shares

Hall of Fame: inducted in 1942

162-game avg.: .358 batting, .434 on-base, .577 slugging, 22 home runs, 338 total bases, 113 runs scored, 114 runs batted in, 210 hits, 73 extra-base hits, 74 BB, 49 K, 10 SB

Career P/E: 1.214; Postseason P/E: .792

The Good. Rogers Hornsby may indeed be the greatest right-handed hitter of all time. His .358 career batting average is second only to Ty Cobb. Hornsby hit above .400 three times, including an astonishing average of .424 in 1924. From '21 through '25, Rogers batted .402, a mark so high that it is hard to comprehend. Twice he was named NL Most Valuable Player, and twice he won the league's Triple Crown honor. He owns the highest P/E Average of any second baseman, 1.214, a mark that is better than those of Cobb, Mantle, Mays, Musial, and Aaron.

From 1920 to 1929, Hornsby put together one of the great runs in the history of the sport. He batted .382 for the decade and managed at least 125 runs scored and batted in for half of those seasons. His combined P/E Average for that span is 1.320, a phenomenal score. Hornsby exceeded 1.400 three times in the '20s, scoring as high as

1.557 in 1925, a year in which he batted .403, slugged .756, and produced 237 net runs in just over 600 plate appearances.

Nineteen twenty-two was another season in which the second baseman reached a .400 batting average and a .700 slugging percentage. He totaled 250 hits, 102 of which went for extra bases. That season, he knocked in 152 and scored 141. When he hit .424 two years later, he did so while fanning only 32 times. For his career, Rajah walked more than he struck out and hit 301 homers.

The Bad. Offensively, Hornsby has to be considered the greatest second baseman ever. Many of his statistics simply dwarf other outstanding players at this position. Still, he wasn't a perfect player. My calculations indicate that he was average in the field. He fielded .965, a mark that just betters the .964 league average of his day. He had fewer than 17 assists for every error. When he was dominant at the plate in '25, he also coughed up 34 balls in the field and ended the season with a relatively low fielding percentage of .954. Hornsby was also quite average in the World Series. He appeared twice, hit .245, slugged .327, and struck out 10 times.

The Verdict. Hornsby is unquestionably one of the three greatest ever at this position. The 450 total bases he accumulated in 1922 are the second most ever behind Ruth's 457 in '21. Naturally, I rate Rogers as Category 5. He was a fierce competitor who also managed more than 1,500 big-league contests. The only question that remains, therefore, is whether Hornsby is the greatest second baseman of all time.

Joe Morgan

Height: 5'7"; Weight: 160; Bats: left; Throws: right

First game: September 21, 1963; Final game: September 30, 1984

Team(s): Houston Colt .45s/Astros (1963–1971, 1980); Cincinnati
Reds (1972–1979); San Francisco Giants (1981–1982); Philadelphia Phillies (1983); Oakland Athletics (1984)

MVP: National League MVP in 1975, 1976; 3.04 career shares

Hall of Fame: inducted in 1990

162-game avg.: .271 batting, .392 on-base, .427 slugging, 16 home
runs, 242 total bases, 101 runs scored, 69 runs batted in, 154 hits,
49 extra-base hits, 114 BB, 62 K, 42 SB

Career P/E: 1.008; Postseason P/E: .811

The Good. Joe Morgan's name often comes up when the discussion
turns to the greatest second baseman in history. He was named to the
All-Star team 10 times and won the National League Gold Glove every
year from 1973 to 1977. Morgan was tremendous both in the field and
at the top of the lineup. He had eight seasons in which he posted on-
base percentages at or above .400, and he stole 689 bases during his
Hall of Fame career. Morgan also scored 1,650 runs.

At his peak, he was able to carry a team. He won back-to-back MVP
honors in 1975 and 1976, and his Cincinnati squad won the World
Series both seasons as well. The first year, Morgan hit .327, had an on-
base mark of .466, drew 132 walks, stole 67 bags, and scored 107 runs.
The next season, '76, he added some power to his game. Joe hit 27
bombs, slugged .576, and knocked in 111 runs, the most ever in his
career. Both years, this smart player won the MVP by comfortable

margins as he posted extremely high P/E Averages of 1.272 and 1.389, which were the two highest marks of his career.

While Morgan did not post great postseason statistics for his career, he was very good when the Reds swept the Yankees in '76. Joe hit .333 and slugged .733 as Cincinnati proved to everyone once again that they were undoubtedly baseball's best team.

The Bad. Morgan had several years in which his statistics were less than spectacular. The 1975 and 1976 seasons marked the only two times in his career when Joe batted above .300. He hit .250 or less in almost half of his seasons, and his average of .95 net runs per game is the lowest of any player listed in this section. Morgan retired with mediocre averages of .271 batting and .427 slugging.

Although his teams often made it into October, Joe wasn't always at the top of his game. He hit less than .200 in more than half of his postseason series. In the '72 World Series, his first with the Reds, the diminutive second baseman hit .125 and slugged .208 as Cincinnati lost to Oakland in seven games. Over back-to-back NLCS visits in '79 and '80, he managed just two hits in 33 plate appearances. His teams lost both times.

The Verdict. Morgan is Category 5 and will be featured a few pages later as one of the top three second basemen in history. He put together his best seasons in the mid-'70s, and his Cincinnati squads were able to win the title both times. Although he wasn't able to sustain that high level past 1976, he remained a very good player, both in the field and at the plate.

Ryne Sandberg

Height: 6'2"; Weight: 180; Bats: right; Throws: right

First game: September 2, 1981; Final game: September 28, 1997

Team(s): Philadelphia Phillies (1981); Chicago Cubs (1982–1994, 1996–1997)

MVP: National League MVP in 1984; 1.98 career shares

Hall of Fame: inducted in 2005

162-game avg.: .285 batting, .344 on-base, .452 slugging, 21 home runs, 284 total bases, 99 runs scored, 79 runs batted in, 179 hits, 57 extra-base hits, 57 BB, 94 K, 26 SB

Career P/E: .971; Postseason P/E: 1.298

The Good. Chicago's original No. 23 won the MVP award in the National League in 1984 and played his entire career in the Windy City after being traded away by Philadelphia following his rookie campaign. In '84 Sandberg was tremendous to say the least. He had 200 hits, batted .314, and scored 114 runs. In the field, he may have been even better. Winning his second Gold Glove, Ryno fielded .993 with 550 assists and only six errors. That computes to a ratio of 91.7 assists per error. He also had 19 triples while grounding into only seven double plays, taking the Cubs into October.

Sandberg was tremendous defensively throughout his career. His overall fielding percentage is .989, and his career ratio of 58.4 assists for every error is the best of any second baseman in this chapter by a wide margin. He had nine full seasons with eight errors or fewer, and he won nine Gold Gloves, trailing only Roberto Alomar on the all-time list for second basemen.

Ryno's teams made the postseason twice but failed to advance both times. It wasn't his fault, however. In the '84 and '89 NLCS, he combined to hit .385 and produce 14 net runs in 10 games. His postseason P/E of 1.298 is more than 300 points higher than his regular-season average, which tells me he was at his best when the games mattered most. That's what every manager hopes to see from the players on his team.

The Bad. It's hard to find fault with Sandberg. He always seemed to say the right thing and to uphold an image of dignified grace, much like Derek Jeter of today. His offensive statistics are not staggering like those of Collins, Hornsby, and Gehringer. He retired with 1,318 runs scored and 1,061 batted in, solid numbers but a far cry from those of the players previously mentioned.

Sandberg struck out more than 1,200 times in his career in comparison with 761 walks. He fanned 90 times or more in six seasons, and that has to count against him when considering his overall place and rank. Furthermore, his average of .97 net runs per game is good but not great. Defensively, it is almost impossible to find any flaws with his game or his career, so I won't even bother.

The Verdict. Ryne Sandberg makes it into the top five at second base. He is Category 5, but I admit he just qualifies for that high of a rating. I think he is probably underrated, at least outside of Wrigley Field and the greater Chicago area. Sandberg, once a twentieth-round pick of the 1978 amateur draft, will always be loved as one of the all-time great Cubs and always remembered by Philadelphia fans as the Hall of Famer they traded away to get Ivan DeJesus.

Second Base: The Top 10

I had 12 second basemen to choose from in organizing my top 10. Bobby Doerr and Tony Lazzeri, both great players, fall short here. Joe Gordon, the great Yankees second baseman, also comes close to earning a spot even though I rate him as Category 3. In selecting this list I looked at a wide range of variables. Second basemen need to be skilled with the leather and the lumber, and they need to be winning ballplayers. Here is the top 10 of a talent-laden position.

10. Craig Biggio

Biggio sneaks in ahead of Doerr and Lazzeri because he has been able to maintain a high level of play for an extended career. He combined solid defense with speed and smarts to provide a spark plug at the top of the Astros lineup for nearly two decades. To me, Biggio is slightly underrated for his career, although I do think he'll earn his way into Cooperstown.

9. Jeff Kent

Jeff Kent edges out Biggio because of his MVP season of 2000 and his better success in the postseason. Biggio never won the prestigious award, so that tips the scales in Kent's favor. Maybe even more important, Kent has been the superior player in October. While he lacks Biggio's glove and speed, he more than makes up for it with power and tremendous RBI numbers.

8. Frankie Frisch

Kent won the MVP battle with Biggio, but he loses that same battle with Frisch. Frankie won the award and finished with 2.58 shares. He was also second and third during his career. Furthermore, Frisch was a .316 lifetime hitter, and he reached the .300 plateau more than a dozen times. Kent only did that three times. Finally, the Fordham Flash was more productive, averaging 1.16 net runs per game to Kent's mark of 1.09.

7. Nap Lajoie

Lajoie, in my opinion, was a better second baseman than Frisch. He produced better, hit for a higher lifetime average, and topped Frisch by more than 50 points in terms of P/E numbers. He doesn't come close to Frisch's MVP accomplishments, but Nap played most of his career without any opportunity to win such an award. They seem to be similar players to me. They were both productive without hitting many homers, and they both consistently hit for high averages. In almost every offensive category, however, Lajoie trumps Frisch. He earns this spot on my top-10 list of second basemen.

6. Roberto Alomar

Alomar betters Lajoie simply because of defense. Roberto holds the record for Gold Gloves won by a second baseman while Napoleon's defensive statistics were contradictory, pointing to a player who was probably average in the field. Alomar was never average. In fact, he is probably one of the best defensive players at the position in history. He had great range, terrific instincts, and the numbers to back up his case. He also hit .313 in the postseason, and Nap never once played beyond the regular season.

5. Ryne Sandberg

Deciding between Sandberg and Alomar for number 5 was very difficult. Both men were tremendous defensively, and both elevated their games and their P/E scores in October. Alomar won ten Gold Gloves, and Sandberg won nine. I finally decided on Sandberg for two reasons. First, his assist-to-error ratio (58.4:1) is superior to Alomar's (36.0:1). And more important, Sandberg won an MVP; Alomar never achieved that distinction.

4. Eddie Collins

It was very hard not to include Eddie Collins in the top three. His statistics are tremendous. Like Sandberg, he won an MVP. He also played well in the World Series, although his postseason P/E does not come close to Ryno's. I chose Collins for fourth place fairly easily simply because Sandberg can't match statistics with him. Collins scored 503 more runs and batted 48 points higher. The Cub's best batting average was .314. Collins bettered that mark in 15 full seasons. There is no shame in finishing behind Collins, who some consider to be the best ever at second base.

The Top Three

My top three includes two men from the first half of the century and one from more modern times. Their styles and statistics were different, but they are all Hall of Famers with loaded résumés. As full of talented players as any infield position in this book, second base guarantees that the man at the top has earned his place by beating out his immortal peers.

The Case for Gehringer

1.30 net runs per game

Eight top-10 MVP finishes and 3.55 career shares

The best walk-to-strikeout ratio of the three men

13 seasons batting above .300

Eight seasons of 200 or more net runs

The Case for Hornsby

Sustained performance: 1920 to 1929

Lifetime efficiency averages of .358 batting, .434 on-base, and .577
slugging

Two MVPs and two Triple Crowns

Three seasons with batting averages above .400, including .424 in
1924

A lifetime P/E Average of 1.214, the highest for any second
baseman

The Case for Morgan

Two MVPs and two World Series titles in back-to-back seasons

Best assist-to-error ratio and five Gold Gloves

689 stolen bases, including nine straight seasons of at least 40
steals

10 All-Star nominations and MVP honors in the 1972 game

Went to the postseason seven times with three different teams

3. Joe Morgan

Joe Morgan did not put up the lifetime numbers of Eddie Collins. However, he was arguably the best player in baseball over the course of two seasons, 1975 and 1976, and I'm not sure Collins can stake that claim. In his prime, Morgan was flawless. He was always on base, he hit for high averages with power, and he was a run-generating machine because of his ability to draw walks, steal bases, and use his instincts to beat his opponent. In the field, he was equally adept at dominating a game. He didn't have the sustainability of Collins, but he did lead his team to consecutive titles as the league's Most Valuable Player. You can't expect anything more from a player. The choice between Morgan and Collins for number 3 wasn't easy by any stretch. In the end, I opted for Joe because of his dominance in the mid-'70s.

2. Rogers Hornsby

It is hard to write a statistical analysis of baseball and not put Hornsby at the top for this position. He put up numbers normally reserved for first basemen and outfielders. In fact, he put up some numbers that no one has ever been able to match. He earns the nod over Joe Morgan fairly easily. Morgan may have been more complete when considering defense and baserunning, but Hornsby is a legendary hitter, perhaps the best ever from his side of the plate. What Joe Morgan did in 1975 and 1976, Hornsby did for a decade. The Cincinnati star had only two seasons in which he surpassed Hornsby's 1.214 career P/E Average, and that fact by itself is more than enough to convince me that I made the right decision here.

1. Charlie Gehringer

I don't imagine many people share my belief that Charlie Gehringer is the greatest second baseman ever. The easy choice is to take Hornsby simply based on his statistics, which no other player at his position, and few other players at any position, can match. Gehringer comes closest of the second basemen. In some respects, he outranks Hornsby. For example, Gehringer produced more net runs per game than Hornsby. He also reached 200 net runs in a season eight times. Rogers reached that plateau only five times.

Charlie doesn't have the offensive résumé of Rajah, but he has the better of him in the field. Hornsby had nine full seasons of at least 100 games played at second. Of those nine, 1928 was arguably his best in terms of errors and fielding percentage. By my count, Gehringer had nine seasons that were better than that. He led his league in assists and fielding percentage several times each and had seven seasons with at least 100 double plays while Hornsby had only two.

To help decide who should own the top spot, I asked myself a simple question: If given the choice, which player would I rather have at second base? Hornsby, despite incomparable statistics, played for five different teams. From 1926 to 1929, he played for a different team in the National League each year. To me, that's a clue that he wasn't a great teammate and maybe wasn't a winning player. Gehringer, on the other hand, played exclusively for Detroit and was known to be a quiet leader, helping the Tigers win three pennants. Second base is a crucial position that demands teamwork and coordination with the rest of the infield. I'll take Gehringer's consistency, defense, baserunning, and per-game production over Hornsby's massive offensive statistics.

Second to None

The Most Valuable Player award has been bestowed on a second baseman 14 times. Larry Doyle won the first in 1912, and Jeff Kent was the
most recent recipient, selected in 2000. The following list briefly summarizes each MVP season in terms of statistical performance, both
offensively and defensively. You can decide for yourself which campaign was most impressive.

- Larry Doyle, 1912 New York Giants (P/E Average: 1.086)
  .330 batting, .393 on-base, .471 slugging, 98 runs, 36 steals, 20 K,
  38 errors, .948 fielding
- Johnny Evers, 1914 Boston Braves (P/E Average: .807)
  .279 batting, .390 on-base, .338 slugging, 81 runs, 87 walks, 26 K,
  17 errors, 73 double plays
- Eddie Collins, 1914 Philadelphia Athletics (P/E Average: 1.186)
  .344 batting, .452 on-base, .452 slugging, 122 runs, 58 steals, 97
  walks, 23 errors, .970 fielding
- Rogers Hornsby, 1925 St. Louis Cardinals (P/E Average: 1.557)
  .403 batting, .489 on-base, .756 slugging, 237 net runs, 90 extra-
  base hits, 34 errors, .954 fielding
- Rogers Hornsby, 1929 Chicago Cubs (P/E Average: 1.445)
  .380 batting, .459 on-base, .679 slugging, 409 total bases, 266 net
  runs, 547 assists to 23 errors
- Frankie Frisch, 1931 St. Louis Cardinals (P/E Average: 1.082)
  .311 batting, .368 on-base, .396 slugging, 96 runs, 28 steals, 13 K,
  19 errors, .974 fielding

- Charlie Gehringer, 1937 Detroit Tigers (P/E Average: 1.244)
  .371 batting, .458 on-base, .520 slugging, 209 hits, 215 net runs,
  12 errors, .986 fielding
- Joe Gordon, 1942 New York Yankees (P/E Average: 1.114)
  .322 batting, .409 on-base, .491 slugging, 103 RBI, 173 hits, 28
  errors, 121 double plays
- Jackie Robinson, 1949 Brooklyn Dodgers (P/E Average: 1.268)
  .342 batting, .432 on-base, .528 slugging, 203 hits, 230 net runs,
  421 assists to 16 errors
- Nellie Fox, 1959 Chicago White Sox (P/E Average: .872)
  .306 batting, .380 on-base, .389 slugging, 191 hits, 84 runs, 13 K,
  453 assists to 10 errors
- Joe Morgan, 1975 Cincinnati Reds (P/E Average: 1.272)
  .327 batting, .466 on-base, .508 slugging, 107 runs, 67 steals, 132
  walks, 11 errors, .986 fielding
- Joe Morgan, 1976 Cincinnati Reds (P/E Average: 1.389)
  .320 batting, .444 on-base, .576 slugging, 111 RBI, 113 runs, 60
  steals, 27 homers, .981 fielding
- Ryne Sandberg, 1984 Chicago Cubs (P/E Average: 1.099)
  .314 batting, .367 on-base, .520 slugging, 200 hits, 19 triples, 114
  runs, 550 assists to 6 errors
- Jeff Kent, 2000 San Francisco Giants (P/E Average: 1.243)
  .334 batting, .424 on-base, .596 slugging, 350 total bases, 206 net
  runs, 33 homers, .986 fielding

Third Base

The hot corner! Playing third base can be a treacherous proposition at times. When a batter squares around to bunt, the third baseman must charge feverishly, putting himself dangerously close to home plate, praying that the hitter doesn't pull the bat back and send a scorching line drive directly at him. Third basemen also need to have catlike reflexes and strong arms.

For this position managers have traditionally favored players with power at the plate. Third basemen are expected to carry the offensive burden more so than the middle infielders, so they need to be as good with the lumber as they are with the leather. My choice for the best third baseman of all time embodied, better than anyone else, that pure blend of glove work and offensive might.

Only four players, George Brett, Eddie Mathews, Brooks Robinson, and Mike Schmidt, earn Category 5 status in my mind. Brett, Robinson, and Schmidt comprise my top three. They distanced themselves from the rest of the pack over their careers. They combined to win five MVPs while delivering World Series glory to their respective cities.

Three current players, Chipper Jones (1.160), Scott Rolen (1.108), and Eric Chavez (1.027), sport extremely high P/E Averages. Jones has accomplished the most of this trio. I already see him as Cooperstown material even though his career has years remaining. Will Rolen and Chavez also be able to rise to Chipper's level?

Others, such as Bob Elliott, Terry Pendleton, and Al Rosen, were able to win Most Valuable Player honors but were not able to flourish over the long run. The demands of the position are often too great for players to overcome beyond a handful of seasons. That is why third base is the position where the fewest Hall of Famers reside.

Third Base: Career P/E Averages

Chipper Jones, 1.160; Mike Schmidt, 1.111; Scott Rolen, 1.108; Al Rosen, 1.079; Eddie Mathews, 1.064; Pie Traynor, 1.044; George Brett, 1.032; Harlond Clift, 1.030; Eric Chavez, 1.027; Bob Elliott, 1.017; Home Run Baker, 1.010; Matt Williams, 1.005; Jimmy Collins, .984; Ken Boyer, .983; Ron Santo, .976; Robin Ventura, .968; Ken Caminiti, .967; Vinny Castilla, .961; Wade Boggs, .960; Ron Cey, .941; Bill Madlock, .937; Stan Hack, .909; Gary Gaetti, .903; Carney Lansford, .903; George Kell, .902; Graig Nettles, .894; Larry Gardner, .872; Terry Pendleton, .869; Doug Rader, .867; Buddy Bell, .861; Heinie Groh, .857; Tim Wallach, .856; Frank Malzone, .853; Brooks Robinson, .834; Ray Knight, .804; Clete Boyer, .775; Howard Johnson, .763; Loren Babe, .648

Category 1–3 Third Basemen

Loren Babe

Career P/E: .648; Postseason P/E: never in the postseason
Notable seasons (P/E): 1952 (.400); 1953 (.663)

As with second base, this section begins with its lowest-ranked player. Babe played two seasons in the AL for the Yankees and the Athletics. In 1952 he appeared in just 12 games for the Bronx Bombers. In April of '53 the Athletics purchased his services, and he appeared in more than 100 contests for Philadelphia. He had 77 hits with the Athletics, including 16 doubles and two triples, and scored 34 runs for his new team.

Loren Babe's career statistics look like an average first half of a season for a marginal player. The 34 runs he scored in 1953 represent all but three of his career total in that category. He hit only two homers and drove home only 26 runs. His career P/E mark of .648 is the lowest of any third baseman in this chapter.

Can a Yankee named Babe really be a Category 1 ballplayer? In this case, the answer is a definitive yes. The 1950s Babe bore no resemblance to the Babe of the '20s and '30s. He lasted for only two seasons, appearing at the plate 426 times and not doing much in those plate appearances to make himself stick around the big leagues longer.

Clete Boyer

Career P/E: .775; Postseason P/E: .738
Notable seasons (P/E): 1962 (.883); 1965 (.856); 1967 (.892)

Clete Boyer played for the Kansas City Athletics, New York Yankees, and Atlanta Braves over 16 years in the majors. He won the Gold

Glove for 1969 with the Braves, fielding successfully .965, almost 20 points higher than the National League average that year. Playing for New York against the San Francisco Giants in the '62 World Series, Boyer was very good at the plate. He hit .318 with a homer and four runs batted in.

Despite occasional success and a few career highlights, Clete Boyer was an average third baseman. He received MVP consideration just once, finishing twenty-first in the 1967 vote, earning the only shares, .02, of his career. He retired with fewer than 700 runs scored and fewer than 700 runs batted in. His efficiency averages are also mediocre.

This Boyer (Ken appears next) rates as a Category 2 selection. He had some success and was able to play well enough to stick around from 1955 to 1971. Offensively, he doesn't have the statistics to warrant a higher rating, and he doesn't have any chance to make it into Cooperstown.

Ken Boyer

Career P/E: .983; Postseason P/E: 1.103

Notable seasons (P/E): 1958 (1.071); 1960 (1.122); 1961 (1.125);
    1964 (1.089)

Ken Boyer played the majority of his career with the St. Louis Cardinals. In 1964 he was selected National League MVP and Major League Player of the Year after scoring 100 runs and driving home 119. That year marked the eighth time in nine seasons that Boyer finished with at least 90 RBI, a solid run of production from the mid-'50s through the mid-'60s. He made seven All-Star teams and won five Gold Gloves.

After 1964, Boyer's career began to decline. He never again hit better than .266, and his production was seriously curtailed. Boyer was never a great on-base player. He never reached the .400 plateau, and his career mark is less than .350.

Ken Boyer, C3, is not in the Hall of Fame, and I don't think he should be, but I do think he's a close call. He won a handful of Gold Gloves, and his career numbers are solid. He was tremendous in '64, a year in which St. Louis also won the World Series.

Howard Johnson

Career P/E: .763; Postseason P/E: .333
Notable seasons (P/E): 1987 (1.087); 1989 (1.173); 1990 (.993);
   1991 (1.169)

HoJo began his career with the Detroit Tigers but spent his best days in Shea Stadium with the Mets. New York traded pitcher Walt Terrell to get him in 1984, and it was a move that paid off very well for them. Johnson finished fifth in MVP voting twice and was in the top 10 on one other occasion. He also won two Silver Slugger awards. In his prime, he was a dangerous combination of power and speed.

When he was good, he was very good. Unfortunately, he also had several seasons that were very bad. In his last four years, HoJo hit .223, .238, .211, and .195 to finish with a career batting average below .250. He never won a Gold Glove. In fact, his ratio of 9.7 assists per error is terrible and ranks far behind his peers. In October ball, Johnson sports a lifetime P/E mark of .333; he managed just one single in 27 plate appearances.

Despite four good offensive seasons, Johnson is Category 2. He was terrible both defensively and in the playoffs. He was never a contact hitter, striking out at least 100 times in five consecutive seasons in the middle of his career. In the late '80s and early '90s, HoJo was a popular and talented player on the Mets. He declined rapidly, though.

Ron Santo

Career P/E: .976; Postseason P/E: never in the postseason

Notable seasons (P/E): 1964 (1.133); 1967 (1.066); 1969 (1.102);
   1970 (1.070)

Ron Santo won five Gold Gloves, was a nine-time All-Star, and drove in 1,331 runs over his 15 seasons in Chicago. From 1963 to 1970, Santo averaged 105 RBI per season, and he had 123 in 1969. During that stretch, he also had five consecutive seasons of 300 or more total bases.

Despite his consistent production and his work in the field, Santo never finished in the top three of MVP voting. He finished fourth in 1967 and fifth in 1969 to pick up the majority of his career shares, which total 1.23. He also failed to lead his teams to a pennant. In 15 seasons, he never played on the big stage of October.

I thought long and hard about his rating. Is he a C3 or a C4? I once heard Mike Francesa, New York radio personality, say that if you have to think too much about whether someone is a Hall of Famer, then he's not. That's the case with Santo.

Matt Williams

Career P/E: 1.005; Postseason P/E: .869

Notable seasons (P/E): 1990 (1.048); 1993 (1.144); 1994 (1.159);
   1999 (1.167)

After three forgettable early seasons, Matt busted out in 1990, knocking in 122 runs and smacking 33 over the fence. That year, he was an All-Star, won the Silver Slugger, and finished sixth in MVP balloting. He was on his way to another great season in '94 when the strike hit. He already had 43 home runs in only 112 games.

Striking out is something this slugger did too often. He fanned 266 times in '90–'91, and he topped 100 Ks on five occasions. He batted .268 for his career and finished with a very low on-base percentage, .317. In the playoffs, his P/E Average was 136 points below his career mark.

Matt Williams is on my top-10 list for the game's best third basemen. I don't think of him as a Hall of Famer, but I do think he was good enough to be considered with the likes of Ron Santo and Ken Boyer. He went above 1.100 several times, and his assist-to-error ratio, 19.0:1, is one of the best in this chapter. It's Category 3 for Mr. Williams.

The Best Third Basemen

162-Game Averages

Player	BA	OBP	SLP	HR	TB	R	RBI	H	XBH	BB	K	SB
Boggs	.328	.415	.443	8	270	100	67	200	50	94	49	2
Brett	.305	.369	.487	19	302	95	95	189	67	66	54	12
Jones	.307	.403	.546	33	322	111	111	181	72	98	92	11
Mathews	.271	.376	.509	35	295	102	98	157	64	98	101	5
Robinson	.267	.322	.401	15	239	69	76	159	46	48	55	2
Schmidt	.267	.380	.527	37	297	101	107	151	68	102	127	12
Traynor	.320	.362	.435	5	275	99	106	202	50	39	23	13

Category 4 Third Basemen

Wade Boggs

Career P/E: .960; Postseason P/E: .764

MVP: never won; 1.20 career shares

Hall of Fame: inducted in 2005

In the 1999 season, Wade Boggs reached baseball immortality by collecting his three thousandth hit. From '83 to '89, he averaged 211 hits per season and never finished a campaign with less than 200. He led the American League in batting over that stretch five times and finished third in both of the other years. His averages were remarkable: .361, .325, .368, .357, .363, .366, and .330. He reached base safely more than 40 percent of the time in 11 of his 18 seasons. From '85 to '88, he posted four straight on-base percentages of at least .450 and averaged 108 walks to only 47 strikeouts per season. Defensively, Boggs was very good. He won two Gold Gloves and posted an assist-to-error ratio of 18.5:1, emblematic of a player that was reliable in the field.

The biggest knock against Boggs is that he lacked power. Only in 1987, when he hit 24 home runs and slugged .588, did he show the type of long-ball ability that normally accompanies third base. Other than '87, the lefty slap-hitter never slugged .500 in his career.

Boggs is Category 4 and ranks as one of the 10 best in history at his position. His lack of power is the only obstacle from rating him a C5. One of the great batsmen ever, Wade hit .357 or better five times.

Year	RBI	R	HR	NR	TB	BB	HBP	SB	CS	CB	PTS	PA	P/E
1986	71	107	8	170	282	105	0	0	4	383	723	693	1.043
1987	89	108	24	173	324	105	2	1	3	429	775	667	1.162
1988	58	128	5	181	286	125	3	2	3	413	775	719	1.078
Career	1,014	1,513	118	2,409	4,064	1,412	23	24	35	5,488	10,306	10,740	.960

Chipper Jones

Career P/E: 1.160; Postseason P/E: 1.010

MVP: National League MVP in 1999; 2.07 career shares (through
'06 voting)

Hall of Fame: possible

Already, Chipper has won an MVP, earned a World Series championship ring, and posted the highest career P/E Average of any third baseman in history. If he is able to continue his outstanding play for a few more seasons, I would rate his Hall of Fame chances as probable or even imminent. I see him as Cooperstown material already. From 1996 through 2003, Chipper knocked in between 100 and 111 runs and hit better than .300 in every season but one. His P/E was above 1.100 every year, climaxing with a score of 1.243 in '99. That season, Jones was awarded the NL Most Valuable Player. He led the Braves to the pennant with 45 homers, 87 extra-base hits, and a .633 slugging percentage.

Very simply, Jones lacks some of the numbers of Brett, Schmidt, Boggs, and Mathews because his career is not yet finished. As of this moment, many voters would probably opt against his induction. He has fewer than 400 homers while playing during a long-ball era. His averages in terms of P/E and net runs (1.17 per game) are tremendous, but it will be interesting to see if he can sustain those levels.

As of now, I rate him as Category 4. I think he is a Hall of Famer; his P/E Average is higher than any third baseman. Incredibly clutch, Chipper makes my top five.

Year	RBI	R	HR	NR	TB	BB	HBP	SB	CS	CB	PTS	PA	P/E
1998	107	123	34	196	329	96	1	16	6	436	828	707	1.171
1999	110	116	45	181	359	126	2	25	3	509	871	701	1.243
2000	111	118	36	193	328	95	2	14	7	432	818	686	1.192
Career	1,299	1,296	386	2,209	3,768	1,152	15	134	43	5,026	9,444	8,143	1.160

Pie Traynor

Career P/E: 1.044; Postseason P/E: .800

MVP: never won; 2.04 career shares

Hall of Fame: inducted in 1948

Harold Joseph Traynor, better known as Pie, was a lifetime .320 hitter who played his entire career with the Pittsburgh Pirates. Traynor was incredibly productive, averaging 1.24 net runs per game despite hitting only 58 home runs and slugging .435. From '27 to '30 he batted .342, .337, .356, and .366 while averaging 114 runs batted in per year. His 1.044 lifetime P/E number places him 12 points ahead of George Brett, 84 points higher than Wade Boggs, and 210 points above Brooks Robinson. He exceeded 1.100 five times and had only one full season below .900.

Traynor's defensive statistics are not very good, however. He averaged less than 11 assists for every miscue, and his overall fielding percentage of .947 only ties the league average for his time. He played shortstop in his first season, 1920, but was quickly moved to a corner position the following year after committing a dozen errors in only 17 games. His postseason P/E stands at just .800, almost 250 points below his regular-season mark.

His per-game production average of 1.24 net runs is higher than any third baseman in history. He was never in the top five of MVP voting, though, and I feel that's a strong indictment against him. After careful scrutiny, I rate him Category 4.

Year	RBI	R	HR	NR	TB	BB	HBP	SB	CS	CB	PTS	PA	P/E
1925	106	114	6	214	274	52	2	15	9	334	762	658	1.158
1929	108	94	4	198	255	30	3	13	7*	294	690	597	1.156
1930	119	90	9	200	253	48	1	7	4*	305	705	569	1.239
Career	1,273	1,183	58	2,398	3,289	472	31	158	85*	3,865	8,661	8,293	1.044

* CS totals estimated based on known statistics

Category 5 Third Basemen

George Brett

Height: 6′0″; Weight: 200; Bats: left; Throws: right

First game: August 2, 1973; Final game: October 3, 1993

Team(s): Kansas City Royals (1973–1993)

MVP: American League MVP in 1980; 3.30 career shares

Hall of Fame: inducted in 1999

162-game avg.: .305 batting, .369 on-base, .487 slugging, 19 home
   runs, 302 total bases, 95 runs scored, 95 runs batted in, 189 hits,
   67 extra-base hits, 66 BB, 54 K, 12 SB

Career P/E: 1.032; Postseason P/E: 1.120

The Good. George Howard Brett played in only 117 games for the
Kansas City Royals in 1980, but it was still one of the great individual
performances in baseball history. Brett flirted with .400 throughout
the season until he finally settled at .390. He knocked in 118 runs,
slugged .664, and averaged more than 1.50 net runs per contest. He
registered a tremendous P/E score of 1.414 during that memorable
year. Despite missing more than a quarter of the season, Brett was
selected as the American League MVP. He collected .85 shares that
year and a total of 3.30 for his career, having finished in the top three
on three other occasions.

Brett is the only player in history to win batting titles in three different decades. In 1976 he hit .333. His .390 average in '80 was easily
the best mark in the league, and he concluded with a .329 average in
1990, capping off a remarkable run of batting prowess spread over a
long and successful career. He retired with a .305 average and more
than 1,500 runs both scored and driven home. The 12-time All-Star
won three Silver Sluggers and the 1985 Gold Glove.

The '85 season was certainly special for Brett. He finished runner-up to Don Mattingly in the MVP vote and, more important, led the Royals to the championship over their in-state rivals, the St. Louis Cardinals. Brett was named ALCS MVP during that run after batting .348 and smacking three home runs against Toronto. His combined P/E Average during the '85 postseason was 1.131 over two seven-game series victories.

The Bad. There is not much to find fault with Brett's career. He hit for average, hit for power, fielded his position well, was frequently dominant in the playoffs, won individual honors, and stole more than 200 bases. He did have two postseason series in which he batted .231 or less without generating any runs. He also hit below .300 during his last three seasons as he approached and passed 3,000 career base knocks. Otherwise, he was a tremendous player.

The Verdict. The greatest Royal of all time, Brett also earns the distinction of being highlighted and considered for the number one spot in this chapter's top three. Naturally, he is a Category 5 third baseman. He was always a fiery competitor who was able to put a team on his back and carry it to great heights, just as he did throughout the 1985 season and into the playoffs that year. Some people will best remember George for tearing out of the Kansas City dugout at Yankee Stadium in a fit of rage during baseball's infamous "Pine Tar Incident," but he should better be recalled as a complete ballplayer who spent his entire career with one team.

Eddie Mathews

Height: 6′1″; Weight: 200; Bats: left; Throws: right

First game: April 15, 1952; Final game: September 27, 1968

Team(s): Boston/Milwaukee/Atlanta Braves (1952–1966); Houston
    Astros (1967); Detroit Tigers (1967–1968)

MVP: never won; 1.61 career shares

Hall of Fame: inducted in 1978

162-game avg.: .271 batting, .376 on-base, .509 slugging, 35 home
    runs, 295 total bases, 102 runs scored, 98 runs batted in, 157 hits,
    64 extra-base hits, 98 BB, 101 K, 5 SB

Career P/E: 1.064; Postseason P/E: .909

The Good. Few players in baseball history began their careers and
flashed early brilliance as well as Eddie Mathews did. He broke into
the big leagues at age 20 and hit 40 or more home runs in three of his
first four seasons. In '53 Mathews was only 21 years old when he
smashed 47 out of the park, drove in 135 runs, and slugged .627 for
the Braves in their first season in Milwaukee. He appeared to be well
on his way to immortality when he blasted 81 more home runs over
the next two seasons. From 1952 to 1960, Eddie was in the top five of
the league for home runs every season and entered the '61 campaign
with 338 dingers, before age 30.

Mathews was a nine-time All-Star and earned 1.61 MVP shares
over his career. He joined exclusive company during the 1967 season
when he hit home run number 500. He went on to strike 12 more to
finish his tenure with as many homers as Ernie Banks and more than
Mel Ott, Lou Gehrig, and Stan Musial. He slugged better than .500 for
his career and drew almost 1,500 career walks, good enough for a .376

lifetime on-base percentage. Mathews, who twice finished second in MVP balloting, averaged 1.02 net runs over his 17 seasons in the majors.

The Bad. Mathews's story bears resemblance to that of Orlando Cepeda. Both started their careers white hot but failed to maintain those levels of success in the latter stages of their playing days. At one point, it looked as if Eddie might be the man to break Ruth's home-run record of 714. Ironically, it was a teammate who took that title away. Hitting 512 home runs is a tremendous accomplishment, but one has to wonder how high that total might have been if the third baseman was able to hit 30 homers more than once over his last seven seasons.

Eddie Mathews never won a Gold Glove, but it should be noted that the award wasn't available during his first five seasons. From '52 to '56, his time in the majors before it was introduced, he committed more than 20 errors three times and had fielding percentages lower than the league average twice. In '54, his defensive statistics were good, but I'm not sure he would have won the honor anyway.

The Verdict. Mathews, who appeared on the first-ever *Sports Illustrated* cover, is a Category 5 ballplayer in my analysis. His career could be considered somewhat of a disappointment based on the amazing start with which it began. Nonetheless, he hit more than 500 home runs and garnered enough MVP shares to be considered one of the five best third basemen ever.

Brooks Robinson

Height: 6′1″; Weight: 190; Bats: right; Throws: right

First game: September 17, 1955; Final game: August 13, 1977

Team(s): Baltimore Orioles (1955–1977)

MVP: American League MVP in 1964; 3.69 career shares

Hall of Fame: inducted in 1983

162-game avg.: .267 batting, .322 on-base, .401 slugging, 15 home
runs, 239 total bases, 69 runs scored, 76 runs batted in, 159 hits,
46 extra-base hits, 48 BB, 55 K, 2 SB

Career P/E: .834; Postseason P/E: .891

The Good. It can be rightfully argued that Brooks Robinson is the greatest defensive player in the history of the game. He won the American League Gold Glove every year from 1960 through 1975, the greatest run ever for an everyday player. Only pitchers Jim Kaat and Greg Maddux have collected as many awards (16 through 2006). Ozzie Smith (13) is the only other nonhurler who comes close to matching Brooks. In the 1970 World Series, Robinson seemed to be everywhere at third, making diving stops and throwing out Cincinnati runners who were incredulous that they were heading back to the dugout instead of rounding first for a double. Robinson also hit .429, after batting .583 in the ALCS, winning the World Series MVP honor without question.

While he piled up Gold Gloves year in and year out, Brooks also was selected to 15 consecutive All-Star Games. In the '66 contest, he was named Most Valuable Player. Two seasons prior, Robinson was selected as the best player in the American League for the regular season almost unanimously. Only Mickey Mantle received any other first-place votes that year. The Orioles legend batted .317 in 1964 and drove home 118 runs while posting the highest P/E score, 1.050, of his career.

In total, Robinson collected 3.69 shares in the balloting. He finished second to teammate Frank Robinson in 1966, third twice, and fourth once. Only Mike Schmidt has more shares to his credit at the position. Brooks Robinson retired with 1,357 runs batted in, 1,232 runs scored, and more than 250 lifetime homers.

The Bad. Robinson's MVP campaign in 1964 was the only time he topped the 1.000 P/E plateau. Often, he was below .850, and his .834 mark is lower than the likes of Buddy Bell, Tim Wallach, and Terry Pendleton. Furthermore, his production average of .80 net runs per game is more likely to be seen by Category 2 and 3 players than by an immortal like Robinson. He hit less than .240 in more than a third of his seasons and retired with very low percentages in terms of on-base, .322, and slugging, .401. Brooks also reached 300 total bases in a season only twice.

The Verdict. Robinson is one of the three best third basemen in history. In my opinion, he is the greatest defensive player ever at any position. He was often at his best when Baltimore needed him the most; his string of consecutive All-Star appearances and Gold Gloves, coupled with his MVP résumé, marks him as an easy choice for Category 5.

Mike Schmidt

Height: 6′2″; Weight: 203; Bats: right; Throws: right

First game: September 12, 1972; Final game: May 28, 1989

Team(s): Philadelphia Phillies (1972–1989)

MVP: National League MVP in 1980, 1981, 1986; 4.96 career shares

Hall of Fame: inducted in 1995

162-game avg.: .267 batting, .380 on-base, .527 slugging, 37 home
   runs, 297 total bases, 101 runs scored, 107 runs batted in, 151
   hits, 68 extra-base hits, 102 BB, 127 K, 12 SB

Career P/E: 1.111; Postseason P/E: .829

The Good. From the mid-1970s to the mid- to late 1980s, Michael
Jack Schmidt was perhaps baseball's most feared hitter. Beginning in
1974 Schmidt generated at least 150 net runs of offense every season
through 1987, except the strike-shortened campaign of '81 and '85,
when he finished with 149. In between, he hit at least 35 homers 11
times, reaching 40 dingers in a trio of years. He consistently posted
high P/E Averages, going above 1.100 almost every year.

The 1980 season was especially meaningful for Schmidt. He won
his first of three MVP awards, and he did so unanimously after belting 48 homers and driving home 121 runs. Schmidt led the Phillies
to the pennant and was then dominant in the World Series, batting
.381 and slugging .714 with two homers as Philadelphia celebrated the
only World Series title in club history. Schmidt walked away with
MVP honors.

He was selected as the NL's best player again in '81. Posting his
highest single-season P/E mark, 1.357, Mike was on his way to tremendous numbers when the strike hit. Again, he was the clear win-

ner in MVP balloting. Between the two years, Schmidt totaled 1.96 shares, earning 45 out of 48 possible first-place votes. In 1986 Schmidt again proved to everyone how great he was by winning his third MVP, sixth Silver Slugger, and tenth Gold Glove.

The righty slugger was also terrific at getting on base safely. Twelve times he finished a season with an on-base percentage of .375 or better. He led the National League in bases on balls four times to go along with eight seasons of hitting the most home runs.

The Bad. The only negatives I can find with Schmidt's Hall of Fame career are with regard to batting average and strikeouts. He hit better than .300 only once, over 102 games in '81, and he retired with a career mark of .267. He had six full seasons in which he batted .255 or less and a dozen years of triple-digit strikeout totals. Schmidt was still developing in 1973 when he batted a dreadful .196 and fanned 136 times in 132 games. In '75 and '76 he whiffed 329 times combined. His career total of 1,883 strikeouts is the seventh most in baseball history.

The Verdict. Despite occasional low batting averages and high strikeout totals, Mike Schmidt was a tremendous third baseman. I have included him, along with Brett and Robinson, in this chapter's top three. Therefore, he is Category 5. He combined offensive punch and defensive poise as well as any player in history. He is the only player in history to have 500 career home runs, 10 Gold Gloves, and three MVPs. Even the immortal Willie Mays can't make that claim to fame.

Third Base: The Top 10

Third base is the only position in this book that needs to draw from Category 3 players to round out my top 10. If you've been reading carefully and can follow my line of thinking, then it should come as no surprise as to whom I have selected as the best player in history at this difficult position. The hot corner calls for tough, instinctive players who aren't afraid to stare down the base line at the batter, who may only be bluffing when squaring around to bunt. Traditionally considered a power position, third base demands a combo of offense and defense rolled into one. Here's my top ten.

10. Ron Santo

Ron Santo begins the list because he was tremendously consistent in terms of run production from 1963 to 1970. He went to nine All-Star Games and won five Gold Gloves, and he retired with 342 home runs and 1,331 runs batted in. He never made the postseason, so that fact makes it a bit more difficult to place him, but I am fairly content with his position. He just beats out Bob Elliott, Scott Rolen, and Al Rosen for spot number 10.

9. Matt Williams

Matt Williams was a slightly better player than Ron Santo in my opinion. He didn't win an MVP, but he did finish in the top three twice, which Santo never did. He was also in the top six four times. He won four Gold Gloves and four Silver Sluggers, emblematic of that offense-defense combo I've mentioned before. In addition, Williams's assist-to-error ratio, 19.0:1, is much better than Santo's, 14.5:1.

8. Ken Boyer

Ken Boyer did what Ron Santo and Matt Williams were unable to do: he won a Most Valuable Player award. In '64 Boyer was also selected Major League Player of the Year, and his Cardinals team won the championship, and that is enough by itself to convince me that he deserves the honor as the highest-ranking Category 3 third baseman. His 1.103 postseason P/E is 234 points higher than Matt Williams's score, and I also think Boyer was a bit more consistent.

7. Pie Traynor

Spot 7 begins the Category 4 players. Traynor's higher rating guarantees him a higher ranking than Boyer. More important, he earns spot number 7 because of his run production. Traynor was more than a quarter of a net run better per game than Boyer, and that's a significant difference. His P/E Average is 61 points better, and he totaled more MVP shares, 2.04 to 1.60.

6. Wade Boggs

I think Boggs was probably a more complete player than Traynor. He won multiple Gold Gloves, multiple Silver Sluggers, and multiple batting titles. Pie was much more productive on a per-game basis, but he also played in an era when offensive statistics were high throughout baseball. After researching both players and thinking carefully about all of the facts, my gut instinct tells me that Boggs is simply the better choice. If it were a horse race, this one would be a photo finish.

5. Chipper Jones

I'd take Chipper over Boggs for two reasons. First of all, he has a considerable advantage in terms of power. Boggs was a great batsman, a real virtuoso with the stick, but Jones has been the more dangerous hitter because of his ability to drive the ball. Second, and more important, Jones has always been extremely clutch. As a Mets fan, I have been scared by no player more than Chipper Jones when the game is on the line.

4. Eddie Mathews

Eddie Mathews ranks ahead of Chipper Jones on my list. I like Mathews's defense and power combination, something neither Jones nor Boggs had in tandem. Chipper could provide the long ball from either side of the plate, but he couldn't pick it in the field like Mathews. That isn't to say Mathews was a perfect ballplayer; he had holes in his career just like almost every other player. In this matchup, however, he's the choice.

The Top Three

The interesting thing about my top three is that each man played exclusively for one team. George Brett, Brooks Robinson, and Mike Schmidt played more than 8,000 combined games without ever switching uniforms. They each earned MVP honors and brought championship glory to their beloved cities. They were different ballplayers, however. Brett was a terrific batsman who combined good power with an ability to hit for high averages. Robinson was incredibly clutch and killed the opposition with his glove better than any player in the game's history. Schmidt, probably the best combination of offense and defense of the three, displayed a great eye at the plate while also hitting for power and fielding his position expertly.

The Case for Brett

Three-time American League batting champion

1980 American League MVP and Major League Player of the Year

Batted .390 with 118 RBI in 117 games in 1980

1985 ALCS Most Valuable Player; 1.120 career postseason P/E
Average

.305 lifetime batting average

The Case for Robinson

16 consecutive Gold Gloves

15 consecutive All-Star selections

MVP honors in 1964 (regular season), 1966 (All-Star), and 1970
(World Series)

3.69 career MVP shares

Batted .485 in the postseason throughout Baltimore's '70
championship run

The Case for Schmidt

Three MVPs and 4.96 career shares

10 Gold Gloves, six Silver Sluggers, and 12 All-Star selections

548 home runs

Lifetime efficiency percentages of .380 on-base and .527 slugging

1.111 P/E Average

3. Brooks Robinson

The Orioles legend is not able to finish any better than third in this race. Obviously, the reason is offense. He simply can't compete with Brett and Schmidt in the batter's box. Mathews was also the better hitter, but he never won an MVP, something that each man in the top three accomplished. Robinson was also a World Series MVP while Mathews was unspectacular on the big stage in October. Brooks takes over at number 3 primarily because of defense. Mathews was solid, but he isn't even close in comparison with Robinson, who just might be the best ever with the leather in the sport's history. Brooks slides in safely to take the bronze, and I'm sure there are people reading this who feel it is an injustice that Robinson doesn't rank even higher.

2. George Brett

In making the decision as to this spot, I asked myself if I'd rather have Brett's or Robinson's combination of offense and defense. I wavered back and forth: Brett was much better offensively, and Robinson was far superior in the field. I think Brett was the better player, though. His lifetime P/E Average is almost 200 points higher, and he comes close to matching Brooks's MVP résumé. Kansas City's favorite son also posted a much better postseason score in terms of production and efficiency, 1.120 to .891. Maybe Brett gets the nod over Brooks simply because I saw him play a lot throughout his career, and I never saw Robinson play a single game. Maybe this ranking would have been reversed, but with my analysis I'm confident to write that George Brett is the second-best third baseman of all time.

1. Mike Schmidt

Like the decision at first base, this was an easy one. Schmidt comes closest to the perfect balance of offense and defense at third base. He hit more homers than Mathews, he is the only other player besides Robinson to have at least 10 Gold Gloves at the position, and he won as many MVPs as the other Category 4 and 5 third basemen combined.

Interestingly, Schmidt and Brett share some territory. Both men retired with exactly 1,595 runs batted in and more than 1,500 runs scored. They both averaged 1.06 net runs per game, and each man was a 12-time All-Star. In 1980 they each won the MVP in their respective league. When they met in the World Series, Schmidt (.381 BA, .462 OBP, .714 SLP) was only slightly better than Brett (.375 BA, .423 OBP, .667 SLP), who nearly mirrored him. In a final example of baseball coincidence, their careers began less than 11 months apart.

Nevertheless, there is no doubt in my mind that Schmidt was the better player throughout their careers. He was better in the field, hit more home runs, won three MVPs, reached base more often, and out-slugged his American League rival. Brett was better in terms of batting average, and he struck out much less. He can also hang his hat on the fact that he, and not Schmidt, was selected as the Player of the Year for 1980. Schmidt got the last laugh that season, however, when Philadelphia won the World Series against Kansas City. He also comes in ahead of Brett in my analysis and search for the best third baseman in baseball history.

A Third of the Time

There are five players not previously included in this chapter who deserve mention at this time. They each played multiple positions but failed to spend at least 60 percent of their games at any one spot. They did, however, have multiple seasons with at least 100 games played at the hot corner, which warrants analysis.

Darrell Evans ('72–'75, Atlanta Braves; '78–'80, San Francisco Giants)

Evans played between 123 and 160 games at third over these years. Yet, he spent less than 54 percent of his career there while also playing 856 games at first base and 253 as a designated hitter. Over his seven full years at third, Evans made one All-Star team and collected just .03 MVP shares. His assist-to-error ratio was 12.7:1. His best single season during that stretch was 1973, when he hit .281 with 41 knocked over the fence. *Combined P/E Average: .941*

Harmon Killebrew ('59, Washington Senators; '66, '69–'70, Minnesota Twins)

Harmon Killebrew is enshrined in Cooperstown as a first baseman, but he also spent about one-third of his career at third. In four full years, he played 105–150 games, smashed 171 home runs, and was an All-Star every time. The '69 AL MVP, he collected 1.73 total shares over this span. Defensively, he was limited, as evidenced by a ratio of 11.1 assists for every error. Offensively, however, he was a nightmare for pitchers. *Combined P/E Average: 1.133*

Paul Molitor ('82–'83, '85, '88–'89, Milwaukee Brewers)

Like Killebrew, Molitor is a Hall of Famer despite not having one main position. With the Brewers in the 1980s, Paul played between 105 and 150 games at third in five seasons, making it to two All-Star squads. He collected only .20 MVP shares during this time, but he did average 105 runs scored. He also stole 171 bases, finishing the season with 41 three times. His ratio of 14.0 assists per error is solid but not spectacular. *Combined P/E Average: .941*

Pete Rose ('75–'78, Cincinnati Reds)

Third base was one of four positions at which Rose played more than 600 games. From 1975 to 1978, he was the regular third baseman for Cincinnati, playing between 137 and 161 games. He made the All-Star team every year and was the '75 World Series MVP. Over this span, he averaged 207 hits per season. He also collected .87 shares, twice finishing in the top five. Good in the field, he averaged 18.4 assists for each error. *Combined P/E Average: .942*

Joe Torre ('71–'72, St. Louis Cardinals)

The former Yankees' skipper had two full seasons at third with the Cardinals, playing 161 and 117 games at this spot. Both years, Torre was an All-Star. In '71 he was the National League MVP and the Major League Player of the Year after batting .363 with 137 runs batted in. He played less than a quarter of his games at third, but he was able to collect .95 MVP shares over those two seasons. He averaged 14.2 assists for each error. *Combined P/E Average: 1.073*

Shortstop

The final infield position is shortstop. Throughout history, shortstops have been more valued for their gloves because good defense is critical at this spot. Shortstops need to have quick feet, good range in both directions, and a strong throwing arm to make plays in the hole and still get the runner at first. The best ever at this spot met all of those requirements and also were productive and efficient with the bat in their hands. A few of them have even become legendary players.

When thinking about defense at short, names such as Ozzie Smith, Luis Aparicio, Mark Belanger, and Omar Vizquel come to mind. They combined to win 41 Gold Gloves and set the bar incredibly high for others to try to reach. That total may even increase, as Vizquel is still active. "Defense, Defense, Defense" summarizes the career accomplishments of the Category 4 and 5 players, along with a few prominent Category 3 shortstops, with respect to their work in the field.

The shortstop position has undergone a transformation over the course of baseball's history. In the early days, Honus Wagner was the game's unquestioned star and the best at his position. Men such as Joe Cronin, Lou Boudreau, and Arky Vaughan came along later to continue in his tradition, but they never reached his level of success. In the '50s, '60s, and '70s, shortstops were often small, slick-fielding, light-hitting players who needed to use their quickness to make up for a deficiency in power. Ripken ushered in a new era in the '80s, one in which shortstops were bigger and hit with authority. Since then, players such as Jeter, Rodriguez, Tejada, and Garciaparra have continued what Ripken began. Today, many of the sport's biggest stars are shortstops.

Shortstop: Career P/E Averages

Alex Rodriguez, 1.234; Nomar Garciaparra, 1.108; Honus Wagner, 1.100; Joe Cronin, 1.089; Arky Vaughan, 1.043; Derek Jeter, 1.039; Miguel Tejada, 1.036; Barry Larkin, .994; Joe Sewell, .980; Travis Jackson, .948; Luke Appling, .946; Cal Ripken Jr., .946; Lou Boudreau, .925; Alan Trammell, .912; Pee Wee Reese, .908; Tony Fernandez, .868; Bobby Wallace, .863; Phil Rizzuto, .843; Joe Tinker, .828; Omar Vizquel, .822; Dave Concepcion, .806; Dave Bancroft, .805; Roger Peckinpaugh, .804; Ozzie Smith, .804; U. L. Washington, .791; Garry Templeton, .785; Charlie Babb, .783; Marty Marion, .779; Zoilo Versalles, .779; Maury Wills, .779; Luis Aparicio, .777; Rabbit Maranville, .767; Dick Groat, .763; Gene Alley, .741; Roy McMillan, .709; Larry Bowa, .702; Rey Ordonez, .675; Mark Belanger, .669

Category 1–3 Shortstops

Charlie Babb

Career P/E: .783; Postseason P/E: never in the postseason
Notable seasons (P/E): 1903 (.880); 1904 (.751); 1905 (.674)

Charlie Babb stole 22 bases as a rookie in 1903 and led the National League in hit by pitch after getting plunked 22 times. He was hit 11 times in '04, but that didn't stop him from setting career highs with 34 steals, 138 hits, and 53 runs batted in. He also hit .265 that year and was on base almost 35 percent of the time.

Babb lasted only three seasons in the pros. He never knew what it felt like to hit a big-league home run, and he slugged just .300 for his career. He committed 121 errors in his first two seasons, and he was later tried at first base for 31 games in his final season, 1905.

He is our Category 1 entry for the shortstop position. Babb had the luxury of playing for John McGraw on the Giants. The '03 Giants sported two 30-game winners, Christy Mathewson and Joe McGinnity, but failed to win the pennant, finishing second in the National League. That was Babb's only season with New York. Along with Uecker, Throneberry, Anderson, and Babe, Charlie Babb rounds out the all-time C1 infield.

Dave Concepcion

Career P/E: .806; Postseason P/E: .946
Notable seasons (P/E): 1974 (.914); 1978 (.907); 1979 (.959); 1981 (.955)

Dave Concepcion was an integral part of the Big Red Machine that won consecutive World Series in the mid-'70s. He played on four pennant-winning teams, won five Gold Gloves, and was a nine-time All-

Star selection. The Reds beat Pittsburgh for the pennant in '75, and Concepcion was tremendous in the NLCS. He hit .455, slugged .727, and reached base safely in half of his plate appearances.

The lifelong Reds player retired with fewer than 1,000 runs both scored and driven in, a fact that hurts his Hall of Fame chances. He averaged only .74 net runs per game, which is not very productive. His .806 P/E Average is only 15 points higher than U. L. Washington, a light-hitting Category 2 player who will be highlighted later in this section. Concepcion also earned only .52 shares in MVP votes over his 19 seasons in the NL.

I can understand why there is some support for Concepcion to be inducted into Cooperstown, but I disagree. Winning five Gold Gloves is an impressive accomplishment, as is nine All-Star appearances. But to me his career statistics are not impressive enough to gain induction in my mind. I think a Category 3 rating is perfect.

Alan Trammell

Career P/E: .912; Postseason P/E: 1.241
Notable seasons (P/E): 1983 (1.007); 1984 (.973); 1986 (1.023);
    1987 (1.172)

The Detroit Tigers have had some tremendous players wear their uniform, but few have been as loved as Alan Trammell. The shortstop spent his entire major league career, 20 years in total, with the Tigers. In '84 he helped lead Detroit to the World Series title. Alan was named WS MVP after posting a remarkable 1.565 P/E versus San Diego.

In terms of MVP voting in the regular season, Trammell was in the top five only once. His total of 1.22 shares is solid but unspectacular.

He won four Gold Gloves but failed to take home that trophy from '85 through '96, his last professional season.

Trammell was an excellent shortstop who played his position well and was a crowd favorite for two decades. He teamed with Lou Whitaker to form one of the best middle infields in the game. I would say his chances of one day getting into Cooperstown are doubtful. I don't think he's a Hall of Famer, so I'll give him a rating of C3.

Zoilo Versalles

Career P/E: .779; Postseason P/E: .933
Notable seasons (P/E): 1963 (.790); 1964 (.864); 1965 (1.025)

Zoilo Versalles played for a handful of teams throughout his career, but he had his best seasons with Minnesota. In 1965 the Cuban shortstop won the AL MVP award, receiving 98 percent of the total available points. Versalles smacked a career-best 76 hits for extra bases and scored 126 runs. He also stole 27 bases in 32 attempts, won his second Gold Glove, and made his second All-Star team.

Versalles won the Gold Glove in '65 despite committing 39 errors and fielding 12 points lower than the league average. In fact, he made at least 30 miscues in a season six times and averaged less than 14 assists per error for his career—hardly impressive statistics. He retired as a .242 batter who reached base safely less than 30 percent of the time.

Versalles had one breakout season, but I still see him as a C2. His MVP casts the only doubt in my mind. I thought of assigning a Category 3 rating, but I don't see him on the same level as Trammell.

U. L. Washington

Career P/E: .791; Postseason P/E: .469

Notable seasons (P/E): 1980 (.853); 1982 (.949); 1983 (.796)

Washington, with his signature style of playing with a toothpick in his mouth, manned the shortstop position for the Royals from the late '70s through the mid-'80s. His best seasons were '80 and '82. He batted .273 and .286 in those years and drove in 113 combined runs. In 1983 U.L. finished seventh in the American League with 40 stolen bases.

His career numbers are quite ordinary. He batted .251 with just 703 hits. He had only four full seasons of at least 100 games played, although he was on pace for a fifth in 1981 when the strike limited him to 98 games. U.L. never received any All-Star selections, Gold Gloves, Silver Sluggers, or MVP consideration over his 11-year career.

When I was a kid, Washington was always one of my favorite players even though he failed to distinguish himself among his peers—maybe it was his name, maybe it was the toothpick. Nonetheless, I can only rate him as high as Category 2.

Maury Wills

Career P/E: .779; Postseason P/E: .607

Notable seasons (P/E): 1961 (.812); 1962 (.984); 1965 (.804); 1967 (.819)

Only four men in the twentieth century stole 100 or more bases in a season. Lou Brock, Rickey Henderson, and Vince Coleman accomplished that feat, but not before Maury Wills did it first in 1962. Wills led the National League that season and took home almost every available piece of individual hardware. He was selected as the league MVP, Player of the Year, and MVP of the All-Star Game, and he won his second straight Gold Glove. From '60 to '65, Maury was the top base stealer in the NL, and he retired with 586 thefts in 14 seasons. He used his speed to score 105 runs in '61, 130 in '62, and 1,067 total.

In the postseason, Wills hit just .244 over four World Series. His .607 lifetime P/E score for October is extremely disappointing for a player with his talent. He also never walked 60 times in any season, reaching safely .330 for his career.

Wills had tremendous talent but was unable to sustain his excellence over the long run. In my opinion, he's C3 and one of the players I would have truly loved to see play.

The Best Shortstops

162-Game Averages

Player	BA	OBP	SLP	HR	TB	R	RBI	H	XBH	BB	K	SB
Aparicio	.262	.311	.343	5	218	83	49	167	36	46	46	32
Appling	.310	.399	.398	3	236	88	75	184	39	87	35	12
Boudreau	.295	.380	.415	7	246	85	78	175	51	78	30	5
Cronin	.301	.390	.468	13	270	94	109	174	61	81	53	7
Jeter	.317	.388	.462	17	303	122	82	208	56	67	114	23
Larkin	.295	.371	.444	15	262	99	71	174	54	70	61	28
Ripken	.276	.340	.447	23	279	89	91	172	58	61	70	2
Rodriguez	.306	.389	.578	44	362	128	128	191	80	78	130	23
Sewell	.312	.391	.413	4	251	97	90	189	47	72	10	6
Smith	.262	.337	.328	2	194	79	50	155	31	67	37	37
Vaughan	.318	.406	.453	9	268	105	83	187	52	84	25	11
Vizquel	.274	.340	.357	5	212	84	54	163	35	59	60	24
Wagner	.327	.391	.466	6	282	101	100	198	58	56	51*	42

* Estimated total for strikeouts based on known statistics

Category 4 Shortstops

Luis Aparicio

Career P/E: .777; Postseason P/E: .467

MVP: never won; 1.24 career shares

Hall of Fame: inducted in 1984

Luis Aparicio won nine Gold Gloves throughout his 18-year career, all of which was spent in the American League. In 1956 he was selected AL Rookie of the Year after collecting 142 hits, stealing 21 bags, and scoring 69 runs. Defense is what made Aparicio a special player, and it's what got him elected to the Hall of Fame in 1984. He averaged almost 22 assists per error, and he had tremendous range at the position. He was quick and agile, the type of player that often comes to mind when thinking of a prototypical slap-hitting shortstop with a great glove. His nine Gold Gloves trail only Ozzie Smith (13) and Omar Vizquel (11 through 2006) on the all-time list.

Aparicio's offensive power and efficiency numbers are not impressive. He slugged just .343 for his career, reaching the .400 level only once. Aparicio never recorded a P/E Average better than the .870 mark he produced in 1960. Had he walked more and reached safely closer to 35 percent of the time, he would undoubtedly have had many more stolen bases, more runs scored, and more wins for his teams.

Aparicio is a C4. Surrounded by offensive stars, he would be a perfect fit at shortstop, able to use his speed and his glove to make a contribution without being relied on to do much more. He lacked offensive punch, but he still makes the top 10.

Year	RBI	R	HR	NR	TB	BB	HBP	SB	CS	CB	PTS	PA	P/E
1956	56	69	3	122	182	34	1	21	4	234	478	583	.820
1959	51	98	6	143	203	53	3	56	13	302	588	686	.857
1960	61	86	2	145	206	43	1	51	8	293	583	670	.870
Career	791	1,335	83	2,043	3,504	736	27	506	136	4,637	8,723	11,230	.777

Luke Appling

Career P/E: .946; Postseason P/E: never in the postseason
MVP: never won; 2.01 career shares
Hall of Fame: inducted in 1964

Appling entered the Hall of Fame in 1964 after collecting more than 2,700 hits and posting a career batting mark of .310. Luke was terrific at getting on base. He finished with a .399 percentage, and he topped .400 in eight full seasons. He didn't hit many homers, but he did drive in more than 1,100 runs and average .99 net runs of offense per game. Without question, Appling's best season came in 1936, one of two times he finished as runner-up in MVP balloting. He paced the American League with a .388 batting average, topped 200 hits, and produced an astounding total of 233 net runs. His P/E Average of 1.332 that year was 287 points higher than any other full season.

Appling appears to be the opposite player from Luis Aparicio when it comes to defense. While Luis was fluid and splendid in the field, Appling was not. He fielded four points lower than the league average for his career, an unusual occurrence for a Hall of Famer. From '31 to '37, Luke made almost 300 miscues in the field.

It would be helpful to know how he would have fared in October when analyzing his career and ranking him against other shortstops; he never appeared in the postseason. He had one breakout season and several very good ones, mostly highlighted by high efficiency averages for batting and on-base ability. He's Category 4.

Year	RBI	R	HR	NR	TB	BB	HBP	SB	CS	CB	PTS	PA	P/E
1936	128	111	6	233	267	85	1	10	6	357	823	618	1.332
1937	77	98	4	171	252	86	1	18	10	347	689	665	1.036
1940	79	96	0	175	250	69	1	3	5	318	668	639	1.045
Career	1,116	1,319	45	2,390	3,528	1,302	11	179	108	4,912	9,692	10,243	.946

Lou Boudreau

Career P/E: .925; Postseason P/E: .833
MVP: American League MVP in 1948; 2.66 career shares
Hall of Fame: inducted in 1970

In 1948 the voters overwhelmingly decided that Lou Boudreau was the best player in the American League. His three efficiency averages, .355 BA, .453 OBP, and .534 SLP, were the highest in his career. He generated 204 net runs of offense for the Indians and fielded above the league average for his position by 11 points. Earning MVP consideration was certainly nothing new to Lou; he finished in the top 10 of the voting eight times throughout his 15 seasons. In the mid-'40s, he hit better than .300 four out of five years, and he reached at least 185 hits three times in that decade. He led the league in batting in 1944 and made eight All-Star teams.

Having appeared at the plate only slightly more than 7,000 times, Boudreau's career numbers look quite ordinary. He finished with less than 1,800 hits and less than 800 runs batted in. Boudreau's .925 P/E is not great either. He topped 1.000 only twice (1.040 in '40 and 1.195 in '48) and was often below .900.

Even though he played in only 1,646 games, Lou Boudreau is a top-five shortstop in my book. His MVP résumé is impressive, and I think he had a very good combination of bat and glove, which is important at this skilled position. Category 4.

Year	RBI	R	HR	NR	TB	BB	HBP	SB	CS	CB	PTS	PA	P/E
1940	101	97	9	189	278	73	2	6	3	356	734	706	1.040
1944	67	91	3	155	255	73	5	11	3	341	651	681	.956
1948	106	116	18	204	299	98	2	3	2	400	808	676	1.195
Career	789	861	68	1,582	2,500	796	34	51	50	3,331	6,495	7,023	.925

Joe Cronin

Career P/E: 1.089 Postseason P/E: .591
MVP: never won; 1.96 career shares
Hall of Fame: inducted in 1956

Over 20 major league seasons, Joe Cronin piled up some tremendous offensive statistics. From 1930 to 1940, Cronin knocked in more than 100 runs eight times. He routinely hit above .300, going as high as .346 in 1930. That season, Cronin also scored 127 runs, walked twice as much as he struck out, and posted the highest P/E Average, 1.261, of any full season. His 1.17 net runs per game average is better than those of Jeter, Sewell, and Vaughan, discussed later in this chapter. He made seven All-Star squads and earned 1.96 career MVP shares, although he never managed to win the award.

He appeared in the World Series only once, when his Washington squad took on the Giants in 1933. Cronin, serving as player-manager, was efficient but failed to hit for any power. His seven hits were all singles, and he generated only three runs for the Senators' scoreboard. The Giants won in five games, and Washington sank to seventh in the AL under his guidance the next year. In terms of defense, I don't think Joe was special. Although he out-fielded the league average for his career, he did commit 485 errors, including 62 in 1929.

I have Cronin, Category 4, ranked in my top 10 for the shortstop position. His defense was poor, but he compensated for his shortcomings with his work at the plate.

Year	RBI	R	HR	NR	TB	BB	HBP	SB	CS	CB	PTS	PA	P/E
1930	126	127	13	240	301	72	5	17	10	385	865	686	1.261
1931	126	103	12	217	293	81	4	10	9	379	813	700	1.161
1932	116	95	6	205	274	66	3	7	5	345	755	629	1.200
Career	1,424	1,233	170	2,487	3,546	1,059	34	87	71	4,655	9,629	8,838	1.089

Barry Larkin

Career P/E: .994; Postseason P/E: .962

MVP: National League MVP in 1995; 1.10 career shares

Hall of Fame: possible

From 1988 to 2004, Larkin appeared in 12 All-Star Games and won nine Silver Slugger honors. In 1990 Barry led the Reds to the World Series and then hit .353 against the Oakland Athletics as Cincinnati swept their way to the title. In 1995 he was again extremely efficient at the plate in the postseason, batting .385 in the NLDS and then .389 in the LCS. That year, this former University of Michigan star received the league's highest individual honor. In a tight race with Dante Bichette, Greg Maddux, and Mike Piazza, Larkin emerged victorious as the MVP. Playing his entire career in Cincy, Larkin collected 2,340 hits, scored 1,329 runs, and stole 379 bases.

Many people will probably disagree with Larkin's inclusion in this section. He only had four seasons with more than 150 games played, and his season-to-season statistics are not overwhelming. He missed considerable time in '89, '97, '01, and '03. He never came very close to 200 hits, 100 runs batted in, or 200 net runs. He won only three Gold Gloves, but he did play in the same league with Ozzie Smith.

Larkin, the fourth overall pick of the '85 draft, should have fared better in MVP balloting, especially in 1996, and he should one day be enshrined. I don't think he's a surefire candidate by any means, but I do think he was good enough to be called C4.

Year	RBI	R	HR	NR	TB	BB	HBP	SB	CS	CB	PTS	PA	P/E
1995	66	98	15	149	244	61	3	51	5	354	652	567	1.150
1996	89	117	33	173	293	96	7	36	10	422	768	627	1.225
1999	75	108	12	171	245	93	2	30	8	362	704	687	1.025
Career	960	1,329	198	2,091	3,527	939	55	379	77	4,823	9,005	9,057	.994

Joe Sewell

Career P/E: .980; Postseason P/E: .644

MVP: never won; 1.08 career shares

Hall of Fame: inducted in 1977

Joe Sewell may have been the toughest batter for pitchers to strike out in the history of baseball. He averaged just 10 Ks per 162 games, and he had five full seasons in which he fanned fewer than five times each. A .312 lifetime hitter, he batted over .300 in 10 of his 14 seasons. From 1923 to 1925, Sewell finished in the top 10 of the MVP vote each year, twice making it into the top four. He hit .353 for Cleveland in '23 and drove home 109. In '25 he batted .336 with 204 hits and only four strikeouts in 699 plate appearances. Sewell used a keen eye at the plate along with great bat control to reach base often and set the table for his teammates. His career on-base percentage, .391, is outstanding.

Even though he generated a lot of runs, Sewell wasn't a base stealer of any renown. He swiped 74 bags but was also caught 72 times. In 1927 he had an unsightly ratio of 3 steals to 16 caught steals. He didn't give away outs at the plate, but at times he gave them away on the base paths. Defensively, Sewell fielded above his league's average, but I don't think he was overly impressive. From '21 to '23 he had 155 errors while being a part of 229 double plays, hardly the type of glove work needed at short.

Sewell rates as Category 4. He struck out less often than any player in history but needed to be better in the field to make it into my top 10.

Year	RBI	R	HR	NR	TB	BB	HBP	SB	CS	CB	PTS	PA	P/E
1921	93	101	4	190	254	80	11	7	6	346	726	683	1.063
1923	109	98	3	204	265	98	7	9	6	373	781	682	1.145
1924	106	99	4	201	255	67	2	3	3	324	726	685	1.060
Career	1,055	1,141	49	2,147	2,945	842	80	74	72	3,869	8,163	8,329	.980

Ozzie Smith

Career P/E: .804; Postseason P/E: .669

MVP: never won; .65 career shares

Hall of Fame: inducted in 2002

The Wizard of Oz won 13 Gold Gloves and is generally considered to be the greatest defensive shortstop ever. He won the coveted award every year from 1980 to 1992, a remarkable run of defensive mastery. Ozzie was as acrobatic and fluid as a shortstop could be. He once made a play where he ranged wide and dove to his left, only to have the ball take a bad hop and shoot off in the opposite direction against his momentum. Smith caught the ball, barehanded, and threw the runner out. ESPN analyst and fellow Hall of Famer Joe Morgan once called it the greatest play he'd ever seen. In '87 Smith scored 104 runs, batted .303, and had an on-base average of .392, all of which were career highs. He finished second in that year's MVP vote.

Aside from 1987, 1991, and his success in NLCS contests, Ozzie Smith was not a good hitter. He hit .230 or below in three of his first four seasons and was below .250 in five of his first six. His career batting average, .262, isn't terrible, but his .328 slugging percentage is extremely low. He never slugged within 15 points of .400, and he never finished a season with more than 230 total bases.

The Wizard's defense is Category 5, but his offense is a 2 or a 3 at best. Thus, I will settle on a final rating of C4 for Smith. He also makes my top 10.

Year	RBI	R	HR	NR	TB	BB	HBP	SB	CS	CB	PTS	PA	P/E
1987	75	104	0	179	230	89	1	43	9	354	712	706	1.008
1988	51	80	3	128	193	74	1	57	9	316	572	669	.855
1991	50	96	3	143	202	83	1	35	9	312	598	641	.933
Career	793	1,257	28	2,022	3,084	1,072	33	580	148	4,621	8,665	10,778	.804

Arky Vaughan

Career P/E: 1.043; Postseason P/E: 1.000
MVP: never won; 1.22 career shares
Hall of Fame: inducted in 1985

Despite missing three full seasons and playing only parts of two others during the 1940s, Arky Vaughan was able to compile some impressive career statistics. The nine-time All-Star selection led the league in batting in 1935 with a .385 average. He also led the Senior Circuit in on-base percentage from '34 to '36, and he retired with outstanding efficiency averages of .318 batting and .406 on-base. For his career, Arky hit .300 or better every year but two, and he hit .333 or better in three consecutive seasons in the mid-'30s. Vaughan was a very productive player, averaging 1.10 net runs per contest.

Arky chose to sit out in the mid-'40s because he clashed with manager Leo Durocher in 1943. Normally quiet and reserved, Vaughan handed in his uniform following a team squabble in which he disagreed with Leo. When he returned in 1947, he failed to regain his previous form, and I suspect he also lost some passion for the game after a three-year layoff. He hit .244 in '48, playing 65 games, before quitting for good.

Vaughan, who was nicknamed Arky because of his home state of Arkansas, had a relatively brief major league career, but he was very successful nonetheless. He was inducted into the Hall in 1985, and I agree with that decision, deeming him Category 4.

Year	RBI	R	HR	NR	TB	BB	HBP	SB	CS	CB	PTS	PA	P/E
1934	94	115	12	197	285	94	2	10	5*	386	780	660	1.182
1935	99	108	19	188	303	97	7	4	2*	409	785	610	1.287
1940	95	113	7	201	269	88	3	12	6*	366	768	689	1.115
Career	926	1,173	96	2,003	3,003	937	46	118	59*	4,045	8,051	7,721	1.043

* CS totals estimated based on 2:1 success ratio

Omar Vizquel

Career P/E: .822; Postseason P/E: .814
MVP: never won; .01 career shares (through '06 voting)
Hall of Fame: possible

Hailing from Caracas, Venezuela, Omar Vizquel has won more Gold Gloves at shortstop than any other player except Ozzie Smith. His .984 fielding percentage and 40.7:1 ratio are the best marks of any shortstop analyzed in this chapter. He has been selected as his league's best defensive shortstop 11 times and deserves consideration with Smith, Aparicio, and Belanger as the elite glove men at position 6 on the diamond. In 2000 he had one of the great seasons ever in the field. Playing 156 games at short for Cleveland that year, Vizquel fielded .995 and made only three errors. His percentage was 22 points higher than the AL average, and he finished the season with an unbelievable ratio of 138.7 assists per error. Vizquel has already put together nine full seasons in which he made less than 10 errors. Ozzie accomplished that feat just once.

Probably the biggest knock against his career is that he has just .01 MVP shares to show for all of his defensive mastery. He finished sixteenth in '99 but has never gained a vote in any other season. He has also made it onto only three All-Star squads, which sounds more like the résumé of a Category 2 or 3 ballplayer.

I believe Vizquel belongs in the Hall of Fame. His work in the field is unparalleled in many ways, and he's been productive enough to earn induction. Omar is C4.

Year	RBI	R	HR	NR	TB	BB	HBP	SB	CS	CB	PTS	PA	P/E
1996	64	98	9	153	226	56	4	35	9	312	618	623	.992
1999	66	112	5	173	250	65	1	42	9	349	695	664	1.047
2000	66	101	7	160	230	87	5	22	10	334	654	717	.912
Career	869	1,337	77	2,129	3,387	941	47	380	152	4,603	8,861	10,782	.822

Category 5 Shortstops

Derek Jeter

Height: 6′3″; Weight: 175; Bats: right; Throws: right

First game: May 29, 1995; Final game: still active

Team(s): New York Yankees (1995–present)

MVP: never won; 2.04 career shares (through '06 voting)

Hall of Fame: imminent

162-game avg.: .317 batting, .388 on-base, .462 slugging, 17 home
    runs, 303 total bases, 122 runs scored, 82 runs batted in, 208 hits,
    56 extra-base hits, 67 BB, 114 K, 23 SB

Career P/E: 1.039; Postseason P/E: .948

The Good. Jeter is the pure embodiment of a winning ballplayer who
rises to the occasion when the game is on the line. He carries himself
much like DiMaggio. He doesn't *think* his team will win. He *knows* it.
To truly appreciate him as a player, you need to look beyond the numbers. Jeter's intangible value was probably best demonstrated in Game
3 of the 2001 ALDS. The Yankees, on the verge of elimination, were
clinging to a 1–0 lead when the A's Terrence Long laced a double to
right. As Jeremy Giambi rounded third, prepared to tie the game, the
throw from the outfield missed the cutoff man. Jeter instinctively
retrieved the loose ball and flipped it backhand to Jorge Posada for
the out. It was the kind of play that only Derek Jeter could make.

The Yankees' captain leads by example, but he has also put together
some impressive statistics over his first 13 seasons. He averages 1.15
net runs per game and is a .317 hitter. He has scored more than 100
runs in a season 11 times, including 134 in 1999, when he posted the
highest Production and Efficiency Average, 1.196, of his career. He

already has nine seasons with at least 190 hits and nine seasons batting over .300. He is a tremendous base runner and is very good in the field. He owns three Gold Gloves through the '06 season to go along with his '96 Rookie of the Year.

Jeter is at his best in the postseason, though. The 2000 World Series MVP, he seems to always be able to reach base, get a big hit, or make an outstanding defensive play at just the right time. His instincts are uncanny, and he is a big reason why the Yankees have won four titles and six pennants with him. If he continues to play at such a high level, and if he continues to win in the playoffs, he will certainly be considered an immortal shortstop after his career is finished.

The Bad. Jeter has good power, but he isn't considered a home-run threat every time he steps to the plate. He has hit as many as 24 homers in a season, but his .462 slugging percentage is far from outstanding. Jeter also strikes out too much. He has fanned 99 times or more in 11 of his 12 full seasons, and he has 96 strikeouts compared with 51 free passes in the postseason. When his '01 Yanks lost to Arizona in the World Series, he batted only .148 and struck out six times.

The Verdict. Jeter is a Category 5 shortstop. He always seems to do whatever it takes to win. In the end, that's about the best thing that can be said about an athlete. I definitely think, when all is said and done, that he'll rank as one of the three greatest in history at the position. For the time being, however, he barely misses making it into that elite company. He is top five, but he's not top three . . . yet. The Yankees' captain is guaranteed a spot in Cooperstown.

Cal Ripken Jr.

Height: 6′4″; Weight: 225; Bats: right; Throws: right

First game: August 10, 1981; Final game: October 6, 2001

Team(s): Baltimore Orioles (1981–2001)

MVP: American League MVP in 1983, 1991; 2.31 career shares

Hall of Fame: inducted in 2007

162-game avg.: .276 batting, .340 on-base, .447 slugging, 23 home
    runs, 279 total bases, 89 runs scored, 91 runs batted in, 172 hits,
    58 extra-base hits, 61 BB, 70 K, 2 SB

Career P/E: .946; Postseason P/E: .855

The Good. Cal Ripken Jr. can truly be called the Iron Man of baseball. He played in more consecutive games, 2,632, than any player in history. His streak began on May 30, 1982, and continued until September 20, 1998. Along the way, Ripken won the Rookie of the Year, two MVPs, and two Major League Player of the Year honors. He made 19 consecutive All-Star teams and was twice (1991 and 2001) selected as the Midsummer Classic's best player.

In '83 Ripken won his first MVP. The Orioles won the pennant and the World Series that magical season. The Maryland native hit .318, scored 121 times, and drove home 102 runs with his 211 hits. He won the award again in 1991 even though Baltimore languished through a disappointing season that saw them lose 95 games. Voters were swayed by Cal's .323 batting average. He also slugged .566, smashing 85 of his 210 hits for extra bases. His P/E that year, 1.100, was the best mark of his legendary career.

Ripken changed the way shortstop was played when he arrived in the early '80s. Traditionally, shortstops were small and light and usually unable to hit with much power. Ripken, standing 6′4″ and weighing 225 pounds, looked more like a first baseman or a corner outfielder who lost his way and ended up between second and third. Derek Jeter and Alex Rodriguez have since come along and mirrored Ripken's image, along with his production, at the shortstop position. His size didn't prevent him from being a solid fielder, however. His ratio of 31.0 assists per error is better than Ozzie Smith's and trails only Omar Vizquel's in this chapter.

The Bad. Ripken's overall P/E score, .946, is not nearly as high as some of the other standout shortstops. He averaged less than one net run per game over his 3,001 major league contests, and he never exceeded 200 net runs in a season. Ripken stole only 36 bases and was caught 39 times. He had consistent power, but he never reached 35 homers in any season.

When Baltimore won the '83 Series, their shortstop hit only .167 and had more strikeouts, four, than total bases, three. When the Orioles fell to the Yankees in the '96 ALCS, Cal hit .250 and generated only one net run of offense in five games.

The Verdict. Cal Ripken Jr. had a tremendous career. He hit 431 homers and approached 1,700 runs both scored and driven in. He joined the 3,000-hit club in the 2000 season and won multiple MVPs. He is Category 5 without any hesitation, and I make a case for him as the best shortstop ever later in this chapter.

Alex Rodriguez

Height: 6′3″; Weight: 190; Bats: right; Throws: right

First game: July 8, 1994; Final game: still active

Team(s): Seattle Mariners (1994–2000); Texas Rangers (2001–2003);
New York Yankees (2004–2007)

MVP: American League MVP in 2003, 2005; 4.05 career shares
(through '06 voting)

Hall of Fame: imminent

162-game avg.: .306 batting, .389 on-base, .578 slugging, 44 home
runs, 362 total bases, 128 runs scored, 128 runs batted in, 191
hits, 80 extra-base hits, 78 BB, 130 K, 23 SB

Career P/E: 1.234; Postseason P/E: .918

The Good. Alex Rodriguez has the highest P/E Average of any short-stop by a wide margin. He is the complete package in terms of speed, power, and glove work. The first overall pick of the 1993 draft, A-Rod burst onto the scene as a highly touted prospect in 1996 with Seattle. He batted .358 that year, smashed 215 hits, and scored 141 runs. His P/E, 1.343, was tremendous but ranks as only the third highest score of his amazing career. In 2000 he generated 225 net runs and slugged .606 en route to a 1.345 P/E. He collected 1.29 combined MVP shares over those two campaigns with the Mariners but failed to walk away with the trophy.

A-Rod has already won two MVPs (although one was as a third baseman, his current position), and I believe he should have won two more. He deserved the honor over Juan Gonzalez in '96, and he was better than Tejada in '02, when he outhomered Miguel 57 to 34 while playing the same position. His 4.05 career share total is tremendous and will likely only increase as he continues to pile up legendary statistics. He will most likely win the '07 honor as well after driving in 156 runs and posting the highest P/E (1.415) of his career.

No one at this position can compete with Rodriguez's numbers. He recently hit his five hundredth home run, and he reached 1,500 runs scored and driven in by the end of the 2007 campaign. His average of 1.31 net runs per game is better than any shortstop in history. A-Rod's efficiency averages (.306 batting, .389 on-base, and .578 slugging), outstanding for any position, are almost unthinkable for a shortstop.

Defensively, Alex is excellent. He owns two Gold Gloves and sports a high ratio of assists to errors. He has good range, dependable hands, and a strong throwing arm. In 2003 he fielded .989 and committed only eight errors in 158 games, earning his second defensive award.

The Bad. When he was traded to New York in 2004, he became a third baseman. Derek Jeter wasn't asked to give up his position, and A-Rod happily agreed to make the switch in order to have a better chance to win a ring. He struggled somewhat in his first season in the Bronx, often leaving runners on base and coming up short against Boston in the playoffs. New York's intense fans and ever-present media have converged to put enormous pressure on A-Rod of late. Despite a huge '07 campaign, he may need to win a World Series title in pinstripes in order to fully validate his career.

The Verdict. Rodriguez is Category 5 and one of the three best shortstops ever, even though he has a handful of years left to play. Currently, he still qualifies as a shortstop, despite the fact that he now patrols the hot corner.

Honus Wagner

Height: 5'11"; Weight: 200; Bats: right; Throws: right

First game: July 19, 1897; Final game: September 17, 1917

Team(s): Louisville Colonels (1897–1899); Pittsburgh Pirates (1900–1917)

MVP: never won; 1.20 career shares

Hall of Fame: inducted in 1936

162-game avg.: .327 batting, .391 on-base, .466 slugging, 6 home runs, 282 total bases, 101 runs scored, 100 runs batted in, 198 hits, 58 extra-base hits, 56 BB, 51 K, 42 SB

Career P/E: 1.100; Postseason P/E: 1.102

The Good. Serious debates raged on during the early days of baseball as to who the game's best player was. Many sided with Detroit's Ty Cobb, but others opted for Wagner, the longtime Pittsburgh shortstop who put up legendary statistics. In 1909 Wagner's Pirates defeated Cobb's Tigers in the World Series. The Flying Dutchman outplayed the Georgia Peach by hitting .333, stealing six bases, and driving home six runs. For some, that Series definitively proved Honus as the best.

Wagner led the National League in batting eight times, and he finished second in 1905 with a .363 mark. He never won an MVP, but it should be noted that 1911 was the first season any such honor was given, and Wagner had already played 13 full seasons by then. He still managed to end his career with 1.20 shares and two finishes in the top three.

The Dutchman posted incredibly high averages year after year, and he matched that efficiency with run production as well. He scored 1,736 runs and drove in 1,732 over his Hall of Fame career. He managed to do so while hitting only 101 round-trippers, which tells me he was probably extremely clutch with runners on base. Honus ended his career as a .327 batter with 3,415 hits. He had 640 doubles, 252 triples, and 722 stolen bases to his credit.

In the field, he made a lot of errors, as did everyone in the early 1900s, but he still fielded well above the National League average, .940 compared to .927. He was inducted into the Hall of Fame in 1936 along with Cobb, Babe Ruth, Walter Johnson, and Christy Mathewson as a member of baseball's first group of immortals.

The Bad. There is not very much to count against the career of Honus Wagner. At retirement, he held career National League records in virtually every significant offensive category, including hits, runs, runs batted in, and stolen bases. He did tail off a bit at the end of his career, however. In 1914 Wagner batted .252, the lowest mark he ever knew. He failed to reach .300 during his last four seasons, and his power numbers waned as well. The only caught-stealing information available was for 1915, when he stole 22 bases but was caught 15 times. That ratio was used in determining his career P/E Average as well as his single-season averages for the other 20 years.

The Verdict. Wagner is Category 5 and deserves serious consideration as the greatest shortstop in history. He hit .330 or better 11 consecutive years from 1899 to 1909 and undoubtedly would have received MVP acclaim frequently during that stretch. He'll battle it out with Cal Ripken Jr. and Alex Rodriguez to determine who claims the number one spot at this glamorous position.

Shortstop: The Top 10

Thirteen shortstops earned Category 4 or 5 status in my opinion and, therefore, also received consideration for the top 10. Although Vaughan, Sewell, and Appling were all great players, they didn't make the list. Once I narrowed the field to 10, finalizing the list was difficult because offensive statistics had to be weighed carefully alongside defensive accomplishments. These are the 10 best shortstops ever.

10. Luis Aparicio

Aparicio just sneaks into the top 10 because of his defensive prowess. He won nine Gold Gloves and was always recognized as a tremendous talent in the field. He certainly didn't have the bat of Arky Vaughan, but he did steal more than 500 bases, score more than 1,300 runs, and accumulate almost 2,700 hits over his career. If given the option, I would choose him over Vaughan to play shortstop on my team. Defense is just too important at this position.

9. Barry Larkin

Larkin beats out Aparicio for number 9 for a couple of reasons. First, he won an MVP, and Aparicio didn't. Second, it would appear from looking solely at Gold Gloves that the American Leaguer was much better, yet Larkin fielded at a higher rate and averaged more assists per error. He also had to compete with Ozzie Smith for the award more than half of his career as well. That doesn't mean I think Larkin was the better defensive player, but I do think it keeps him close. Offensively, there is no ambiguity. The Cincinnati star's P/E is 217 points higher in the regular season and nearly 500 points better in October.

8. Ozzie Smith

Ozzie comes in ahead of Larkin because he won 10 more Gold Gloves and was clearly the better defensive player. Smith's '87 season was just as good as Larkin's '95 campaign, and Ozzie won a postseason MVP, something Larkin never did. At the plate, Larkin was better, and he may have been a more complete player. Ozzie is number 8, however, simply because of his glove.

7. Omar Vizquel

Surprise! I think Omar Vizquel deserves to be ranked higher than Ozzie Smith. I also see Vizquel as the better defensive player. He may not be able to match the Wizard's flair for the spectacular, but he has been better at fielding the shortstop position than any player in history. Ozzie never had more than one full season with less than 10 errors; Vizquel has nine. Ozzie's highest fielding percentage was .987, a score eclipsed by Omar seven times and nearly matched by his .984 career mark. Vizquel's 2000 defensive season is the best ever at shortstop in my opinion, and it might be the best ever at any position. Vizquel was also slightly more productive on offense, although Smith has him by a wide margin in stolen bases. He has my vote, though, and he has spot number 7.

6. Joe Cronin

Cronin was not in the same league as Vizquel defensively, but his offensive numbers are just too good to overlook. His P/E is 267 points higher, and he generated .35 more net runs every game on average. He also tops Vizquel by a wide margin when it comes to MVP shares. Cronin's bat is the choice over Vizquel's glove.

5. Lou Boudreau

Cronin doesn't hold the same advantage over Lou Boudreau. Boudreau won an MVP, collected 2.66 shares, and finished in the top 10 eight times. In '48 the voters decided he was the best player in either league, and Cronin can't make that claim. Boudreau's P/E doesn't stand up well against Cronin's, but he was far better in the field, averaging almost 10 more assists per error. Both men had 22 World Series at-bats, but Boudreau was more efficient in terms of total bases. I like his combination of offense and defense, and I think the sportswriters in his day did too.

4. Derek Jeter

Even though his career is not yet through, I believe Derek Jeter is the fourth best shortstop in history. He exudes a winning aura, and he has the statistics to back it up. Jeter's P/E Average is 114 points better than Boudreau's, and he averages 1.15 net runs per game. Jeter has topped 150 net runs in a season 11 times, and his Cleveland counterpart did it only three. Unlike Boudreau, he has never won an MVP in the regular season, but he has taken home that trophy as World Series MVP.

The Top Three

The top three begins in 1897 and comes right up to the present moment. Their statistics and their accomplishments are legendary, and a strong case can be made for each to be number 1. The argument is slightly muddied by the fact that A-Rod is now playing third but still qualifies here with more than 60 percent of his games played at shortstop. Right now, it's time to take a summarized look at the strongest arguments in favor of each.

The Case for Ripken

Two MVP/Player of the Year seasons

19 consecutive All-Star nominations

Two Gold Gloves and a ratio of 31.0 assists per error

2,632 consecutive games played

More than 3,100 hits, 600 doubles, and 400 home runs

The Case for Rodriguez

Two MVPs, five top-three finishes, and 4.05 total shares (and still
counting)

1.234 career P/E Average

Seven seasons with more than 200 net runs produced; 1.31 net runs
per game

Eight 40-homer seasons and 109 home runs from 2001 and 2002

Eight seasons with P/E scores above 1.200, three above 1.300, and
one above 1.400

The Case for Wagner

3,415 hits and more than 1,700 runs both scored and driven home

.327 lifetime batting average and six seasons at .350 or better

Eight-time league batting champion

1.21 net runs per game over 21 seasons in the dead-ball era

No MVP given until 1911

3. Cal Ripken Jr.

The greatest Orioles player finishes ahead of Derek Jeter on the strength of his two MVP/Player of the Year campaigns in '83 and '91. Jeter has been in the top five only twice, as a third-place finisher in '98 and runner-up in '06. Ripken also finished third, in 1989, but had two seasons in which he was judged to be the best player in the game. Jeter can't make that assertion, and that by itself is enough to make this a fairly easy choice. Furthermore, I think Cal was probably a little more solid in the field, and he hit for more power at the plate. He also maintained a high standard of play over 21 seasons. Jeter may one day prove to be the better player, but he falls shy of Ripken at this time.

2. Alex Rodriguez

A-Rod wins the silver, edging out Cal but unable to overtake Honus for the top spot. Like Ripken, Rodriguez won two MVPs and finished third once. Alex also was runner-up twice, and I think he deserved the award in both of those seasons. Two other top-10 finishes (with the '07 vote still to be determined) give A-Rod a comfortable advantage, 4.05 to 2.31, in terms of MVP shares. When you consider that he rivals Ripken in the field and eclipses him at the plate, the decision to put Rodriguez in second place becomes fairly obvious. A career P/E Average of 1.234 puts the superstar slugger in elite company with the best players of all time regardless of position. His lifetime score is higher than those of Rogers Hornsby, Ty Cobb, and Mickey Mantle, and it's 288 points better than Ripken's, which is enough to earn him this place on my top 10 list for shortstops.

1. Honus Wagner

It wasn't easy to decide between Rodriguez and Honus Wagner for number 1. First of all, they played more than 75 years apart. When the Flying Dutchman played, the game was entirely different from today; Rodriguez hit more home runs in his first two years in Texas than Wagner did in 21 seasons. Therefore, I needed to compare their careers less with one another and more with their peers.

Wagner was arguably the greatest player of his generation, and he was definitely regarded as the best in the game until Ty Cobb came along, established himself as a superstar, and clouded the issue. Despite playing during a time when runs were scored at one of the lowest levels in the sport's history, Wagner still managed to produce 1.21 net runs per game. He was able to average that over more than two decades throughout the dead-ball era, a fact that is quite remarkable and lends support to his number 1 ranking. Rodriguez's average, 1.31, is higher but has also been formulated since '94 and has not yet been maintained over the course of a long career.

I think Wagner would have won some MVPs if the award had been made available earlier in his career. He led the National League in batting seven times prior to 1911, the year the award was introduced. He finished third in that year's vote, second in 1912, and eighth in 1913. Wagner had 100 or more runs batted in eight times from 1898 to 1909, yet he had no chance to earn any MVP shares during his prime.

Finally, A-Rod may need to win a World Series ring to truly validate his career. Honus played poorly in the 1903 Series, and his team lost to Boston. But he rebounded six years later against Ty Cobb's Tigers, posting a 1.400 P/E mark and leading his Pittsburgh team to victory. A-Rod hasn't yet proven he can do that.

Defense, Defense, Defense

In the real-estate game, the saying is "location, location, location." In the game of baseball, the property where shortstops reside calls for defense, defense, and more defense. Shortstops, normally the best athletes on the field, must have quick feet, strong arms, and the ability to range to both sides to turn potential hits into outs. While I believe that catcher is the most important position because it is involved in every pitch, I also believe that it takes the most skill to play shortstop.

I have compared this position's Category 4 and 5 players, along with a few C3s, with respect to defense. Each player has been analyzed according to three defensive categories. The first, assist-to-error ratio, represents how many positive plays were made in relation to each miscue. The second measure, fielding percentage, looks at the player's career mark in relation to his league's average over the same time period. Finally, the number of Gold Gloves won gives a good indication of how well that player defended his position relative to other top shortstops in the league that season. For those players who had limited or no opportunity to win any Gold Gloves (the award did not start until 1957) I have noted that in their column.

Player	Ratio	FP (Lg. Avg.)	Gold Gloves*
Luis Aparicio	21.9:1	.972 (.963)	9 (began in '56)
Luke Appling	11.2:1	.948 (.952)	no opportunity
Mark Belanger	27.6:1	.977 (.964)	8
Lou Boudreau	21.3:1	.973 (.954)	no opportunity
Larry Bowa	32.5:1	.980 (.965)	2
Dave Concepcion	21.2:1	.971 (.964)	5
Joe Cronin	12.0:1	.951 (.946)	no opportunity
Derek Jeter	24.2:1	.975 (.972)	3 (still active)
Barry Larkin	24.9:1	.975 (.968)	3
Cal Ripken Jr.	31.0:1	.979 (.969)	2
Alex Rodriguez	27.5:1	.977 (.972)	2 (still active)
Joe Sewell	11.8:1	.951 (.944)	no opportunity
Ozzie Smith	29.8:1	.978 (.966)	13
Arky Vaughan	12.0:1	.951 (.949)	no opportunity
Omar Vizquel	40.7:1	.984 (.972)	11 (still active)
Honus Wagner	8.9:1	.940 (.927)	no opportunity

* accurate through 2006 balloting

7

Left Field

We now move into the outfield, where we will begin in left. At this point, it is important to mention a slight change in how I have organized the outfielders in the next three chapters. Until now, a player had to play at least 60 percent of his games at one specific defensive position to be included at that spot. With the outfielders, it's a little bit different. As long as 60 percent of their games were played in the outfield, they will be recognized at the outfield position they played most often. There is little difference between playing left field and playing right field. On the other hand, there is a great difference between being a shortstop and being a catcher. Naturally, if a player did not play 60 percent of his games in the outfield, then he is considered multiposition.

The left-field position is loaded with superstars from the past right up to the present. My top three, which includes Barry Bonds, Stan Musial, and Ted Williams, have combined to amass the most impressive MVP credentials of any position. They each have a legitimate claim to the top spot, and the choice was not an easy one. In fact, it was one of the more difficult decisions of any position, a fact that is noted later in the book when I list my top 100 baseball players in the history of the game.

So it was with the rest of my top 10. The left fielders analyzed include leadoff speedsters such as Lou Brock and Rickey Henderson, middle-of-the-order muscle such as Jim Rice and Al Simmons, and power hitters such as Albert Belle and Ralph Kiner, whose careers burned brightly but didn't last as long as they would have liked.

More than any other position, left fielders need to be offensively gifted. Whether generating runs with quick feet on the bases or with power at the plate, the best at this position added runs to the scoreboard and kept opposing pitchers up at night.

Left Field: Career P/E Averages

Ted Williams, 1.346; Barry Bonds, 1.264; Al Simmons, 1.199; Albert Belle, 1.161; Stan Musial, 1.151; Ralph Kiner, 1.141; Ken Williams, 1.134; Bob Johnson, 1.131; Goose Goslin, 1.130; Chick Hafey, 1.128; Joe Jackson, 1.123; Joe Medwick, 1.116; Bob Meusel, 1.099; Heinie Manush, 1.071; Rickey Henderson, 1.062; Kevin Mitchell, 1.060; Dante Bichette, 1.059; Jim Rice, 1.046; Minnie Minoso, 1.044; Tim Raines, 1.020; Billy Williams, 1.012; George Foster, 1.006; Sherry Magee, .997; Carl Yastrzemski, .993; Bob Cerv, .992; Greg Luzinski, .991; Garret Anderson, .979; Zack Wheat, .968; Sandy Amoros, .958; Kevin McReynolds, .939; Ben Oglivie, .936; Lou Brock, .926; Dusty Baker, .922; Joe Rudi, .891; Vince Coleman, .882

Category 1–3 Left Fielders

Sandy Amoros

Career P/E: .958; Postseason P/E: .763
Notable seasons (P/E): 1954 (.993); 1955 (.927); 1956 (1.108)

Playing for the '55 Brooklyn Dodgers, Amoros appeared in 119 games, collecting 96 hits in the regular season. He stole 10 bases and scored 59 runs. These were all career highs. Most important, Amoros came up big in Game 7 of the World Series against the hated Yankees. Two men were on base in the sixth inning when Yogi Berra hit a shot to left that looked like it had a chance to tie the game. Amoros, however, made the catch and then threw back into the infield for a double play. Brooklyn won 2–0, finally overcoming the Yanks.

Unfortunately for Amoros and Dodgers fans, there wasn't much else to get excited about regarding his playing career. The Cuban left fielder played in only 517 games over seven seasons. He never distinguished himself as a bona fide everyday corner outfielder. Amoros never had 60 runs either scored or driven home.

Amoros is a Category 1 outfielder according to the system I've organized. He would probably be a C2 if he had stayed around a little bit longer or put up better offensive numbers.

Bob Cerv

Career P/E: .992; Postseason P/E: .484
Notable seasons (P/E): 1958 (1.185); 1959 (1.008); 1960 (.944)

Playing for the Kansas City Athletics in 1958, Bob Cerv became a textbook example of a player with a true breakout season. The righty outfielder set career highs in virtually every offensive category. He batted .305, hit 38 homers, and knocked in 104 runs en route to an impressive P/E score of 1.185. That season, Bob received his only All-Star nomination as well as the only Most Valuable Player shares (.49) of his career by finishing fourth in the vote.

After '58 Cerv was decent the following season but never came close to matching his levels of production and efficiency from his breakout campaign. He had less than 45 RBI every season but two throughout his career and frequently had low batting averages. He was out of baseball by '62, appearing in only 33 games and retiring with fewer than 400 runs either scored or driven in.

Despite one memorable season, Bob Cerv rates as Category 2. He was great in '58, good in '59, and marginal at best for the remainder of his career. He hit .357 in the '60 Series for the Yankees, but he generated only one net run.

Vince Coleman

Career P/E: .882; Postseason P/E: .793
Notable seasons (P/E): 1985 (.925); 1986 (.849); 1987 (1.004)

In 1985 the St. Louis Cardinals were led by a speedy rookie named Vince Coleman. Nicknamed Vincent Van Go, Coleman hit leadoff and led the National League with 110 stolen bases. St. Louis won the pennant, and Coleman was given the Rookie of the Year award while also finishing eleventh in the MVP vote. He led the league in swipes for his first six years, averaging more than 90 steals per season.

While his first three seasons were electrifying, the rest of his career wasn't. He played three seasons for the Mets from 1991 to 1993 but failed to play 100 games in any of those campaigns. Vince reached base safely less than a third of the time for his career, and he averaged only .85 net runs per game.

The '85 World Series may have turned out differently had Coleman been able to play in it. He injured himself in the NLCS and didn't appear in the Fall Classic against the Royals. I see him as Category 2 with no chance for enshrinement.

George Foster

Career P/E: 1.006; Postseason P/E: .941

Notable seasons (P/E): 1976 (1.155); 1977 (1.303); 1978 (1.108);
    1979 (1.147)

Throughout the mid- to late '70s, George Foster was one of the best sluggers in the NL. He led the league in runs batted in for three consecutive seasons and was named MVP in 1977 after belting 52 homers and driving in 149. The year before, Foster had finished second in the vote, losing out to teammate Joe Morgan. In the '76 World Series, George terrorized Yankees pitching with a .429 batting average and seven net runs over the Reds' four-game sweep, reaching base in 50 percent of his plate appearances.

Foster was on his way to a big season when the strike hit in 1981, but his career took a turn for the worse after being traded to the Mets. His production tailed off, his strikeouts remained high, and his batting averages were below .270 the rest of his career.

For a while during his playing days in the late '70s, it looked as if George Foster would end up as an all-time great. The strike of '81 seemed to be a line of demarcation in his career, after which he was never the same player. He rates as Category 3.

Joe Jackson

Career P/E: 1.123; Postseason P/E: 1.035

Notable seasons (P/E): 1911 (1.265); 1912 (1.253); 1919 (1.109);
    1920 (1.270)

Shoeless Joe has the third-highest batting average in history, yet he isn't in the Hall of Fame. Accused of throwing the 1919 World Series with seven others, Jackson was banned from baseball for life. Had he not been banned, Jackson would be in the Hall. Immortals such as Cobb and Ruth pointed to Jackson as a tremendous hitter, one they emulated and respected greatly. Shoeless Joe hit better than .350 six times.

Jackson's name will always be linked to the infamous Black Sox Scandal. He admitted under oath that he had involvement with the fix, but he also pleaded his innocence throughout his life after being banned. His performance in the 1919 Series—a .375 average, 12 hits, 6 RBI, and no errors—speaks for itself. Sadly, the speculation and doubt will probably hover around this great player forever.

I think it's doubtful that Jackson will ever make it into the Hall of Fame. If it hasn't happened yet, then it most likely never will. It would take a strong commissioner to lift his ban. Jackson, considered Category 3, insisted his innocence until his death.

Tim Raines

Career P/E: 1.020; Postseason P/E: .732
Notable seasons (P/E): 1983 (1.165); 1984 (1.033); 1985 (1.065);
    1987 (1.219)

Rock stole more than 800 bases, scored almost 1,600 runs, and used his 2,605 hits to average .294 at the plate over 23 seasons. His best years came in Montreal in the 1980s, when he teamed with Andre Dawson to form a terrific corner outfield duo. Raines served notice to the National League in the strike-shortened season of '81, when he swiped 71 bags in only 88 games. He went on to record five more consecutive seasons with at least 70 steals, peaking at 90 in 1983. His 84 percent success rate is one of the best ever.

Raines never finished better than fifth in MVP balloting, a feat that he accomplished in 1983. He also finished sixth and seventh, but his career total of .99 MVP shares is low. His postseason P/E is almost 300 points below his regular-season number.

As a few more years pass, I believe Tim Raines will begin to gain serious consideration for Cooperstown. As one of the game's all-time best base stealers, he ranks as one of only five men to top 800 career thefts. Raines also hit for good averages, scored a ton of runs, and made seven straight All-Star Games. Raines is Category 3 in my book.

The Best Left Fielders

162-Game Averages

Player	BA	OBP	SLP	HR	TB	R	RBI	H	XBH	BB	K	SB
Belle	.295	.369	.564	40	347	103	130	182	83	72	101	9
Bonds	.298	.444	.607	41	324	121	108	159	78	139	83	28
Brock	.293	.343	.410	9	262	100	56	187	48	47	107	58
Goslin	.316	.387	.500	18	306	105	114	194	65	67	41	12
Henderson	.279	.401	.419	16	241	121	59	161	46	115	89	74
Kiner	.279	.398	.548	41	314	107	112	160	69	111	82	2
Manush	.330	.377	.479	9	296	104	95	204	62	41	28	9
Medwick	.324	.362	.505	17	315	98	113	202	70	36	45	3
Musial	.331	.417	.559	25	328	104	104	194	73	86	37	4
Rice	.298	.352	.502	30	320	97	113	190	65	52	110	4
Simmons	.334	.380	.535	22	343	110	134	214	72	45	54	6
B. Williams	.290	.361	.492	28	299	92	96	177	62	68	68	6
T. Williams	.344	.482	.634	37	345	127	130	188	79	143	50	2
Yastrzemski	.285	.379	.462	22	271	89	90	167	57	90	68	8

Category 4 Left Fielders

Albert Belle

Career P/E: 1.161; Postseason P/E: 1.114
MVP: never won; 2.38 career shares
Hall of Fame: doubtful

I imagine many people reading this are somewhat surprised to find Albert Belle included in this section. He only played a dozen seasons, but he put up tremendous offensive numbers during that stretch. He hit for high averages with terrific power and averaged 1.19 net runs per game. His 1.161 lifetime P/E is the fourth highest score at this position, better than even Stan Musial's 1.151. It is also higher than the career averages of such immortals as Willie Mays, Hank Aaron, and Frank Robinson. I don't think he is their equal, but I do think he's a Hall of Famer. His average of 83 extra-base hits per 162 games is better than any left fielder in history.

Belle's overall numbers will count heavily against him when voters consider him for Cooperstown. He scored less than 1,000 runs and collected only 1,726 hits. He had three seasons when he hit 48 or more homers but retired with just 381, a total that might not be enough for him to gain the necessary votes. Moreover, Belle's personality and surliness may be the prime factors that ultimately keep him out.

I think it is doubtful that Belle will make it into Cooperstown. He didn't play very long, and he made too many enemies. However, I believe his career warrants induction one day. I rate him as Category 4.

Year	RBI	R	HR	NR	TB	BB	HBP	SB	CS	CB	PTS	PA	P/E
1995	126	121	50	197	377	73	6	5	2	459	853	629	1.356
1996	148	124	48	224	375	99	7	11	0	492	940	715	1.315
1998	152	113	49	216	399	81	1	6	4	483	915	706	1.296
Career	1,239	974	381	1,832	3,300	683	55	88	41	4,085	7,749	6,673	1.161

Lou Brock

Career P/E: .926; Postseason P/E: 1.348

MVP: never won; 1.60 career shares

Hall of Fame: inducted in 1985

The St. Louis Cardinals were on the better end of one of baseball's most lopsided trades in 1964 when they received Louis Clark Brock, a speedy, young Chicago Cubs outfielder as part of a package for Ernie Broglio. As soon as Brock joined the Cardinals, his career blossomed. He hit .348 in 103 games and helped lead them to the World Series, where he batted .300 as the Cardinals defeated the Yankees in seven games. He would return to the Fall Classic two other times, winning in '67 and losing in '68. Both times, Brock batted well over .400 with 25 combined hits over those back-to-back Series. He generated 25 net runs in 21 postseason games. Brock was most dangerous to the opposition when he was on the base paths. He stole 938 career bags and led the league in that category eight times. In 1974 he broke Maury Wills's record by swiping 118 bases.

Brock never walked very much. Therefore, his career on-base percentage finished at just .343—he never came close to a .400 mark in that important category. Had he been able to reach base at a higher clip, he could have been Rickey Henderson. The Cardinals legend struck out almost 1,000 times more than he walked.

Brock has the lowest P/E Average and the lowest average net runs per game in this section. He finished in the top five of the MVP once and made six All-Star teams.

Year	RBI	R	HR	NR	TB	BB	HBP	SB	CS	CB	PTS	PA	P/E
1965	69	107	16	160	281	45	10	63	27	372	692	697	.993
1967	76	113	21	168	325	24	6	52	18	389	725	724	1.001
1971	61	126	7	180	272	76	1	64	19	394	754	720	1.047
Career	900	1,610	149	2,361	4,238	761	49	938	307	5,679	10,401	11,235	.926

Goose Goslin

Career P/E: 1.130; Postseason P/E: .895

MVP: never won; .76 career shares

Hall of Fame: inducted in 1968

Long before there was a Goose Gossage blowing away hitters, Goose Goslin was terrorizing pitchers. He was a steady run producer, knocking in at least 100 runs 11 times. For his career, he drove home more than 1,600 runs while batting .316 lifetime. He hit as high as .379, which he did as a member of the Washington Senators in 1928. Goslin averaged 1.24 net runs per game over his major league tenure. In 1924 he generated 217 net runs, and he bettered that total a dozen years later when he was responsible for 223 runs to Detroit's scoreboard in 1936. When he retired, he had more than 2,700 hits.

Goslin played in an era when offensive statistics were high, and he was never able to distinguish himself from his peers. He made only one All-Star appearance, although the game was not around for much of his career. More important, he never finished in the top five of the American League's MVP vote. His .76 career shares point to a player with big statistics who wasn't recognized as one of the best players of his time. When he was finally inducted into Cooperstown, it was already 30 years past his retirement.

His statistics point to a player who had a tremendous career, but I think they were probably a bit inflated by the era in which he played. Still, his production numbers are impressive, good enough for a Category 4 rating but not good enough for the top 10.

Year	RBI	R	HR	NR	TB	BB	HBP	SB	CS	CB	PTS	PA	P/E
1925	113	116	18	211	329	53	6	27	8	407	829	670	1.237
1930	138	115	37	216	351	67	3	17	11	427	859	668	1.286
1936	125	122	24	223	301	85	0	14	4	396	842	660	1.276
Career	1,609	1,483	248	2,844	4,325	949	55	175	89	5,415	11,103	9,822	1.130

Ralph Kiner

Career P/E: 1.141; Postseason P/E: never in the postseason
MVP: never won; 1.31 career shares
Hall of Fame: inducted in 1975

Ralph Kiner wasted no time in establishing himself as a legitimate power hitter and a star when he broke in with the Pirates in 1946. He led the league in home runs that year, something that he would do every year through 1952, a remarkable string of seven consecutive seasons. He hit over .300 three times, scored 100 or more runs six times, and reached base routinely. His career on-base percentage (.398) is outstanding, especially for a middle-of-the-order slugger like Ralph. The righty's rate of one home run per 14.1 times at bat is one of the best in history, better than Killebrew, Mantle, and Foxx. Kiner was an All-Star every year from 1948 to 1953.

Kiner was not an early selection for Cooperstown because he simply didn't play very long. He retired with less than 1,000 runs scored and fewer than 1,500 hits. Numbers like that make it difficult to earn the necessary votes.

I think Kiner deserves to be a Hall of Famer. He was the best slugger in the National League in the late '40s and early '50s, and he complemented his power with excellent plate discipline and run production. A longer career would have been nice, just as a postseason appearance would have been. Nonetheless, Kiner is a C4 and in my top 10.

Year	RBI	R	HR	NR	TB	BB	HBP	SB	CS	CB	PTS	PA	P/E
1947	127	118	51	194	361	98	2	1	0*	462	850	666	1.276
1949	127	116	54	189	361	117	1	6	1*	484	862	667	1.292
1951	109	124	42	191	333	137	2	2	1	473	855	670	1.276
Career	1,015	971	369	1,617	2,852	1,011	24	22	5*	3,904	7,138	6,256	1.141

* CS totals estimated based on known statistics

Heinie Manush

Career P/E: 1.071; Postseason P/E: .400

MVP: never won; 2.25 career shares

Hall of Fame: inducted in 1964

Henry Emmett Manush made his major league debut on April 20, 1923, as a member of the Detroit Tigers. He hit .334 during his rookie campaign, and it was certainly a sign of things to come. A lifetime .330 batter, Manush frequently hit for high averages. He hit .378 for the '26 Tigers and then matched that two years later in St. Louis by batting .378 for the '28 Browns. In both seasons, he walked more than he struck out and reached base more than 40 percent of the time. Although Manush never won an MVP, he did finish in the top five four times, including a second-place finish in '28 and back-to-back third-place finishes in '32 and '33. In total, he earned 2.25 career shares in the balloting.

Left field is a power position, meaning that home-run ability is usually stressed. Manush was never a big home-run threat. He hit only 110 for his career and never had 15 in any single season. That lack of power also contributed to his RBI totals being average. In '31, for example, he had 70 RBI to go along with a P/E Average of just .991.

Manush retired with solid career numbers and an outstanding batting average. I think he was a very good player but probably not quite as good as Joe Medwick or Goose Goslin, a pair of left fielders who played during a similar time.

Year	RBI	R	HR	NR	TB	BB	HBP	SB	CS	CB	PTS	PA	P/E
1928	108	104	13	199	367	39	0	17	5	418	816	697	1.171
1932	116	121	14	223	325	36	5	7	2	371	817	677	1.207
1933	95	115	5	205	302	36	2	6	4	342	752	704	1.068
Career	1,183	1,287	110	2,360	3,665	506	70	114	62*	4,293	9,013	8,416	1.071

* CS totals estimated based on known statistics

Joe Medwick

Career P/E: 1.116; Postseason P/E: .854

MVP: National League MVP in 1937; 2.27 career shares

Hall of Fame: inducted in 1968

With 31 home runs, 154 driven in, and a .374 batting average, Joseph Michael Medwick won the 1937 National League Triple Crown. The outfielder, better known as Ducky, won the Most Valuable Player award that year, collecting 88 percent of the available votes. His 1.357 P/E score that season was the highest of his career and marked the second time in three years that he reached 1.300. Medwick was tremendously productive in the mid- to late '30s. Beginning in 1935 and continuing through 1939, Ducky generated more than 200 net runs each year.

Medwick had dominant years in the 1930s but failed to sustain that level of excellence. For that reason, he fails to rank with the likes of Al Simmons and Rickey Henderson, who both compiled more impressive career numbers. After the '42 season, Ducky's production tailed off dramatically.

Joe Medwick rates as a Category 4 left fielder according to my analysis. His numbers are very similar to Goose Goslin's, but I think he was a better player. He won an MVP and was recognized more frequently for that honor than Goslin. Coincidentally, both men were inducted into Cooperstown in 1968.

Year	RBI	R	HR	NR	TB	BB	HBP	SB	CS	CB	PTS	PA	P/E
1935	126	132	23	235	365	30	4	4	2*	401	871	670	1.300
1936	138	115	18	235	367	34	4	3	2*	406	876	677	1.294
1937	154	111	31	234	406	41	2	4	2*	451	919	677	1.357
Career	1,383	1,198	205	2,376	3,852	437	26	42	21*	4,336	9,088	8,142	1.116

* CS totals estimated based on 2:1 success ratio

Jim Rice

Career P/E: 1.046; Postseason P/E: .913

MVP: American League MVP in 1978; 3.15 career shares

Hall of Fame: possible

In the midst of one of baseball's great pennant races, Jim Rice was at his best for the 1978 Red Sox. The left fielder eclipsed 400 total bases, generated 214 net runs of offense, and was selected as the AL's Most Valuable Player even though Boston failed to make the playoffs thanks to Bucky Dent's improbable home run over the Green Monster. That year was one of eight in which Rice topped 100 runs batted in and one of four years in which he reached 200 hits. I believe his career numbers are good enough to warrant induction into Cooperstown. He batted .298 lifetime and slugged just over .500. Rice finished his playing days with 382 home runs while playing during an era when 30–40 dingers in a season were near the top of the league leaders.

Jim Rice has been retired since the '89 season, and he has yet to earn the necessary votes to enter the hallowed halls of Cooperstown. He was never a favorite of many sportswriters, and that fact may permanently keep him out of the Hall. Statistically, Rice fell short of some offensive milestones. He was just shy of hitting .300 for his career and missed 400 home runs by 18, 2,500 hits by 48, and 1,500 runs batted in by 49.

I see Rice as Category 4. I think he did just enough to be in the Hall of Fame, but I'm not sure he'll ever get in. I also have him ranked in my top 10 for left field.

Year	RBI	R	HR	NR	TB	BB	HBP	SB	CS	CB	PTS	PA	P/E
1978	139	121	46	214	406	58	5	7	5	471	899	746	1.205
1979	130	117	39	208	369	57	4	9	4	435	851	688	1.237
1983	126	90	39	177	344	52	6	0	2	400	754	689	1.094
Career	1,451	1,249	382	2,318	4,129	670	64	58	34	4,839	9,475	9,058	1.046

Billy Williams

Career P/E: 1.012; Postseason P/E: .125
MVP: never won; 1.61 career shares
Hall of Fame: inducted in 1987

The Cubs must have known they had something special in the early '60s with Billy Williams. He won the National League Rookie of the Year in 1961 after belting 25 home runs and driving in 86 runs. He was an All-Star in three of the next four seasons. Williams went on to hit 426 home runs and surpass 1,400 runs both scored and driven in for his career. He was inducted into the Hall of Fame in 1987. Twice, Williams finished second in the MVP vote. In 1970 he reached 200 hits in a season for the third time, batting .322 and generating 224 net runs. He was runner-up to Johnny Bench. In 1972 Billy again played second fiddle to the Cincinnati catcher despite batting .333 and slugging .606 with 122 runs batted in. While he failed to win the MVP, he was named Major League Player of the Year for that season.

Williams played for the Cubs for 16 seasons but was never able to get them into the playoffs. The only time he reached the postseason was when he joined the Oakland Athletics in 1975. Against Boston in the ALCS, Williams went 0 for 7 with only one walk throughout the three-game sweep by the Red Sox.

Williams, C4, had two outstanding seasons surrounded by some very good ones. He was steady, consistent, and reliable, and he could play for my team any time.

Year	RBI	R	HR	NR	TB	BB	HBP	SB	CS	CB	PTS	PA	P/E
1965	108	115	34	189	356	65	3	10	1	433	811	719	1.128
1970	129	137	42	224	373	72	2	7	1	453	901	714	1.262
1972	122	95	37	180	348	62	6	3	1	418	778	650	1.197
Career	1,475	1,410	426	2,459	4,599	1,045	43	90	49	5,728	10,646	10,519	1.012

Category 5 Left Fielders

Barry Bonds

Height: 6′1″; Weight: 228; Bats: left; Throws: left

First game: May 30, 1986; Final game: still active

Team(s): Pittsburgh Pirates (1986–1992); San Francisco Giants (1993–2007)

MVP: National League MVP in 1990, 1992, 1993, 2001, 2002, 2003, 2004; 9.30 career shares (through '06 voting)

Hall of Fame: imminent

162-game avg.: .298 batting, .444 on-base, .607 slugging, 41 home runs, 324 total bases, 121 runs scored, 108 runs batted in, 159 hits, 78 extra-base hits, 139 BB, 83 K, 28 SB

Career P/E: 1.264; Postseason P/E: 1.120

The Good. Barry Bonds has now passed Hank Aaron to become the career home-run leader. No player comes close to matching his record of seven MVPs. He has walked more than any player in history, has scored more than 2,200 runs, and has been awarded the Gold Glove eight times. Only Ted Williams has a higher lifetime P/E Average for left fielders.

In 2001 Bonds was at his absolute best. He set the single-season record by smacking 73 home runs, a feat that might never be duplicated. He slugged .863 that year, the highest such percentage in the history of baseball. In fact, three of the five best seasons in terms of slugging percentage were accomplished by Barry Bonds. He also slugged .799 in '02 and .812 in '04.

Barry has won the National League MVP award seven times and finished second on two other occasions. Every time he has won, he has garnered at least 90 percent of the available votes. In other words, no one was close to winning the award in those seven years, and that remarkable achievement has helped account for his record of 9.30 career MVP shares.

From 2001 to 2004 Bonds had tremendous efficiency averages. He batted between .328 and .370, reached safely well over 50 percent of the time each season, and never slugged lower than .749. His P/E Averages over that stretch ranged from 1.398 to 1.495, and he was named the best player in the National League each season.

The Bad. Perhaps no player's career has been tainted by steroid allegations more than Bonds's. Before 2001 he was a tremendous player destined for the Hall of Fame. Since then, he has become an immortal and vaulted himself into the same class as Ruth, Williams, and the other truly elite players in history. However, it is widely speculated that Bonds has risen to that level because of performance-enhancing supplements.

Outside of San Francisco, he is booed and jeered every time he steps to the plate, and opposing fans love to see him fail. Prior to 2005, failure was something Bonds rarely experienced. Since then, however, he has begun to break down, possibly the result of years of steroid abuse and the stress that accompanies the nonstop allegations, questions, and doubt.

The Verdict. Bonds is one of the great players in history, but the steroid controversy hovers over his head and will probably forever mar his legacy. His statistics and accomplishments are without peer. I see him as one of the three best left fielders in history and an easy choice for C5.

Rickey Henderson

Height: 5'10"; Weight: 195; Bats: right; Throws: left

First game: June 24, 1979; Final game: September 19, 2003

Team(s): Oakland Athletics (1979–1984, 1989–1993, 1994–1995, 1998); New York Yankees (1985–1989); Toronto Blue Jays (1993); San Diego Padres (1996–1997, 2001); Anaheim Angels (1997); New York Mets (1999–2000); Seattle Mariners (2000); Boston Red Sox (2002); Los Angeles Dodgers (2003)

MVP: American League MVP in 1990; 2.46 career shares

Hall of Fame: imminent

162-game avg.: .279 batting, .401 on-base, .419 slugging, 16 home runs, 241 total bases, 121 runs scored, 59 runs batted in, 161 hits, 46 extra-base hits, 115 BB, 89 K, 74 SB

Career P/E: 1.062; Postseason P/E: 1.099

The Good. No one in the history of major league baseball has stolen more bases or scored more runs than Rickey Henderson. The prototypical leadoff man, Henderson had a great knack for getting on, getting over, and getting in. In 1982 Rickey set the all-time single-season mark for stolen bases when he swiped 130 bags. It marked the third time in four seasons that he walked more than 100 times and stole at least 100 bases. His career mark of 1,406 thefts is almost 500 more than Lou Brock's total and is likely to remain the record for quite a long time.

Henderson reached base better than 40 percent of the time for his career by using a great eye at the plate with a low, crouched stance that made it difficult for pitchers to locate strikes. He hit .300 or better seven times, including his .325 average in 1990, the year he was selected as the American League's Most Valuable Player. In just 136 games that season, the speedster scored 119 runs and had an on-base percentage of .439, which was the highest of his career. Rickey stole 65 bags and knocked 28 over the fence, displaying good power and an ability to jump-start his team with first-inning leadoff homers, something he did more often than anyone in history.

In the postseason, this future Hall of Famer has often been at his best. His P/E Average in the playoffs, 1.099, is higher than his regular-season average. He was named ALCS MVP in 1989 against Toronto. In typical Henderson fashion, he walked seven times, stole eight bases, and scored eight runs. He smacked two home runs, didn't strike out, and wasn't caught stealing. His P/E for that series was a remarkable 2.304.

The Bad. Henderson was not the same player over the last few years of his career. From 2000 through 2003, his batting averages were .233 or lower each year. He also failed to reach base as often as he did throughout the earlier stages of his career. Henderson played 25 major league seasons, and he probably would have stayed around even longer. He bounced around the minors trying to earn another shot, but that opportunity never happened again after '03.

The Verdict. Rickey should get into Cooperstown on the first ballot without question. He was a great run producer who was truly unique. He walked 2,190 times, stole 1,406 bases, and scored 2,295 runs. A manager can't ask for anything more from a leadoff hitter. He's Category 5 and top five.

Stan Musial

Height: 6′0″; Weight: 175; Bats: left; Throws: left

First game: September 17, 1941; Final game: September 29, 1963

Team(s): St. Louis Cardinals (1941–1944, 1946–1963)

MVP: National League MVP in 1943, 1946, 1948; 6.96 career
   shares

Hall of Fame: inducted in 1969

162-game avg.: .331 batting, .417 on-base, .559 slugging, 25 home
   runs, 328 total bases, 104 runs scored, 104 runs batted in, 194
   hits, 73 extra-base hits, 86 BB, 37 K, 4 SB

Career P/E: 1.151; Postseason P/E: .788

The Good. Along with Willie Mays and Hank Aaron, Stan Musial is one of only three players in major league history with more than 6,000 total bases. Stan the Man led the National League in so many different categories over his career that it's virtually impossible to list them all here. Seven times he led the league in extra-base hits and six times he led in total bases. Until Barry Bonds came along, Musial held the all-time record in terms of career MVP shares with 6.96. He collected 3,630 hits and retired with 1,951 runs batted in and 1,949 runs scored.

Stan won his first MVP in 1943 after leading the league with 220 hits and a .357 average. Three years later, Musial again topped the NL in those two categories and again walked away as the MVP. He was named Major League Player of the Year in '46 as well. He wasn't finished, though. The best season of his career was still to come. In 1948 he put together a season for the ages. Musial led the league in virtually every offensive category: batting average, on-base percentage, slugging percentage, hits, extra-base hits, total bases, runs scored, runs batted in, doubles, and triples. It was indicative of how special of a player he was.

Musial dominated the National League in the 1940s. His Cardinals won four pennants and three World Series from '42 to '46. He won three MVPs in the decade and routinely led the league in a variety of offensive categories. He never wore another uniform, establishing himself as probably the greatest Cardinals player in history and one of the best players to ever take the field.

The Bad. There is certainly not much negative associated with Musial's career. He never hit 40 homers in a season, although he was steady enough to amass 475 by the end of his playing days. He was never a great base stealer, and I estimated through known seasons that he was caught more often than he was successful. Furthermore, he batted just .256 in his World Series career, but his St. Louis squads were able to overcome his lack of efficiency and prevail three out of four times anyway.

The Verdict. Not only did Stan the Man win three MVPs, but he also was runner-up every year from 1949 through 1951 and again in 1957. Had the voting gone a little bit differently, Musial might have won a couple more times. Without question, he is an immortal, Category 5 player. He made 20 All-Star teams and splashed his name all over the record book year after year. He routinely smashed extra-base hits and was a perfect fit in the middle of a lineup. Amazingly, he only struck out more than 40 times twice, in the last two seasons he played. In my opinion, Stan Musial is one of the three greatest left fielders in baseball history.

Al Simmons

Height: 5′11″; Weight: 190; Bats: right; Throws: right

First game: April 15, 1924; Final game: July 1, 1944

Team(s): Philadelphia Athletics (1924–1932, 1940–1941, 1944);
Chicago White Sox (1933–1935); Detroit Tigers (1936);
Washington Senators (1937–1938); Boston Braves (1939);
Cincinnati Reds (1939); Boston Red Sox (1943)

MVP: never won; 2.43 career shares

Hall of Fame: inducted in 1953

162-game avg.: .334 batting, .380 on-base, .535 slugging, 22 home
runs, 343 total bases, 110 runs scored, 134 runs batted in, 214
hits, 72 extra-base hits, 45 BB, 54 K, 6 SB

Career P/E: 1.199; Postseason P/E: 1.325

The Good. Only two men in baseball history have ever achieved a
1.600 P/E Average for an entire season. One of them is Babe Ruth, and
the other is Al Simmons. Simmons played only 138 games in 1930 but
put up one of the great years in the history of the sport. Bucketfoot
Al batted .381, slugged .708, and had 211 hits. Most impressive was
his level of production. He scored 152 runs, drove in 165, and hit 36
homers for a total of 281 net runs, which works out to an average of
2.04 net runs per game, an amazing total. His P/E that season was
1.638.

Unlike some of the other big stars of his day who had tremendous
individual seasons, Al was able to maintain his level of success beyond
a handful of years. He knocked in more than 100 runs in 12 of his first
13 seasons, going over 150 three times from '29 to '32 when his
Philadelphia Athletics were at their best. Simmons had four seasons

in which he hit better than .380, and he led the AL in batting in consecutive seasons in '30 and '31.

Al Simmons appeared in the World Series four times, and he batted .300 or better in three of them. From '29 to '31, the Athletics won the pennant every year, and Al hit two home runs in each World Series. Philadelphia won the first two, establishing themselves as a legendary squad.

The Bad. There is not much wrong with Simmons's offensive numbers. He paired with Jimmie Foxx to form one of the most feared combinations in the sport's history. Critics can find fault with his meager total of 88 career stolen bases or his .380 lifetime on-base percentage, a very good mark but not quite on the same level as the game's other immortal players. Simmons didn't walk very much. He was a slugger, and he came to bat to swing, not to let pitchers off the hook by innocently strolling 90 feet down to first base when there were extra-base hits to be had.

In the latter part of his career, Simmons was tamer at the plate. The '36 season was the last time he reached 100 runs batted in, and he played only 90 games from '40 to '44. Al Simmons just missed joining the 3,000-hit club, failing to reach that milestone by 73 knocks.

The Verdict. Simmons's statistics are amazing. At 1.37 net runs per game, he remains one of the game's best run producers. He topped 1.400 P/E in four of five years in the late '20s and early '30s and had one of the truly great seasons ever in 1930. He cracks my top five for this corner outfield spot, and I will assign him a rating of Category 5 without any hesitation.

Ted Williams

Height: 6'3"; Weight: 205; Bats: left; Throws: right

First game: April 20, 1939; Final game: September 28, 1960

Team(s): Boston Red Sox (1939–1942, 1946–1960)

MVP: American League MVP in 1946, 1949; 6.43 career shares

Hall of Fame: inducted in 1966

162-game avg.: .344 batting, .482 on-base, .634 slugging, 37 home
    runs, 345 total bases, 127 runs scored, 130 runs batted in, 188
    hits, 79 extra-base hits, 143 BB, 50 K, 2 SB

Career P/E: 1.346; Postseason P/E: .533

The Good. Many people believe Ted Williams to be the greatest hitter
in the history of baseball, and it is not hard to understand why after
perusing his statistics. He combined great power and an uncanny eye
at the plate with a tremendous understanding of hitting. His .482 lifetime on-base percentage is the highest mark in history, and his 1.346
P/E score trails only Ruth and Gehrig. He won the MVP twice, the
Triple Crown twice, and the Major League Player of the Year five
times. He finished as runner-up in MVP balloting four times and
owns 6.43 career shares, the third highest total in history. He did all
of this despite missing three entire seasons and the majority of two
others defending his country in battle.

In 1941 Williams put together one of the great individual seasons
in the sport's history. He batted .406 for the season, the last man to
achieve that feat. When he had the option to sit out Boston's final two
games on the last day of the season to preserve a .400 average,
Williams balked at the chance. Instead, he went 6 for 8 and raised his

average to that legendary score. He walked 147 times that year and had more homers, 37, than strikeouts, 27.

To truly appreciate Williams's accomplishments, you must study his numbers, especially those posted from '39 through '49 when he was at his absolute best. Teddy Ballgame was a perfect blend of production and efficiency. He batted .353 in the eight seasons he played over that stretch and averaged 232 net runs per year. The Boston legend has the highest batting average (.344) of any player with 500 or more career home runs. He homered in his last at-bat.

The Bad. Offensively, Williams was a complete hitter. You cannot find fault with his work at the plate. Defensively, he wasn't great. He also wasn't fast, stealing only 24 bases. But that doesn't matter at all. His offensive prowess far overshadowed any deficiencies he had in the field or on the bases. The one glaring weakness from his illustrious career came in the postseason. Williams never won a World Series, and he was terrible on the game's biggest stage in his only appearance. Against St. Louis in the '46 Classic, he hit just .200, managing only five singles, five walks, two runs scored, and one run driven home over seven games.

The Verdict. The Splendid Splinter may have been the game's greatest hitter. Had he not missed time in the war effort, especially from 1943 to 1945, his statistics would be even more mind-boggling. He easily rates as Category 5 and ranks as one of the three greatest left fielders ever. Some experts have even supported his case as the greatest player in history regardless of position.

Carl Yastrzemski

Height: 5'11"; Weight: 182; Bats: left; Throws: right

First game: April 11, 1961; Final game: October 2, 1983

Team(s): Boston Red Sox (1961–1983)

MVP: American League MVP in 1967; 2.23 career shares

Hall of Fame: inducted in 1989

162-game avg.: .285 batting, .379 on-base, .462 slugging, 22 home
     runs, 271 total bases, 89 runs scored, 90 runs batted in, 167 hits,
     57 extra-base hits, 90 BB, 68 K, 8 SB

Career P/E: .993; Postseason P/E: 1.240

The Good. The city of Boston and Red Sox Nation fell in love with
Yaz in 1967, and they had every reason in the world to validate their
affection. Winning the MVP, Player of the Year, and the AL Triple
Crown, Yastrzemski led the Red Sox to the pennant and into the World
Series against the Cardinals. In the Fall Classic, the left fielder batted
.400 and slugged .840, doing everything possible to win the title. His
efforts were in vain, however, as Bob Gibson and St. Louis prevailed
in a decisive Game 7. Yaz, who also won the Gold Glove in that magical season, paced the league with a .326 average, 44 round-trippers,
and 121 runs driven home. His P/E mark in the regular season was
1.228. In the World Series, it was 1.310.

   The beloved outfielder also topped 1.200 P/E three years later. In
1970 Carl set career highs in batting average, .329, and on-base percentage, .452, a mark that was tops in the American League. He finished fourth in the MVP ballot, adding .40 shares to his career total,
which amounted to 2.23. Boston failed to make the postseason that
year, but Yaz returned to the October stage in '75. Again, he was tre-

mendous. After batting .455 in the ALCS, Yaz generated 11 net runs and hit .310 against the Reds in a dramatic seven-game World Series. Fisk's homer in Game 6 was Boston's final highlight as Cincinnati won Game 7 by a score of 4–3.

Throughout his career, which was spent entirely in Boston, Yaz was an 18-time All-Star and the winner of seven Gold Gloves. He was MVP of the '70 Midsummer Classic between the rival leagues and topped 1,800 runs both scored and driven in over his 23 seasons.

The Bad. Yastrzemski compiled great overall numbers, but he had some years in which he wasn't great. In 1968, for example, Carl generated only 141 net runs. He also had similar years in the early '70s. At the end of his career, he batted less than .280 in eight of his last nine seasons.

This player exemplifies the value of P/E Average in determining a player's overall worth. Yaz's career score, .993, is good, but it trails behind those of George Foster, Minnie Minoso, and Tim Raines. Just looking at his career numbers may give the indication that he was a dominant player, but I think that was only the case for a few years. His P/E numbers support my opinion.

The Verdict. Yaz retired with more than 3,400 hits, which is a remarkable accomplishment. He was great in the playoffs, and he will always remain a Fenway legend. He's Category 5 in my book, just making it to the top level based on Gold Gloves, postseason excellence, overall numbers, and his '67 masterpiece.

Left Field: The Top 10

The first outfield position is loaded with heavy hitters and MVPs. Perhaps more than any other position, left field places a premium on offense over defense. This outfield spot is so full of talent that players such as Billy Williams, Goose Goslin, and Lou Brock don't make it onto the list that follows. My top 10 left fielders look like this.

10. Joe Medwick

Medwick beats out Lou Brock for spot number 10 because he generated 33 percent more net runs per game, and that is a tremendous advantage in his favor. He also won an MVP, something Brock didn't, and made four more All-Star appearances. Brock was tremendous in the World Series, but Ducky was also exceptional in the '34 Classic despite being removed from the seventh game by Commissioner Kenesaw Mountain Landis after sliding in hard to third, which prompted Detroit fans to throw garbage at him. In terms of P/E Averages, Medwick betters his fellow Cardinals left fielder by nearly 200 points, enough to sway the decision slightly in his favor.

9. Albert Belle

Albert Belle bumps out Ducky for number 9 on the strength of his power numbers. He slugged .564 to Medwick's .505, a figure that Belle routinely eclipsed. Medwick's highest percentage (.641) was bettered by Albert three times. Furthermore, Belle averaged 23 more homers and 13 more extra-base hits per 162 games. Medwick hit for higher averages, but he comes up short trying to outmuscle Albert Belle in this analysis.

8. Ralph Kiner

The comparison between Kiner and Belle is interesting because both men had tremendous power but didn't play very long. Neither won an MVP, and they are very close in terms of P/E Average, net runs per game, and slugging percentage. Kiner was much better at reaching base, but Belle had postseason success to help strengthen his claim. I finally chose Kiner over Belle because of one important fact: Ralph led the National League in home runs for seven straight seasons. Kiner edges out Belle because he was more dominant in relation to his peers.

7. Jim Rice

I'll take the lifelong Boston left fielder here because he won an MVP and helped get the Red Sox into the playoffs twice and into the Series once. Kiner didn't do any of that. Kiner had better power, and that's significant. He was also better at reaching base, but Rice's slight edge in net run production combines with his MVP résumé (3.15 career shares in balloting) to earn the nod over the Pirates slugger.

6. Carl Yastrzemski

Yaz and Rice comprise two-thirds of the Green Monster Trio and rank back-to-back on this list. Like Rice, Yaz won an MVP and helped lead the Sox into the postseason. When he got there, however, he was tremendous, while Rice was average. Yaz dominated in the '67 Series (P/E Average of 1.310) even though Boston came up short yet again. Yaz also won seven Gold Gloves, and Rice never earned that defensive honor. Add in 10 more All-Star selections and a Triple Crown and Yaz is the choice.

5. Al Simmons

Simmons is a legitimate Category 5 player. He put up huge statistics year in and year out. Yaz was dominant in '67 and had several other very good years; he never approached Simmons's numbers beyond his MVP campaign, however. Al Simmons has more than a 200-point advantage in terms of career P/E Average, and that is simply too much for the Boston star to overcome. Both men were great in the postseason, and they both earned nearly the same number of career MVP shares.

4. Rickey Henderson

The fact that a player of Henderson's stature only ranks fourth speaks volumes about the talent at the left field position. Al Simmons had better power numbers and P/E Averages than Rickey, but he wasn't the type of player who stood out among his peers the way Henderson did. No one was better at getting on base and generating runs for his team than Henderson. He was the consummate leadoff man, and he perfected his art over a quarter of a century. Rickey also won an MVP, something that Simmons didn't. Henderson prevails here because he was so unique. There will never be another Rickey.

The Top Three

Barry Bonds, Stan Musial, and Ted Williams make up my top three and are as talented as any final grouping at any position on the field; they combined to win 12 Most Valuable Player awards. In terms of career MVP shares, they rank one, two, and three all-time, totaling 22.69 shares between them. They each hit from the left side of the plate and had legendary careers. Only Musial, however, ever won a World Series ring.

The Case for Bonds

Seven-time MVP with 9.30 career shares

Eight Gold Gloves and 12 Silver Sluggers

762 career home runs including 73 in 2001

High 2001–2004 efficiency averages

More than 500 stolen bases; three seasons with 40 or more steals

The Case for Musial

Three MVPs and three World Series championships

3,630 career hits; six seasons with 200 or more hits

20 All-Star selections

Seven National League batting titles

Seven seasons leading the league in extra-base hits

The Case for Williams

Career averages: 1.346 P/E, .344 batting, .482 on-base, .634
   slugging

Missed three full seasons and parts of two others in his prime

Two-time AL MVP; five-time Major League Player of the Year; two
   Triple Crowns

1.36 net runs per game; nine years with more than 200 net runs

Highest on-base percentage of any player in history

3. Stan Musial

Unfortunately for Stan the Man, he was up against two players who each make strong claims as the greatest player in history. Musial was extraordinary, but he comes up short when compared with Bonds and Williams. However, he betters Henderson for this spot for a couple of reasons. First, he won three MVPs to Rickey's one, and his advantage in career shares (6.96 to 2.46) clearly marks him as the superior player. He also batted 52 points higher, made twice as many All-Star appearances, and had P/E Averages higher than Rickey's lifetime number for the first 16 years of his career. The Cardinals legend was also a master batsman while Henderson was prone to the strikeout. Rickey was a special player, but he wasn't Stan Musial.

2. Barry Bonds

It was as close as a coin flip for the top spot. Bonds could easily be ranked as the greatest left fielder ever, but he only comes in at number 2 on my list. In comparison with Musial, on the other hand, Bonds wins fairly easily. He hit with more power, was better defensively, and was much better running the bases. He won as many MVPs as Musial even before winning four in a row from 2001 through 2004, vaulting himself to the top of the class of the all-time greats. At one time, Musial held the record with 6.96 career MVP shares. Bonds has since come along and shattered that mark, registering 9.30 shares over his major league tenure. Musial was far easier to root for, but Bonds is the better choice here.

1. Ted Williams

The last member of the Green Monster trio is the greatest of them all. Deciding between Bonds and Williams for the top spot was extremely difficult. Both players have statistics that are out of this world, and both of them repeatedly won individual honors and major awards. Bonds was much better in the field and on the bases. Williams may have been the greatest pure hitter the game has ever seen, he missed more than 500 games in the prime of his career, and he doesn't have a cloud of steroid speculation looming over him. Interestingly, Bonds also struggled in the postseason early in his career, but he later had the chance to redeem himself and prove his critics wrong when they said he wilted under the bright lights of October. Williams never had that opportunity for redemption. He also never had the chance to recoup the years lost to the war effort. Had he played uninterrupted in the mid-'40s and early '50s, his numbers would be even more staggering, perhaps the best ever.

Williams didn't win as many MVPs as Bonds, but he also played alongside much tougher competition. Berra, Mantle, and DiMaggio all won multiple MVP awards during Williams's playing days while players such as Terry Pendleton, Ken Caminiti, and Jeff Kent won the honor during Bonds's era. Twice, Williams won the Triple Crown but finished second in the MVP race. If he wasn't in the shadow of the Yankees stars, and if he hadn't missed major time at the peak of his career, Ted would have been more decorated.

I think choosing between the two is very tricky, and I can certainly understand why many people would select Bonds. In my opinion, though, Williams is the best left fielder of all time. His P/E Average is the third highest in history, and he was much more productive than Barry.

What Might Have Been

Many players, including Joe DiMaggio, Bob Feller, and Warren Spahn, missed portions of their major league careers while serving their country in times of war. But perhaps no player gave more of himself than Ted Williams. Williams missed three full seasons, 1943–1945, at the zenith of his career to serve in World War II. He also missed time during the Korean War in the early '50s. What would his career statistics have looked like had he not served? I thought about that while I was analyzing his numbers, so I decided to do some statistical maneuvering to estimate what might have been.

First, I calculated Williams's totals from the four years (1939–1942) prior to his first leave of absence and his totals from the four years (1946–1949) immediately following his return. I then averaged them by dividing by eight to get an estimate of what he might have produced on a yearly basis. Since he missed three full seasons, I multiplied the yearly averages by 3 and added them to his total. I performed a similar routine for his second hiatus from baseball, when he played only 43 combined games in '52 and '53. In total, I estimated that Ted missed about four and a half years of his career. By figuring out yearly averages and then giving him credit for his time missed from the sport, I arrived at the following career statistics:

664 home runs (would have ranked fourth all-time)

2,364 runs scored (would have ranked first all-time)

2,390 runs batted in (would have ranked first all-time)

2,640 bases on balls (would have ranked first all-time)

6,300 total bases (would have ranked second all-time)

3,433 hits (would have ranked sixth all-time)

684 doubles (would have ranked fifth all-time)

If Ted Williams did not have to leave baseball to serve in two different wars, it is quite possible that he would be considered the greatest player of all time. The estimated statistics above, especially in terms of run production and reaching base, are emblematic of a player who by many accounts fulfilled his desire to be known as the greatest hitter to ever live.

Center Field

Center field—the glamour position! Some of the game's biggest stars patrolled the area at this outfield spot. Names such as Mantle, Mays, DiMaggio, and Cobb are instantly recognizable, even by the most casual of baseball fans. Center fielders are the leaders in the outfield and are often extremely athletic and talented in all different aspects of the game. The position demands tremendous range, instincts, and strong throwing arms. At the plate, they are supposed to be heavy hitters.

Chapter 8 is probably more loaded with talent, especially at the top, than any other position. Tris Speaker, Mickey Mantle, and Ken Griffey Jr. have all had tremendous careers yet fail to make it into the top three. Cobb, DiMaggio, and Mays have a stranglehold on it, and they also rank very high in terms of the 100 greatest players ever.

Center field in Yankee Stadium has always been hallowed ground. From Earle Combs to Joe DiMaggio to Mickey Mantle, Hall of Famers seemed to continually patrol the outfield in the Bronx throughout the '20s, '30s, '40s, '50s, and '60s. These three great players, who all have a place in my top 10, never wore another uniform. Aside from the years devoted to World War II, their careers blended seamlessly with one another from 1924, Combs's first season, until 1968, Mantle's last.

Center fielders are often the most gifted players on a team in a position that calls for speed and offensive punch, as well as the mental fortitude to be seen as stars, highlighted as the centerpieces of their outfield trios. It's a select group that makes it into my top 10, and even a more select group that earns consideration for the number one overall position. In the end, that honor went to a man with an outstanding résumé, both in terms of statistics and championships.

Center Field: Career P/E Averages

Joe DiMaggio, 1.295; Hack Wilson, 1.209; Ty Cobb, 1.204; Earl Averill, 1.179; Mickey Mantle, 1.178; Willie Mays, 1.154; Ken Griffey Jr., 1.136; Duke Snider, 1.123; Carlos Beltran, 1.116; Jim Edmonds, 1.113; Tris Speaker, 1.107; Larry Doby, 1.094; Bernie Williams, 1.060; Earle Combs, 1.059; Andruw Jones, 1.052; Kirby Puckett, 1.011; Fred Lynn, 1.009; Kenny Lofton, 1.000; Dale Murphy, .992; Johnny Damon, .989; Dom DiMaggio, .978; Andy Van Slyke, .978; Bobby Murcer, .967; Edd Roush, .967; Amos Otis, .965; Vada Pinson, .926; Max Carey, .914; Marquis Grissom, .913; Willie McGee, .891; Garry Maddox, .879; Tommie Agee, .878; Brett Butler, .871; Richie Ashburn, .853; Mickey Rivers, .853; Lloyd Waner, .850; Doc Cramer, .841; Curt Flood, .832; Paul Blair, .806; Al Heist, .793

Category 1–3 Center Fielders

Tommie Agee

Career P/E: .878; Postseason P/E: 1.083
Notable seasons (P/E): 1966 (.990); 1969 (.978); 1970 (.987)

Mets fans will always have a place in their hearts for Tommie Agee, who helped secure the team's '69 championship with his outstanding play in Game 3. Agee made two unbelievable catches, saving a handful of runs, and led off the bottom of the first with a homer off Orioles starter Jim Palmer. The Mets won the Series 4–1, and that critical game served as the high point of Tommie's career. The '69 season was his best since '66, when he won the Rookie of the Year, made the first of two All-Star teams, and won the first of two Gold Gloves.

Agee had only three seasons ('66, '69, and '70) when his statistics were good. Although he made the All-Star team in 1967, he batted only .234 with 52 RBI and had less than 200 total bases. In 1968 Agee batted .217 with 30 runs and 17 RBI in his first season in New York. He hit .227 in 1972 in his last season with the Mets and just .222 combined for St. Louis and Houston in '73.

Tommie Agee was instrumental in New York's '69 championship run, and he has a Rookie of the Year award, two Gold Gloves, and two All-Star nominations to his credit. However, his statistics are mediocre, leaving him as Category 2.

Al Heist

Career P/E: .793; Postseason P/E: never in the postseason
Notable season (P/E): 1961 (.872)

After making a name for himself as a talented defensive center fielder in the Pacific Coast League, Al Heist broke into the majors with the Cubs in 1960. Although he had just over 100 at-bats, Heist set career highs in the three efficiency averages (.275 batting, .339 on-base, and .412 slugging) and made just one error in the field.

Alfred's career ended almost as soon as it began. He played in only 27 games in 1962, this time for Houston. That season would be his last. This little-known center fielder retired with 126 hits.

The point of including a C1 player like Heist is simply for comparative purposes. By looking at players of this lowest rating, we can better understand why other players are rated in certain ways. Category 1 players are those with mostly unknown names, paltry statistics, and short-lived tenures in professional baseball.

Fred Lynn

Career P/E: 1.009; Postseason P/E: 1.197
Notable seasons (P/E): 1975 (1.228); 1979 (1.322); 1982 (1.123)

In 1975 Fred Lynn became the first player in major league history to win the MVP and the Rookie of the Year in the same season. He hit .331 with 47 doubles, 103 runs scored, and 105 RBI. Lynn posted a tremendous P/E of 1.228 and also won the first of four Gold Gloves. The lefty had possibly his best season in 1979. A .333 batting average, combined with 199 net runs, earned him .41 shares and a fourth-place finish in the AL MVP race. Always good in October, Lynn batted .517 over two AL Championship Series.

It looked as if Fred Lynn might one day be mentioned with the game's greatest center fielders as the 1980s rolled around. Yet, his career never actualized to the point that some had predicted. From '80 to '90, Lynn never again reached 150 hits or 90 runs either scored or driven in, and he had batting averages below .275 all but three years.

Lynn's career got off to as good a start as possible, but he wasn't able to sustain that level after the 1970s, when he was at his best. Injuries always took their toll. His defense and clutch hitting in the playoffs combine with his early success to earn a rating of C3.

Garry Maddox

Career P/E: .879; Postseason P/E: .719
Notable seasons (P/E): 1976 (.988); 1977 (.978); 1978 (.853)

"Two-thirds of the Earth is covered by water. The rest is covered by Garry Maddox." This witty quote, which explains Maddox in a nutshell, was delivered by either Phillies broadcaster Harry Kalas or Hall of Famer Ralph Kiner. I have seen it attributed to both men in various sources. Those who watched Maddox play center field from the mid-'70s into the early '80s know how good he was defensively. Maddox won the Gold Glove every year from 1975 to 1982. Garry used his speed to run down balls in the gaps. His best season was 1976; he was fifth in the MVP race after batting .330 with 29 steals.

Maddox was never a great run producer, averaging just .81 net runs per game, a deficiency in production that helps explain a very modest .879 career P/E. His batting averages were usually solid, but he never scored more than 85 runs or drove home more than 76. The .29 shares he earned in '76 represent all but .02 of his total.

The offensive numbers and lack of MVP acclaim in every year but one suggests Category 2. However, Maddox was tremendous with the glove, and center field is an important position defensively. Therefore, the Secretary of Defense earns a rating of C3.

Mickey Rivers

Career P/E: .853; Postseason P/E: .677

Notable seasons (P/E): 1975 (.842); 1976 (1.003); 1977 (.926); 1980
(.915)

Mick the Quick starred in center field for the Angels, Yankees, and
Rangers throughout the '70s and into the mid-'80s. In 1976 the speedy
lefty hit .312, stole 43 bags, and scored 95 runs. Rivers usually performed at his best in ALCS play, where he went 3–0 and batted .386
for the Yankees from '76 to '78.

Rivers hit only 61 homers over 15 seasons. His career slugging percentage (.397) is low but not as disappointing as his .327 on-base
mark. Leadoff hitters, ideally, approach .400 in that critical category.
Rivers was never higher than .353 in any full year and reached base
less than a third of the time in many seasons. The problem is that
Mick never walked much. The 43 free passes he received in '75 repre-
sented his highest single-season total. In fact, he only had one other
season in which he walked at least 30 times.

Rivers is Category 2. He only scored 785 runs, and he drove in less
than 500. His impressive stolen-base totals were limited to only a few
years, and he never received much individual acclaim in terms of
MVP, All-Star, or Gold Glove nominations.

Hack Wilson

Career P/E: 1.209; Postseason P/E: .660

Notable seasons (P/E): 1927 (1.297); 1929 (1.412); 1930 (1.540)

There are several major league records that have stood for quite a
long time and may never be broken. One of them is Hack Wilson's
mark of 191 RBI in 1930. That year, Wilson put together one of the

best campaigns of all time, hitting .356, slugging .723, and accumulating 423 total bases. He also had 208 hits, including 56 homers, and he scored 146 times. His 1.540 P/E for that season stands as one of the highest scores in baseball history.

After 1930 Wilson's numbers went down dramatically. His Hall of Fame induction came in 1979, 45 years after his retirement. In other words, baseball writers didn't see Wilson as a Hall of Famer for nearly four decades.

I understand why Wilson, C3, is in the Hall. He put together two tremendous years back-to-back and had enough other very good ones to earn the necessary votes.

The Best Center Fielders

162-Game Averages

Player	BA	OBP	SLP	HR	TB	R	RBI	H	XBH	BB	K	SB
Averill	.318	.395	.534	23	329	119	113	196	74	75	50	7
Cobb	.366	.433	.512	6	312	120	103	224	61	67	29*	48
Combs	.325	.397	.462	6	296	132	70	208	57	75	31	11
DiMaggio	.325	.398	.579	34	368	130	143	207	82	74	34	3
Griffey	.290	.374	.553	40	333	105	116	174	75	79	109	13
Mantle	.298	.421	.557	36	304	113	102	163	64	117	115	10
Mays	.302	.384	.557	36	328	112	103	178	72	79	83	18
Puckett	.318	.360	.477	19	314	97	99	209	62	41	88	12
Snider	.295	.380	.540	31	292	95	101	160	64	73	94	7
Speaker	.345	.428	.500	7	296	109	89	204	66	80	16*	25

* Estimated total for strikeouts based on known seasons

Category 4 Center Fielders

Earl Averill

Career P/E: 1.179; Postseason P/E: .000

MVP: never won; 1.85 career shares

Hall of Fame: inducted in 1975

From 1929 through 1938 Averill put up tremendous numbers with the Cleveland Indians. As a rookie, Earl batted .332, scored 110 runs, and had 74 extra-base hits. He would hit better than .300 seven other times throughout his career, retiring with a terrific .318 average. He had two extraordinary seasons at the plate. In 1931, he surpassed 200 hits for the first time en route to a .333 batting average. He reached safely more than 40 percent and slugged .576, the second highest mark of his career. His other dominant season was '36. Earl set career highs in the three standard efficiency averages: .378 batting, .438 on-base, and .627 slugging. Again, his production was outstanding, producing 234 runs for Cleveland.

After '38 Averill's numbers fell off dramatically. He was dealt to Detroit in 1939, after the season had begun, and he batted just .262 for the Tigers. His lifetime production totals are solid but not spectacular, especially in comparison with some of the immortals at this position.

I see him as Category 4, and I have placed him in my top 10 for center field. It took until 1975 to induct Averill into Cooperstown. I'm not sure what took so long.

Year	RBI	R	HR	NR	TB	BB	HBP	SB	CS	CB	PTS	PA	P/E
1931	143	140	32	251	361	68	6	9	9	435	937	701	1.337
1934	113	128	31	210	340	99	4	5	3	445	865	702	1.232
1936	126	136	28	234	385	65	1	3	3	451	919	682	1.348
Career	1,164	1,224	238	2,150	3,390	774	33	70	57*	4,210	8,510	7,215	1.179

* CS totals estimated based on known statistics

Earle Combs

Career P/E: 1.059; Postseason P/E: 1.222

MVP: never won; .29 career shares

Hall of Fame: inducted in 1970

Earle Combs, the Kentucky Colonel, played his entire career with the New York Yankees and was at the heart of their World Series successes in the 1920s and 1930s. Combs played center field and hit leadoff, winning four pennants and three World Series in pinstripes. He reached base often, walked almost 400 more times than he struck out, and scored between 113 and 143 runs for eight consecutive seasons beginning in 1925. With Ruth, Gehrig, Meusel, and Lazzeri at the heart, the Yankees put together one of the game's great lineups, and Combs was the spark plug. For his career, Earle averaged 1.21 net runs per game, a score symbolic of a very productive player.

Certainly, Combs benefited greatly from two of the greatest run producers in history, Ruth and Gehrig, hitting behind him. His entire career was spent with at least one, if not both, of those Hall of Famers driving him home. If he had played for another team that lacked sluggers, then his career numbers would probably not be as good. The center fielder failed to reach 2,000 hits, falling shy by about a full season's worth.

Combs's career wasn't very long, but he was very successful in his limited time. For eight straight years, he was a perfect leadoff man at the top of a potent lineup. In my analysis, he deserves to be in Cooperstown. I see him as a Category 4 center fielder.

Year	RBI	R	HR	NR	TB	BB	HBP	SB	CS	CB	PTS	PA	P/E
1927	64	137	6	195	331	62	2	15	6	404	794	724	1.097
1930	82	129	7	204	278	74	0	16	10	358	766	617	1.241
1932	65	143	9	199	269	81	2	3	9	346	744	675	1.102
Career	632	1,186	58	1,760	2,657	670	17	96	71	3,369	6,889	6,507	1.059

Kirby Puckett

Career P/E: 1.011; Postseason P/E: 1.055
MVP: never won; 2.56 career shares
Hall of Fame: inducted in 2001

The best thing that can be said about a professional athlete, in my opinion, is that he played at his best when the games mattered most. Kirby Puckett was that kind of player. In the 1991 World Series, the Minnesota Twins faced elimination against Atlanta in Game 6. Puckett accounted for every single Twins run, going three for four with two runs scored and three batted in. In the third inning, he robbed Ron Gant of an extra-base hit as he leaped, crashed into the wall, and made a terrific catch. When he came to bat in the bottom of the eleventh, the score was tied, and the tension was palpable. No sooner did the inning begin than Puckett sent everyone home with a dramatic walk-off homer to force Game 7. Puckett won six Gold Gloves and six Silver Sluggers and made 10 straight All-Star teams.

There are people who don't think Puckett deserves to be in Cooperstown. He only topped 100 RBI three times, and he didn't have the power numbers of other Hall of Fame center fielders. Glaucoma caused Kirby to lose vision, which forced him into early retirement after he played 137 games in 1995.

Puckett was a tremendous talent whose career was unfortunately cut short. I think he would have easily reached 3,000 hits had he not lost vision, and then there would be no question regarding his enshrinement. I rate him Category 4 and a top-10 center fielder.

Year	RBI	R	HR	NR	TB	BB	HBP	SB	CS	CB	PTS	PA	P/E
1988	121	109	24	206	358	23	2	6	7	382	794	691	1.149
1992	110	104	19	195	313	44	6	17	7	373	763	696	1.096
1994	112	79	20	171	237	28	7	6	3	275	617	482	1.280
Career	1,085	1,071	207	1,949	3,453	450	56	134	76	4,017	7,915	7,831	1.011

Duke Snider

Career P/E: 1.123; Postseason P/E: 1.114

MVP: never won; 1.97 career shares

Hall of Fame: inducted in 1980

The mid-'50s belonged to Duke Snider. He hit 40 or more home runs five consecutive seasons from '53 to '57, exceeding 200 net runs by a wide margin three times during that span. Yankees fans had Mantle and Giants fans had Mays, but Brooklyn was proud to call Duke Snider their own. With Snider in center, Brooklyn won five National League pennants between 1949 and 1956. The Silver Fox never won an MVP, but he did finish in the top 10 six times, and he was in the top four each year from 1953 to 1955. His consistency was apparent in the regular season and the World Series. Duke had four straight seasons in which he topped 100 runs scored and driven home in the same year, and he had four straight World Series with 7 to 10 hits and 7 to 9 net runs.

Once the 1960s rolled around, Duke was not the same player. He hit just 53 homers during his last five seasons and batted less than .250 three times in the first half of that decade. When the Dodgers left Brooklyn, his slide downhill had already begun.

Snider was a very good player, and during the mid-'50s he was exceptional. However, he is not on the same level as Mantle and Mays. I have him rated as Category 4, and I think he should have been inducted before 1980.

Year	RBI	R	HR	NR	TB	BB	HBP	SB	CS	CB	PTS	PA	P/E
1953	126	132	42	216	370	82	3	16	7	464	896	680	1.318
1954	130	120	40	210	378	84	4	6	6	466	886	679	1.305
1955	136	126	42	220	338	104	1	9	7	445	885	653	1.355
Career	1,333	1,259	407	2,185	3,865	971	21	99	76*	4,880	9,250	8,237	1.123

* CS totals estimated based on known statistics

Category 5 Center Fielders

Ty Cobb

Height: 6'1"; Weight: 175; Bats: left; Throws: right

First game: August 30, 1905; Final game: September 11, 1928

Team(s): Detroit Tigers (1905–1926); Philadelphia Athletics
   (1927–1928)

MVP: American League MVP in 1911; 1.43 career shares

Hall of Fame: inducted in 1936

162-game avg.: .366 batting, .433 on-base, .512 slugging, 6 home
   runs, 312 total bases, 120 runs scored, 103 runs batted in, 224
   hits, 61 extra-base hits, 67 BB, 29 K, 48 SB

Career P/E: 1.204; Postseason P/E: .845

The Good. When the Hall of Fame opened its doors for the first time in 1936, Ty Cobb was one of five immortal players inducted, and he received the most votes of them all. Cobb's status is legendary. He owns the highest career batting average, .366, of any player to ever step into the batter's box. Generally considered to be the best player of his time, Cobb dominated the dead-ball era. After hitting .240 as a rookie in 1905, Cobb went on to hit better than .315 in every other season of his 24-year career. He hit .350 or higher 16 times, a feat that is hard to comprehend and will likely never be duplicated. The Georgia Peach led the league in batting 11 times and never finished worse than second in that category from 1907 to 1919.

   Undoubtedly, Cobb's best year was 1911. In my opinion, it remains one of the great individual seasons ever. Ty hit .420 and slugged .621. Of his 248 hits, 79 went for extra bases, and he added to his value by swiping 83 bases. In terms of production, Cobb was tremendous. He scored 147 times and drove in 127 runs with only eight homers. His average net runs per game for that season was 1.82, a tremendous mark. Although he didn't know it at the time, Cobb joined elite company by becoming one of a select group of players to surpass 1.500 P/E in a single season. He was the unanimous selection to receive the first MVP awarded in the AL.

At his retirement, Ty Cobb was the most decorated player of all time. As his Hall of Fame plaque notes, Tyrus "created or equaled more major league records than any other player." In 1909 he won the American League's Triple Crown. He led the league in on-base percentage seven times and in slugging percentage eight times. His 1.204 lifetime P/E Average is the third best in this chapter.

The Bad. Cobb was a tough man to like. He had a vicious temper, and he placed winning and on-field success above all else. Perhaps more than any other player, Cobb played the villain well. In terms of his play, however, there is little with which to find fault. He slugged above .500 for his career, but he never hit more than a dozen home runs in any season. More important, Cobb never won a World Series. He had three chances from '07 to '09, but his Tigers squad failed each time. In two of those appearances, he batted a combined .217 with nine net runs in 12 games.

The Verdict. Despite his personality and his inability to win a championship, Cobb still ranks as one of the great baseball players in history. His statistics and achievements are legendary. There will probably never be another player like him. He's Category 5 with a place in this chapter's top three.

Joe DiMaggio

Height: 6'2"; Weight: 193; Bats: right; Throws: right
First game: May 3, 1936; Final game: September 30, 1951
Team(s): New York Yankees (1936–1942, 1946–1951)
MVP: American League MVP in 1939, 1941, 1947; 5.43 career
    shares
Hall of Fame: inducted in 1955
162-game avg.: .325 batting, .398 on-base, .579 slugging, 34 home
    runs, 368 total bases, 130 runs scored, 143 runs batted in, 207
    hits, 82 extra-base hits, 74 BB, 34 K, 3 SB
Career P/E: 1.295; Postseason P/E: .918

The Good. Throughout the summer of '41, baseball fans awoke each
morning and checked their newspapers to find out if DiMaggio did
it again. For 56 consecutive games, Joltin' Joe hit safely, captivating the
city of New York and the entire baseball world with his remarkable
accomplishment. DiMaggio went on to win the AL MVP that year,
beating out runner-up Ted Williams for the award as the Yankees won
yet another pennant and yet another World Series championship. The
MVP was DiMaggio's second, having already won one in 1939, and
he would finish his career with three MVPs, a Player of the Year, and
5.43 MVP shares.

Almost as soon as DiMaggio took his place in the Yankees outfield,
he was a star. In his rookie season, Joe D. batted .323 with 206 hits and
132 runs scored. The '36 Yankees won 102 regular-season games
before winning the title, establishing themselves as one of the great
teams of all time. They repeated the trick the next year, 102 wins and
a championship parade, as DiMaggio had arguably his best season.

The Yankee Clipper stroked 215 hits, 96 of which went for extra bases, to go along with 151 runs scored and 167 RBI. Baseball fans soon realized, if they hadn't already, that a very special player was in center field in the Bronx.

DiMaggio owns the highest career P/E Average of any center fielder in history, and he owns it by a wide margin. His 1.295 score is more than 140 points higher than that of Willie Mays, considered by many to be the greatest center fielder, if not the greatest player, in history. Like Williams and other stars from the '40s, DiMaggio missed considerable time due to World War II. If he had not left the game for three full seasons, then I think it is fair to assume that he could have approached 2,000 career RBI. He battled through injuries and pain later in his career, which also stunted his lifetime numbers. Nevertheless, DiMaggio achieved more in 13 seasons than almost any player in history. His statistics are fabulous, he won three MVPs, and his squads won 10 pennants and nine World Series championships. He also married Marilyn Monroe.

The Bad. Joe DiMaggio wasn't the friendliest or the most accommodating superstar that New York has ever seen. He was very careful in maintaining a certain image, and that probably rubbed many people the wrong way. On the field, he didn't hit 600 homers, steal 100 bases in a season, or hit .400. Other players had more flash or more power or better numbers, but they weren't Joe.

The Verdict. The Yankee Clipper is Category 5. A case on his behalf is presented later in this chapter in consideration of the best center fielder ever. To me, he was the pure embodiment of a winner.

Ken Griffey Jr.

Height: 6′3″; Weight: 205; Bats: left; Throws: left

First game: April 3, 1989; Final game: still active

Team(s): Seattle Mariners (1989–1999); Cincinnati Reds
(2000–present)

MVP: American League MVP in 1997; 3.20 career shares (through
'06 voting)

Hall of Fame: imminent

162-game avg.: .290 batting, .374 on-base, .553 slugging, 40 home
runs, 333 total bases, 105 runs scored, 116 runs batted in, 174
hits, 75 extra-base hits, 79 BB, 109 K, 13 SB

Career P/E: 1.136; Postseason P/E: 1.206

The Good. If you were given the opportunity to build the perfect baseball player, he might very well look exactly like Ken Griffey Jr. The son
of a major league father, Junior had great genes right from the beginning. He matured into a complete athlete, gifted with great speed,
range, and leaping ability. At the plate, he used his effortless swing to
hit for high averages with tremendous power. In short, there's almost
nothing Junior can't do on the diamond, which is why the Mariners
used the first pick of the '87 draft to select him. After batting .264 as
a rookie, Griffey responded by hitting .300 or better in seven of his
next eight seasons. In 1993 he found his power stroke. Junior blasted
45 homers that season and then added 40 more in 111 games in '94.
From 1996 to 2000, a five-year stretch, he hit 249 homers, including
56 in both '97 and '98.

Griffey has been an extremely well decorated player in terms of
individual awards throughout his major league tenure. From 1990 to
2000, he made every All-Star team, and he also made the squad in

2004 and 2007. He has already won seven Silver Sluggers. Griffey won the Gold Glove every year in the 1990s, 10 in a row. In '97 he was the unanimous Most Valuable Player as well as the Major League Player of the Year, and he has finished in the top five of the MVP ballot five times, earning a total of 3.20 career shares with years left to play.

The first time this superstar had the chance to appear in the post-season, he made the most of it. Against the Yankees, Junior smacked five home runs, scored nine runs, and slugged 1.043 in the '95 ALDS. His P/E Average for that series was 1.852, and he scored the winning run on Edgar Martinez's double to send New York home in a decisive and thrilling Game 5 victory for Seattle.

The Bad. After leaving the Mariners, the star center fielder hasn't enjoyed the same level of success. He played in only 206 games with the Reds from 2002 to 2004, as it looked as if his career might be over prematurely. Griffey's first season in Cincinnati, 2000, was good, but things haven't gone as well since. He failed to reach 100 runs either scored or driven in from 2001 to 2006, and he has only .01 MVP shares to his credit since joining the National League.

The Verdict. Perhaps Junior should have stayed in the Pacific North-west instead of following in his father's footsteps by joining the Cincinnati Reds. At one time, he looked like a sure bet to challenge the career home-run totals of Mays, Ruth, and even Henry Aaron. Although he has regained some of his power, he hasn't been able to come fully back to the player he was in Seattle. Nonetheless, he is a Category 5 center fielder and, in my opinion, one of the five best ever at the position.

Mickey Mantle

Height: 5'11"; Weight: 198; Bats: both; Throws: right

First game: April 17, 1951; Final game: September 28, 1968

Team(s): New York Yankees (1951–1968)

MVP: American League MVP in 1956, 1957, 1962; 5.79 career
   shares

Hall of Fame: inducted in 1974

162-game avg.: .298 batting, .421 on-base, .557 slugging, 36 home
   runs, 304 total bases, 113 runs scored, 102 runs batted in, 163
   hits, 64 extra-base hits, 117 BB, 115 K, 10 SB

Career P/E: 1.178; Postseason P/E: 1.073

The Good. The game of baseball may have never witnessed a more talented player than No. 7, Mickey Mantle. Mantle was blessed with one of the great combinations of speed and power in history. He could hit a ball 500 feet from either side of the plate just as easily as he could beat out a drag bunt, racing down the first-base line as fast as anyone in the game. In the mid-'50s, there was no bigger star and no better player than Mantle. In 1956 he won the AL Triple Crown, batting .353 with 52 round-trippers and 130 runs batted in, leading the Yanks to the World Series title. The Mick was the unanimous MVP that year, and he won his second trophy the following season after batting .365 and reaching base well over half the time thanks in part to a league-high 146 bases on balls. By the end of his playing days, Mickey had three MVPs, three second-place finishes, and 5.79 career shares, good for fifth place all-time.

Mantle virtually lived in the World Series. He appeared in the Fall Classic 12 times, winning seven of them. His name is plastered all over the record books. In terms of World Series play, Mantle is first in home runs (18), RBI (40), extra-base hits (26), walks (43), runs (42), and total bases (123). Twice, he had 10 hits in the Series, including the 1960 championship against the Pirates when Mantle registered a P/E score of 1.788 in a losing effort.

The Mick retired with outstanding career efficiency averages, especially in terms of on-base (.421) and slugging (.557). He joined the 500-home-run club in 1967 and ended up with 536 career dingers. He scored 1,677 runs, made 16 All-Star teams, and owns the fifth best P/E Average in this chapter. Fans idolized him, teammates loved him, and pitchers feared seeing him in the batter's box. Mickey Mantle was inducted into the Hall of Fame in 1974.

The Bad. Mantle had some bad luck with injuries, and he didn't take care of himself very well. In '51, as a rookie playing right field in the World Series, Mick stepped awkwardly onto a drainage ditch and hurt his knee. From '62 to '63, he played only 188 combined games as he again battled injuries and ailments with his legs, ankles, and feet. It was a well-known fact that Mantle also drank too much and stayed up too late too often. He lived life at a feverish pace, and it caught up with him in the end. Mantle died in 1995 at the age of 63.

The Verdict. Although he is a certain Category 5 player, Mantle could have been even better had he been able to avoid injuries and the bottle. He was as gifted as any player in history, yet the brilliance he flashed in the mid-'50s and early '60s wasn't sustained. Still, he ranks in this position's top five.

Willie Mays

Height: 5'11"; Weight: 180; Bats: right; Throws: right

First game: May 25, 1951; Final game: September 8, 1973

Team(s): New York/San Francisco Giants (1951–1952, 1954–1972);
   New York Mets (1972–1973)

MVP: National League MVP in 1954, 1965; 6.06 career shares

Hall of Fame: inducted in 1979

162-game avg.: .302 batting, .384 on-base, .557 slugging, 36 home
   runs, 328 total bases, 112 runs scored, 103 runs batted in, 178
   hits, 72 extra-base hits, 79 BB, 83 K, 18 SB

Career P/E: 1.154; Postseason P/E: .859

The Good. Many people consider Willie Mays to be the greatest center fielder of all time. When you look at his statistics and his accomplishments and consider his tremendous talent, it's not hard to understand why. He hit 660 home runs, made 20 consecutive All-Star squads from 1954 to 1973, and played the position with more skill and flair than anyone before or since. From '57 through '68 Mays won every Gold Glove that was awarded for center field. Willie combined remarkable range, hustle, instincts, and a terrific throwing arm to become one of the game's best defensive players in history. In the '54 Series against Cleveland, he made one of the most famous and improbable catches ever in deep center field at the Polo Grounds. Racing with his back to home plate, Mays robbed Vic Wertz (who already had three hits) with an over-the-shoulder basket catch. Then he whirled around and fired the ball back into the infield before anyone knew what had happened. The Giants won the game and swept the Indians, who had won 111 games.

The '54 season also witnessed Mays win his first of two MVP awards. After batting .345 with 41 homers and a .667 slugging percentage, Mays earned 84 percent of the available points while also being named Major League Player of the Year. He won the Rookie of the Year honor in '51 and was twice named MVP of the All-Star Game. In terms of MVP balloting, Willie finished in the top six a dozen times, helping account for 6.06 career shares, the fourth best total in history.

Willie Mays scored more than 2,000 runs, drove in more than 1,900, and surpassed 6,000 total bases. Hank Aaron is the only other player in history that can make that claim. Willie scored more than 100 runs for 12 straight seasons, and he reached 40 homers six times, including two years with more than 50.

The Bad. From 1967 to 1973 Mays failed to bat .300, hit 30 home runs, reach 150 hits, or score or drive in 100 runs in each season. When he finished his career with the Mets in '73, he wasn't nearly the same player. The other knock I can find with his résumé is that he won only one championship. Willie went 1-for-3 in four World Series attempts, and he batted just .239 with no home runs on the biggest stage. After winning Rookie of the Year, Mays hit and slugged .182 against the '51 Yankees in defeat. His postseason P/E is 295 points lower than his regular-season score.

The Verdict. Mays is an easy pick for Category 5. He ranks in my top three and deserves serious consideration as the best center fielder ever. There will never be another Say Hey Kid.

Tris Speaker

Height: 6'0"; Weight: 193; Bats: left; Throws: left

First game: September 14, 1907; Final game: August 30, 1928

Team(s): Boston Red Sox (1907–1915); Cleveland Indians
(1916–1926); Washington Senators (1927); Philadelphia Athletics
(1928)

MVP: American League MVP in 1912; 1.72 career shares

Hall of Fame: inducted in 1937

162-game avg.: .345 batting, .428 on-base, .500 slugging, 7 home
runs, 296 total bases, 109 runs scored, 89 runs batted in, 204 hits,
66 extra-base hits, 80 BB, 16 K, 25 SB

Career P/E: 1.107; Postseason P/E: .855

The Good. Tris Speaker is one of only five men in the history of major
league baseball to reach 3,500 hits. He also scored 1,882 runs, batted
.345 with a .428 on-base mark, and hit more doubles (792) than any
player ever. Speaker was an outstanding center fielder in the early part
of the twentieth century, playing the majority of his career with the
Red Sox and Indians. He hit .380 or better five times, winning the AL
batting crown with a .386 average in 1916, his first season in Cleveland. Speaker had great speed and was terrific at reaching base and
scoring runs. From 1910 through 1927, Tris had on-base percentages
that ranged from .395 to .483, and he scored more than 100 runs in a
season seven times during that stretch. He walked often and seldom
struck out. Speaker received as many as 97 free passes in a season, yet
available statistics show that he never struck out more than 25 times
in any year. He also stole 432 bags, making him a nightmare for
opposing pitchers to worry about, both at the plate and on the bases.

In 1912 Tris won the AL MVP in just the second year of the award's existence. He had 222 hits, including 53 doubles, and scored 136 runs in leading Boston to the pennant. Facing the New York Giants in the World Series, Speaker batted .300 with nine hits and four walks as he won the first of his three championships. The Grey Eagle would never lose a postseason series.

In terms of production and P/E scores, his best years came in Cleveland. Speaker generated 236 net runs in 1920, which helped account for his impressive 1.307 P/E. Three years later he was even better, contributing 246 runs to the Indians scoreboard while racking up the highest Production and Efficiency Average (1.354) of his Hall of Fame career. Cooperstown opened its doors to this outstanding player in 1937, the Hall's second year of existence.

The Bad. Speaker's lifetime P/E Average, 1.107, is very good but falls short of some of the other Hall of Fame center fielders. He hit more than 10 homers in a season only once. His .500 lifetime slugging percentage is due in large part to his ability to hit the ball into the gaps and down the lines, legging out doubles and triples as well as anyone in history. While he hit .306 and never lost in the World Series, his .855 postseason P/E score is more than 250 points lower than his regular-season number. Tris had only three RBI in 20 World Series contests.

The Verdict. The Red Sox had the opportunity to have Speaker and Babe Ruth in the same outfield. What a duo that would have been. Tris is Category 5 and one of the 10 best ever in center.

Center Field: The Top 10

Exactly 10 center fielders were mentioned in the previous two sections, making it clear as to who comprises the top 10. But what is the order? It wasn't easy to decide between such a talented group. In all, six center fielders earned Category 5 status. Three Yankees outfielders highlight the list that follows, while Snider and Mays do their part to give it even more of a New York feel. In my opinion, these are the 10 best center fielders in baseball history.

10. Earle Combs

The Kentucky Colonel begins my list. He deserves to be in the Hall of Fame, and he edges out the other contenders for this spot based on his run production and consistency with the Yankees from the mid-'20s through the mid-'30s. Combs was a perfect leadoff man, routinely topping a .400 on-base percentage and staying in the lineup enough to score 996 runs from 1925 through 1932, a stretch that witnessed the Bronx Bombers win four pennants and three World Series.

9. Kirby Puckett

Imagine what Puckett's numbers would have been if he had Ruth, Gehrig, Meusel, and Lazzeri hitting behind him. Puckett proved he could take over and win games single-handedly, and I'm not sure Combs had that same ability. I'm uncertain about Combs's defensive prowess, but I can't imagine he was Kirby's equal. Ironically, both men had their careers suddenly cut short by injuries that quickly forced retirement on them. I think Puckett probably had a little more pop in his bat and a better glove in the field, making him my choice for ninth by a close margin.

8. Earl Averill

Earl Averill's numbers are just too good not to place him ahead of Puckett. His 1.179 lifetime P/E score was bettered only once by the Minnesota star, in the strike-shortened 1994 campaign. Averill slugged much higher and averaged .20 net runs per game more than Kirby. Both men hit .318 for their careers, but Earl reached base at a much better clip and had three seasons that bettered Kirby's top RBI year. Puckett's postseason success is a big advantage in his favor, but I'm willing to give Averill the benefit of the doubt that he would have performed well on the big stage had he been given more opportunity.

7. Duke Snider

Two words explain why Snider comes in at number 7 over Averill: power and postseason. Duke hit 40 or more homers five times, something Earl can't come close to claiming. He also hit for high batting and slugging averages in the World Series. That, in itself, is enough for me.

6. Tris Speaker

I see Tris Speaker as a much better player than Duke Snider. First, he batted 50 points higher and had about 1,400 more hits. He won an MVP, had a higher net-runs-per-game average, and simply had more good seasons than Duke. In my opinion, Speaker has always been underappreciated, despite his tremendous statistics and accomplishments. I have found that many casual fans simply don't know the name Tris Speaker, and that's a shame.

5. Ken Griffey Jr.

Starting with Speaker at number 6, we're left with only Category 5 center fielders, and it's not easy to rank them against one another. Junior edges out Speaker in my mind because of power. He equals Tris as a fielder, matched his MVP with one of his own, and hit above .300 for his postseason career, just like Speaker. Speaker's top home-run season was 17, however, a number that Junior reached in just 72 games in '95. The Grey Eagle's 117 career dingers are only five more than Griffey hit over two seasons, '97–'98, in Seattle.

4. Mickey Mantle

Griffey toppled the immortal Speaker, but he can't eclipse Mantle. While they're both Category 5, Mantle was clearly the superior player. He won three MVPs and was runner-up three other times. The Mick owns so many World Series records that it's almost unbelievable. Interestingly, Mantle hit 536 home runs in 18 seasons. Through 2005, Junior hit exactly 536 home runs in 17 seasons. Their P/E Averages are similar (slight edge to Mickey), but the Yankees legend walked a lot more. Both players had injury issues, so that argument essentially cancels itself out.

The Top Three

I think if you gave a hundred people my top three and asked them to rank these superstars, you'd get every possible combination over and over without a clear consensus. Cobb, DiMaggio, and Mays are the three best ever in center. Even the great Mantle can't break into this top grouping. My top three is legendary. Each one enjoyed his status as the game's best player at one time or another, but only one can be the winner.

The Case for Cobb

.366 lifetime batting average and 11 league batting titles

892 stolen bases; 4,189 hits; 2,246 runs scored

Tremendous 1911 season (unanimous MVP and P/E Average of 1.512)

No MVP given in his 1909 Triple Crown season

On retirement, held or shared more major league records than any player

The Case for DiMaggio

10 pennants and nine World Series championships

Three MVPs despite missing three full seasons in his prime

1.295 P/E, .579 slugging, and 1.48 net runs per game career averages

361 career home runs with only 369 strikeouts

Made the All-Star team every year that he played

The Case for Mays

6.06 MVP shares

660 home runs and more than 6,000 total bases

20 consecutive All-Star nominations

12 straight Gold Gloves (1957–1968)

Rookie of the Year, Player of the Year, two-time MVP, and two-time All-Star MVP

3. Willie Mays

When they were both at their best, I think Mickey was probably a better player than Willie, but Mays clearly had the better career. He avoided injuries and was able to put up bigger numbers more consistently, and that's why he edges out Mantle for number 3. The similarities between the two stars are fascinating. They began their careers less than a mile apart in New York City within six weeks of each other. Their P/E Averages are less than 25 points apart, and both averaged 1.10 net runs per game. They batted within four points of one another while both slugging .557 for their careers. When looking at total bases, however, Mays emerges as the winner. The Mick topped 300 total bases in a season five times. Say Hey accomplished that feat for 13 straight years.

2. Ty Cobb

I admit, it wasn't easy choosing Cobb over Mays for number 2, but I think it was the correct decision nonetheless. Cobb's career was one of a kind, and I just think he was the better player, albeit slightly, than Mays. The fact that he received more Hall of Fame votes than Babe Ruth and Walter Johnson in 1936 says something to me that I can't ignore. At his retirement, Cobb was thought by many to be the game's greatest of all time, and I'm not sure the same case can be made for the Say Hey Kid. Coming in behind Ty Cobb is no injustice. Mays had the advantages in terms of defense and power, and that is hard to overlook. I just think Ty Cobb was that special and that dominating; he deserves to be placed ahead of the National League star by the slimmest of margins.

1. Joe DiMaggio

The greatest center fielder in history is Joe DiMaggio, and I feel quite confident stating that as my opinion. DiMaggio had the statistics, and, more important, he had the championships to back it up. He won 10 pennants and nine World Series titles. He also ranks number one in terms of P/E Average and net runs per game for this position. What else can you ask of your star center fielder? Like Jeter and a handful of select players over baseball's history, DiMaggio exuded a winning persona. His Yankees weren't just favored to win, they were destined to, with no doubt about it, and he made sure that it happened. True, he was surrounded by talented players. But that shouldn't take away from Joltin' Joe's greatness. As I said before, all he did was win. His 1937 season ranks as one of the greatest of all time, and you have to take into account the years he lost during WWII.

He was more productive than Cobb (1.48 net runs per game to 1.34), he was better defensively, and he won and won and won. His career statistics don't seem as impressive as they could have been because he served in the war effort, missing three full seasons, which may have thrown off his momentum and prevented him from compiling truly legendary numbers. You can't go wrong with either one playing center field and hitting in the middle of your lineup, but I'm taking DiMaggio if given the chance.

The Center of It All

In the mid-1950s, several major league cities witnessed great center-field play, but nowhere was the talent more concentrated than in New York. From 1954 through 1957, Mickey Mantle, Willie Mays, and Duke Snider all were superstars for their respective teams while playing within a stone's throw of one another. Those four years were the only ones in which each played a full season (at least 100 games) in NYC. Mantle played in less than 100 games in '51, the year he and Willie broke into the majors. Mays appeared in only 34 games in '52 and didn't play at all in '53. After '57, Duke went to L.A. with the Dodgers while the Giants departed for San Francisco. But they were all together, playing full-time, from '54 to '57. So which one was the best over that span? Let's take a look at each player's four-year average.

Per-Year Offensive Averages (1954–1957)

Player	BA	OBP	SLP	HR*	R*	RBI*	H*	TB*	P/E
Mantle	.330	.453	.625	38	126	106	171	323	1.310
Mays	.323	.397	.627	41	114	105	187	362	1.231
Snider	.305	.403	.616	41	112	115	166	335	1.241

* Rounded off to the nearest whole number

Production and Efficiency Averages indicate that Mantle was the best of the three as a result of much higher walk totals and more runs scored. Mick, who won the Triple Crown in '56, also batted the highest and was at least 50 points ahead of both Willie and Duke in terms of on-base percentage. The idea that Mantle was the best center fielder in New York over that time frame is also supported by each player's individual awards and team success.

Player	MVP: shares	POY	All-Star Appearances	Pennants	WS Titles
Mantle	2 MVP: 2.08	1	4	3	1
Mays*	1 MVP: 1.89	1	4	1	1
Snider	0 MVP: 1.25	1	3	2	1

* Mays also won the Gold Glove in 1957, the only one of the three to do so during the four-year span. The Gold Glove was first given in '57 as a combined award for both leagues.

Right Field

Power and production. Above everything else, that's what this position is about. The right-field position is dominated by heavy hitters and legendary run producers, including Ruth, Aaron, Ramirez, Sosa, Robinson, and Ott. Like those at first base and left field, right fielders need to wield powerful bats.

There are eight right fielders who have received Category 5 status, more than any other position. In addition, 12 other players are Category 4. I didn't go into this chapter with a predisposition toward anointing so many Hall of Famers; I simply couldn't help it. The position is loaded with power and production.

Tony Gwynn and Roberto Clemente, included in the top 10, are exceptions to the rule. What they lacked in home-run power and monster RBI numbers, they made up for with scintillating defense, multiple batting titles, and more than 6,000 combined hits between the two of them. Do they have enough to push ahead of the heavy hitters and into the top five? The answer to that question awaits you.

Henry Aaron, Frank Robinson, and Babe Ruth comprise the top three, and it should come as little surprise that I have chosen them for this elite group. They are legends, and their names are plastered all over baseball's record books. The trio combined to hit more than 2,000 home runs and generate more than 10,000 runs for their teams' scoreboards. No other top three comes close to matching those numbers.

As we wind down our analysis of the outfield, it becomes clear, to me at least, that right field has been dominated by sluggers, more so than any other position. It was very difficult to put together the top-10 list because so many players were worthy.

Right Field: Career P/E Averages

Babe Ruth, 1.436; Manny Ramirez, 1.234; Vladimir Guerrero, 1.174; Mel Ott, 1.171; Chuck Klein, 1.160; Juan Gonzalez, 1.155; Harry Heilmann, 1.144; Hank Aaron, 1.140; Frank Robinson, 1.126; Bobby Abreu, 1.123; Gary Sheffield, 1.120; Sammy Sosa, 1.100; Kiki Cuyler, 1.092; Darryl Strawberry, 1.081; Paul Waner, 1.050; Bobby Bonds, 1.048; Elmer Flick, 1.040; Enos Slaughter, 1.040; Ken Griffey Sr., 1.036; Reggie Jackson, 1.033; Sam Crawford, 1.028; Dave Winfield, 1.025; Al Kaline, 1.023; Paul O'Neill, 1.018; Wally Post, 1.016; Roger Maris, 1.015; Rocky Colavito, 1.013; Ross Youngs, 1.007; Andre Dawson, .998; Roberto Clemente, .994; Carl Furillo, .994; Dave Parker, .986; Tony Gwynn, .981; Tony Oliva, .979; Sam Rice, .977; Ichiro Suzuki, .953; Harry Hooper, .883; Cory Snyder, .854; Mike Vail, .807

Category 1–3 Right Fielders

Cory Snyder

Career P/E: .854; Postseason P/E: never in the postseason
Notable seasons (P/E): 1986 (.991); 1987 (.886); 1988 (.957)

Cory Snyder's career got off to a tremendous start with the Cleveland Indians in the mid- to late 1980s. Finishing fourth in the '86 AL Rookie of the Year vote, the young right-field prospect had Indian fans excited. He hit 83 home runs over his first three seasons, including 33 in 1987. That season also saw Cory set career highs in RBI (82), runs (74), and total bases (263).

Unfortunately for Cleveland, Snyder was never able to propel his game to the next level. After '88, he never again hit 20 homers in any season, and he never made an All-Star team, won a Gold Glove, or received any MVP support. Furthermore, Snyder had a penchant for striking out. He fanned almost 1,000 times in his career to just 226 walks.

Snyder is Category 2. At one time, he was a highly touted prospect with a bright future. As is normally the case with C2 players, however, he never reached his potential.

Vladimir Guerrero

Career P/E: 1.174; Postseason P/E: .672
Notable seasons (P/E): 1999 (1.212); 2000 (1.254); 2004 (1.265); 2005 (1.207)

There aren't many current stars in baseball bigger or better than Vladimir Guerrero. Having begun his career in '96 with the Expos, Vlad has since moved out to the West Coast, where he now patrols the outfield for the Angels. In 2004 he generated 211 net runs for his team's scoreboard, a fact that impressed the MVP voters; Guerrero won the prestigious award with a 100-point advantage over runner-up Gary Sheffield. Vlad has a tremendous throwing arm, and he's known for being able to hit balls all over, and sometimes out of, the strike zone.

Despite owning a cannon for a right arm, Vladimir has as many errors (119) as assists (119) for his career. With seven seasons of at least 10 errors, he has never been able to win a Gold Glove even though base runners know better than to test his arm when going from first to third or trying to score from second on a single to right. Guerrero also hasn't been able to carry his prowess at the plate into October on a consistent basis.

If he continues on his current pace, Guerrero will end up in Cooperstown. He already has 2.32 MVP shares and 1,177 RBI. Currently, I see him as a C3 outfielder. If he can stay healthy, however, he has a chance to have his name immortalized in the Hall of Fame once he hangs up his spikes for good.

Roger Maris

Career P/E: 1.015; Postseason P/E: .877
Notable seasons (P/E): 1960 (1.220); 1961 (1.279); 1962 (1.016)

There may have been a few numerologists who saw it coming, but for the rest of the world, Roger Maris's accomplishment of 61 homers in 1961 was a complete shock. Even after winning the American League MVP in 1960 (39 home runs and 112 RBI), Roger's '61 masterpiece left the country in awe. For his outstanding campaign, Maris won another MVP, topping a 1.200 P/E for the second time in as many seasons.

After '61 Maris never came close to reaching the same level of power and production. He did knock in 100 runs in 1962, but he never came close to that mark again. To this day, Roger Maris has failed to receive enough support to enter the Hall of Fame, and it's very possible that he will never make it in.

I think Maris had one very good year ('62), one great year ('60), and one magical year ('61). To me, he's Category 3 with a doubtful chance of enshrinement.

Wally Post

Career P/E: 1.016; Postseason P/E: 1.000
Notable seasons (P/E): 1955 (1.168); 1956 (1.027); 1959 (1.022)

Walter Charles Post was a tall, strong right fielder who played the majority of his career in Cincinnati. In 1955 he had his best season when he smacked 40 homers, drove in 109, and scored 116, leading to the highest P/E Average (1.168) of his career. The next season, the righty slugger hit 36 more out of the park. In the field, Wally possessed a powerful throwing arm; he had at least a dozen outfield assists every year from '54 to '59.

Post was terrific in 1955 but then failed to come close to those numbers again throughout his career. He retired with fewer than 700 RBI, fewer than 600 runs, and a batting average of .266; he fanned more than 800 times while only drawing 331 bases on balls—not a good ratio. In MVP balloting, Post was almost nonexistent.

Wally Post is a good example of a Category 2 player. He played for a long time (15 seasons) but never put up great numbers, other than '55. Even when he hit 36 homers in 1956, he hit just .249 and drove in only 83 runs. His lifetime statistics are quite ordinary.

Darryl Strawberry

Career P/E: 1.081; Postseason P/E: 1.028

Notable seasons (P/E): 1983 (1.059); 1986 (1.101); 1987 (1.225);
1988 (1.133)

The New York Mets used the first pick of the 1980 draft to select Darryl Strawberry, a tall outfield prospect with a powerful bat and all the tools a player could ask for. Darryl first appeared in the majors in '83 and proceeded to hit more than 25 homers every season through 1991. He was selected Rookie of the Year with the Mets and went on to make eight consecutive All-Star teams beginning in 1984. Straw had probably his best season in '87. He hit .284, walked 97 times, and had 151 hits, 76 of which went for extra bases.

The negatives with Darryl Strawberry were usually off the field, where he has struggled with spousal abuse issues, alcohol, and narcotics. He has been arrested and in and out of rehab several times. Considering his immense talent, Strawberry's career could definitely be viewed as a disappointment. Once seen as a can't-miss prospect, he never hit 40 home runs, and he had only a few really big years in terms of production.

Strawberry deserves a Category 3 nomination, but he is nowhere near a Hall of Famer. In his first year of eligibility, he failed to receive the minimum 5 percent of votes from the baseball writers, meaning that only the Veteran's Committee can induct him once 20 years have passed following his retirement. That probably won't happen, however.

Mike Vail

Career P/E: .807; Postseason P/E: never in the postseason
Notable seasons (P/E): 1975 (.813); 1977 (.782); 1980 (.872)

The New York Mets must have thought they had something special in Mike Vail in 1975. The rookie outfielder was named International League Player of the Year before joining the major league Mets. He then put together a 23-game hitting streak throughout the summer, captivating Mets fans and making them believe he was the real thing.

Vail's career never took hold after his rookie year in '75. After three seasons in New York, he bounced around six other teams between 1978 and 1984, playing mostly as a pinch hitter and fourth outfielder. He sports unsightly lifetime ratios of 81 walks to 317 strikeouts and 3 stolen bases to 17 times caught stealing.

Sorry, Mike, but it's the dreaded Category 1 label for you. Maybe a few breaks here or there would have steered his career in a different direction. Unfortunately for Vail, the hot start he enjoyed in '75 ended up being the highlight of a 10-year career.

The Best Right Fielders

162-Game Averages

Player	BA	OBP	SLP	HR	TB	R	RBI	H	XBH	BB	K	SB
Aaron	.305	.374	.555	37	337	107	113	185	73	69	68	12
Clemente	.317	.359	.475	16	299	94	87	200	56	41	82	6
Crawford	.309	.362	.452	6	279	90	98	191	55	49	27*	24
Dawson	.279	.323	.482	27	295	85	98	171	64	36	93	19
Gonzalez	.295	.343	.561	42	353	102	135	186	81	44	122	2
Gwynn	.338	.388	.459	9	283	92	76	209	51	52	29	21
Heilmann	.342	.410	.520	14	306	97	116	201	66	65	41	9
Jackson	.262	.356	.490	32	278	89	98	148	62	79	149	13
Kaline	.297	.376	.480	23	277	93	90	172	55	73	58	8
Klein	.320	.379	.543	28	325	108	111	192	72	56	48	7
Ott	.304	.414	.533	30	299	110	110	171	63	101	53	5
Parker	.290	.339	.471	22	289	84	98	178	62	45	101	10
Ramirez	.313	.409	.593	41	348	111	133	184	81	93	128	3
Rice	.322	.374	.427	2	267	102	73	201	48	48	19	24
Robinson	.294	.389	.537	34	310	106	105	170	68	82	88	12
Ruth	.342	.474	.690	46	375	141	143	186	88	133	86	8
Slaughter	.300	.382	.453	12	245	85	89	162	50	69	37	5
Sosa	.273	.344	.534	42	324	102	115	166	71	64	159	16
Waner	.333	.404	.473	7	285	103	83	200	57	69	24	7
Winfield	.283	.353	.475	25	284	91	100	169	59	66	92	12

* Estimated total for strikeouts based on known seasons

Category 4 Right Fielders

Sam Crawford

Career P/E: 1.028; Postseason P/E: .778
MVP: never won; .75 career shares
Hall of Fame: inducted in 1957

It's often said that the triple is the prettiest play in all of baseball. If that's true, then Sam Crawford was one good-looking ballplayer. With 309 three-baggers to his credit, Wahoo Sam is the game's all-time leader in that category. He led the league in triples six times and topped 20 five times. In every full season that he played, Crawford was in double digits. If you think that an inside-the-park homer is even prettier than a triple, then Crawford is still your man. He holds the major league record for home runs not going over the fence in a season (12 in 1901) as well as in a career (51). Teaming with Cobb for the 1911 Tigers, Wahoo Sam batted .378 and set important career highs in net runs (217) and P/E Average (1.252).

Despite his impressive career numbers and records, Sam Crawford wasn't elected to the Hall of Fame until 1957. Voting for Cooperstown began in '36, almost 20 years after his retirement, so he certainly had plenty of time for induction. I think that may be a telling fact about the opinions of the writers of his day.

Wahoo Sam is C4. I think he would have been an exciting player to watch, legging out triples and inside-the-park homers.

Year	RBI	R	HR	NR	TB	BB	HBP	SB	CS	CB	PTS	PA	P/E
1901	104	91	16	179	270	37	3	13	8*	315	673	559	1.204
1910	120	83	5	198	249	37	1	20	12*	295	691	650	1.063
1911	115	109	7	217	302	61	0	37	23*	377	811	648	1.252
Career	1,525	1,391	97	2,819	4,328	760	23	366	225*	5,252	10,890	10,594	1.028

* CS totals estimated based on known statistics

Andre Dawson

Career P/E: .998; Postseason P/E: .516
MVP: National League MVP in 1987; 2.36 career shares
Hall of Fame: possible

Ideally, right fielders should be able to drive the ball deep, produce runs, and have cannons for arms to cut down base runners. Andre Dawson exemplified those qualities. Dawson hit 438 home runs and knocked in almost 1,600 runs over his 21 seasons. In the field, he was known for a powerful arm; he won eight Gold Gloves from 1980 through 1988. Dawson left Montreal for Chicago beginning in 1987, and he made an immediate impact with his new team, the Cubs. The Hawk set career highs in homers (49), RBI (137), slugging percentage (.568), and total bases (353). Despite Chicago finishing 18½ games back and in last place in the National League East, Dawson won the NL MVP.

Dawson's lifetime averages in terms of P/E (.998) and net runs per game (.96) are solid but unspectacular, especially for a corner outfielder who often hit in the middle of his teams' lineups. He never came close to 200 net runs in any year, topping out at 185 for the '83 Expos. Andre also had only one season, 1987, with great home-run numbers.

I think it's possible that Dawson will one day make it into the Hall, but I also wouldn't be surprised if he didn't. I see him as Category 4 because of his career home-run and RBI totals, his Gold Gloves, and his MVP success. He may ultimately come up short, however, because he failed to produce in the postseason, where he was just a .186 batter.

Year	RBI	R	HR	NR	TB	BB	HBP	SB	CS	CB	PTS	PA	P/E
1983	113	104	32	185	341	38	9	25	11	402	772	698	1.106
1987	137	90	49	178	353	32	7	11	3	400	756	662	1.142
1990	100	72	27	145	283	42	2	16	2	341	631	581	1.086
Career	1,591	1,373	438	2,526	4,787	589	111	314	109	5,692	10,744	10,769	.998

Juan Gonzalez

Career P/E: 1.155; Postseason P/E: 1.303
MVP: American League MVP in 1996, 1998; 2.76 career shares
Hall of Fame: possible

In 1996 Juan Gonzalez won the American League Most Valuable Player award with the Texas Rangers. The Puerto Rican slugger batted .314 and slugged .643. He smacked 47 long balls and drove home 144 runs despite playing in only 134 games. Two years later, Gonzalez repeated his '96 performance, again taking home the AL MVP. Juan hit .318 in '98 and set a career best with 157 runs batted in, one of five times he exceeded 125 RBI in a six-year stretch from 1996 to 2001. The '96 Yankees eventually went on to win the World Series, but Juan Gonzalez did everything in his power to derail them in the AL Division Series. In four games, Juan hit five home runs and knocked in nine. He batted .438 against New York and slugged 1.375. Juan's P/E for that series was 2.263.

Gonzalez may fall short of Cooperstown for several reasons. First, he failed to reach 2,000 hits. He also scored just over 1,000 runs, not a very big number for a Hall of Famer. While he had two great postseason series, he also had two very bad ones. In back-to-back ALDS against the Yankees in '98 and '99, Juan Gone batted .083 and .182.

Dale Murphy and Roger Maris also won two MVPs, and I don't think they are Hall of Famers. Gonzalez, C4, is different in my mind, however, because he has superior numbers in terms of power, production, and P/E. I'll list his chances to get in as possible.

Year	RBI	R	HR	NR	TB	BB	HBP	SB	CS	CB	PTS	PA	P/E
1996	144	89	47	186	348	45	3	2	0	398	770	592	1.301
1998	157	110	45	222	382	46	6	2	1	435	879	669	1.314
2001	140	97	35	202	314	41	6	1	0	362	766	595	1.287
Career	1,404	1,061	434	2,031	3,676	457	62	26	19	4,202	8,264	7,155	1.155

Tony Gwynn

Career P/E: .981; Postseason P/E: .778
MVP: never won; 1.93 career shares
Hall of Fame: inducted in 2007

Playing his entire career with the Padres, Gwynn hit .309 or better in 19 of his 20 major league seasons, retiring as a .338 batter. He exceeded 200 hits five times, including his career-high 220 in 1997, which may have been his best season. The former San Diego State star scored 97 runs and drove home 119, by far the highest output of his career. His '97 masterpiece came exactly 10 years after another great season. The '87 campaign saw Tony collect 218 hits, score 119 runs, and steal 56 bases. Again, his batting average (.370) was tops in the National League. With 15 All-Stars, five Gold Gloves, seven Silver Sluggers, and eight league batting titles, Gwynn was a lock for the HOF.

Power and production. That's the theme of this chapter, and unfortunately Tony Gwynn was lacking in both categories. He reached double figures in homers only five times, never hitting more than 17 in a season. Furthermore, his '97 campaign was the only time he topped 90 RBI.

Gwynn, C4, deserves his status as a first-ballot Hall of Famer without question. With eight batting titles under his belt, he has to be considered as one of the finest pure hitters ever. Add to that the facts that he was great in the field and, at one time, a very good base stealer, and it's easy to see why I've included him in my top 10 for right field.

Year	RBI	R	HR	NR	TB	BB	HBP	SB	CS	CB	PTS	PA	P/E
1987	54	119	7	166	301	82	3	56	12	430	762	680	1.121
1995	90	82	9	163	259	35	1	17	5	307	633	577	1.097
1997	119	97	17	199	324	43	3	12	5	377	775	651	1.190
Career	1,138	1,383	135	2,386	4,259	790	24	319	125	5,267	10,039	10,232	.981

Harry Heilmann

Career P/E: 1.144; Postseason P/E: never in the postseason

MVP: never won; 1.91 career shares

Hall of Fame: inducted in 1952

Heilmann broke in with the Tigers in 1914, playing his final season in Detroit in 1929. In between, he won four American League batting titles and finished in the top five of the MVP vote four times. Harry was runner-up to Lou Gehrig in '27, a year in which the Detroit outfielder batted .398, one of four times throughout his Hall of Fame career that he hit better than .390. Throughout the 1920s, Heilmann was very good most years and simply dominant every other year beginning in 1921. In '21, '23, '25, and '27, the Detroit star averaged 219 hits, 127 RBI, and 44 doubles per season. He hit between .393 and .403 over those years and slugged better than .600 three times.

Heilmann was never in the postseason, so it is difficult to fully analyze his career without knowing how he might have fared on the game's biggest stage. He also never won an MVP, which tells me that his statistics, although very impressive, weren't necessarily overwhelming for the era in which he played. Of course, the fact that he never played on a pennant-winning squad would also hurt his chances to win the award.

It's a rating of C4 for Heilmann. Success in the postseason or an MVP would have certainly justified making him Category 5, but that's not the case.

Year	RBI	R	HR	NR	TB	BB	HBP	SB	CS	CB	PTS	PA	P/E
1921	139	114	19	234	365	53	2	2	6	416	884	672	1.315
1923	115	121	18	218	331	74	5	9	7	412	848	626	1.355
1927	120	106	14	212	311	72	2	11	5	391	815	596	1.367
Career	1,539	1,291	183	2,647	4,053	856	40	113	102*	4,960	10,254	8,960	1.144

* CS totals estimated based on known statistics

Al Kaline

Career P/E: 1.023; Postseason P/E: 1.154
MVP: never won; 2.92 career shares
Hall of Fame: inducted in 1980

Kaline erupted in '55, breaking out with 200 hits, 121 runs, and a
.340 batting average, the highest of his Hall of Fame career. The next
season, '56, was equally good. Again, Kaline hit well above .300 and
produced 197 net runs after 196 the previous year. His P/E scores were
1.172 for 1955 and 1.152 for 1956, and Kaline eclipsed 1.100 five other
times throughout the '50s and '60s. In the field, Kaline was superb. In
1957 he won the Gold Glove as the best defensive right fielder in all
of baseball, as only one award was granted to each position in that
first year. He won the Gold Glove again in '58 and was named the best
center fielder in the American League in '59. Then, Kaline won seven
consecutive outfield Gold Gloves from '61 to '67.

Although Kaline hit 399 career homers, he never had that one huge
power season that set him apart from the rest of the league. Al never
hit 30 homers in any season, and he never slugged .600. Furthermore,
Kaline compiled excellent production numbers over a long career but
wasn't great on a per-game basis (average of .99 net runs per contest).

Kaline's career would be even more impressive had he secured an
MVP honor for himself. He was runner-up twice and in the top five
four times. While that doesn't detract from a great career, it does prevent me from rating him higher than C4.

Year	RBI	R	HR	NR	TB	BB	HBP	SB	CS	CB	PTS	PA	P/E
1955	102	121	27	196	321	82	5	6	8	406	798	681	1.172
1956	128	96	27	197	327	70	1	7	1	404	798	693	1.152
1961	82	116	19	179	302	66	4	14	1	385	743	665	1.117
Career	1,583	1,622	399	2,806	4,852	1,277	55	137	65	6,256	11,868	11,597	1.023

Chuck Klein

Career P/E: 1.160; Postseason P/E: 1.083

MVP: National League MVP in 1932; 2.46 career shares

Hall of Fame: inducted in 1980

Only two men in the history of major league baseball have reached 400 total bases in a season three times. One of them is Lou Gehrig (who did it five times), and the other is Chuck Klein. From 1929 to 1933, he starred for the Philadelphia Phillies and was a dominant player. Klein's 1930 season remains one of the game's great individual campaigns of all time. With 445 total bases, Klein recorded 250 hits, 107 extra-base hits, 288 net runs of offense, and 44 outfield assists. His P/E Average that season (1.503) stands as one of the highest ever for a single season. No MVP was awarded in '30, but Klein surely would have had a great chance to take home the hardware. He won the MVP in 1932 and followed up by winning the Triple Crown the next year.

After 1933 Klein's career began a sudden and drastic downturn. Although he put up good numbers in '36, he was a shell of his former self throughout the rest of his career. He appeared in less than 200 games in the '40s, hitting below .220 every year from '40 through '44.

Klein, C4, didn't make it into Cooperstown until 1980, approximately three and a half decades after his retirement. He had a truly dominant stretch in the early part of his career, and he held on just long enough to reach 300 home runs and eclipse 2,000 hits.

Year	RBI	R	HR	NR	TB	BB	HBP	SB	CS	CB	PTS	PA	P/E
1929	145	126	43	228	405	54	0	5	2*	462	918	679	1.352
1930	170	158	40	288	445	54	4	4	2*	505	1,081	719	1.503
1932	137	152	38	251	420	60	1	20	10*	491	993	711	1.397
Career	1,201	1,168	300	2,069	3,522	601	12	79	39*	4,175	8,313	7,168	1.160

* CS totals estimated based on 2:1 success ratio

Dave Parker

Career P/E: .986; Postseason P/E: .713
MVP: National League MVP in 1978; 3.19 career shares
Hall of Fame: possible

Dave Parker is not currently in the Hall of Fame, but he should be. With 3.19 MVP shares, more than 2,700 hits, and almost 1,500 RBI, Parker accomplished enough in his 19 major league seasons to stand alongside the game's greatest. The 1978 campaign saw him take home National League Most Valuable Player honors. The Cobra stroked 194 hits to the tune of a .334 batting average, which again led the league. He stole 20 bags and generated 189 net runs of offense for Pittsburgh while winning the second of his three consecutive Gold Gloves. After a few down seasons in the early '80s, Parker responded with a gem in 1985. The slugger finished second in the MVP vote, driving home 125 runs with 350 total bases, the best mark of his career.

Parker had several disappointing years in the middle of his career. Between '81 and '82, he played in only 140 games, although it should be noted that the first of those two seasons was cut short for everyone by a strike. Even in '83, when Dave was able to play a full season, his numbers were less than extraordinary, batting .279 with 69 RBI.

In the end, I chose him as a Hall of Famer because he won two batting titles, earned considerable MVP acclaim, and had very good career numbers in terms of hits, RBI, and batting average. His three Gold Gloves don't hurt either. I see him as Category 4.

Year	RBI	R	HR	NR	TB	BB	HBP	SB	CS	CB	PTS	PA	P/E
1978	117	102	30	189	340	57	2	20	7	412	790	642	1.231
1979	94	109	25	178	327	67	9	20	4	419	775	707	1.096
1985	125	88	34	179	350	52	3	5	13	397	755	694	1.088
Career	1,493	1,272	339	2,426	4,405	683	56	154	113	5,185	10,037	10,184	.986

Sam Rice

Career P/E: .977; Postseason P/E: .687
MVP: never won; .28 career shares
Hall of Fame: inducted in 1963

Thirteen hits. That's how close Edgar Charles Rice (better known as Sam) came to joining the 3,000-hit club. Rice had six seasons with more than 200 hits, including 227 in 1925. Playing for the Washington Senators that year, Rice batted .350, scored 111 runs, and set a career high with 87 runs batted in. He generated 197 net runs of offense for Washington's scoreboard, which was also a career high. For his career, Rice hit .322 and struck out far less than he walked. Always a tough out, he enjoyed many seasons with 20 or fewer strikeouts while reaching base at a good clip throughout his major league tenure. Rice also stole 351 bases, including 63 in 1920.

Rice had very little power, and that is a serious knock against any corner outfielder, regardless of the era in which he played. In the postseason, Rice was purely a singles hitter. Of his 19 World Series hits, none went for extra bases. He also wasn't a great run generator in October. Therefore, his lifetime Offensive Production and Efficiency Average for the postseason stands at .687, a very mediocre score.

Rice is Category 4. His totals for hits and runs scored are impressive, as are his .322 lifetime average and ratio of walks to strikeouts. He deserves to be in the Hall of Fame.

Year	RBI	R	HR	NR	TB	BB	HBP	SB	CS	CB	PTS	PA	P/E
1923	75	117	3	189	268	57	6	20	8	343	721	671	1.075
1925	87	111	1	197	287	37	4	26	11	343	737	709	1.039
1930	73	121	1	193	271	55	3	13	8	334	720	668	1.078
Career	1,078	1,514	34	2,558	3,955	708	56	351	176*	4,894	10,010	10,246	.977

* CS totals estimated based on known statistics

Enos Slaughter

Career P/E: 1.040; Postseason P/E: 1.010
MVP: never won; 2.10 career shares
Hall of Fame: inducted in 1985

In 1985 Enos Slaughter entered into baseball immortality when he was inducted into the Hall of Fame. Over his career, Slaughter was able to accumulate 2.10 shares in MVP voting despite missing three full seasons in the mid-'40s serving in the Army Air Corps.

Slaughter ended the 1946 season, his first one back after the war effort, with a P/E mark of 1.140, the highest of his career. When St. Louis faced Boston in the World Series, Enos was terrific, with eight hits, a .320 average, and five runs scored. In Game 7, the score was tied in the eighth inning. Slaughter singled and then took off for second on a hit-and-run. He rounded second and then third, completely ignoring his coach's signal to stop. Catching the fielders off guard, Slaughter scored the eventual winning run.

Slaughter was never a big power hitter, as evidenced by 169 career home runs and a career slugging percentage of .453. He never reached 300 total bases in a season, although he did have 290 or more three times. In 1946 Slaughter was very good, but he lacked that one outstanding season.

When I first looked at Slaughter's numbers, I didn't consider him to be a Hall of Famer. Then I realized he missed three full seasons because of WWII. It's C4 for Enos.

Year	RBI	R	HR	NR	TB	BB	HBP	SB	CS	CB	PTS	PA	P/E
1942	98	100	13	185	292	88	6	9	6*	389	759	687	1.105
1946	130	100	18	212	283	69	2	9	6*	357	781	685	1.140
1947	86	100	10	176	249	59	4	4	2*	314	666	619	1.076
Career	1,304	1,247	169	2,382	3,599	1,018	37	71	44*	4,681	9,445	9,084	1.040

* CS totals estimated based on known statistics

Paul Waner

Career P/E: 1.050; Postseason P/E: .706

MVP: National League MVP in 1927; 2.86 career shares

Hall of Fame: inducted in 1952

With 3,152 hits and more than 1,600 runs scored to his credit, Paul Waner was an easy choice for the Hall of Fame. Also known as Big Poison, he played the majority of his career with the Pirates. His best season was probably 1927. He reached his best P/E score that year (1.240) while taking home NL MVP honors as Pittsburgh won the pennant. Waner registered 237 hits and generated an impressive total of 236 net runs in leading the league in batting with a .380 average. Paul hit well above .300 in each of his first 12 seasons (including six years above .350) and retired as a .333 batter. Averaging 1.11 net runs per game over 20 seasons, Waner reached 100 RBI twice and topped 100 runs scored nine times, including eight out of his first nine years with the Pirates.

Paul appeared in the postseason only once, in 1927, when his overmatched Pirates were swept by the Yankees. He batted .333, but he hit with little power (.400 slugging) against New York. A lack of long-ball ability was also evident throughout his career.

Big Poison was a three-time league batting champion who put together some outstanding career numbers. Waner lacked power and postseason success, however, so I have not included him in my top 10 for this position. I see him as a Category 4 player.

Year	RBI	R	HR	NR	TB	BB	HBP	SB	CS	CB	PTS	PA	P/E
1927	131	114	9	236	342	60	3	5	3*	407	879	709	1.240
1928	86	142	6	222	329	77	5	6	3*	414	858	697	1.231
1929	100	131	15	216	318	89	3	15	7*	418	850	703	1.209
Career	1,309	1,627	113	2,823	4,478	1,091	38	104	52*	5,659	11,305	10,762	1.050

* CS totals estimated based on 2:1 success ratio

Dave Winfield

Career P/E: 1.025; Postseason P/E: .741
MVP: never won; 2.20 career shares
Hall of Fame: inducted in 2001

With a cannon for an arm, good speed, and home-run power, David Mark Winfield was a manager's dream in right field. Winfield won seven Gold Gloves for his outstanding outfield play and also earned six Silver Sluggers for his prowess at the plate. A 12-time All-Star, Winfield entered the Hall of Fame in 2001 on the strength of 3,110 hits, 1,833 RBI, and 465 home runs. After the strike in '81, Winfield went on an RBI spree from '82 to '88, averaging 106 runs knocked in each season over that span. In '84 he teamed with Don Mattingly to form a lethal one-two punch in the middle of the Yankees lineup. Dave batted .340 for the season and reached 100 runs both scored and batted in.

Although he won a World Series title with the Blue Jays in '92 and appeared in 26 postseason games, Winfield was not usually a big-time player in October. He batted .208 for his playoff career and owns a postseason P/E Average of just .741. Dave's career would also have been more impressive had he been able to win an MVP. He never finished in the top two, and his 2.20 career shares fail to establish him as a true superstar.

Winfield, C4, who was also a basketball star at the University of Minnesota, is deserving of his Hall of Fame status but doesn't rank in my top 10. Although he was immensely talented, he failed to separate himself from this pack of gifted right fielders.

Year	RBI	R	HR	NR	TB	BB	HBP	SB	CS	CB	PTS	PA	P/E
1979	118	97	34	181	333	85	2	15	9	426	788	686	1.149
1985	114	105	26	193	298	52	0	19	7	362	748	689	1.086
1992	108	92	26	174	286	82	1	2	3	368	716	670	1.069
Career	1,833	1,669	465	3,037	5,221	1,216	25	223	96	6,589	12,663	12,358	1.025

Category 5 Right Fielders

Hank Aaron

Height: 6'0"; Weight: 180; Bats: right; Throws: right

First game: April 13, 1954; Final game: October 3, 1976

Team(s): Milwaukee/Atlanta Braves (1954–1974); Milwaukee
Brewers (1975–1976)

MVP: National League MVP in 1957; 5.45 career shares

Hall of Fame: inducted in 1982

162-game avg.: .305 batting, .374 on-base, .555 slugging, 37 home
runs, 337 total bases, 107 runs scored, 113 runs batted in, 185
hits, 73 extra-base hits, 69 BB, 68 K, 12 SB

Career P/E: 1.140; Postseason P/E: 1.297

The Good. With 755 career home runs to his name, Henry Aaron
reigned as baseball's king of the long ball until 2007. Aaron also ranks
number one in RBI (2,297), extra-base hits (1,477), and total bases
(6,856), as well as third in hits (3,771) and fourth in runs scored
(2,174). He compiled those one-of-a-kind totals over 23 seasons, during which time Aaron also made 21 consecutive All-Star teams
('55–'75) and earned MVP votes in 19 straight seasons ('55–'73). Year
after year, he was a strong run producer with excellent batting averages. From 1955 through 1970, he scored at least 100 runs each year
except one, and he knocked in more than 105 runs 11 times. Aaron
retired as a .305 lifetime hitter, batting as high as .355 in 1959.

In '57 Aaron won the National League MVP. He hit 44 homers, one
of eight times he'd hit 40 or more in a season, and knocked in 132
runs, the highest total ever in his career. With a P/E Average of 1.241,
Hank led his Milwaukee Braves into the World Series against the Yan-

kees. Batting .393 with three homers and seven RBI, Aaron led the Braves to the championship in seven games. The Yanks got their revenge in '58, but Aaron was again a solid hitter, with a .333 average and a .419 on-base mark in defeat. When the Mets beat the Atlanta Braves in 1969 to capture the pennant, it was in spite of Aaron's heroics to derail New York. The righty slugger hit .357 with three homers and seven RBI in only 14 plate appearances.

Henry Aaron was a complete ballplayer. He hit for high averages, stole bases, and played tremendous defense. Playing in Milwaukee, he won three consecutive Gold Gloves from 1958 to 1960, with more than twice as many assists as errors each season. On the bases, Aaron was a smart runner with good speed. In '63 Hank stole 31 bases and was caught only five times. For his career, Aaron was successful 76 percent of the time, finishing with 240 stolen bases.

The Bad. Probably the biggest knock against Aaron's career is that he won only one MVP in almost a quarter of a century. In fact, Aaron never finished as runner-up in the league balloting, although he did finish third six times. His career total of 5.45 MVP shares is outstanding but would look even more impressive had he been able to win another individual honor. Aaron's career P/E score doesn't rank in the all-time top 25.

The Verdict. While he didn't homer at the rate of Ruth or win as many MVPs as Mantle, Hank Aaron was nevertheless a tremendous ballplayer. A case for him as the greatest right fielder ever will be made in this chapter's top-three analysis. Aaron's an easy choice for C5.

Roberto Clemente

Height: 5'11"; Weight: 175; Bats: right; Throws: right

First game: April 17, 1955; Final game: October 3, 1972

Team(s): Pittsburgh Pirates (1955–1972)

MVP: National League MVP in 1966; 2.80 career shares

Hall of Fame: inducted in 1973

162-game avg.: .317 batting, .359 on-base, .475 slugging, 16 home
    runs, 299 total bases, 94 runs scored, 87 runs batted in, 200 hits,
    56 extra-base hits, 41 BB, 82 K, 6 SB

Career P/E: .994; Postseason P/E: .814

The Good. Perhaps no other right fielder in history ever played the position with more flair than Roberto Clemente. Clemente starred for the Pirates from 1955 to 1972, making 12 All-Star teams and winning 12 consecutive Gold Gloves. He is probably the best defensive player at his position ever. Longtime broadcaster Vin Scully once quipped that Roberto "could field the ball in New York and throw out a guy in Pennsylvania." In 1961 Clemente had 27 assists.

Roberto's powerful arm and great range in the outfield were paired with a dynamic bat. The Puerto Rican star hit .317 for his career, winning four league batting titles and going above a .350 average on three occasions. He had more than 200 hits in a season four times and ended his career with exactly 3,000 base knocks.

In 1966 Clemente won the National League MVP after batting .317 and setting career highs in runs scored (105) and runs batted in (119). The next season, Clemente may have been even better. With 209 hits and a .357 batting average, Roberto proved that '66 was no fluke. He finished the season with a P/E of 1.196, the highest score of his career and one of four times that the right fielder topped the 1.100 plateau.

Clemente was a career .318 hitter in the postseason, and he was at his best in the '71 Fall Classic versus Baltimore. With 12 hits, including 5 for extra bases, Roberto walked away with Series MVP honors (P/E: 1.097) and earned his second championship ring. Clemente played in a total of 14 World Series contests, and he got at least one hit in each game.

The Bad. Other than 1966 and 1967, when he combined to generate 385 net runs, Clemente was never a big run producer. Throughout the other 16 years of his career, he never exceeded 170 net runs in a season. His 1.02 per-game average is good but trails the marks of several other right fielders in this section. He also never hit 30 homers in a season or came close to slugging .600, topping out at .559 in 1961. Therefore, his lifetime Production and Efficiency Average falls below the 1.000 level.

Roberto Clemente died in an airplane crash on December 31, 1972, while trying to deliver supplies and aid to earthquake victims in Nicaragua. His body was never recovered.

The Verdict. In terms of legend and aura, Clemente ranks as high as almost any player. Although I don't see him as high as Aaron or Ruth, I do see him as Category 5. His defense was superb, and he often played big on the big stage. In my opinion, he's one of the 10 best right fielders in history.

Reggie Jackson

Height: 6'0"; Weight: 200; Bats: left; Throws: left

First game: June 9, 1967; Final game: October 4, 1987

Team(s): Kansas City/Oakland Athletics (1967–1975, 1987);
   Baltimore Orioles (1976); New York Yankees (1977–1981);
   California Angels (1982–1986)

MVP: American League MVP in 1973; 3.28 career shares

Hall of Fame: inducted in 1993

162-game avg.: .262 batting, .356 on-base, .490 slugging, 32 home
   runs, 278 total bases, 89 runs scored, 98 runs batted in, 148 hits,
   62 extra-base hits, 79 BB, 149 K, 13 SB

Career P/E: 1.033; Postseason P/E: 1.035

The Good. Reginald Martinez Jackson earned one of the best nick-
names in baseball history, Mr. October, by twice winning MVP honors in the World Series. In 1973 Jackson won after batting .310 with
six runs batted in and five extra-base hits against the Mets. He was
even better in '77, this time playing in pinstripes, terrorizing Dodgers
pitching with five Series homers (including three in a decisive Game
6 victory) and 10 runs scored. Reggie's P/E for the '77 Series was a
remarkable 2.292, symbolic of one of the great postseason series of all
time.

Jackson's best season may have been 1969, a year in which he posted
his best P/E score (1.264). The A's outfielder hit 47 homers, scored 123
runs, and drove home 118. He led the league in slugging (.608) and
drew 114 free passes to help account for a .410 on-base percentage.
Somehow, he finished only fifth in the MVP race. But he would make
up for that four years later. The '73 campaign was special for Reggie

because it found him walking away with the unanimous MVP honor as well as Player of the Year recognition. When he won the World Series MVP, it must have felt like the icing on a perfect cake.

Mr. October finished his career with some very impressive regular-season statistics, including 563 round-trippers, 1,702 RBI, and more than 2,500 hits. Jackson was a 14-time All-Star, won two Silver Sluggers, and earned 3.28 career MVP shares by finishing in the top five on five occasions. He was a well-known superstar, and he was elected to the Hall of Fame in 1993.

The Bad. No player in the history of baseball has struck out more than Reggie Jackson. In fact, no other player is even close to his career total of 2,597 whiffs. Jackson played for 21 seasons, and he fanned at least 105 times in 18 of them. He avoided that dubious distinction in only his first season (35 games played), his last season (115 games), and 1981 (94 games in a strike-shortened year). In 1968 Jackson struck out 171 times. For his career, the lefty slugger averaged 149 strikeouts per 162 games. Mr. October wasn't much better in the postseason either, having fanned 70 times in 77 career playoff games. Jackson's reputation is also hurt by his .262 career batting average and a relatively low average of .95 net runs per contest.

The Verdict. Reggie is C5 in my eyes. His MVP résumé is outstanding, and 563 homers qualify him for a top-10 spot. Players need to play at their best in the postseason, and that's exactly what Jackson did on a regular basis.

Mel Ott

Height: 5′9″; Weight: 170; Bats: left; Throws: right

First game: April 27, 1926; Final game: July 11, 1947

Team(s): New York Giants (1926–1947)

MVP: never won; 2.75 career shares

Hall of Fame: inducted in 1951

162-game avg.: .304 batting, .414 on-base, .533 slugging, 30 home
runs, 299 total bases, 110 runs scored, 110 runs batted in, 171
hits, 63 extra-base hits, 101 BB, 53 K, 5 SB

Career P/E: 1.171; Postseason P/E: .971

The Good. It's rare for a superstar player to spend his entire career in
one uniform, but that's exactly what Mel Ott did, playing 22 major
league seasons exclusively with the New York Giants from 1926 to
1947. Although small in stature, Ott possessed great power and was
extremely productive. The Giants outfielder averaged 1.18 net runs
per game for his career and had five years with more than 200. His
best statistical season was 1929, a year in which Ott posted the highest P/E Average (1.427) of his career. He batted .328 and set personal
bests in homers (42), runs scored (138), RBI (151), and slugging percentage (.635), although he failed to finish in the top 10 of the
National League's MVP vote. That year also marked the first in a string
of 10 that saw Ott drive in at least 95 runs per season, averaging 121
RBI over that span. Mel also topped 100 runs scored nine times, finishing his career with 1,859 runs and 1,860 RBI.

In 1945 Melvin Thomas Ott joined elite company when he
smacked his five hundredth home run. He wound up with 511, cur-

rently good for a top-25 all-time ranking in that category. With 25 or more homers 13 times and 30 or more eight times, Ott was a consistent threat to go deep. Impressively, he also had great plate discipline for someone with long-ball power. In '29, for example, Mel homered 4 more times (42) than he struck out (38) while drawing 113 walks. Ten seasons, Ott drew at least 100 free passes, yet he never struck out 70 times. For his career, he walked 812 times more than he fanned. In terms of on-base percentage, the right fielder was frequently above .400, finishing with a lifetime average of .414.

The Bad. Ott's career would certainly look more impressive had he been able to win an MVP. His best finish was third in 1942, and he was in the top five only three times. He made 12 consecutive All-Star appearances but wasn't able to secure his league's top honor, something that prevents him from cracking the top three for this position.

In '36 and again in '37 Ott's Giants lost to the Yankees in the World Series. He combined to bat .256, striking out more than he walked and producing only nine net runs in 11 games. His postseason P/E is 200 points lower than his regular-season average.

The Verdict. Mel Ott's lack of MVP success prevents him from being in the top three, but it doesn't stop him from earning a rating of C5. His overall numbers are great. He hit for high averages, reached base often, and was a consistent threat in terms of power and production, exactly what a manager wants from a corner outfielder. I think he's top five for this position.

Manny Ramirez

Height: 6'0"; Weight: 200; Bats: right; Throws: right

First game: September 2, 1993; Final game: still active

Team(s): Cleveland Indians (1993–2000); Boston Red Sox
   (2001–present)

MVP: never won; 2.75 career shares (through '06 voting)

Hall of Fame: imminent

162-game avg.: .313 batting, .409 on-base, .593 slugging,
   41 home runs, 348 total bases, 111 runs scored,
   133 runs batted in, 184 hits, 81 extra-base hits,
   93 BB, 128 K, 3 SB

Career P/E: 1.234; Postseason P/E: 1.028

The Good. Manny Ramirez is an RBI machine, plain and simple. Beginning in 1995 Manny has topped the century mark for runs batted in every season except two. In 1998 and 1999 the Dominican outfielder drove home 310 runs in 297 combined games. He has knocked in more than 120 runs six times, and he averages 133 per 162 games for his career. His ability to bring runners around is largely responsible for his gaudy average of 1.26 net runs per game. That is a figure that tops every right fielder in this section not named Ruth. He's been one of the leading offensive players in the sport for many years and doesn't seem to be slowing down very much.

Ramirez combines amazing run production with great power and the ability to hit for high averages and reach base often. Five times he has hit more than 40 homers in a season, and he has hit more than 30 in 11 of the past 13. A .313 career batter, Ramirez has hit as high as .351, a mark he posted in 2000, his last season with the Indians.

In terms of P/E Average, Manny is superb. His 1.234 lifetime mark is better than those of Ty Cobb and Mickey Mantle. In 1999 and 2000 the slugger finished with P/Es above 1.400 in back-to-back seasons, a rare and significant accomplishment. The 252 net runs his bat produced in 1999 helped push his season P/E to 1.495, the highest mark of his Hall of Fame career.

Manny was named MVP of the 2004 World Series after his Boston squad swept the Cardinals. He hit .412, reached base safely in half of his plate appearances, and drove in four runs as the Red Sox finally broke the curse to win it all.

The Bad. Ramirez's World Series MVP notwithstanding, his postseason numbers pale in comparison with his regular-season stats. His 1.028 P/E in October is more than 200 points lower than his number from April through September, and he has driven in just 64 runs in 95 playoff games. Furthermore, Manny has been unable to win an MVP in the regular season, never having finished better than third on the American League ballot. Finally, Manny is not a very good fielder or base runner.

The Verdict. While he currently plays left field in front of the Green Monster at Fenway Park, Manny still has more career games played in right, so he's included here rather than Chapter 7. Forget about Ramirez's quirky personality or the fact that he isn't a model teammate at all times. The guy can hit, driving in runs at a tremendous pace and owning a career slugging percentage of .593. His lethal bat qualifies him for Category 5 and a top-five spot. Cooperstown awaits him.

Frank Robinson

Height: 6′1″; Weight: 195; Bats: right; Throws: right

First game: April 17, 1956; Final game: September 18, 1976

Team(s): Cincinnati Reds (1956–1965); Baltimore Orioles
    (1966–1971); Los Angeles Dodgers (1972); California Angels
    (1973–1974); Cleveland Indians (1974–1976)

MVP: National League MVP in 1961/American League MVP in
    1966; 4.83 career shares

Hall of Fame: inducted in 1982

162-game avg.: .294 batting, .389 on-base, .537 slugging,
    34 home runs, 310 total bases, 106 runs scored,
    105 runs batted in, 170 hits, 68 extra-base hits,
    82 BB, 88 K, 12 SB

Career P/E: 1.126; Postseason P/E: 1.060

The Good. In 1956 a young rookie outfielder in Cincinnati stole the headlines after scoring 122 runs, batting .290, and hitting 38 home runs. Frank Robinson won the Rookie of the Year honor that season, and he would go on to become one of Cincinnati's best players ever. Frank won the Gold Glove in 1958, and he drove in 125 runs and batted .311 the next season. As the early '60s rolled around, Robinson was quickly establishing himself as one of the National League's best players. He won the MVP in '61, helping lead the Reds to the pennant. The next season may have been his best ever as Robinson stroked 208 hits, including 92 for extra bases, and generated 231 net runs of offense. Both seasons, Robinson's P/E Average topped 1.300.

After the 1965 season, Cincinnati traded Robinson to Baltimore for three players, including pitcher Milt Pappas, and it turned out to be a huge mistake. Frank immediately made his impact felt with the Orioles in '66 by winning the AL Most Valuable Player, the Triple Crown, and eventually the World Series MVP as Baltimore upset the Dodgers to win the title. By winning the MVP in the American League, Robinson became the first player to win that prestigious honor in both leagues. He was a unanimous winner in addition to being named Player of the Year.

Frank Robinson made six NL All-Star teams and six AL All-Star teams and finished with 586 round-trippers. At the time of his retirement, Robinson was number four on the all-time home-run list, trailing only Hank Aaron, Babe Ruth, and Willie Mays. He also topped 1,800 runs both scored and driven in and came very close (2,943) to 3,000 hits.

The Bad. Robinson had some disappointing seasons over the second half of his career. In 1968, for example, Frank hit .268 with only 52 RBI. Returning to the National League as a Dodger in '72, he played in just over 100 games, batting .251 with only 26 extra-base hits. Two years later, Robinson suited up for California and Cleveland and combined to hit below .250 for the first time in his career. For those three seasons, Robinson's P/E Averages fell below 1.000.

Although he was named MVP of the '66 Fall Classic, Robinson struggled in the World Series in 1961 with the Reds and in 1969 with the Orioles. Frank hit .200 against the '61 Yankees and .188 against the '69 Mets. He batted .200 or lower in half of his eight postseason series.

The Verdict. Robinson is C5. He put up great numbers and was enormously successful in both the American and National Leagues. In my opinion, he is one of the three best right fielders ever.

Babe Ruth

Height: 6'2"; Weight: 215; Bats: left; Throws: left

First game: July 11, 1914; Final game: May 30, 1935

Team(s): Boston Red Sox (1914–1919); New York Yankees (1920–1934); Boston Braves (1935)

MVP: American League MVP in 1923; 1.82 career shares

Hall of Fame: inducted in 1936

162-game avg.: .342 batting, .474 on-base, .690 slugging, 46 home runs, 375 total bases, 141 runs scored, 143 runs batted in, 186 hits, 88 extra-base hits, 133 BB, 86 K, 8 SB

Career P/E: 1.436; Postseason P/E: 1.449

The Good. If you asked 100 people who they thought was the best baseball player of all time, I expect a very large percentage of them would name Babe Ruth as the sport's brightest star. It would be hard to argue with them. Ruth single-handedly changed baseball after he arrived in the Bronx in 1920. Prior to him donning the pinstripes, baseball was dominated by singles hitters and high-average stars with little power. Ruth altered baseball forever by introducing the long ball on a consistent basis. When he hit 54 homers in '20, he finished 35 ahead of his nearest American League competitor, George Sisler (19 home runs). Babe went on to hit 59 the next year in what may be the single greatest season a baseball player has ever enjoyed. In terms of P/E Averages, his '21 campaign (1.714) reigns supreme. Ruth scored 177 runs, batted in 171, and had tremendous efficiency averages (.378 BA, .512 OBP, and .846 SLP). The sport of baseball would never be the same again.

The Sultan of Swat led the league in on-base percentage 10 times, in slugging 13 times, in runs scored 8 times, in home runs 12 times, and in bases on balls 11 times. There was no other player like him, and he simply dominated the nation's attention. In 1927 Babe did the unthinkable when he hit 60 home runs in a single season. His 1.562 P/E score that year was one of eight times when he surpassed 1.500, a feat that no other player can even come close to claiming. The Babe's lifetime P/E of 1.436 is by far the highest mark in the history of the sport; only Lou Gehrig is within 50 points of him.

Before Ruth became an immortal hitter, he was an excellent pitcher with the Red Sox. He won 23 games in 1916 and 24 the next year, topping 320 innings pitched both times. His career winning percentage (.671) and his lifetime ERA (2.28) are both outstanding. Babe also went 3–0 in two Fall Classic visits with Boston, both wins, in 1916 and 1918. He pitched 31 innings in World Series play to an ERA of 0.87.

The Bad. Ruth didn't take care of himself physically as well as he could have, and he certainly wasn't in line for sainthood. In 1925 Babe played in only 98 games and had his worst season in New York (P/E: 1.075) after suffering stomach cramps and fever early in the year.

The Verdict. There has never been another player like Babe Ruth, and there probably never will. He put up numbers and influenced the game beyond compare, and his name is synonymous with the sport he transformed. Naturally, he's a C5 and one of the three best right fielders ever.

Sammy Sosa

Height: 6'0"; Weight: 220; Bats: right; Throws: right

First game: June 16, 1989; Final game: still active

Team(s): Texas Rangers (1989); Chicago White Sox (1989–1991); Chicago Cubs (1992–2004); Baltimore Orioles (2005); Texas Rangers (2007)

MVP: National League MVP in 1998; 2.46 career shares (through '06 voting)

Hall of Fame: probable

162-game avg.: .273 batting, .344 on-base, .534 slugging, 42 home runs, 324 total bases, 102 runs scored, 115 runs batted in, 166 hits, 71 extra-base hits, 64 BB, 159 K, 16 SB

Career P/E: 1.100; Postseason P/E: .910

The Good. Sammy Sosa is the only player in major league history to have hit more than 60 home runs in three different seasons. The stoutly built Dominican, who hails from San Pedro de Macoris like so many other professional ballplayers, accomplished that feat in three of the four years from 1998 to 2001. With 50 home runs in 2000, Sosa clubbed an amazing 243 out of the park over that storied period. What Roger Maris miraculously accomplished in 1961, Sammy Sosa averaged for four years. Slammin' Sammy reached the 500-home-run club early in 2003, one of seven seasons in which the Wrigley favorite hit 40 or more, and after missing the 2006 season entirely, returned to the game in 2007 to join the exclusive 600-home-run club with the Texas Rangers.

Throughout the summer of '98, Sosa and Mark McGwire went back and forth with one another trying to break Roger Maris's home-run record. While Big Mac ultimately prevailed, Sosa was the one to walk away with National League MVP honors, the Player of the Year award, and a postseason berth with the Cubs. Sammy finished the year with 66 bombs and 158 runs knocked in. His 226 net runs of offense helped account for a very high P/E of 1.317.

Even 1998 wasn't Sosa's best season statistically, however. In 2001 he registered a P/E of 1.447 after slugging .737 with 425 total bases, 64 home runs, and 242 net runs of offense for Chicago's scoreboard. The Cubs' right fielder also set career highs in walks (116), RBI (160), and runs scored (146), as well as batting average (.328) and on-base percentage (.437). He finished second in the MVP vote as the Cubbies finished in third place in the National League Central Division.

The Bad. After 2001 Sosa's numbers fell each year, although he still maintained great statistics in '02 and '03. The 2004 season was Sammy's final year in Wrigley, and he hit just .253 with 80 RBI. He suited up for Baltimore in 2005 and had his worst season since the very early stages of his career. With a .221 batting average and 14 homers, he sank to a .764 P/E in Camden Yards.

Steroid allegations have tainted Sosa, just like many of the other superstars of the past five to ten years. When he appeared before Congress with McGwire, Palmeiro, and Canseco, among others, Sosa didn't present himself very well. A corked bat incident in 2003 also painted this Dominican legend in a bad light.

The Verdict. Sosa is one of the 10 best right fielders in history according to my analysis. His statistics over a four-year period are as good as anyone's, but there is strong doubt that his accomplishments were gained fairly. In my opinion, Sosa is Category 5 due to his tremendous power numbers.

Right Field: The Top 10

It was very difficult to come up with this chapter's top 10. While the top three were fairly easy to rank, I had a hard time deciding who else belonged here and an even harder time coming up with the exact order. It's a position dominated by sluggers, but there is also a significant number of skilled glove men (Kaline, Clemente) and those with impressive batting averages (Gwynn, Waner). Here's how I see the 10 best right fielders.

10. Tony Gwynn

Tony Gwynn won eight league batting titles and five Gold Gloves. He was a dominant hitter in his era, even if he never hit with a tremendous amount of power. He gets the nod for number 10 over Kaline, Waner, and other C4 players because of his consistency. Gwynn hit .309 or higher, often much higher, every season after his rookie campaign. That's 19 straight years with extremely impressive batting averages. Add to that the facts that he was great in the field and stole as many as 56 bases in one year and his value to a team is apparent.

9. Harry Heilmann

Like Gwynn, Heilmann hit for an extremely high average (.342), and he won multiple batting titles (four). I chose the longtime Tigers' right fielder as the better choice for ninth place because of run production. Harry averaged 1.23 net runs per contest to Tony's .98, and that advantage of a quarter of a run per game is significant enough in my mind to separate the two. Gwynn definitely holds the upper hand in the postseason; Heilmann's teams never played in October. However, I would still choose Harry over the career National Leaguer, by a slim margin, if given the opportunity.

8. Reggie Jackson

While Reggie never hit for exceedingly high averages like Gwynn or Heilmann, he did hit with power (563 career homers). Furthermore, he won an MVP, something that the previous two weren't able to accomplish. Most important, I felt that Jackson's multiple World Series MVPs were enough to push him into a Category 5 ranking and ahead of Harry Heilmann for this spot.

7. Roberto Clemente

Clemente also won a regular-season MVP and one World Series MVP. He didn't hit with the same power as Jackson, but I prefer him for this spot because of his defense and his ability to hit for average. Clemente led the NL in batting four times and won the Gold Glove every year from 1961 to 1972, making him arguably the greatest defensive outfielder in history. Roberto also averaged more net runs per game, 1.02 to Jackson's .95. I think many people would probably put Clemente even higher on this list.

6. Sammy Sosa

In placing Sosa ahead of Clemente, I have tried my best to ignore steroid allegations and simply focus on the numbers and the accomplishments. Slammin' Sammy put together years that Clemente never did. In fact, he put together years that no one else in history is able to match. While Roberto never hit 30 homers in a season, Sammy hit more than double that amount three times. From 1998 to 2001 Sosa hit more balls out of the park (243) than the Pittsburgh right fielder hit in 18 seasons (240). In terms of P/E, Sosa's score is more than 100 points ahead of Clemente's.

5. Mel Ott

I chose Mel Ott over Sosa for a few reasons. First, his lifetime numbers are better. Ott scored 1,859 runs and drove in 1,860. Sosa doesn't come close to those totals. Second, the lifelong Giants teammate was more productive, averaging 1.18 net runs to 1.08 for Sosa. Finally, I love Ott for the top five based on the fact that their walks-to-strike-outs ratios are nearly identical . . . in reverse. Ott received 1,708 free passes while fanning 896 times. Sammy walked 929 times while whiffing on more than 2,300 occasions. P/E Averages don't take strikeouts into account. If they did, Ott's lead in that statistic would be much higher than the 69-point advantage he currently owns.

4. Manny Ramirez

Manny earns this ranking over Ott for one reason: run production. Ramirez will one day retire and go down as one of the great RBI men of all time. While he hasn't yet reached Ott's lifetime numbers, he does better his National League peer in terms of net runs per game. Ramirez averages more than a run and a quarter (1.26) per contest.

The Top Three

Hank Aaron, Frank Robinson, and Babe Ruth each put together incredible careers and were able to distance themselves from a talented field with their unparalleled numbers. The section titled "Power and Production" at the end of this chapter clearly illustrates just how dominant this trio was in comparison with the other top groups of the infield and outfield. At one time, Aaron, Ruth, and Robinson ranked one, two, and four, respectively, on the all-time home-run list. They currently rank two, three, and seven.

The Case for Aaron

755 home runs; 2,297 runs batted in; 6,856 total bases

21 consecutive All-Star nominations (1955–1975)

19 consecutive years earning MVP votes (1955–1973)

Three National League Gold Gloves for right field (1958–1960)

3,771 career hits (third most in baseball history)

The Case for Robinson

Won MVP in both National League and American League

National League Rookie of the Year in 1956

Player of the Year/Triple Crown winner in 1966 (.316 BA, 49 home
    runs, 122 RBI)

Most Valuable Player of '66 World Series

Six All-Star appearances in each league

The Case for Ruth

P/E Averages: 1.436 career; 1.449 postseason; eight seasons above
    1.500

1.47 net runs per game

Lifetime averages of .342 batting, .474 on-base, and .690 slugging

Nine seasons with more than 45 home runs; led league in homers
    12 times

Played in 10 World Series and won 7

3. Frank Robinson

Frank Robinson won two MVPs, and Manny Ramirez hasn't won any as of yet. Therefore, the decision to put him in the top three over Manny was fairly easy. Most Valuable Player success, in my opinion, is an important indicator of a player's effectiveness. In addition, Robinson won a Gold Glove in the outfield. While I don't think Manny is as poor defensively as people often think, he wasn't nearly as good as Robinson. Granted, if Ramirez continues to put up incredible production numbers year after year, then he may one day deserve a spot ahead of Frank. It will take a lot for that to occur, however. Ramirez's best chance, in my eyes, is to take home some MVP hardware, something Frank Robinson did in each league.

2. Hank Aaron

It's the silver medal for Henry Aaron. The man with more All-Star appearances than any other deserves spot number 2. True, Frank Robinson won two MVPs to Aaron's sole award in '57. However, Aaron also finished third six times, and he owns more career shares (5.45 to 4.83). In the final analysis, I simply couldn't overlook Aaron's substantial lead in the lifetime numbers. While the two are similar in terms of P/E Average and the three standard efficiency measures, Frank is way behind Henry in overall statistics. Aaron hit 169 more homers, drove in 485 more runs, and registered 828 more hits. Aaron was slightly more productive on a per-game basis (1.13 net runs per contest to 1.09), but it's the longevity and sustainability that won me over. In their prime, I think they were probably similar players, about even in terms of their overall ability and worth. Hank Aaron simply had more good years, and that's the reason for his placement here.

1. Babe Ruth

Was there ever really any doubt? For as great as Hank Aaron was, Ruth was even better. He didn't hit as many homers, but he did hit them at a far superior rate. Aaron averaged a home run every 16.38 at-bats while Ruth hit one every 11.76 at-bats, the second best rate in history. Aaron hit more than 45 homers once; Ruth achieved that feat nine times. Hank hit 41 more home runs than Babe, approximately one good season's worth. However, he appeared in almost 800 more games, approximately five full seasons.

When it came to run production, it wasn't much of a contest either. The Sultan of Swat averaged 1.47 net runs per game, a mark 30 percent higher than Aaron's average of 1.13. It can certainly be argued that Ruth benefited from Gehrig hitting behind him, yet I think that the difference in run production goes beyond the Iron Horse's protection. Remember, Ruth's 1921 season, in which he scored 177 and drove in 171, occurred without Gehrig's presence. In 3,324 fewer plate appearances, Ruth scored as many runs as Aaron and only drove in 80 fewer. In substantially more time at the plate, Aaron produced only 39 more net runs than the Sultan of Swat, a gap that Ruth probably could have closed in approximately one month of playing time.

You can go through the numbers however you'd like, but I still see Ruth as the clear-cut choice for the top spot. Aaron fans shouldn't lament. There are worse things that can be said about a ballplayer than he finished second to Babe Ruth.

Power and Production

More than any other position, the top three right fielders were legends when it came to power and production. The chart below lists my top three at each position and notes their combined totals for home runs, runs scored, RBI, and net runs. As you can see, no other spot in either the infield or the outfield can match the trio of Hank Aaron, Frank Robinson, and Babe Ruth in terms of knocking the ball over the fence and putting runs on the scoreboard.

Position	My Top 3 Players	HR	Runs Scored	RBI	Net Runs
C	Bench, Berra, Campanella	866	3,307	3,638	6,079
1B	Foxx, Gehrig, Greenberg	1,358	4,690	5,193	8,525
2B	Gehringer, Hornsby, Morgan	753	5,003	4,144	8,394
3B	Brett, Robinson, Schmidt	1,133	4,321	4,547	7,735
SS	Ripken, Rodriguez, Wagner	1,050	4,884	4,930	8,764
LF	Bonds, Musial, Williams	1,732	5,900	5,709	9,877
CF	Cobb, DiMaggio, Mays	1,138	5,698	5,377	9,937
RF	Aaron, Robinson, Ruth	2,055	6,177	6,326	10,448

Multiposition

Some people simply have no place to go. Such is the case with this chapter's players, men who never found one position on the field at which to spend at least 60 percent of their games. For the sake of organization, I've also included designated hitters in this chapter; if a player was primarily a DH, even for more than 60 percent of his total games played, you will find him here with the multiposition athletes.

Perhaps the biggest complaint my readers may have will focus on Ernie Banks. I'm sure there will be those who feel that Banks should be included with the shortstops, where he would give Wagner, A-Rod, Ripken, and Jeter a good run for their money. After all, he won back-to-back MVPs and a Gold Glove at that position. I understand the thinking, but it doesn't meet the criteria I have set forth. Not only did Banks fail to play 60 percent of his games at short, but he actually played more career games at first base.

I have also decided not to include a top-10 list for this chapter. With each player appearing in a variety of positions spanning different eras in baseball history, I felt it would be fruitless and unfair to rank them against one another. Do I give a player credit for jumping from one position to another, or should that be looked on as a negative? I wasn't sure how to answer that question, so I'm not even going to try. Besides, if you've read this far, then you are probably very familiar with my thinking and analysis. I prefer players who are run producers, have MVP credentials, and have succeeded in October.

Although it may appear as if these players have no place to call home, the more appropriate perspective is that this chapter focuses on some of the most talented and versatile players the game has ever known. Think of them as jacks-of-all-trades and enjoy the analyses that follow.

Multiposition: Career P/E Averages

Frank Thomas, 1.169; Jim Thome, 1.168; David Ortiz, 1.163; Richie Allen, 1.108; Jose Canseco, 1.107; Jackie Robinson, 1.094; Edgar Martinez, 1.090; Willie Stargell, 1.078; Harmon Killebrew, 1.052; Jack Clark, 1.030; Ernie Banks, 1.000; Paul Molitor, .993; Freddie Lindstrom, .981; Harold Baines, .971; Al Oliver, .952; Darrell Evans, .941; Rod Carew, .938; Robin Yount, .938; Joe Torre, .940; Pete Rose, .890; Hubie Brooks, .850; Joel Youngblood, .833; Joe McEwing, .752

Category 1–3 Multiposition Players

Harold Baines

Career P/E: .971; Postseason P/E: .982

Notable seasons (P/E): 1982 (1.016); 1985 (1.004); 1999 (1.156)

With 2,866 hits and more than 1,600 RBI, there is legitimacy to any claim to induct Harold Baines into the Hall of Fame. Throughout the 1980s and occasionally in the 1990s, Baines was a solid run producer, playing the majority of his career with the White Sox. Harold topped 100 runs batted in three times, including 113 in 1985 and 103 near the end of his career in 1999, the year in which he posted his highest P/E. Most impressive is the fact that he hit better than .350 in five different postseason series.

Baines finished in the top 10 of the MVP vote twice but earned only .29 shares over 22 seasons in the big leagues. Aside from leading the AL in slugging in '84 (.541), Harold was never among the league leaders in the major offensive categories. For his career, he averaged .90 net runs per game, a respectable but not overwhelming score.

Looking quickly at his career statistics, it might appear that he was Hall of Fame material. On closer inspection, however, you find a very good ballplayer, but one who didn't distinguish himself among his peers. Therefore, I've decided on a rating of C3.

Hubie Brooks

Career P/E: .850; Postseason P/E: never in the postseason

Notable seasons (P/E): 1985 (.911); 1988 (.900); 1990 (.917)

The New York Mets must have felt that they let another talented player slip away after they witnessed what Hubie Brooks did for the

Montreal Expos in 1985. Traded north after the '84 season in a package for Gary Carter, Brooks showed his former team that he could put up big numbers. Hubie knocked in 100 runs, reached 250 total bases for the season, and legged out 34 doubles. In limited action, Brooks hit .340 in 1986.

The Mets brought Brooks back for the '91 campaign after watching him perform very well in the second half of the 1980s. It turned out to be a bad move. Brooks batted just .238 with 50 RBI for New York. As it turned out, 1991 was Brooks's last noteworthy season. The Mets parted ways with him after one year, and then Hubie headed to the Angels and Royals for his last three seasons, playing 82 games or less in each one.

Brooks is a Category 2. He has no chance for Cooperstown; no C2 player does. Hubie had some good seasons in baseball, but he certainly can't be rated any higher. Brooks played in more than 500 games in both the outfield and at third base while also spending considerable time (371 games) at shortstop.

Edgar Martinez

Career P/E: 1.090; Postseason P/E: 1.014
Notable seasons (P/E): 1995 (1.340); 1996 (1.300); 1997 (1.174);
    2000 (1.266)

At DH, Martinez was a hitting machine. He won two batting titles and led the league in on-base percentage three times. Edgar retired with tremendous efficiency averages in the regular season (.311 BA, .418 OBP, .515 SLP), but his display in the first round of the '95 playoffs truly showed his worth. In addition to his game-winning double in Game 5, Martinez also smacked two homers with seven RBI in Game 4 to keep hope alive.

Martinez's chances for Cooperstown will probably be hurt by two facts: he was primarily a designated hitter, and he earned only 1.01 career shares in MVP voting.

I always loved watching Martinez hit. He routinely killed the Yankees and was one of the few batters to give Mariano Rivera trouble. However, I don't see Edgar as a Hall of Famer. His chances are in the doubtful to possible range, and he's C3.

Joe McEwing

Career P/E: .752; Postseason P/E: 3.500
Notable seasons (P/E): 1999 (.791); 2001 (.887)

The player with the highest postseason P/E score in this entire book is Joe McEwing, who registers a huge number of 3.500. Why is his average so high? Simple. McEwing frequently appeared in games as a pinch-runner, thereby scoring runs without accumulating plate appearances. In the 2000 postseason, Super Joe scored three runs while only appearing twice in the batter's box. Therefore, his P/E number is inflated.

The 141 hits Joe laced in 1999 represent almost a third of his career base knocks. He has failed to stake a claim for himself in a team's lineup on a daily basis, even though he is versatile and has a reputation for hitting Randy Johnson.

McEwing is Category 1 for the multiposition chapter. A true jack-of-all-trades, Super Joe has been a valuable complementary player on some talented teams, but he has never really established himself as an everyday player.

Joe Torre

Career P/E: .940; Postseason P/E: never in the postseason

Notable seasons (P/E): 1964 (1.071); 1966 (1.075); 1970 (1.028); 1971 (1.191)

Before he won multiple championships as skipper of the Yankees, Joe Torre had a very successful playing tenure in the 1960s and 1970s. Torre, who played his entire career as a National Leaguer, had unquestionably his best season in 1971. Walking away with a near-unanimous MVP (he received .95 shares) as well as Major League Player of the Year honors, Torre established himself as a top player. He led the NL with a .363 average and set career highs in runs (97), hits (230), RBI (137), and on-base percentage (.421). Although he played third and first, he spent the most career games behind the plate.

Torre will certainly make it into the Hall of Fame one day, but that will come as a result of his managerial résumé and not his playing one. Although his career numbers are very good, they are probably a little shy of what's needed for induction. Joe just missed hitting .300 for his career by three points and was only four runs short of 1,000. Ironically, Joe Torre the player never once appeared in the postseason, a place that has become like a second home to him since becoming the manager of the New York Yankees.

Joe Torre had a C3 playing career. Like many baseball writers, I think he was just a notch below a Hall of Famer. Certainly, his MVP season of '71 was spectacular. I just think he needed a couple more big seasons to earn my vote. In terms of managerial success, however, Joe has an imminent induction ceremony in Cooperstown, New York, awaiting him one day in the future.

Joel Youngblood

Career P/E: .833; Postseason P/E: never in the postseason
Notable seasons (P/E): 1979 (.898); 1980 (.851); 1983 (1.005)

Joel Youngblood played 14 major league seasons, enjoying limited success over a fairly long career. Mainly an outfielder, Youngblood also saw significant time at third and second. For the '79 Mets, he scored 90 runs, hit 16 homers, and batted .275. Two years later, Joel made the All-Star team despite playing only 43 games for New York.

Youngblood was a relatively well-known name in baseball in the '70s and '80s, but his career totals are nothing to write home about. He retired with less than 1,000 hits even though he appeared in more than 1,400 games.

Were it not for a 14-year stay in the big leagues, Youngblood would be C1. Being good enough to play professionally for almost a decade and a half earns him Category 2.

The Best Multiposition Players

162-Game Averages

Player	BA	OBP	SLP	HR	TB	R	RBI	H	XBH	BB	K	SB
Banks	.274	.330	.500	33	302	84	105	166	65	49	79	3
Carew	.328	.393	.429	6	262	93	67	200	42	67	67	23
Killebrew	.256	.376	.509	38	276	85	105	139	59	104	113	1
Molitor	.306	.369	.448	14	293	108	79	200	58	66	75	30
Robinson	.311	.409	.474	16	271	111	86	178	54	87	34	23
Rose	.303	.375	.409	7	262	98	60	194	47	71	52	9
Stargell	.282	.360	.529	33	288	82	106	153	66	64	133	1
Thomas	.303	.421	.561	37	321	106	120	173	73	117	96	2
Yount	.285	.342	.430	14	268	93	80	178	54	55	77	15

Category 4 Multiposition Players

Rod Carew

Career P/E: .938; Postseason P/E: .618

MVP: American League MVP in 1977; 1.80 career shares

Hall of Fame: inducted in 1991

The best quote I ever read about Rod Carew was delivered by Alan Bannister, also a multiposition player from the '70s and '80s. Describing Carew's uncanny hitting ability, Bannister quipped, "He's the only guy I know who can go four for three." That short, witty description perfectly described Carew; he was one of the game's most deft and skilled hitters, a maestro with a bat in his hand. He was never better than in 1977. Ending the season with a .388 average, Carew set career highs in virtually every major offensive category. His 239 hits included 68 that went for extra bases. He drove in 100, scored 128, and surpassed 350 total bases. Rod walked away with the AL MVP trophy.

Other than in '77, Carew never reached 100 runs either scored or driven in. His career average of .95 net runs per game fails to distinguish him among the game's elite run producers. Furthermore, Carew lacked power, hitting more than nine homers in a season only twice and playing in 142 games in 1972 without a single long ball over the fence.

Carew's lack of power and production relegate him to C4 status. Granted, I was very tempted to make him a C5 based on his batting titles and expertise with the lumber. Another MVP, a few Gold Gloves, or postseason success would have pushed him higher.

Year	RBI	R	HR	NR	TB	BB	HBP	SB	CS	CB	PTS	PA	P/E
1975	80	89	14	155	266	64	1	35	9	357	667	617	1.081
1976	90	97	9	178	280	67	1	49	22	375	731	687	1.064
1977	100	128	14	214	351	69	3	23	13	433	861	694	1.241
Career	1,015	1,424	92	2,347	3,998	1,018	25	353	187	5,207	9,901	10,550	.938

Paul Molitor

Career P/E: .993; Postseason P/E: 1.326
MVP: never won; 1.43 career shares
Hall of Fame: inducted in 2004

Like wine, some athletes seem to get better with age. Such was the case with Paul Molitor. Playing for the Twins in 1996, the 40-year-old Molitor had arguably his best season, setting career bests in hits (225) and RBI (113). He batted .341 and was directly responsible for more than 200 runs on Minnesota's scoreboard. October is when Molitor normally was at his best. Joining the Blue Jays just in time to win a championship with them in 1993, Molitor was selected World Series MVP after batting .500, generating 16 net runs, and producing an eye-popping P/E Average of 2.179, making his performance one of the greatest ever in the history of the Fall Classic. In '87, a season in which he hit .353, Paul captured the nation's attention with a 39-game hitting streak.

I think there are probably two knocks that can be made against Molitor's career. First, he never won an MVP, finishing second in '93 and earning only 1.43 career shares. Second, he never hit with a lot of power, except perhaps in his first season with Toronto (22 homers, .509 slugging). He averaged only 14 long balls every 162 games.

Molitor is a no-doubt Hall of Famer, but I don't think he's on the elite level in terms of my rating system. Without an MVP, a Gold Glove, or a batting title, I am forced to relegate him to Category 4.

Year	RBI	R	HR	NR	TB	BB	HBP	SB	CS	CB	PTS	PA	P/E
1987	75	114	16	173	263	69	2	45	10	369	715	542	1.319
1993	111	121	22	210	324	77	3	22	4	422	842	725	1.161
1996	113	99	9	203	309	56	3	18	6	380	786	728	1.080
Career	1,307	1,782	234	2,855	4,854	1,094	47	504	131	6,368	12,078	12,160	.993

Jackie Robinson

Career P/E: 1.094; Postseason P/E: .863

MVP: National League MVP in 1949; 1.74 career shares

Hall of Fame: inducted in 1962

When Robinson appeared in a Dodgers uniform in '47 (originally at first base), his impact became readily apparent. He walked away with the NL's Rookie of the Year honor while also finishing fifth in the MVP race. Two years later, Robinson turned in a virtuoso performance. The 1949 campaign saw Jackie dominate National League pitching to the tune of a .342 batting average, 203 hits, and 230 net runs of offense. The voters had no choice but to select him as the league's Most Valuable Player. In only his third season, Robinson had done the unthinkable. Not only had he survived the insults and threats and obvious racism that plagued society, but he had also risen to the top of his profession, earning recognition as the best player in the National League.

Robinson's career lasted only 10 seasons, so many of his cumulative statistics are not overwhelmingly impressive. For example, he failed to reach 1,000 runs scored, and he recorded just over 1,500 hits. In five of his six World Series, Jackie batted less than .260.

Robinson's amazing determination and bravery cannot be measured; it can only be appreciated and learned from. On the diamond, he was a multitalented player who should have been able to display his talents sooner. It's C4 for baseball's ultimate hero.

Year	RBI	R	HR	NR	TB	BB	HBP	SB	CS	CB	PTS	PA	P/E
1947	48	125	12	161	252	74	9	29	9*	355	677	701	.966
1949	124	122	16	230	313	86	8	37	11*	433	893	704	1.268
1953	95	109	12	192	243	74	7	17	4	337	721	574	1.256
Career	734	947	137	1,544	2,310	740	72	197	61*	3,258	6,346	5,802	1.094

* CS totals estimated based on known statistics

Willie Stargell

Career P/E: 1.078; Postseason P/E: .967
MVP: National League co-MVP in 1979; 3.30 career shares
Hall of Fame: inducted in 1988

Not many athletes have ever been as beloved as Willie Stargell in Pittsburgh. Pops played his entire 21 years with the Pirates, belting 475 homers and driving in 1,540 runs over his tenure. Despite winning co-MVP honors with Keith Hernandez in '79, Stargell's best seasons were probably 1971 and 1973, years in which the lovable Pirates outfielder finished as runner-up in league balloting. Willie hit 48 home runs in '71 and then connected for another 44 two years later, establishing himself as one of the game's best long-ball threats. His blasts didn't just clear the fences either; he hit some of the longest home runs in National League history. Both seasons, Stargell generated 181 net runs while finishing the season with remarkably similar P/E numbers.

I think Hernandez definitely had the better year in '79 and probably deserved the MVP outright. Keith hit .344 with 210 hits and 210 net runs, but his Cardinals finished in third place in their division. Stargell, conversely, generated exactly 100 fewer net runs and played in only 126 games, yet his Pirates ball club won 98 games and made the playoffs.

For me, Stargell's most impressive number is 3.30; that's his career total of MVP shares. Willie, Category 4, finished in the top three four times and in the top 10 seven times.

Year	RBI	R	HR	NR	TB	BB	HBP	SB	CS	CB	PTS	PA	P/E
1971	125	104	48	181	321	83	7	0	0	411	773	606	1.276
1973	119	106	44	181	337	80	3	0	0	420	782	609	1.284
1979	82	60	32	110	234	47	3	0	1	283	503	480	1.048
Career	1,540	1,195	475	2,260	4,190	937	78	17	16	5,206	9,726	9,026	1.078

Robin Yount

Career P/E: .938; Postseason P/E: 1.000

MVP: American League MVP in 1982, 1989; 1.80 career shares

Hall of Fame: inducted in 1999

The 1982 Milwaukee Brewers were led by shortstop Robin Yount, who was named American League MVP. That year, Yount set career highs in batting average (.331), net runs (214), and P/E Average (1.223). In a loaded lineup that featured Paul Molitor, Cecil Cooper, Ben Oglivie, and Ted Simmons, Yount was the unquestioned star, and his near-unanimous MVP win (he earned .98 shares) demonstrated that. Although the Cardinals won the World Series in seven games, Yount was nonetheless magnificent, with 12 hits, 11 net runs, and a .414 batting average. His P/E against St. Louis in '82 was 1.355. Robin proved his first MVP was no fluke when he won the honor again in '89. For the second time, Yount surpassed 100 runs both scored and driven home in the same season.

Yount never hit with a tremendous amount of power, although his 29 homers and .578 slugging average in '82 were impressive. He hit 251 career round-trippers but only topped 20 four times, never reaching 30. Surprisingly, Yount accumulated only 1.80 career MVP shares despite twice taking home the trophy.

Yount is Category 4. He starred at both shortstop and center field, winning two MVPs, but failed to have enough other great seasons to warrant a higher rating.

Year	RBI	R	HR	NR	TB	BB	HBP	SB	CS	CB	PTS	PA	P/E
1980	87	121	23	185	317	26	1	20	5	359	729	647	1.127
1982	114	129	29	214	367	54	1	14	3	433	861	704	1.223
1989	103	101	21	183	314	63	6	19	3	399	765	690	1.109
Career	1,406	1,632	251	2,787	4,730	966	48	271	105	5,910	11,484	12,249	.938

Category 5 Multiposition Players

Ernie Banks

Height: 6′1″; Weight: 180; Bats: right; Throws: right

First game: September 17, 1953; Final game: September 26, 1971

Team(s): Chicago Cubs (1953–1971)

MVP: National League MVP in 1958, 1959; 2.83 career shares

Hall of Fame: inducted in 1977

162-game avg.: .274 batting, .330 on-base, .500 slugging,
  33 home runs, 302 total bases, 84 runs scored,
  105 runs batted in, 166 hits, 65 extra-base hits, 49 BB,
  79 K, 3 SB

Career P/E: 1.000; Postseason P/E: never in the postseason

The Good. Let's play two! Ernie Banks was the well-known and much-loved face of the Chicago Cubs franchise for almost two decades, earning him the nickname Mr. Cub. Banks played mostly shortstop from 1953 to 1961, yet he wasn't the conventional player at this position normally reserved for light-hitting, slick-fielding glove men. In 1955, playing every game at short, Banks hit 44 homers, knocked in 117, and slugged .596, unheard-of numbers for his position.

Three years later, in 1958, Banks won the first of his two consecutive Most Valuable Player awards. Mr. Cub again topped 40 homers (47) while generating 201 net runs of offense. He led the league in long balls as well as runs batted in (129). In '59 Banks again led the league in RBI, this time knocking in 143 runs. Ernie reached 350 total bases for the third time in his career, winning another MVP. In both '58 and '59 Banks hit better than .300 and posted P/E Averages above 1.200.

Mr. Cub finished his career with 1,636 RBI, more than 1,300 runs scored, more than 2,500 hits, and 512 home runs. In addition to his back-to-back MVPs, he also finished third, fourth, and sixth, totaling 2.83 career shares. Banks was runner-up for the 1954 Rookie of the Year honor, won a Gold Glove at shortstop in 1960, and made 11 All-Star contests between 1955 and 1969. He led the league in homers twice and was a mainstay in the Cubs lineup, playing in at least 150 games in a season a dozen times.

The Bad. Ernie Banks never appeared in the postseason. By far, that is the biggest hole in his great, Hall of Fame career. The Cubs posted losing records in each of Banks's first 10 seasons and were below .500 in 13 of 14 years to begin his career. Notably, Chicago finished with a winning record in each of Banks's last five major league seasons, but they were unable to make the playoffs every time.

After 1961 Ernie Banks never appeared at shortstop again. Aside from a few games at third, Banks became a first baseman. Interestingly, he ended up with more games played at first (1,259) than short (1,125), a fact I didn't realize until I began my research for this book.

The Verdict. Mr. Cub deserves C5 status. He drove in more than 100 runs eight times and hit more than 40 homers five times from '55 to '60, when Banks was truly a dominant player in the National League. It's a shame we can't talk about his postseason record, however, but that fact doesn't hold me back from placing him among the game's best with a Category 5 rating.

Harmon Killebrew

Height: 5'11"; Weight: 213; Bats: right; Throws: right

First game: June 23, 1954; Final game: September 26, 1975

Team(s): Washington Senators (1954–1960); Minnesota Twins
(1961–1974); Kansas City Royals (1975)

MVP: American League MVP in 1969; 3.23 career shares

Hall of Fame: inducted in 1984

162-game avg.: .256 batting, .376 on-base, .509 slugging, 38 home
runs, 276 total bases, 85 runs scored, 105 runs batted in, 139 hits,
59 extra-base hits, 104 BB, 113 K, 1 SB

Career P/E: 1.052; Postseason P/E: .963

The Good. Hitting 40 home runs in a season is a major accomplishment. Back in the '50s, '60s, and '70s, it was an even rarer occurrence, normally reserved for baseball's true superstars. Harmon Clayton Killebrew accomplished that feat eight times from 1959 to 1970, establishing himself as one of the game's most feared hitters during that span. Killebrew also smacked 25 or more out of the park in five other seasons, and he hung up his spikes with 573 dingers, more than Reggie Jackson, Mike Schmidt, and Mickey Mantle.

Harmon began his career with the Senators but became best known (and entered the Hall of Fame) as a member of the Minnesota Twins. When he joined the team in 1961, he was an instant success, hitting 46 home runs and knocking in 122 while reaching base safely more than 40 percent of the time. Throughout the 1960s, Harmon continued to terrorize AL pitchers, who often steered clear of him by issuing free passes to first. He capped the decade off with his best season (P/E: 1.233). In 1969 Killer was named American League MVP after leading the league in on-base percentage (.427), walks (145), home runs (49), and runs batted in (140).

The stocky power hitter from Idaho made 11 All-Star teams over his major league tenure. He led the league in RBI three times and in home runs six times. In the second half of his career especially, Killer often walked far more than he struck out, including a ratio of 273 bases on balls to 168 whiffs in '69 and '70, especially good for a power hitter. In addition to his MVP, Killebrew also finished in the top four on five other occasions, earning 3.23 career shares.

The Bad. Harmon's teams went 0–3 in the postseason, and he wasn't much of a factor in any of those appearances. In the '65 World Series, he knocked in only two runs over seven games. In back-to-back ALCS in '69 and '70, Killebrew batted a combined .211, although he did hit two home runs against Baltimore pitching in their 1970 meeting.

Harmon Killebrew never hit better than .288, and he retired as a .256 lifetime batter. He had a rough year in 1968, playing in only 100 games and batting .210 with 40 RBI (P/E: .868). With almost no speed to speak of, he managed just 19 career steals.

The Verdict. Killebrew's power and MVP success make him Category 5. Most impressive are his eight 40-homer and nine 100-RBI seasons. The quiet man with the powerful stroke was a fearsome hitter in the American League and should have been inducted earlier than 1984.

Pete Rose

Height: 5′11″; Weight: 200; Bats: both; Throws: right

First game: April 8, 1963; Final game: August 17, 1986

Team(s): Cincinnati Reds (1963–1978, 1984–1986); Philadelphia
   Phillies (1979–1983); Montreal Expos (1984)

MVP: National League MVP in 1973; 3.68 career shares

Hall of Fame: doubtful

162-game avg.: .303 batting, .375 on-base, .409 slugging, 7 home
   runs, 262 total bases, 98 runs scored, 60 runs batted in, 194 hits,
   47 extra-base hits, 71 BB, 52 K, 9 SB

Career P/E: .890; Postseason P/E: .797

The Good. With 4,256 career base knocks, Pete Rose is officially baseball's hit king. Over the course of 24 seasons, Rose accumulated some
tremendous numbers. In addition to ranking number one all-time in
hits, Rose also ranks sixth in runs scored and first in at-bats. Perhaps
most impressive, Rose's total of 5,929 times on base is the highest in
history, with Ty Cobb in second place almost 400 behind. Rose was
an integral piece on Cincinnati's championship teams of the 1970s.
In 1973 Charlie Hustle won the NL Most Valuable Player award after
hitting .338 on 230 hits while scoring 115 runs. Rose hit .381 throughout the NLCS that year against the Mets.

Over the course of his major league tenure, Rose won three batting
titles, two Gold Gloves (both as an outfielder), and the 1963 Rookie
of the Year honor. He made his way onto 17 All-Star teams as well.
When Cincinnati's Big Red Machine won the World Series in 1975,
Pete Rose was named MVP. He batted .370 with 10 hits and five walks
against the Red Sox after hitting .357 in the National League Cham-

pionship Series. For his career, Rose batted .321 in the postseason, going 6–1 in NLCS play and winning three championship rings.

Rose was always known for his hustling, hard-nosed style of play. His longevity and ability to stay in the lineup day after day was remarkable. Fifteen times, Rose had 700 or more plate appearances in a season. He accomplished that feat every year from 1969 to 1980, an amazing run of playing nearly every single day for a dozen years.

Charlie Hustle hustled his way to 3.68 career MVP shares. In addition to winning the award in '73, Rose also finished second in '68, in the top five three other times, and in the top 10 a total of 10 times. He led the NL in runs scored four times, in hits seven times, and in doubles five times.

The Bad. Rose's lack of power is the reason for his .890 career P/E mark. He hit singles and doubles almost exclusively, which explains his career slugging percentage of .409. Pete topped a 1.000 P/E only twice in his career despite frequently batting above .300.

The Verdict. If Pete Rose is ever to be inducted into the Hall of Fame, then he will need to be reinstated first. He received a lifetime ban from baseball in 1989 after gambling allegations and evidence thereof continued to mount. I think that baseball may one day reinstate him and allow him to enter Cooperstown. His play on the field unmistakably made him a Hall of Famer. Unfortunately, other actions may have sealed his fate. I believe Rose is Category 5.

Frank Thomas

Height: 6′5″; Weight: 257; Bats: right; Throws: right

First game: August 2, 1990; Final game: still active

Team(s): Chicago White Sox (1990–2005); Oakland Athletics
(2006); Toronto Blue Jays (2007–present)

MVP: American League MVP in 1993, 1994; 4.79 career shares
(through '06 voting)

Hall of Fame: imminent

162-game avg.: .303 batting, .421 on-base, .561 slugging, 37 home
runs, 321 total bases, 106 runs scored, 120 runs batted in, 173
hits, 73 extra-base hits, 117 BB, 96 K, 2 SB

Career P/E: 1.169; Postseason P/E: .794

The Good. Big Hurt has been injuring the careers of American League
pitchers for almost two decades. The former first-round pick (seventh
overall) of the 1989 amateur draft by the White Sox has put together
a legendary career, evidenced by a lifetime P/E of 1.169 and almost
five full career shares (4.79) in balloting.

Twice named American League MVP, Thomas first won the prestigious award in 1993. The Chicago slugger batted .317 and used his
41 home runs to help generate 193 runs of offense for his club.
Impressively, he walked far more often (112 times) than he struck out
(54) that season. His ability to draw free passes and avoid swinging at
pitchers' pitches has stayed with him throughout much of his career;
his lifetime on-base percentage of .421 is outstanding.

Baseball came to a grinding halt in the strike-shortened season of
1994, but Frank Thomas kept chugging along. Again walking away
with AL MVP honors, Thomas recorded the best P/E Average (1.429)

of his career. In only 113 games, Big Hurt scored 106 times and drove in 101. He batted .353 that season and slugged .729 while reaching base safely in nearly half of his plate appearances (.487).

When it looked as if Thomas's career was headed south, he put up huge numbers in 2000. Frank set career marks in home runs (43), extra-base hits (87), runs (115), and RBI (143). The 2006 season was also one that witnessed a resurgence in his career. Playing in an Oakland uniform, the former Auburn University star drove home 114 runs and finished fourth in league balloting for Most Valuable Player.

The Bad. In the postseason, Thomas has been up and down. Although he was great in the '93 ALCS and the '06 ALDS, he also had two other postseason series, the '00 ALDS and the '06 ALCS, in which he failed to register a hit, a run, or an RBI. A player of Thomas's stature occupying a prime spot in the middle of a lineup needs to be more consistent in October. In a twist of unfortunate irony for Frank, the 2005 White Sox won the World Series without him on their postseason roster.

The Verdict. Thomas should be a first-ballot Hall of Famer when his turn comes up. He was simply dominant in the 1990s, and he's had enough other success ('00, '03, and '06) to guarantee himself a place in Cooperstown. According to my system, he rates as Category 5 and would be the top-ranked player in this chapter if a top-10 list were given.

Jack-of-All-Trades

So exactly where did these multiposition stars play? Some spread themselves thin at a variety of positions while others just missed reaching 60 percent of their total games played at one spot. Perhaps by looking at where they played, we can more accurately assess their worth. For example, a shortstop with a .285 batting average and 175 net runs is probably far more valuable than a left fielder with the same statistics. The following list offers the career games played at each position by every Category 4 and 5 player from this chapter. Simply adding each position's total will not result in total games played. Pinch-hitting, pinch-running, and single games played at more than one position affect each player's career total, from which the 60 percent threshold is calculated.

- Ernie Banks

    1B—1,259; SS—1,125; 3B—69; OF—23; 2,528 total games played

- Rod Carew

    1B—1,184; 2B—1,130; DH—68; SS—4; 3B—2; OF—1; 2,469 total games played

- Harmon Killebrew

    1B—969; 3B—791; OF—470; DH—158; 2B—11; 2,435 total games played

- Paul Molitor

    DH—1,174; 3B—791; 2B—400; 1B—197; SS—57; OF—50; 2,683 total games played

- Jackie Robinson

  2B—748; 3B—256; 1B—197; OF—162; SS—1; 1,382 total games played

- Pete Rose

  OF—1,327; 1B—939; 3B—634; 2B—628; 3,562 total games played

- Willie Stargell

  OF—1,296; 1B—848; 2,360 total games played

- Frank Thomas

  DH—1,242; 1B—971; 2,251 total games played

- Robin Yount

  SS—1,479; OF—1,218; DH—138; 1B—12; 2,856 total games played

11

Nineteenth-Century Stars

Perhaps more than any other sport, baseball has a history and a past second to none. Essentially, all you really need to play is a ball, a bat, some willing participants, and enough open space for a field. Although simple bat and ball games have been around for hundreds (and probably even thousands) of years, the organized game we know so well today took root in the 1840s in New York City. The New York Knickerbockers were founded on September 23, 1845, adopting a set of rules by which they would be governed. One of the most important guidelines restricted players from throwing the ball at one another; players needed to be either tagged or forced out. Ever since, the rules have transformed, and the game has evolved, but the essence of baseball has remained the same.

In this chapter, I have analyzed 20 Hall of Famers who played before the turn of the twentieth century. Some of them date back to the 1870s, while others played well into the modern era. I felt it was appropriate to give these players special recognition in their own chapter. They each played a part in laying the foundation for the sport they loved. Many of them played for teams unknown to most people, such as the Boston Beaneaters and the Louisville Colonels. From Cap

Anson to Monte Ward, Chapter 11 provides a brief glimpse into the careers of the stars from the nineteenth century.

Statistical record keeping was not always what it is today. Many of the players featured in the upcoming pages had incomplete stats, especially for stolen bases, strikeouts, and hit by pitch. Furthermore, there was a time in the 1800s when bases on balls were counted as hits, thereby inflating batting averages. Therefore, I have kept my comments on these players brief and have avoided calculating P/E Averages, which I thought would be quite futile. In terms of statistical commentary, I have abided by the numbers set forth by baseball-reference.com, an outstanding Internet resource for anyone interested in anything about baseball.

The game has changed since the days of Dan Brouthers, King Kelly, and Wee Willie Keeler, but the essential nature of the sport has remained. Baseball is beautiful because there is no clock, and it is a natural human instinct to pick up an object (like a ball) and hurl it through the air to someone else trying to either hit it or catch it. The sport owes a great deal to the 20 men featured here. They helped pave the way for today's generation of ballplayers.

Cap Anson

Born in 1852, Cap Anson played professional ball for 27 seasons. He retired with a .333 lifetime average, just under 2,000 runs scored, and 2,076 RBI. Cap hit .415 in 46 games for the Philadelphia Athletics in 1872. The majority of his career was played in Chicago with the White Stockings and the Colts of the National League. Anson, unfortunately, often refused to play against teams with players of dark skin color, which somewhat marred a tremendous career.

Jake Beckley

Nicknamed Eagle Eye, Jacob Peter Beckley played all but one of his seasons in the National League. He scored exactly 1,600 career runs and just missed inclusion in the 3,000-hit club (2,930). Beckley played almost exclusively at first base, where he recorded more than 1,500 putouts in 1892 and again in 1904. Cooperstown welcomed him in 1971.

Dan Brouthers

Slight controversy surrounds this player, as various sources list his career batting average differently due to the fact that walks were once counted as hits. The source I have used throughout this book, baseball-reference.com, lists it as .342, and that sounds good to me. Big Dan originally broke into organized ball with the Troy Trojans in 1879.

Jesse Burkett

In 1895 and 1896 Jesse Burkett led the National League in batting with averages of .409 and .410, respectively. An outfielder for the Cleveland Spiders, Burkett scored a remarkable combined total of 313 runs over those two years. His Hall of Fame induction came in 1946.

Fred Clarke

Fred Clarke played in the 1900s but had his most productive seasons before the turn of the century. Playing for the 1897 Louisville Colonels, Clarke batted .390 with 202 hits and 120 runs scored. In 1900 Clarke shared the outfield with a young player who would later be moved to shortstop, Honus Wagner. He also served as a very successful player-manager for almost two decades, winning three straight pennants from 1901 to 1903 and a World Series in 1909.

Roger Connor

Until Babe Ruth began his onslaught on the record books with the Yankees in the 1920s, Roger Connor was baseball's home-run king. His total of 138 long balls was tops until Ruth broke it in '21. Connor played all but one year of his career in the National League, scoring more than 100 runs eight times. Mainly a first baseman, Connor led his leagues in slugging percentage twice and in extra-base hits three times.

George Davis

George Davis was a true multiposition star before the turn of the century. While he played more than 300 games in the outfield and more than 500 at third base, Davis was primarily a shortstop, a position he played for the New York Giants and Chicago White Sox. In 1897 George batted .353 and drove in 136 runs. He also stole more than 600 bases in his career.

Ed Delahanty

Big Ed, who also had four brothers who played professionally, batted .397 or higher four times in his career, including three years that saw him hit better than .400. Mainly an outfielder, Delahanty amassed some tremendous lifetime numbers: 1,599 runs, 2,596 hits, and a .346 batting average. He was inducted into the Hall of Fame in 1945.

Hugh Duffy

Duffy began his career in the National League with the Chicago White Stockings. After two years, he joined the Players' League for one season and then the American Association for one before finally settling back into the NL with the Boston Beaneaters. In his first season, Boston went 102–48, winning the pennant. Then, in 1894, he made Beaneaters fans ecstatic as he put up one of the greatest seasons ever. Duffy batted .440, the highest mark in history, and generated 287 net runs for his team's scoreboard.

Buck Ewing

Before there was Berra or Bench there was Buck, considered one of the greatest players ever from the nineteenth century. Playing for the Cleveland Spiders in 1893, Ewing set career bests in runs (117), hits (172), runs batted in (122), and batting average (.344). He became the first catcher to enter the Hall of Fame when he was inducted in 1939.

Billy Hamilton

Born in Newark, New Jersey, Sliding Billy Hamilton stole more than 100 bases in each of his first three full seasons. His career total of 912 swipes ranks third all-time. In addition to stealing bases, Hamilton was known for scoring runs. Over 14 seasons, Billy scored 1,690 runs in 1,591 games, including his remarkable total of 192 in 1894. From 1894 to 1897, he averaged more than 165 runs scored per year while playing in only 123–131 games each season.

Hughie Jennings

Also a great manager, Hughie Jennings was inducted into Cooperstown in 1945 after playing most of his career as a shortstop. Hughie led the National League in being hit by pitches for five straight years from 1894 to 1898. Plunked an amazing 202 times over that short span, he is also baseball's all-time leader in that painful category, although Craig Biggio came close to breaking his record.

Willie Keeler

Wee Willie Keeler is the man who advised to "hit 'em where they ain't." He certainly took those words to heart, compiling a .341 lifetime average. Keeler posted eight consecutive 200-hit seasons from 1894 to 1901. He batted .424 in 1897 and scored more than 1,700 runs over his professional career. This outfielder joined baseball's elite in Cooperstown in 1939.

Joe Kelley

Always a great on-base player, Joe Kelley outdid himself in 1894 when he reached safely in more than half of his plate appearances (.502). The Orioles left fielder also scored 165 runs, helping Baltimore to win the National League pennant. Kelley batted .317 for his career and was inducted into Cooperstown in 1971, exactly 100 years after he was born.

King Kelly

Michael Joseph Kelly began his professional career all the way back in 1878 as a right fielder for the Cincinnati Reds. Often given credit for inventing the hit-and-run, Kelly was an extremely popular player in his day. The 1886 season witnessed King Kelly bat .388 and score 155 runs in only 118 games. The Boston Beaneaters were so in love with this player that they paid $10,000 to secure his services on Valentine's Day in 1887.

Tommy McCarthy

Hall of Famer Tommy McCarthy played from 1884 until 1896 in three different professional leagues. Mainly a corner outfielder, McCarthy also pitched early in his career, but that did not work out. Much better with the bat in his hands, Tommy proceeded to hit .310 or higher in four seasons between 1890 and 1894. He was immortalized in Cooperstown in 1946.

Bid McPhee

Recently inducted into the Hall of Fame (2000), John Alexander McPhee was baseball's last gloveless second baseman. Bid played his entire career in Cincinnati, first with the Red Stockings of the American Association and then with the better-known Reds of the National League. He stole 568 bases and scored almost 1,700 career runs.

Jim O'Rourke

On April 22, 1876, the National League began play for the first time, and Jim O'Rourke got the first hit. O'Rourke played baseball for 23 seasons, originally appearing with the 1872 Middletown Mansfields of the National Association. His best season may have been 1890; he batted .360, scored 112 runs, and knocked in 115.

Sam Thompson

Sam Thompson comprised one-third of a legendary outfield for the 1894 Philadelphia Phillies. Thompson (.407), Billy Hamilton (.404), and Ed Delahanty (.407) each eclipsed .400 batting averages for the season. Even the team's fourth outfielder, Tuck Turner (.416), managed to top that magical mark. The entire Philadelphia team combined to bat .349. Thompson posted a .331 career average and was inducted in 1974.

Monte Ward

John Montgomery Ward was originally a pitcher but then became a middle infielder for the majority of his career. He won 47 games on the mound in 1879, then added another 39 victories the following year. Ward scored 100 or more runs five times and batted as high as .338, which he did in 1887. Monte Ward became a Hall of Famer during Cooperstown's annual ceremony in 1964.

Negro League Stars

From spitballs, corked bats, and labor stoppages to the Chicago Black Sox and the tainted 1919 World Series, a tied All-Star Game, and steroids, baseball has suffered through and survived much negativity and shame. More than anything else, however, baseball will never be able to fully escape the disgrace it brought upon itself by not allowing black players to participate until Jackie Robinson changed the sport and the country in 1947. While men such as Bud Fowler and Moses Fleetwood Walker played organized ball before the turn of the century, it wasn't until Robinson's debut on April 15, 1947, that baseball officially ended its unwritten policy of not allowing black players to participate.

The Negro Leagues were a natural and necessary reaction to baseball's racism. The players featured in this chapter were stars in those leagues and were deserving of better treatment than they received. Of the 20 players analyzed here, 19 are Hall of Famers. Buck O'Neill, not yet enshrined in Cooperstown, was an important figure in Negro League history as both a player and a manager, so he has been included as well.

As with the nineteenth-century stars of the previous chapter, the ballplayers listed here are analyzed briefly. Without full statistical data, I have again decided not to attempt to calculate P/E Averages. Also similar to the players from the 1800s, I have refrained from assigning ratings or ranking a top-10 list. I admit that my knowledge of many of these men is elementary. Therefore, I thought it only fair to present quick sketches of their careers and not attempt to go beyond my capabilities. Trying to do too much, in my opinion, runs the risk of discrediting their careers, and that has certainly been done enough already.

In his *Illustrated History of Baseball* (1995), author Alex Chadwick, referring to the racial integration of the sport, made the following remark: "History has shown us that if Branch Rickey and Jackie Robinson were not the first men to attempt to break baseball's self-imposed color line, they definitely had the best timing." Unfortunately, the timing of that integration occurred after countless other players had suffered and were alienated, not able to showcase their talents on a bigger stage with the other great athletes of the sport. Baseball can only be thankful that Branch Rickey was wise and that Jackie Robinson was courageous. They certainly did their parts to ensure that baseball's cloud of racism wouldn't linger forever.

Cool Papa Bell

Josh Gibson claimed that Bell was so fast he could turn out the lights and be under the covers of his bed before it got dark. Blessed with tremendous speed, James Thomas Bell played mostly in center field for a number of teams, including the Kansas City Monarchs, the Homestead Grays, and the St. Louis Stars, his primary team. Bell was a prototypical leadoff man with great range in the outfield.

Willard Brown

Home Run Brown played center field and was known for his out-standing skills at home plate. He played briefly in the major leagues, signing with the St. Louis Browns in 1947, but he was most recognized for his time spent with the Kansas City Monarchs and several teams in the Puerto Rican League. Brown helped the Monarchs win six pennants in the '30s and '40s.

Oscar Charleston

Charleston spent 40 years in the Negro Leagues as both player and manager. An outstanding center fielder earlier in his career, he was a part of the 1932 Pittsburgh Crawfords, playing first base. That team won 99 games, and Oscar batted .363, one of many years in which he topped a .300 average.

Ray Dandridge

At the hot corner, nothing got by Ray Dandridge, a tremendous defensive star who spent a half-dozen seasons with the Newark Eagles in the 1930s and 1940s. Purported to be the best ever defensively at his position by many who either played with him or watched him, Dandridge earned his due recognition in 1987, the year he gained entrance into Cooperstown.

Josh Gibson

Perhaps the greatest of them all, catcher Josh Gibson played for the Pittsburgh Crawfords and the Homestead Grays from 1930 to 1946. Accounts of his statistics and accomplishments range widely, some crediting him with hitting more home runs than any player in history, including Hank Aaron. Especially lethal in the mid-'30s, at the height of his career, Gibson is widely regarded as the greatest power hitter in Negro League history. Tragically, he died in January of '47, only months before Jackie Robinson stepped onto the field in a Dodgers uniform.

Frank Grant

A recent inductee into Cooperstown (2006), Ulysses F. Grant was a gifted middle infielder, playing primarily at second base before the twentieth century. Despite being small in stature, Grant had good power and was excellent defensively. In reading about his career, I was reminded of Joe Morgan as probably a similar player, and that's quite a compliment.

Pete Hill

Like Grant, Hill was inducted to the Hall of Fame in 2006 as part of a long list of players of color. Hill was an outfielder who threw right-handed but swung from the left side of the plate. A skilled batsman, Hill played for several teams in the early half of the twentieth century and also managed the Milwaukee Bears. Notably, Hill was made captain of the 1910 Leland Giants, a team that allegedly went 123–6, a fact substantiated by several sources during my research.

Monte Irvin

It's been a while since I've noted a P/E Average, but I can do so here. Monte Irvin (lifetime score of 1.037) played for eight seasons in the majors with the Giants and the Cubs. In 1951 he finished third in the

MVP race after knocking in 121 runs and batting .312 (P/E: 1.183). In the World Series that year, he hit .458 versus the Yankees in defeat. Before joining the Giants, Irvin was a high-average hitter for the Newark Eagles.

Judy Johnson

Inducted into the HOF in 1975, Johnson was a standout third baseman, playing the majority of his career with the Hilldale Daisies. In 1924 the first Negro World Series was played, and Judy Johnson batted .341. As player-coach for the Homestead Grays, Johnson discovered an up-and-coming star named Josh Gibson.

Buck Leonard

Walter Fenner Leonard, better known as Buck, was a part of nine consecutive pennant winners with the Homestead Grays of the '30s and '40s. The legacy of Leonard, who played first base, is succinctly captured on his Hall of Fame plaque, which includes the following: "Teamed with Josh Gibson to form most feared batting twosome in Negro baseball from 1937 to 1946." I can only wonder how Leonard and Gibson would have fared against Gehrig and Ruth.

Pop Lloyd

One of the best black players in the dead-ball era, Pop often drew favorable comparisons to Honus Wagner, one of the greatest players of that time. At shortstop, Lloyd was blessed with soft hands and great range. He played for many teams over the course of 27 seasons, many of which saw him bat above .400. The Hall of Fame welcomed him in 1977.

Biz Mackey

Biz was a tremendous catcher who once mentored a young Roy Campanella, a legendary player who went on to win three MVPs with the Brooklyn Dodgers. Mackey hit better than .400 several times and won the nomination as the starting catcher over Josh Gibson on the inaugural 1933 Negro League All-Star squad.

Buck O'Neill

Buck O'Neill is the only player in this chapter not to be in the Hall of Fame, but I think he may one day get there. O'Neill batted well over .300 several times and also made a name for himself as a major league scout after signing Lou Brock to his first contract. In 2006 he became the oldest person ever to step to the plate when, at age 94, he appeared in an All-Star Game as a member of the Kansas City T-Bones. Buck O'Neill drew an intentional walk.

Louis Santop

Louis Santop was a left-handed-hitting catcher who played from 1909 to 1926. Blessed with tremendous power at the plate, Santop was enshrined as part of the 2006 induction class in Cooperstown, New York. Santop hit .470 in 1911, although statistics from Negro teams in that era were often less than complete. Regardless of that fact, it can be stated with confidence that he was a great hitter and a top star in his day.

Turkey Stearnes

This gifted center fielder won several home-run titles and hit better than .300 in 14 of 19 seasons. Primarily, Stearnes played for the

Detroit Stars, but he also spent time with many other squads throughout the '20s, '30s, and '40s. A quiet and unassuming man in his day, Stearnes reportedly hit .350 for his career. He entered the Hall of Fame in 2000 after receiving the necessary votes from the Veterans Committee.

Mule Suttles

George Suttles was a power-hitting first baseman who starred for a number of teams as a player and also managed the Newark Eagles. Suttles was a huge man, standing 6′6″ and weighing 250 pounds. Mule was especially brilliant in the East-West All-Star Games of the Negro Leagues. He hit the first home run ever in that contest and won the '35 game with a three-run blast in the eleventh inning.

Ben Taylor

Like Suttles, Ben Taylor was a first baseman who recently entered the Hall of Fame as a member of the 2006 class. Great in the field, Taylor was also a great role model and teacher to younger players. That reputation helped earn him managerial positions with several teams. Negro League star Buck Leonard credited Taylor with being instrumental to his development.

Cristobal Torriente

Born in Cuba in 1893, Torriente went on to establish an outstanding career both on his home island and in the United States. Cristobal, inducted into Cooperstown in 2006, was a member of Cuba's inaugural class for its own baseball Hall of Fame in 1939. Torriente excelled at the plate as well as in the outfield.

Willie Wells

This eight-time Negro League All-Star was an all-around talent at the shortstop position in the '20s, '30s, and '40s. Wells had range in the field and power at the plate, a combination of Ozzie Smith and Ernie Banks rolled into one. He also played in the Cuban Winter League, where he won two MVPs.

Jud Wilson

Jud Wilson played mostly as a third baseman, although his talents were such that he could handle several infield positions. Wilson played for the Baltimore Black Sox, the Homestead Grays, the Pittsburgh Crawfords, and the Philadelphia Stars from the 1920s into the 1940s. He was a line-drive hitter from the left side of the plate, respected greatly by opposing pitchers, including Satchel Paige. Paige claimed he was one of the two toughest hitters he had ever faced.

The Top 100

One of the major goals of this book has been to systematically determine the 100 best baseball players in the sport's history. It certainly wasn't easy. I had to compare players at all different positions ranging from the dead-ball era to today, all the while taking into consideration several important factors, which I feel determine a player's overall worth. Most notably, I focused on the following areas in organizing my list:

- **Statistics.** Numbers don't often lie in baseball. P/E Averages, as well as more formal statistical categories, weighed heavily in determining value.
- **MVP Résumé.** By this I am referring to regular-season and postseason awards as well as career shares. All-Star MVPs don't matter very much to me, but it is fair to mention it for players who have won them. Special attention needed to be given to those who played prior to 1931, the year MVP voting was streamlined.
- **Postseason Performance.** This carried a lot of weight in my analyses. After all, winning championships is the objective at the major league level.

- **Defense.** P/E Averages are based solely on offense, but that's only half the game. In terms of defense, I focused on Gold Gloves, assist-to-error ratios at second base, third base, and shortstop, and overall quality of play in the field.
- **Individual Success.** This includes league leadership in offensive and defensive categories, All-Star nominations, and Hall of Fame voting.
- **Intangibles and Special Considerations.** Some players outperform their statistics by saving their best for when it matters most. Consideration also needed to be given to the time in which the athlete played and whether he was a truly unique player for his position or generation.

In ranking the top 100, I have not included players from the nineteenth century or the Negro League simply because they competed in settings far different from modern ballplayers. Therefore, I focused only on the men from Chapters 2–10. To form my list, I started at 1, taking the player I considered the best available choice at each stop along the way. However, I have presented it by beginning at 100 and finishing with my pick for the top spot, with detailed explanations for each selection. The top 100 includes the 50 Category 5 players (1–50) and 50 of the Category 4 (51–100). In my opinion, these are the 100 best players ever.

100. Tony Lazzeri

I'll begin with Lazzeri, a terrific second baseman for the Yankees in the '20s and '30s. He had some outstanding offensive seasons, with great numbers for a middle infielder. Impressively, he averaged 1.15 net runs per contest. Poosh 'Em Up Tony starts the top 100.

99. Luis Aparicio

Like Lazzeri, Aparicio was a middle infielder. Although he lacked the offensive might of the man at number 100, he was tremendous in the field. Aparicio won nine Gold Gloves and stole more than 500 bases. I opt for his speed and defense over Lazzeri's bat.

98. Enos Slaughter

Slaughter outgained Aparicio in terms of MVP shares (2.10 to 1.24) despite missing three full seasons in the middle of his career. They played different positions, a fact that always makes it hard to compare players. Nevertheless, I like Slaughter's track record in the postseason (4–1 in the World Series with a P/E of 1.010), and I like him over Luis for number 98.

97. Chuck Klein

Klein has a lifetime P/E Average (1.160) that is much higher than Slaughter's (1.040). He also won an MVP and a Triple Crown. Overall, I think Klein was probably more dynamic and more dominant in his prime than Slaughter. That's good enough for me to place him at number 97.

96. Barry Larkin

Larkin lacks the offensive numbers of Klein, but he played well enough at a premium position to warrant a higher ranking. The era in which Chuck Klein played also has to be considered here. Offensive statistics were inflated in the 1930s. I like Larkin's combination of leadership, speed, glove work, and pop at the plate.

95. Dave Winfield

Winfield gets the nod over Larkin based on his longevity and power. Like Larkin, Winfield made a dozen All-Star squads, and he betters the Reds shortstop in Gold Gloves, seven to three. Although he never won a Most Valuable Player award, he did reach 3,000 hits and came within one good season of 500 homers (465). I'll take Winfield in right over Larkin at short . . . but only by a little.

94. Dave Parker

The Cobra is my choice here because of his MVP résumé. Parker won the award in '78 with a 95 percent share of the available points. He also finished runner-up once and in third place twice. In all, Parker collected 3.19 career shares to Winfield's 2.20. Both were Gold Glove corner outfielders. At peak performance, I think Parker was probably the better player.

93. Pie Traynor

I wasn't exactly sure where Traynor belonged. He played in the '20s and '30s and put up some terrific offensive statistics. Most impressive is his lifetime average of 1.24 net runs per game, which is more than a quarter of a run better than Parker's average (.98). And although there have been many, many talented players in right field, third base is sparse. My ranking of Pie as the seventh-best third baseman ever gives the edge to him over Dave Parker, who failed to make it into the top 10 for his position.

92. Craig Biggio

Craig Biggio comes in at spot 92, ahead of Traynor. Biggio has scored a ton of runs in his career, reaching 100 in a season eight times, including 146 in 1997. Defensively, he has four Gold Gloves to his credit. He only made 10 errors in '95 and again in '96 while winning the award and fielding .986 and .988 respectively. His glove and run-scoring consistency win out here.

91. Wade Boggs

The lifetime P/E Averages for Boggs and Biggio are extremely close, as are their MVP shares and average net runs per game. I chose Wade as the superior player for a couple of reasons. First, he won five batting titles. He also made a dozen consecutive All-Star appearances from the mid-'80s through the mid-'90s. Finally, Boggs averaged 211 hits a season from 1983 to 1989, a time when he was probably the best pure hitter in the game. Can you imagine a lineup with Biggio leading off and Boggs hitting second?

90. Andre Dawson

The Hawk earns my vote over Boggs. He betters Wade slightly in terms of lifetime P/E (.998 to .960), but it's his MVP season of 1987 that tipped the scales in his favor. Dawson won the award while languishing on a team that was terrible, which shows you how truly dominant he was that year. He was also runner-up in the balloting twice. Add in eight Gold Gloves and the choice is clear. Dawson is number 90 on my all-time list.

89. Gabby Hartnett

Obviously, Hartnett lacks the offensive numbers of Dawson, although his 1930 campaign (.339 BA, .404 OBP, .630 SLP, 122 RBI, 1.235 P/E) was tremendous. Catcher is such a tough position to play. Therefore, Gabby edges Andre based on position value. I think having Hartnett behind the plate would better serve a team than having Dawson in right field.

88. Billy Williams

I like Williams's consistency. From '61 through '73, the Cubs' star averaged 98 runs batted in per season in an era when pitchers dominated. He also won Rookie of the Year and Player of the Year honors during that stretch as well. While he didn't make my top 10 for left field, he does come in ahead of Hartnett for spot 88.

87. Paul Waner

Amazingly, Big Poison reached 200 hits in a season eight times, finishing his career with 3,152 base knocks. I prefer him over Williams because he was more productive (1.11 net runs to .99) and sported much better batting averages. Waner retired with a mark of .333, and he hit above .350 six times. Paul had the advantage of playing in the '20s and '30s, but I still consider him the better choice.

86. Orlando Cepeda

Cepeda had an interesting run. Like Waner, he had his best seasons in the first half of his career. Baby Bull also had an outstanding campaign in 1967, winning the MVP and helping to lead the Cardinals to the

World Series title over Boston. Cepeda had much better power than Waner (379 homers to 113) and had better RBI totals (1,365 to 1,309) despite 2,000 fewer plate appearances.

85. Goose Goslin

Goslin's 1.130 lifetime P/E is terrific, and it's more than 100 points higher than Cepeda's. Goose topped 200 net runs in five different seasons; Cepeda reached that number only once. On a per-game basis, Goslin averaged almost a quarter net run more while amassing more than 1,600 runs batted in throughout the '20s and '30s. Goose Goslin slides in safely at number 85.

84. Juan Gonzalez

Juan begins a short run of more recent players on my list. Gonzalez won two MVPs and was an RBI machine throughout his career. He had one of the great postseason series ever against the Yankees in the '96 ALDS (2.263 P/E). Although he wasn't a polished ballplayer in terms of defense and baserunning, I would opt for him over Goslin if I were picking a team.

83. Mike Piazza

Like Hartnett, Piazza earns points for being a catcher. I see him as a superior player to Gonzalez because he distinguished himself as his position's best offensive force in history. True, his defense hurts his case. Nevertheless, Piazza enters the list at number 83, just ahead of the powerful slugger.

82. Jeff Kent

Kent and Piazza have both been recognized for great offense at positions normally known for defense. Jeff Kent knocked in more than 100 runs every year from 1997 to 2005 except one, tremendous production for a second baseman. I chose him over Piazza for three reasons. First, he won an MVP. Second, he has been slightly better in the postseason. Third, he is better defensively at second than Piazza is behind the plate.

81. Ozzie Smith

This is an interesting one. Obviously, Ozzie has the glove while Kent has the bat. I opt for the defensive master at shortstop, the position that probably requires the most skill to play. Smith's Gold Glove collection is extremely impressive. The Wizard never won an MVP, but he was instrumental on several Cardinals teams that went deep into the postseason.

80. Omar Vizquel

If I had the chance, I'd take Vizquel over Ozzie. His defensive numbers are just better. Offensively, they have similar résumés. For a more detailed comparative analysis, check out the top-10 list for shortstop, where Omar is seventh and Ozzie is eighth.

79. Paul Molitor

At number 79, I'm going with offense over defense. Molitor racked up more than 3,300 hits over his career, seemingly getting better with age. Paul also scored 1,782 runs and registered more than 600 lifetime doubles. I'll take his offense, leadership, and postseason success (1.326 P/E in the playoffs) over Vizquel's glove and range at short.

78. Robin Yount

Both members of the 3,000-hit club, Yount and Molitor were long-time teammates in Milwaukee, which makes this an interesting comparison. Yount wins here because he won two Most Valuable Player awards and because he played his career at short and in center field. Molitor played mostly as a DH. Therefore, Yount is the better choice.

77. Willie McCovey

Stretch was a dominant player in the late '60s and early '70s; he was one of the most feared hitters in the game. I'm not sure the same can be said for Yount, a great hitter but not the same threat in terms of power. McCovey's production average of .87 net runs per game is disappointing for a first baseman, but he did play in a pitcher's era, and he was a platoon player for much of his early career. In the final analysis, 521 homers are hard to overlook.

76. Chipper Jones

Many people probably won't agree with this ranking, but I can't ignore how clutch Chipper has been. From both sides of the plate, he has gotten big hits in big spots. Jones is also helped by the fact that he's played the majority of his games at third, a position that is not as deep in talent as first base. Finally, he's been more productive on a per-game basis than Stretch.

75. Lou Brock

I left Lou Brock out of my top 10 for left field, which was a very difficult decision. Here, he comes in ahead of Jones for spot 75. Most notably, Brock was tremendous in the World Series as evidenced by a 1.348 P/E mark in the Fall Classic. That's a terrific average, especially considering that Brock was a speedster and not a slugger. If I had the opportunity, I'd take Lou at the top of my lineup rather than Chipper in the middle of it.

74. George Sisler

Gorgeous George was a tremendously skilled batsman who hit better than .300 13 times. Twice, he batted over .400, including his .420 mark in 1922. A great run producer as well, Sisler is my choice over Brock. While Sisler walked more than he whiffed, Brock was just the opposite, registering almost 1,000 more strikeouts than bases on balls.

73. Joe Medwick

Sisler (with the Browns) and Medwick (with the Cardinals) both played the majority of their careers in St. Louis. Both won MVPs and finished with terrific lifetime batting averages. Medwick, however, was a little more productive and hit with a little more power, two facts that contribute to his 86-point advantage in terms of career Production and Efficiency Average.

72. Earle Combs

I'll take Combs over Medwick. Earle scored more than 100 runs in eight consecutive seasons. More important, he was great in the World

Series, batting .350 and scoring 17 runs in 16 games. In the '32 Classic, he helped the Yanks to a sweep over the Cubs with a P/E of 1.800. Medwick was very good, but I think Combs was a little bit better.

71. Jim Bottomley

Bottomley didn't have the same World Series success as Combs, but he was a great player nonetheless. Sunny Jim put up great numbers in terms of batting average and on-base percentage and was a consistent run producer. In 1928 he was the NL MVP, generating 228 net runs of offense while posting his career-best P/E Average (1.339). Sunny Jim is the choice for position 71 on my top 100 list.

70. Albert Belle

Although Belle wasn't a widely popular player in his day, it's hard to ignore his numbers. In '95 he reached 50 homers and 52 doubles while slugging .690. Albert averaged 40 homers per 162 games played and owns a very high career P/E mark (1.161). His power and postseason production earn him the higher placement over Bottomley.

69. Joe Cronin

One of the best offensive shortstops in history, Joseph Edward Cronin was a lifetime .301 batter with eight seasons of more than 100 RBI. He never hit for as much power as Belle, but he played a tremendously demanding position on the diamond while Belle was a corner outfielder and a designated hitter.

68. Kirby Puckett

Puckett had a great combination of glove work and prowess at the plate. He won six Gold Gloves and had a penchant for making the big catch at the big moment, just as he did in Game 6 of the 1991 World Series. Cronin, in my opinion, doesn't stand up against Kirby when defense is included in the analysis.

67. Gary Carter

Like Puckett, Gary Carter was clutch in the big game and was a terrific team leader. He's my choice here, however, simply because of the position he played. Getting 100 or more RBI in from the catcher spot, something Carter did four times, is tremendous production. The Kid also won three consecutive Gold Gloves (1980–1982) and was a perennial All-Star selection in the National League.

66. Earl Averill

Earl Averill was a name I knew very little about before writing this book. He had some huge seasons in the 1930s, including his '31 showing (251 net runs). His lifetime averages of 1.179 P/E and 1.29 net runs were too impressive when comparing him with Carter.

65. Frankie Frisch

Frisch was a great combination of offense and defense. Considering he was a second baseman, I think he would have been more valuable to a team than Averill. Four times, Frankie finished in the top 10 of MVP balloting, including a first-place finish in '31. The Fordham Flash is my choice for number 65.

64. Nap Lajoie

As with Omar Vizquel and Ozzie Smith, Frisch and Lajoie are a pair of players from the same position who piggyback one another on my list. I like the fact that Nap led his league in batting five times. His Triple Crown season in 1901 may have been against lesser competition but was miraculous nonetheless.

63. Ralph Kiner

Many people don't see Kiner as a Hall of Famer, but I do. Although he didn't play that long, he was lethal when he was in the lineup. And he wasn't one dimensional either. He scored runs, drew a lot of walks, and hit for good averages. Against Lajoie, he wins out simply based on his power numbers (.548 lifetime slugging and five straight seasons with 40 or more homers).

62. Duke Snider

I chose Snider over Kiner for a couple of reasons. First, he played 18 seasons and topped 400 career homers. He was the Major League Player of the Year in '55, a year in which his Brooklyn squad finally overcame the Yankees in the World Series. Duke hit .320 with four home runs in that Series. Kiner never appeared in the postseason, a fact that hurts him in this comparison.

61. Al Kaline

Like Snider, Kaline was a popular outfielder who enjoyed some of his best seasons in the mid-'50s. He also played well in big games. Against the Cardinals in the '68 Series, Al batted .379 with 11 hits, good enough for a 1.467 P/E over seven games. The choice between the two wasn't easy. Ultimately, I selected Kaline as the better player based on 10 Gold Gloves and 15 All-Star appearances.

60. Rod Carew

Carew was a great batsman who had one unbelievable season in 1977. Rodney batted .388 with 239 hits and 128 runs scored in winning the American League MVP. His consistently high batting averages led to 18 All-Star nominations and seven league batting titles. That's enough convincing for me. Carew enters my list ahead of Al Kaline at number 60.

59. Tony Gwynn

As hitters, Gwynn and Carew were two peas in a pod. Both were artists with a bat in their hands. In my opinion, Gwynn was the better player, however. He hit 10 points higher for his career and was slightly more productive. While Tony also has a higher lifetime P/E mark (.981 to .938), I made my final decision based on defense. The lifetime Padre won the Gold Glove five times, something Carew never did once during his career.

58. Willie Stargell

Like Gwynn, Pops played his entire career for one team, becoming a legendary figure in Pittsburgh. If given the choice between the two, I'd take him over Tony because of power considerations. Stargell led the NL in homers twice and finished with 475 for his career. His longball ability also accounts greatly for an advantage of almost 100 points in terms of P/E.

57. Bill Terry

Terry didn't have the same power as Stargell, but he was a tremendous hitter nonetheless. He batted .350 or higher four times and was over .300 11 times. My mind was made up when comparing Terry and Stargell in terms of production. Memphis Bill averaged 1.19 runs for his team's scoreboard each game, almost a quarter run per game higher than Pops.

56. Lou Boudreau

Boudreau's status as a shortstop helps him greatly here. I like his combination of glove and stick better than Terry's. He also won an MVP, which Terry didn't, and was in the top 10 of the balloting eight times. I think Lou Boudreau is an underrated ballplayer in most circles, but he comes in quite high on my list.

55. Eddie Murray

At number 55, Steady Eddie makes the list. Most impressive about Murray was his ability to be a consistent run producer over many, many seasons. Add in his three Gold Gloves ('82–'84), Rookie of the Year, All-Star accomplishments, and 3.33 career shares in MVP voting, and you can understand why he's so high on my top 100.

54. Harry Heilmann

Heilmann narrowly beats out Murray for this spot. He won four batting titles and retired with a .342 lifetime mark. His career P/E Average, 1.144, is also outstanding. Murray has consistency on his side, but I think Heilmann was probably more exceptional. Just take a look at his numbers in the 1920s. Despite not being a home-run hitter, Heil-mann sports a higher career slugging percentage (.520) than Murray (.476).

53. Jim Rice

Rice isn't in the Hall of Fame, but I definitely think he should be. Rice hit for power and high averages, and he delivered in the clutch. When the Red Sox were battling the Yankees for the division title in '78, Rice eclipsed 400 total bases, slugged .600, and won the AL MVP. Unlike Heilmann, he didn't have the luxury of playing during a high-scoring era like the 1920s.

52. Johnny Mize

Mize missed three full years ('43, '44, and '45) in the prime of his career. Just imagine how impressive his numbers would be had he not missed that time. The Big Cat tops Rice in terms of lifetime postsea-son P/E (1.064 to .913). He also has him by 139 points for their regu-lar-season averages (1.185 to 1.046).

51. Jackie Robinson

Jackie comes in as the highest-ranked Category 4 player on my list, a distinction that lands him firmly at number 51. It's hard to say exactly what Robinson would have accomplished had he been able to join the Dodgers before 1947 and had he not needed to endure the endless onslaught of racial prejudice. His MVP campaign of '49 has to be con-sidered one of the great individual seasons of all time. Robinson's speed, ability to play multiple positions, and courage to fight through 10 heroic seasons give him the nod over Mize.

50. Pete Rose

Rose begins the discussion of the Category 5 players. I felt that his overwhelming numbers (4,256 hits, 2,165 runs, 746 doubles, and so on) were worthy of that highest rating even though he may never have been a truly dominant player, and his lifetime P/E number is below .900. Rose played two dozen seasons and accumulated some unparalleled statistics that earn him a spot in my top 50.

49. Mark McGwire

McGwire comes in ahead of Rose based on his power advantage. Rose's MVP campaign of '73 helps his case considerably, but I can't ignore Big Mac's advantage of 423 lifetime homers. Whether or not McGwire belongs in the Hall of Fame based on steroid allegations is an argument for another time. This analysis has been formulated strictly by the numbers and on-field accomplishments.

48. Carl Yastrzemski

Yaz won an MVP and was a terrific defensive outfielder (seven Gold Gloves). Moreover, he was tremendous in the postseason, sporting a lifetime P/E of 1.240 when it mattered most. In the '67 Series Yaz nearly beat the Cardinals single-handedly (P/E: 1.310). McGwire can't boast that, and that's enough ammunition to put the Boston legend at number 48.

47. Eddie Mathews

The decision between Yaz and Mathews was a hard one for me to make. Ultimately, I chose Mathews based on his position and better home-run numbers. A third baseman with long-ball power like Mathews doesn't come along very often. His ranking as the fourth best at the hot corner earns him a slight advantage over Yastrzemski.

46. Roberto Alomar

Alomar is my choice because he did so many things well on the diamond. He was a tremendous fielder, a smart base runner, and a clutch hitter with enough power to make him dangerous to opposing pitchers. Arguably, he is the greatest defensive second baseman of all time. He's also my choice as the forty-sixth best baseball player in history.

45. Ryne Sandberg

The argument for Sandberg over Alomar was spelled out in greater detail in the second base top 10. I don't expect many to agree with Sandberg's high ranking. However, when considering his defense, postseason success, and '84 MVP campaign, I think 45 is a deserving spot for Ryno.

44. Reggie Jackson

While Sandberg played well in the playoffs twice, Reggie was a two-time World Series MVP. In and of itself, that counts heavily in his favor. He also hit 563 homers and drove in more than 1,700 runs. Too many strikeouts? Yes. A lifetime batting average of just .262? Yes. Nevertheless, Mr. October is my choice for number 44, the same number the Yankees retired in honor of him.

43. Bill Dickey

Also a Yankees legend, Dickey splits the two right fielders. I'll take him over Jackson because of position. Having a catcher with Dickey's bat is a tremendous advantage for any manager. Extremely productive, he averaged 1.08 net runs per game, an outstanding mark for a backstop. From 1929 to 1939, the lifelong pinstriper hit over .300 10 out of 11 seasons.

42. Roberto Clemente

Clemente holds the MVP advantage over Dickey. He won the regular-season award in '66 and the World Series version in '71. Dickey never won, although it can certainly be argued that his greatness was often overshadowed by the likes of Ruth, Gehrig, and DiMaggio. Nevertheless, I'd take Clemente on my team to play right field if both players were available.

41. Harmon Killebrew

Killebrew's 58-point advantage in terms of lifetime P/E isn't enough by itself for him to better Clemente on my list. Both men won MVPs and both had their moments in the postseason. What impressed me most about Harmon's career was eight seasons with more than 40 home runs from the late '50s through the early '70s. In today's game, he probably would have routinely knocked 50–55 balls over the fence year in and year out.

40. Sammy Sosa

While I think Killebrew would have been a 50-homer player today, I'm not sure he'd be able to hit 60, which Sosa did three times. In those three years ('98, '99, '01), Sammy hit 193 round-trippers, a remarkable achievement. Did performance-enhancing substances have anything to do with it? Possibly and maybe even probably. However, my choice has been to focus on what we know for sure. Although he may be guilty in the eyes of the public, he accomplished enough on the field to warrant a top-40 ranking.

39. Jeff Bagwell

When the strike hit in 1994, Bagwell was on his way to one of the great seasons in the sport's history (P/E of 1.549 in 110 games). He was the unanimous MVP that year and was in the top 10 of the vote five other times. The lifelong Astros teammate eclipses Sosa based on better production (1.21 net runs per game to 1.08) and better consistency. Year in and year out, Bagwell was a nightmare for opposing pitchers to handle.

38. Derek Jeter

The main reason Jeter ranks ahead of Bagwell and so many other notable players is that he is incredibly clutch when games are on the line. His leadership, other intangibles, and sheer will to win make him a legendary player. With very good defense at a premium position as well, Jeter deserves to be this high on my list.

37. Ivan Rodriguez

I have to opt for I-Rod's defense and MVP résumé. Having Rodriguez behind the plate would be more valuable, albeit slightly, than having Jeter at short in my opinion. In winning the 2003 NLCS Most Valuable Player award, Rodriguez was a one-man wrecking crew, driving in 10 runs over seven games against the Cubs.

36. Roy Campanella

Here's another case where two players from the same position are back-to-back. While Rodriguez's career has been longer and more distinguished in terms of overall All-Star appearances and Gold Gloves, it must also be noted that Campy's last year (1957) was the first in which the defensive award was given. I can't ignore his three MVPs, the fact that he made eight straight All-Star teams, and his impressive 1.069 lifetime Production and Efficiency Average.

35. Mel Ott

Ott doesn't have the advantage of playing at a premium defensive position like Campanella, and he never even won an MVP. However, he was a tremendous power hitter and run producer for the Giants from the late 1920s. Beginning in '29, Ott averaged more than 120 RBI per season for the next 10 years. Mel also hit over .300 in half of his 22 major league seasons. Campanella, while great in '51, '53, and '55, didn't display the consistency of Ott.

34. Brooks Robinson

In my opinion, Robinson is the greatest defensive player in baseball history. That unique distinction is enough to warrant placing him ahead of Ott. He won the Gold Glove every year from 1960 through 1975, a tremendous achievement at an extremely demanding infield position. In the 1970 World Series, he made one miraculous play after another, almost sucking the will out of the Cincinnati hitters. He doesn't compare with many players on this list in terms of P/E, but sometimes looking beyond the numbers is necessary for measuring greatness. Having a player of Robinson's caliber at the hot corner is a tremendous advantage for any team.

33. Cal Ripken Jr.

One of the most difficult decisions was choosing between Ripken and Robinson for spot 33. Both Baltimore immortals, they would team to form a dynamic left side of the infield on the ultimate Orioles squad. I selected Ripken as the superior player, however. Cal won two MVPs and was the Major League Player of the Year in both of those seasons as well. With almost 1,700 career RBI and 431 home runs, Ripken's offensive prowess at the shortstop position won out over Brooks.

32. Ernie Banks

Even though Banks played more career games at first base, he won his back-to-back Most Valuable Player honors as a shortstop. Therefore, the comparison between him and Ripken is fairly easy. Banks had much better power and was a better run producer. Mr. Cub led the NL in RBI twice and in home runs twice despite never playing on a team talented enough to make it into October. He would be the number 3 shortstop on that top-10 list if he had played at least 60 percent of his games there. He didn't, so Cal ended up there, but Banks prevails in this head-to-head comparison.

31. George Brett

Brett's case is helped by the fact that I ranked him as the second best third baseman of all time. Incredibly clutch, he proved himself over and over again in his team's biggest games. In terms of P/E, he betters Banks slightly, 1.032 to 1.000 for their careers. If Banks had remained a shortstop for his entire career, then I might opt for him over Brett. I'll take the lifelong Royals infielder to anchor third base on my team anytime.

30. Manny Ramirez

Manny is not a good fielder, can be a clubhouse distraction, and always seems to be mentioned in various trade rumors. So why is he positioned so high on my list? Simply because he's one of the best run producers the game has ever known. With a lifetime P/E score of 1.234, Ramirez is an offensive force. Brett was a great hitter, but I'd take Manny based on his penchant for plating runs on such a consistent basis.

29. Eddie Collins

There are probably many baseball experts who would rate Eddie Collins as the best second baseman ever, and it would be hard to argue with them. Collins had a long career, consistently hitting for high averages while generating runs for his team. He had a .400 or better on-base percentage in 15 full seasons. He's my choice ahead of Ramirez based on his steadiness, defense, and status as a second baseman.

28. Albert Pujols

Deciding where to include Pujols in the top 100 was one of the harder decisions I had to make when writing this book. Obviously, he still has years to play, and no one knows how many more championships or how many more MVPs he'll win. I think twenty-eighth is a good spot for him now. Ten or fifteen years in the future, I think it's conceivable that Pujols could be in the top 10; he's that good. His power and run production are too much for Eddie Collins to overcome.

27. Frank Thomas

Thomas has enjoyed a late-career resurgence, which helps him to be ranked so high. In 2006 he smacked 39 homers and drove in 114 for Oakland, leading them into the playoffs without much protection around him. In the 1990s Thomas was arguably the best player in baseball. He won back-to-back MVPs and routinely put up huge offensive numbers. One day, Pujols will pass him on my list. For the time being, though, Big Hurt's overall numbers win out.

26. Mickey Cochrane

As with Collins, some people feel Cochrane is the best ever at his position. He was certainly a unique ballplayer, reaching base often and hitting for incredibly high averages (.331 or better in five of his first seven seasons) year in and year out. I like Cochrane's toughness, leadership, and defense behind the plate over Big Hurt's power. Finding a player like Cochrane is more difficult than finding one like Thomas.

25. Joe Morgan

The top 25 begins with Morgan, the two-time MVP spark plug who ignited Cincinnati's Big Red Machine of the 1970s. In the mid-'70s especially, Morgan was a lethal combination of defensive mastery, speed, power, and intelligence on the diamond. He's another player who would get a lot of acclaim as the best ever at his position, although I have him ranked third in that discussion. His back-to-back MVP seasons in '75 and '76 give him the edge over Black Mike.

24. Tris Speaker

Like Morgan, Speaker had a great combination of glove and bat. I favor him here, however, because he simply had more good seasons than Joe. Was he as dominant as Morgan in the prime of their careers? I doubt it. But Speaker was much more consistent, in the regular season as well as in the World Series, and that fact convinced me that he was the better choice.

23. Al Simmons

Other than Babe Ruth, Simmons is the only man in history to record a P/E mark above 1.600 (1.638 in 1930) for an entire season. That year, Simmons averaged more than two full net runs per contest (281 in 138 games), a phenomenal accomplishment. He also maintained an average of 1.37 net runs per game for his career. In comparison with Speaker, Simmons was more productive, more powerful, and my choice for 23 on the top-100 list.

22. Ken Griffey Jr.

For a while it looked as if Junior would be the best candidate to break Aaron's home-run record. From '96 through '99 he knocked 209 balls over the fence while also driving in 567 runs for Seattle. With the Reds he hasn't been able to stay healthy and maintain that same level of dominance. Nevertheless, membership in the 500-home-run club along with 10 Gold Gloves gives him the nod over Al Simmons.

21. Hank Greenberg

The only reason Greenberg doesn't rank higher on my list is longevity. Hank played in fewer than 1,400 career games, but he was a legendary hitter and run producer. His 1.318 lifetime P/E trails only Ruth, Gehrig, and Ted Williams. In the postseason, he was even better, sporting a 1.356 mark in the World Series. For those reasons, I rank him ahead of Junior.

20. Rickey Henderson

The reason Greenberg fails to come in higher is the same reason Henderson makes my top 20. Henderson played at a high level over an extremely long career. He amassed unbelievable numbers in terms of runs scored, stolen bases, and walks. More important, he established himself as a truly unique player, the greatest leadoff hitter of all time. The Man of Steal was the pure embodiment of what a table setter should be, getting on, getting over, and getting in better than anyone in history. And he did it for a quarter of a century.

19. Frank Robinson

Robinson won two MVPs to Henderson's one, hit with much more power, and was simply more dangerous offensively. Frank's 1.126 lifetime P/E is outstanding, buoyed by 586 homers and more than 1,800 runs both scored and driven home. Henderson was a leadoff hitter while Robinson was a middle-of-the-order threat, so it's sort of an apples and oranges thing. My gut instinct tells me that Robinson was the superior player.

18. Rogers Hornsby

Not only did Hornsby put up better numbers than Robinson, but he also did so while playing mainly at second base, a position normally highlighted by defensive-minded fielders. In fact, Hornsby put up some of the great offensive seasons, regardless of position, in the history of baseball. In 1925 he finished the season with a P/E score of 1.557, a tremendously high average. He wasn't the greatest teammate, and he wasn't a virtuoso in the field, but his phenomenal offensive numbers warrant this high of a ranking.

17. Charlie Gehringer

My reasons for selecting Gehringer over Hornsby were spelled out in detail in Chapter 4. I don't think there's another player in baseball history more underrated than Charlie Gehringer. He was a complete ballplayer, and he was tremendously consistent, earning the nickname the Mechanical Man for his steady play year after year.

16. Alex Rodriguez

When all is said and done, A-Rod may indeed rank as one of the top 5 players of all time. His power advantage over Gehringer is the main reason he is ranked ahead of the lifelong Detroit second baseman.

15. Johnny Bench

Arguably the greatest defensive catcher in history, Bench was also incredibly clutch. His 1970 campaign (45 homers, 148 RBI, 355 total bases) may be the best ever for a backstop. I guess I'd take Bench's combination of power, production, and defense behind the plate over A-Rod's skill set on the left side of the infield. But it's not an easy choice.

14. Yogi Berra

This is another case of players from the same position back-to-back on my list. Ranking Bench at number 15 and Berra at number 14 just goes to show how I view these players in comparison with one another. There probably wasn't a closer call in the entire book. I'll use Berra's rings and extra MVP as evidence to support my decision.

13. Honus Wagner

The greatest shortstop as well as the greatest middle infielder of all time is up next. If MVPs had been awarded throughout Wagner's career, he no doubt would have won one, if not many. He led the league in batting eight times and was considered a giant in the game. Although he can't match Berra in terms of championships, he did have so many outstanding seasons that I feel he deserves this spot.

12. Mike Schmidt

The gap between Schmidt and the next-best third baseman (Brett) is wider than at any other position. I can't imagine anyone with a solid knowledge of baseball history making a logical argument that Michael Jack Schmidt isn't the greatest third baseman ever. His defense, power, and MVP résumé make him a solid choice over Wagner. The fact that his career P/E is 11 points higher just adds fuel to the fire. The Philadelphia legend is one of the best dozen ever.

11. Stan Musial

Musial has the edge over Schmidt in terms of lifetime P/E (by 40 points), career net runs per game (by .07), and by a wide margin in the three efficiency averages (.331 BA, .417 OBP, and .559 SLP vs. .267, .380, and .527). My final choice, however, was also based on MVP shares. Both men won the award three times, but Musial holds a distinct advantage with 6.96 career shares to 4.96 for Schmidt.

The Top 10

If you've been paying close attention, then you can probably predict who is still left. Leaving Musial out was hardest of all. Several times I had him in, and several times I had him out. His exclusion is certainly no knock against his outstanding Hall of Fame career. Someone had to be number 11.

Four of my top 10 wore pinstripes in the Bronx. Four were center fielders. Only two were infielders, and they were both first basemen. Therefore, you won't find any catchers, second basemen, third basemen, or shortstops.

10. Mickey Mantle

The Mick begins the top 10. Cardinals fans reading this book are probably not pleased that Stan the Man didn't make it in. I just think Mantle was better. He was a great defensive center fielder while Musial played left and first base. Mickey hit for better power and was better on the bases. In his prime, Mantle was without peer in the mid-'50s. Finally, the man who wore number 7 was simply better in the big games, bettering Musial in terms of postseason P/E scores by a comfortable margin (1.073 to .788).

9. Hank Aaron

I don't think Hank Aaron was better than Mantle when both were at their best, but he wins out over the course of a long and storied career. Aaron's accomplishments are just too noteworthy not to give him the edge over Mickey. Both were complete players in terms of power, average, defense, and speed. Aaron merely did it longer.

8. Jimmie Foxx

Some might argue that Foxx's numbers are inflated by the era in which he played and that, therefore, this is too high of a ranking. I don't care if Foxx played softball. His power and production numbers are awesome, as is his 1.315 career Production and Efficiency Average. Double X won three MVPs and nearly came away with a fourth. Aaron only won the award once. That is enough to convince me that Foxx was better.

7. Willie Mays

I'm sure there will be several outcries against various rankings, ratings, and opinions in this work. I'm also sure that none will be louder than those speaking out against Mays at number 7. Most baseball experts would certainly put Mays in their top five if not higher. I don't agree, which isn't to say that Mays wasn't an immortal ballplayer. His speed and defense are obvious advantages over Foxx. To rank higher on my list, however, he needed to win more than one championship, and he needed to hit better than the .247 lifetime average he managed in the postseason.

6. Ty Cobb

My reasoning for Cobb over Mays has already been discussed, so I will keep this explanation brief. Despite hitting only 117 home runs and playing a large portion of his career in the dead-ball era, Cobb still averaged almost a quarter of a net run better per game than Mays and bettered him by 50 points in lifetime P/E.

5. Barry Bonds

In selecting Bonds as the fifth best player in history, I have ignored the issue of steroids and looked only at the numbers and on-field accomplishments. I don't know if that's the best way to do it, but it was the only way I felt I could be fair and objective. He ranks ahead of Cobb because he played better defense, hit with tremendous power, and won seven Most Valuable Player awards, a fact that is the strongest argument in his favor.

4. Ted Williams

This is the final case of two same-position players coming in together in the top 100. I think Williams was the better hitter and played in a better league, coming up short against DiMaggio on more than one occasion. If he hadn't missed so many games in two separate war efforts, then he might own records that no one else, not even Barry Bonds, could touch.

The Top Three

In my opinion, the three greatest baseball players of all time are Joe DiMaggio, Lou Gehrig, and Babe Ruth. You might find it amazing, based on that opinion, that I am not a Yankees fan. My team, for better or worse, is the Mets. Yet I cannot let fan loyalty sway my judgment. What is amazing is that these three immortals came within an eyelash of all playing with one another. Ruth played with the Yankees through 1934 and was still in baseball in 1935, the year before Joltin' Joe appeared on the scene. Gehrig knew what it was like to play with them both. Imagine a lineup with Ruth batting third, DiMaggio hitting cleanup, and Gehrig providing ultimate protection in the fifth spot. It almost happened. The stars nearly aligned, but it wasn't quite meant to be. Nevertheless, the fact they all wore pinstripes in the mid-'30s paved the way for the sport's greatest dynasty. It also created a great ending to my top-100 list.

The Case for DiMaggio

Three American League MVPs (1939, 1941, and 1947)

Three full seasons missed in the prime of his career (1943–1945)

An All-Star nomination in every season he played

The best defense at the most critical position of the three players

10 pennants and nine World Series championships

The Case for Gehrig

Averaged 1.57 net runs per game as the most productive player ever

1.493 career P/E Average in the World Series

Averaged 250 net runs per season from 1926 to 1938

5.44 career MVP shares and the 1934 Triple Crown

2,130 consecutive games played

The Case for Ruth

1.436 lifetime P/E, the highest average in history

714 home runs and a .690 career slugging percentage

His 1921 season, arguably the greatest ever (P/E: 1.714)

Revolutionized the sport, hitting more home runs than entire teams
  early in his career

94–46 lifetime record as a pitcher and 0.87 ERA over 31 World
  Series innings

3. Joe DiMaggio

The Yankee Clipper comes in third, unable to wrestle away one of the top two spots from Gehrig and Ruth. DiMaggio put up tremendous numbers beginning in his rookie year. Had he not left for the war effort, or had he not suffered from various pain and injuries at the end of his career, his lifetime statistics would be even more impressive. I chose him over Williams for a couple of reasons. First, from '36 to '42, the years before his career was interrupted, Joe was unbelievable, averaging 224 net runs per season and batting .339 over that span. He earned 3.97 MVP shares and had a combined P/E of 1.358 for those first seven seasons. Second, and more important, DiMaggio's teams won 10 pennants and nine World Series. While he wasn't always great in October, he did play center field and hit in the middle of the Yankees' lineup. Ted Williams never won a championship, and he hit .200 in his only postseason appearance. Ted was the better hitter, but Joe was more complete in terms of defense and leadership. It would be a very difficult decision, but if I needed to win one game, I'd take DiMaggio in center over Williams in left.

2. Lou Gehrig

The Iron Horse didn't have DiMaggio's flair, and he didn't win as many titles. He also wasn't as important in the field. Nonetheless, it can easily be argued that Gehrig was the most productive player ever, and that is extremely impressive. His average of 1.57 net runs generated per game is better than any player in history. I simply can't ignore that level of production. Need more proof that Gehrig deserves to be number 2? Consider this. Imagine a "perfect" offensive season in which the following conditions were met: 165 or more RBI, more than 400 total bases, more than 90 extra-base hits, more than 100 walks, less than 85 strikeouts, an on-base percentage above .440 with a batting average above .340, more than 40 home runs, and at least 210 hits. Only one player in history has ever achieved this amazing combination of production and efficiency in the same season. That man was Lou Gehrig, and he did it four times (1927, 1930, 1931, and 1934).

1. Babe Ruth

In my opinion, it would be extremely difficult to analyze baseball history and all of its players and their statistics and accomplishments and not come to the conclusion that Babe Ruth was the best ever. In terms of P/E Average, no one is close to Ruth's 1.436 lifetime mark or his standard of eight seasons above 1.500. I believe his 1921 campaign (171 RBI, 177 runs, 457 total bases, 1.714 P/E) is the greatest individual season in the sport's history, not likely to ever be matched. Ruth changed the face of baseball, taking it out of its dead-ball era and into a brave new world where 50 and 60 home runs in a season were possible. When you factor in Ruth's achievements as a pitcher, which I have done, I think the choice becomes quite clear. Babe Ruth is the greatest baseball player in history.

Conclusion

Baseball is our greatest sport. The NFL is organized and run the best, there's nothing quite like March Madness, and a bad day of golf will always beat a good day of work. Nevertheless, baseball, in its purest form, reigns supreme in my eyes. I truly consider it an honor to have written this book and, in some small way, contributed something to this great American pastime.

As I stated at the beginning, my objective in this endeavor has been twofold. First, I wanted to formulate and introduce Offensive Production and Efficiency Average as a new tool in determining and quantifying a baseball player's value, worth, and contributions. Because it is comprehensive, incorporating both measures of production and efficiency, I feel it is the single most telling statistic available to date. My second goal was to use P/E Averages, in combination with a variety of other objective and subjective data, to rate, rank, and compare the greatest (and some of the not-so-great) players in baseball history. I hope that you have enjoyed reading my book, and I also hope that you continue to use it as a resource any time you have a question or need to settle an argument regarding the game's biggest stars.

One of the best aspects of my statistic is that it is extremely easy to use. If you want to calculate the P/E Average for a certain player not already listed, then you can do it in a matter of seconds. All you need is the formula, access to the necessary statistics, and a calculator. I think it also works well for anyone involved in a fantasy baseball league. If you can dominate your fellow fantasy owners in P/E Average at each position, then you deserve your league's crown—with an eye for talent worthy of GM status.

There will never be a clear consensus on many of the arguments I have posed and tried to answer in this work. Someone who saw Mays play in the 1950s and 1960s, I'm sure, will not be swayed by my opinion that Joe DiMaggio and Ty Cobb were both better center fielders. In fact, I imagine that my opinions have caused more than a few readers to slam the book shut and proclaim that I don't know what the hell I'm talking about. And that's fabulous. A big part of baseball's charm rests with the fact that it's fun to pore over the statistics and debate the best catcher of all time, Williams versus Musial, and who does and doesn't belong in Cooperstown.

Thank you for taking the time to read my book. And thank you for continuing to be a part of baseball, the greatest sport ever imagined.

Appendix A

Career P/E Averages

The following are the top 25 players of all time in terms of career Production and Efficiency Average. While obvious candidates such as Gehrig, Foxx, and Bonds make the list, you may be surprised not to see the names of Aaron, Mays, or Schmidt.

1.	Babe Ruth	1.436
2.	Lou Gehrig	1.387
3.	Ted Williams	1.346
4.	Hank Greenberg	1.318
5.	Jimmie Foxx	1.315
6.	Joe DiMaggio	1.295
7.	Albert Pujols*	1.271
8.	Barry Bonds*	1.264
9.	Manny Ramirez*	1.234 (tie)
9.	Alex Rodriguez*	1.234 (tie)
11.	Rogers Hornsby	1.214
12.	Hack Wilson	1.209
13.	Ty Cobb	1.204
14.	Todd Helton*	1.202
15.	Al Simmons	1.199
16.	Johnny Mize	1.185

17. Earl Averill (tie)   1.179
17. Mark McGwire (tie)   1.179
19. Mickey Mantle   1.178
20. Vladimir Guerrero*   1.175
21. Jeff Bagwell   1.173
22. Mel Ott   1.171
23. Frank Thomas*   1.169
24. Jim Thome*   1.168
25. David Ortiz*   1.163

* Active player

Appendix B

Single-Season P/E Averages

According to my research, a P/E Average above 1.500 has been attained only 23 times in major league history. Barry Bonds (1.495 in 2001), Manny Ramirez (1.495 in 1999), Joe DiMaggio (1.494 in 1937), and Babe Ruth (1.493 in 1928) all had years that just failed to make it onto this list. Bagwell's '94 masterpiece was in a strike-shortened season, while every other instance was in the first half of the twentieth century. In terms of P/E, these are the best seasons ever.

Babe Ruth, 1921	1.714
Babe Ruth, 1920	1.663
Al Simmons, 1930	1.638
Babe Ruth, 1931	1.563
Babe Ruth, 1927	1.562
Rogers Hornsby, 1925	1.557
Lou Gehrig, 1927	1.555
Nap Lajoie, 1901	1.550
Jeff Bagwell, 1994	1.549
Hack Wilson, 1930	1.540
Lou Gehrig, 1931	1.537
Jimmie Foxx, 1932	1.532
Babe Ruth, 1926	1.531

Jimmie Foxx, 1938	1.527
Lou Gehrig, 1930	1.526
Hank Greenberg, 1937	1.522
Ted Williams, 1941	1.517
Babe Ruth, 1930	1.515
Ty Cobb, 1911	1.512
Babe Ruth, 1923	1.504
Babe Ruth, 1929	1.504
Chuck Klein, 1930	1.503
Lou Gehrig, 1936	1.501

Appendix C

Career MVP Shares

I have relied heavily on Most Valuable Player data to rate and rank the players in this book. The following table lists the 15 best in terms of career MVP shares; the data is accurate only through the 2006 season. Next to each player's name, I have given his career total of shares along with the number of times he has finished first, second, third, in the top five, and in the top 10. Frank Thomas, Alex Rodriguez, and Albert Pujols are all still active, so their totals will likely increase in coming years.

Player	Shares	First	Second	Third	Top 5	Top 10
1. Barry Bonds	9.30	7	2	0	12	13
2. Stan Musial	6.96	3	4	0	9	14
3. Ted Williams	6.43	2	4	1	9	12
4. Willie Mays	6.06	2	2	2	9	12
5. Mickey Mantle	5.79	3	3	1	9	9
6. Hank Aaron	5.45	1	0	6	8	13
7. Lou Gehrig	5.44	2	2	0	8	9
8. Joe DiMaggio	5.43	3	2	1	6	10
9. Mike Schmidt	4.96	3	0	2	5	9
10. Frank Robinson	4.83	2	0	2	6	10
11. Frank Thomas	4.79	2	1	2	6	9
12. Jimmie Foxx	4.21	3	1	0	4	6

Player	Shares	First	Second	Third	Top 5	Top 10
13. Alex Rodriguez	4.05	2	2	1	5	7
14. Yogi Berra	3.98	3	2	1	7	7
15. Albert Pujols	3.96	1	3	1	6	6

Appendix D

C5 P/E Calculations

Fifty players in my book have been rated Category 5. All of these players' statistics necessary for calculating P/E Averages are listed here. The following formulas have been listed to serve as reminders to you of how P/E Average is calculated:

$$NR = \text{net runs (RBI + R − HR)}$$
$$CB = \text{complete bases (TB + BB + HBP + SB − CS)}$$
$$PTS = \text{points (NR + NR + CB)}$$
$$P/E = \text{production and efficiency average (PTS ÷ PA)}$$

The production aspect of my statistic comes from net runs, which I have also called "scoreboard runs" at various times throughout the book. Net runs are calculated by adding a player's total for runs batted in and runs scored and then subtracting home runs.

Efficiency is measured by complete bases. This refers to the sum total of bases a player accumulates through a variety of means. Adding total bases, walks, hit by pitch, and stolen bases, and then subtracting times caught stealing, gives you a player's complete bases. When this is achieved, the second component of P/E Average is in place.

Offensive Production and Efficiency Average is derived by assigning two points for every net run and one point for every complete base. In this way, an equitable 50/50 balance is approximated as best as possible. A player's total number of points is then divided by the number of times he appeared at the plate. The quotient, rounded off to the nearest thousandth, is the P/E Average. It's easy to calculate and understand, and it's a very telling statistic.

You may find it helpful to flip back and forth between the players' statistical pages in this appendix with the individual pages devoted to them in their respective chapters. In this way, my commentaries in "The Good," "The Bad," and "The Verdict" sections may make more sense when reading them in combination with the numbers.

This book has been heavily saturated with statistics. What better way to end it than with the numbers that have served as the backbone to this entire project. Enjoy!

Hank Aaron

Year	RBI	R	HR	NR	TB	BB	HBP	SB	CS	CB	PTS	PA	P/E
1954	69	58	13	114	209	28	3	2	2	240	468	509	.919
1955	106	105	27	184	325	49	3	3	1	379	747	665	1.123
1956	92	106	26	172	340	37	2	2	4	377	721	660	1.092
1957	132	118	44	206	369	57	0	1	1	426	838	675	1.241
1958	95	109	30	174	328	59	1	4	1	391	739	664	1.113
1959	123	116	39	200	400	51	4	8	0	463	863	693	1.245
1960	126	102	40	188	334	60	2	16	7	405	781	664	1.176
1961	120	115	34	201	358	56	2	21	9	428	830	671	1.237
1962	128	127	45	210	366	66	3	15	7	443	863	667	1.294
1963	130	121	44	207	370	78	0	31	5	474	888	714	1.244
1964	95	103	24	174	293	62	0	22	4	373	721	634	1.137
1965	89	109	32	166	319	60	1	24	4	400	732	639	1.146
1966	127	117	44	200	325	76	1	21	3	420	820	688	1.192
1967	109	113	39	183	344	63	0	17	6	418	784	669	1.172
1968	86	84	29	141	302	64	1	28	5	390	672	676	.994
1969	97	100	44	153	332	87	2	9	10	420	726	639	1.136
1970	118	103	38	183	296	74	2	9	9	381	747	598	1.249
1971	118	95	47	166	331	71	2	1	1	404	736	573	1.284
1972	77	75	34	118	231	92	1	4	4	328	564	544	1.037
1973	96	84	40	140	252	68	1	1	1	321	601	465	1.292
1974	69	47	20	96	167	39	0	1	1	207	399	382	1.045
1975	60	45	12	93	165	70	1	0	0	235	421	543	.775
1976	35	22	10	47	100	35	0	0	0	134	228	308	.740
Career	2,297	2,174	755	3,716	6,856	1,402	32	240	73	8,457	15,889	13,940	1.140

Roberto Alomar

Year	RBI	R	HR	NR	TB	BB	HBP	SB	CS	CB	PTS	PA	P/E
1988	41	84	9	116	208	47	3	24	6	276	508	611	.831
1989	56	82	7	131	234	53	1	42	17	313	575	702	.819
1990	60	80	6	134	223	48	2	24	7	290	558	646	.864
1991	69	88	9	148	278	57	4	53	11	381	677	719	.942
1992	76	105	8	173	244	87	5	49	9	376	722	671	1.076
1993	93	109	17	185	290	80	5	55	15	415	785	683	1.149
1994	38	78	8	108	177	51	2	19	8	241	457	455	1.004
1995	66	71	13	124	232	47	0	30	3	306	554	577	.960
1996	94	132	22	204	310	90	1	17	6	412	820	699	1.173
1997	60	64	14	110	206	40	3	9	3	255	475	469	1.013
1998	56	86	14	128	246	59	2	18	5	320	576	657	.877
1999	120	138	24	234	300	99	7	37	6	437	905	694	1.304
2000	89	111	19	181	290	64	6	39	4	395	757	697	1.086
2001	100	113	20	193	311	80	4	30	6	419	805	677	1.189
2002	53	73	11	115	222	57	1	16	4	292	522	655	.797
2003	39	76	5	110	180	59	3	12	2	252	472	598	.789
2004	24	18	4	38	67	14	1	0	2	80	156	190	.821
Career	1,134	1,508	210	2,432	4,018	1,032	50	474	114	5,460	10,324	10,400	.993

Jeff Bagwell

Year	RBI	R	HR	NR	TB	BB	HBP	SB	CS	CB	PTS	PA	P/E
1991	82	79	15	146	242	75	13	7	4	333	625	650	.962
1992	96	87	18	165	260	84	12	10	6	360	690	697	.990
1993	88	76	20	144	276	62	3	13	4	350	638	609	1.048
1994	116	104	39	181	300	65	4	15	4	380	742	479	1.549
1995	87	88	21	154	222	79	6	12	5	314	622	539	1.154
1996	120	111	31	200	324	135	10	21	7	483	883	719	1.228
1997	135	109	43	201	335	127	16	31	10	499	901	717	1.257
1998	111	124	34	201	301	109	7	19	7	429	831	661	1.257
1999	126	143	42	227	332	149	11	30	11	511	965	729	1.324
2000	132	152	47	237	363	107	15	9	6	488	962	719	1.338
2001	130	126	39	217	341	106	6	11	3	461	895	717	1.248
2002	98	94	31	161	296	101	10	7	3	411	733	691	1.061
2003	100	109	39	170	317	88	6	11	4	418	758	702	1.080
2004	89	104	27	166	266	96	8	6	4	372	704	679	1.037
2005	19	11	3	27	38	18	1	0	0	57	111	123	.902
Career	1,529	1,517	449	2,597	4,213	1,401	128	202	78	5,866	11,060	9,431	1.173

Ernie Banks

Year	RBI	R	HR	NR	TB	BB	HBP	SB	CS	CB	PTS	PA	P/E
1953	6	3	2	7	20	4	0	0	0	24	38	39	.974
1954	79	70	19	130	253	40	7	6	10	296	556	649	.857
1955	117	98	44	171	355	45	2	9	3	408	750	646	1.161
1956	85	82	28	139	285	52	0	6	9	334	612	593	1.032
1957	102	113	43	172	344	70	3	8	4	421	765	674	1.135
1958	129	119	47	201	379	52	4	4	4	435	837	682	1.227
1959	143	97	45	195	351	64	7	2	4	420	810	671	1.207
1960	117	94	41	170	331	71	4	1	3	404	744	678	1.097
1961	80	75	29	126	259	54	2	1	2	314	566	573	.988
1962	104	87	37	154	307	30	7	5	1	348	656	657	.998
1963	64	41	18	87	174	39	4	0	3	214	388	484	.802
1964	95	67	23	139	266	36	3	1	2	304	582	637	.914
1965	106	79	28	157	277	55	6	3	5	336	650	680	.956
1966	75	52	15	112	221	29	5	0	1	254	478	554	.863
1967	95	68	23	140	261	27	3	2	2	291	571	615	.928
1968	83	71	32	122	259	27	5	2	0	293	537	595	.903
1969	106	60	23	143	235	42	7	0	0	284	570	629	.906
1970	44	25	12	57	102	20	1	0	0	123	237	247	.960
1971	6	4	3	7	27	6	0	0	0	33	47	92	.511
Career	1,636	1,305	512	2,429	4,706	763	70	50	53	5,536	10,394	10,395	1.000

Johnny Bench

Year	RBI	R	HR	NR	TB	BB	HBP	SB	CS	CB	PTS	PA	P/E
1967	6	7	1	12	22	5	0	0	1	26	50	93	.538
1968	82	67	15	134	244	31	2	1	5	273	541	607	.891
1969	90	83	26	147	259	49	4	6	6	312	606	592	1.024
1970	148	97	45	200	355	54	0	5	2	412	812	671	1.210
1971	61	80	27	114	238	49	0	2	1	288	516	613	.842
1972	125	87	40	172	291	100	2	6	6	393	737	652	1.130
1973	104	83	25	162	239	83	0	4	1	325	649	651	.997
1974	129	108	33	204	315	80	3	5	4	399	807	708	1.140
1975	110	83	28	165	275	65	2	11	0	353	683	605	1.129
1976	74	62	16	120	183	81	2	13	2	277	517	552	.937
1977	109	67	31	145	267	58	1	2	4	324	614	560	1.096
1978	73	52	23	102	190	50	1	4	2	243	447	451	.991
1979	80	73	22	131	213	67	0	4	2	282	544	538	1.011
1980	68	52	24	96	174	41	2	4	2	219	411	407	1.010
1981	25	14	8	31	87	17	0	0	2	102	164	196	.837
1982	38	44	13	69	158	37	0	1	2	194	332	439	.756
1983	54	32	12	74	134	24	0	0	1	157	305	334	.913
Career	1,376	1,091	389	2,078	3,644	891	19	68	43	4,579	8,735	8,669	1.008

Yogi Berra

Year	RBI	R	HR	NR	TB	BB	HBP	SB	CS	CB	PTS	PA	P/E
1946	4	3	2	5	15	1	0	0	0	16	26	23	1.130
1947	54	41	11	84	136	13	0	0	1	148	316	306	1.033
1948	98	70	14	154	229	25	1	3	3	255	563	497	1.133
1949	91	59	20	130	199	22	6	2	1	228	488	443	1.102
1950	124	116	28	212	318	55	4	4	2	379	803	656	1.224
1951	88	92	27	153	269	44	3	5	4	317	623	594	1.049
1952	98	97	30	165	255	66	4	2	3	324	654	605	1.081
1953	108	80	27	161	263	50	3	0	3	313	635	557	1.140
1954	125	88	22	191	285	56	4	0	1	344	726	652	1.113
1955	108	84	27	165	254	60	7	1	0	322	652	615	1.060
1956	105	93	30	168	278	65	5	3	2	349	685	597	1.147
1957	82	74	24	132	211	57	1	1	2	268	532	545	.976
1958	90	60	22	128	204	35	2	3	0	244	500	476	1.050
1959	69	64	19	114	218	43	4	1	2	264	492	521	.944
1960	62	46	15	93	160	38	3	2	1	202	388	404	.960
1961	61	62	22	101	184	35	2	2	0	223	425	437	.973
1962	35	25	10	50	90	24	2	0	1	115	215	263	.817
1963	28	20	8	40	73	15	1	1	0	90	170	164	1.037
1965	0	1	0	1	2	0	0	0	0	2	4	9	.444
Career	1,430	1,175	358	2,247	3,643	704	52	30	26	4,403	8,897	8,361	1.064

Barry Bonds

Year	RBI	R	HR	NR	TB	BB	HBP	SB	CS	CB	PTS	PA	P/E
1986	48	72	16	104	172	65	2	36	7	268	476	484	.983
1987	59	99	25	133	271	54	3	32	10	350	616	611	1.008
1988	58	97	24	131	264	72	2	17	11	344	606	614	.987
1989	58	96	19	135	247	93	1	32	10	363	633	679	.932
1990	114	104	33	185	293	93	3	52	13	428	798	621	1.285
1991	116	95	25	186	262	107	4	43	13	403	775	634	1.222
1992	103	109	34	178	295	127	5	39	8	458	814	612	1.330
1993	123	129	46	206	365	126	2	29	12	510	922	674	1.368
1994	81	89	37	133	253	74	6	29	9	353	619	474	1.306
1995	104	109	33	180	292	120	5	31	10	438	798	635	1.257
1996	129	122	42	209	318	151	1	40	7	503	921	675	1.364
1997	101	123	40	184	311	145	8	37	8	493	861	690	1.248
1998	122	120	37	205	336	130	8	28	12	490	900	697	1.291
1999	83	91	34	140	219	73	3	15	2	308	588	434	1.355
2000	106	129	49	186	330	117	3	11	3	458	830	607	1.367
2001	137	129	73	193	411	177	9	13	3	607	993	664	1.495
2002	110	117	46	181	322	198	9	9	2	536	898	612	1.467
2003	90	111	45	156	292	148	10	7	0	457	769	550	1.398
2004	101	129	45	185	303	232	9	6	1	549	919	617	1.489
2005	10	8	5	13	28	9	0	0	0	37	63	52	1.212
2006	77	74	26	125	200	115	10	3	0	328	578	493	1.172
2007	66	75	28	113	192	132	3	5	0	332	558	477	1.170
Career	1,996	2,227	762	3,461	5,976	2,558	106	514	141	9,013	15,935	12,606	1.264

George Brett

Year	RBI	R	HR	NR	TB	BB	HBP	SB	CS	CB	PTS	PA	P/E
1973	0	2	0	2	7	0	0	0	0	7	11	41	.268
1974	47	49	2	94	166	21	0	8	5	190	378	486	.778
1975	89	84	11	162	289	46	2	13	10	340	664	697	.953
1976	67	94	7	154	298	49	1	21	11	358	666	705	.945
1977	88	105	22	171	300	55	2	14	12	359	701	627	1.118
1978	62	79	9	132	238	39	1	23	7	294	558	558	1.000
1979	107	119	23	203	363	51	0	17	10	421	827	701	1.180
1980	118	87	24	181	298	58	1	15	6	366	728	515	1.414
1981	43	42	6	79	168	27	1	14	6	204	362	379	.955
1982	82	101	21	162	279	71	1	6	1	356	680	629	1.081
1983	93	90	25	158	261	57	1	0	1	318	634	525	1.208
1984	69	42	13	98	173	38	0	0	2	209	405	422	.960
1985	112	108	30	190	322	103	3	9	1	436	816	665	1.227
1986	73	70	16	127	212	80	4	1	2	295	549	529	1.038
1987	78	71	22	127	212	72	1	6	3	288	542	508	1.067
1988	103	90	24	169	300	82	3	14	3	396	734	681	1.078
1989	80	67	12	135	197	59	3	14	4	269	539	528	1.021
1990	87	82	14	155	280	56	0	9	2	343	653	607	1.076
1991	61	77	10	128	203	58	0	2	0	263	519	572	.907
1992	61	55	7	109	235	35	6	8	6	278	496	637	.779
1993	75	69	19	125	243	39	3	7	5	287	537	612	.877
Career	1,595	1,583	317	2,861	5,044	1,096	33	201	97	6,277	11,999	11,624	1.032

Roy Campanella

Year	RBI	R	HR	NR	TB	BB	HBP	SB	CS	CB	PTS	PA	P/E
1948	45	32	9	68	116	36	1	3	3*	153	289	321	.900
1949	82	65	22	125	217	67	3	3	2*	288	538	507	1.061
1950	89	70	31	128	241	55	2	1	1*	298	554	494	1.121
1951	108	90	33	165	298	53	4	1	2	354	684	562	1.217
1952	97	73	22	148	212	57	3	8	4	276	572	533	1.073
1953	142	103	41	204	317	67	4	4	2	390	798	590	1.353
1954	51	43	19	75	159	42	2	1	4	200	350	446	.785
1955	107	81	32	156	260	56	6	2	3	321	633	522	1.213
1956	73	39	20	92	153	66	1	1	0	221	405	461	.879
1957	62	31	13	80	128	34	4	1	0	167	327	380	.861
Career	856	627	242	1,241	2,101	533	30	25	21*	2,668	5,150	4,816	1.069

* CS totals estimated based on known statistics

Roberto Clemente

Year	RBI	R	HR	NR	TB	BB	HBP	SB	CS	CB	PTS	PA	P/E
1955	47	48	5	90	181	18	2	2	5	198	378	501	.754
1956	60	66	7	119	234	13	4	6	6	251	489	572	.855
1957	30	42	4	68	157	23	0	0	4	176	312	475	.657
1958	50	69	6	113	212	31	0	8	2	249	475	556	.854
1959	50	60	4	106	171	15	3	2	3	188	400	456	.877
1960	94	89	16	167	261	39	2	4	5	301	635	620	1.024
1961	89	100	23	166	320	35	3	4	1	361	693	614	1.129
1962	74	95	10	159	244	35	1	6	4	282	600	581	1.033
1963	76	77	17	136	282	31	4	12	2	327	599	642	.933
1964	87	95	12	170	301	51	2	5	2	357	697	683	1.020
1965	65	91	10	146	273	43	5	8	0	329	621	642	.967
1966	119	105	29	195	342	46	0	7	5	390	780	690	1.130
1967	110	103	23	190	324	41	3	9	1	376	756	632	1.196
1968	57	74	18	113	242	51	1	2	3	293	519	557	.932
1969	91	87	19	159	276	56	3	4	1	338	656	570	1.151
1970	60	65	14	111	229	38	2	3	0	272	494	455	1.086
1971	86	82	13	155	262	26	0	1	2	287	597	553	1.080
1972	60	68	10	118	181	29	0	0	0	210	446	413	1.080
Career	1,305	1,416	240	2,481	4,492	621	35	83	46	5,185	10,147	10,212	.994

Ty Cobb

Year	RBI	R	HR	NR	TB	BB	HBP	SB	CS	CB	PTS	PA	P/E
1905	15	19	1	33	45	10	0	2	1*	56	122	164	.744
1906	34	45	1	78	141	19	3	23	13*	173	329	394	.835
1907	119	97	5	211	283	24	5	49	27*	334	756	646	1.170
1908	108	88	4	192	276	34	6	39	21*	334	718	635	1.131
1909	107	116	9	214	296	48	6	76	42*	384	812	651	1.247
1910	91	106	8	189	279	64	4	65	36*	376	754	590	1.278
1911	127	147	8	266	367	44	8	83	45*	457	989	654	1.512
1912	83	120	7	196	323	43	5	61	33*	399	791	609	1.299
1913	67	70	4	133	229	58	4	51	28*	314	580	501	1.158
1914	57	69	2	124	177	57	6	35	17	258	506	414	1.222
1915	99	144	3	240	274	118	10	96	38	460	940	700	1.343
1916	68	113	5	176	267	78	2	68	24	391	743	636	1.168
1917	102	107	6	203	335	61	4	55	30*	425	831	669	1.242
1918	64	83	3	144	217	41	2	34	18*	276	564	473	1.192
1919	70	92	1	161	256	38	1	28	15*	308	630	545	1.156
1920	63	86	2	147	193	58	2	15	10	258	552	495	1.115
1921	101	124	12	213	302	56	3	22	15	368	794	581	1.367
1922	99	99	4	194	297	55	4	9	13	352	740	612	1.209
1923	88	103	6	185	261	66	3	9	10	329	699	647	1.080
1924	78	115	4	189	281	85	1	23	14	376	754	726	1.039
1925	102	97	12	187	248	65	5	13	9	322	696	490	1.420
1926	62	48	4	106	119	26	1	9	4	151	363	273	1.330
1927	93	104	5	192	236	67	5	22	16	314	698	574	1.216
1928	40	54	1	93	152	34	4	5	8	187	373	393	.949
Career	1,937	2,246	117	4,066	5,854	1,249	94	892	487*	7,602	15,734	13,072	1.204

* CS totals estimated based on known statistics

Mickey Cochrane

Year	RBI	R	HR	NR	TB	BB	HBP	SB	CS	CB	PTS	PA	P/E
1925	55	69	6	118	188	44	2	7	4	237	473	474	.998
1926	47	50	8	89	151	56	0	5	2	210	388	452	.858
1927	80	80	12	148	214	50	2	9	6	269	565	507	1.114
1928	57	92	10	139	217	76	3	7	7	296	574	568	1.011
1929	95	113	7	201	244	69	2	7	6	316	718	606	1.185
1930	85	110	10	185	256	55	1	5	0	317	687	561	1.225
1931	89	87	17	159	254	56	3	2	3	312	630	521	1.209
1932	112	118	23	207	264	100	4	0	1	367	781	625	1.250
1933	60	104	15	149	221	106	3	8	6	332	630	542	1.162
1934	76	74	2	148	180	78	4	8	4	266	562	524	1.073
1935	47	93	5	135	185	96	4	5	5	285	555	522	1.063
1936	17	24	2	39	48	46	0	1	1	94	172	178	.966
1937	12	27	2	37	48	25	1	0	1	73	147	126	1.167
Career	832	1,041	119	1,754	2,470	857	29	64	46	3,374	6,882	6,206	1.109

Eddie Collins

Year	RBI	R	HR	NR	TB	BB	HBP	SB	CS	CB	PTS	PA	P/E
1906	0	2	0	2	3	0	0	0	0*	3	7	18	.389
1907	2	0	0	2	10	0	0	0	0*	10	14	24	.583
1908	40	39	1	78	125	16	3	8	4*	148	304	364	.835
1909	56	104	3	157	257	62	6	67	36*	356	670	660	1.015
1910	81	81	3	159	243	49	6	81	43*	336	654	658	.994
1911	73	92	3	162	237	62	15	38	20*	332	656	588	1.116
1912	64	137	0	201	236	101	0	63	34*	366	768	673	1.141
1913	73	125	3	195	242	85	7	55	29*	360	750	652	1.150
1914	85	122	2	205	238	97	6	58	30	369	779	657	1.186
1915	77	118	4	191	227	119	5	46	30	367	749	680	1.101
1916	52	87	0	139	216	86	3	40	21	324	602	673	.895
1917	67	91	0	158	205	89	3	53	28*	322	638	689	.926
1918	30	51	2	79	109	73	0	22	12*	192	350	425	.824
1919	80	87	4	163	210	68	2	33	19*	294	620	628	.987
1920	76	117	3	190	297	69	2	20	8	380	760	706	1.076
1921	58	79	2	135	223	66	2	12	10	293	563	607	.928
1922	69	92	1	160	241	73	3	20	12	325	645	701	.920
1923	67	89	5	151	229	84	4	48	29	336	638	632	1.009
1924	86	108	6	188	253	89	3	42	17	370	746	676	1.104
1925	80	80	3	157	188	87	4	19	6	292	606	533	1.137
1926	62	66	1	127	172	62	3	13	8	242	496	455	1.090
1927	15	50	1	64	93	56	0	6	2	153	281	290	.969
1928	7	3	0	10	13	4	0	0	0	17	37	37	1.000
1929	0	0	0	0	0	2	0	0	0	2	2	9	.222
1930	0	1	0	1	1	0	0	0	0	1	3	2	1.500
Career	1,300	1,821	47	3,074	4,268	1,499	77	744	398*	6,190	12,338	12,037	1.025

CS totals estimated based on known statistics

Bill Dickey

Year	RBI	R	HR	NR	TB	BB	HBP	SB	CS	CB	PTS	PA	P/E
1928	2	1	0	3	6	0	0	0	0	6	12	15	.800
1929	65	60	10	115	217	14	1	4	3	233	463	473	.979
1930	65	55	5	115	178	21	0	7	1	205	435	396	1.098
1931	78	65	6	137	211	39	0	2	1	251	525	523	1.004
1932	84	66	15	135	204	34	0	2	4	236	506	459	1.102
1933	97	58	14	141	234	47	2	3	4	282	564	532	1.060
1934	72	56	12	116	195	38	2	0	3	232	464	438	1.059
1935	81	54	14	121	205	35	6	1	1	246	488	491	.994
1936	107	99	22	184	261	46	3	0	2	308	676	472	1.432
1937	133	87	29	191	302	73	4	3	2	380	762	608	1.253
1938	115	84	27	172	258	75	2	3	0	338	682	532	1.282
1939	105	98	24	179	246	77	4	5	0	332	690	565	1.221
1940	54	45	9	90	132	48	2	0	3	179	359	424	.847
1941	71	35	7	99	145	45	3	2	1	194	392	397	.987
1942	37	28	2	63	100	26	1	2	2	127	253	295	.858
1943	33	29	4	58	119	41	0	2	1	161	277	284	.975
1946	10	10	2	18	49	19	1	0	1	68	104	156	.666
Career	1,209	930	202	1,937	3,062	678	31	36	29	3,778	7,652	7,060	1.084

Joe DiMaggio

Year	RBI	R	HR	NR	TB	BB	HBP	SB	CS	CB	PTS	PA	P/E
1936	125	132	29	228	367	24	4	4	0	399	855	668	1.280
1937	167	151	46	272	418	64	5	3	0	490	1,034	692	1.494
1938	140	129	32	237	348	59	2	6	1	414	888	660	1.345
1939	126	108	30	204	310	52	4	3	0	369	777	524	1.483
1940	133	93	31	195	318	61	3	1	2	381	771	572	1.348
1941	125	122	30	217	348	76	4	4	2	430	864	621	1.391
1942	114	123	21	216	304	68	2	4	2	376	808	680	1.188
1946	95	81	25	151	257	59	2	1	0	319	621	567	1.095
1947	97	97	20	174	279	64	3	3	0	349	697	601	1.160
1948	155	110	39	226	355	67	8	1	1	430	882	669	1.318
1949	67	58	14	111	162	55	2	0	1	218	440	329	1.337
1950	122	114	32	204	307	80	1	0	0	388	796	606	1.314
1951	71	72	12	131	175	61	6	0	0	242	504	482	1.046
Career	1,537	1,390	361	2,566	3,948	790	46	30	9	4,805	9,937	7,671	1.295

Jimmie Foxx

Year	RBI	R	HR	NR	TB	BB	HBP	SB	CS	CB	PTS	PA	P/E
1925	0	2	0	2	7	0	0	0	0	7	11	9	1.222
1926	5	8	0	13	14	1	0	1	0	16	42	35	1.200
1927	20	23	3	40	67	14	1	2	1	83	163	146	1.116
1928	79	85	13	151	219	60	1	3	8	275	577	473	1.220
1929	118	123	33	208	323	103	2	9	7	430	846	638	1.326
1930	156	127	37	246	358	93	0	7	7	451	943	673	1.401
1931	120	93	30	183	292	73	1	4	3	367	733	593	1.236
1932	169	151	58	262	438	116	0	3	7	550	1,074	701	1.532
1933	163	125	48	240	403	96	1	2	2	500	980	670	1.463
1934	130	120	44	206	352	111	1	11	2	473	885	652	1.357
1935	115	118	36	197	340	114	0	6	4	456	850	649	1.310
1936	143	130	41	232	369	105	1	13	4	484	948	693	1.368
1937	127	111	36	202	306	99	1	10	8	408	812	673	1.207
1938	175	139	50	264	398	119	0	5	4	518	1,046	685	1.527
1939	105	130	35	200	324	89	2	4	3	416	816	563	1.449
1940	119	106	36	189	299	101	0	4	7	397	775	618	1.254
1941	105	87	19	173	246	93	0	2	5	336	682	582	1.172
1942	33	43	8	68	105	40	2	1	0	148	284	347	.818
1944	2	0	0	2	2	2	0	0	0	4	8	22	.364
1945	38	30	7	61	94	23	0	0	0	117	239	248	.964
Career	1,922	1,751	534	3,139	4,956	1,452	13	87	72	6,436	12,714	9,670	1.315

Lou Gehrig

Year	RBI	R	HR	NR	TB	BB	HBP	SB	CS	CB	PTS	PA	P/E
1923	9	6	1	14	20	2	0	0	0	22	50	29	1.724
1924	5	2	0	7	7	1	0	0	0	8	22	13	1.692
1925	68	73	20	121	232	46	2	6	3	283	525	497	1.056
1926	112	135	16	231	314	105	1	6	5	421	883	696	1.269
1927	175	149	47	277	447	109	3	10	8	561	1,115	717	1.555
1928	142	139	27	254	364	95	4	4	11	456	964	677	1.424
1929	126	127	35	218	323	122	5	4	4	450	886	692	1.280
1930	174	143	41	276	419	101	3	12	14	521	1,073	703	1.526
1931	184	163	46	301	410	117	0	17	12	532	1,134	738	1.537
1932	151	138	34	255	370	108	3	4	11	474	984	708	1.390
1933	139	138	32	245	359	92	1	9	13	448	938	687	1.365
1934	165	128	49	244	409	109	2	9	5	524	1,012	690	1.467
1935	119	125	30	214	312	132	5	8	7	450	878	672	1.307
1936	152	167	49	270	403	130	7	3	4	539	1,079	719	1.501
1937	159	138	37	260	366	127	4	4	3	498	1,018	700	1.454
1938	114	115	29	200	301	107	5	6	1	418	818	689	1.187
1939	1	2	0	3	4	5	0	0	0	9	15	33	.455
Career	1,995	1,888	493	3,390	5,060	1,508	45	102	101	6,614	13,394	9,660	1.387

Charlie Gehringer

Year	RBI	R	HR	NR	TB	BB	HBP	SB	CS	CB	PTS	PA	P/E
1924	1	2	0	3	6	0	0	1	1	6	12	13	.923
1925	0	3	0	3	3	2	0	0	1	4	10	20	.500
1926	48	62	1	109	183	30	1	9	7	216	434	517	.839
1927	61	110	4	167	224	52	2	17	8	287	621	571	1.088
1928	74	108	6	176	272	69	6	15	9	353	705	691	1.020
1929	106	131	13	224	337	64	6	27	9	425	873	715	1.221
1930	98	144	16	226	326	69	7	19	15	406	858	699	1.227
1931	53	67	4	116	165	29	0	13	4	203	435	414	1.051
1932	107	112	19	200	307	68	3	9	8	379	779	692	1.126
1933	105	103	12	196	294	68	3	5	4	366	758	705	1.075
1934	127	134	11	250	311	99	3	11	8	416	916	708	1.294
1935	108	123	19	212	306	79	3	11	4	395	819	709	1.155
1936	116	144	15	245	356	83	4	4	1	446	936	731	1.280
1937	96	133	14	215	293	90	1	11	4	391	821	660	1.244
1938	107	133	20	220	276	113	4	14	1	406	846	688	1.230
1939	86	86	16	156	221	68	1	4	3	291	603	486	1.241
1940	81	108	10	179	230	101	3	10	0	344	702	629	1.116
1941	46	65	3	108	132	95	3	1	2	229	445	537	.829
1942	7	6	1	12	15	7	0	0	0	22	46	52	.885
Career	1,427	1,774	184	3,017	4,257	1,186	50	181	89	5,585	11,619	10,237	1.135

Hank Greenberg

Year	RBI	R	HR	NR	TB	BB	HBP	SB	CS	CB	PTS	PA	P/E
1930	0	0	0	0	0	0	0	0	0	0	0	1	.000
1933	87	59	12	134	210	46	1	6	2	261	529	498	1.062
1934	139	118	26	231	356	63	2	9	5	425	887	667	1.330
1935	170	121	36	255	389	87	0	4	3	477	987	710	1.390
1936	16	10	1	25	29	9	0	1	0	39	89	55	1.618
1937	183	137	40	280	397	102	3	8	3	507	1,067	701	1.522
1938	146	144	58	232	380	119	3	7	5	504	968	681	1.421
1939	112	112	33	191	311	91	2	8	3	409	791	604	1.310
1940	150	129	41	238	384	93	1	6	3	481	957	670	1.428
1941	12	12	2	22	31	16	0	1	0	48	92	83	1.108
1945	60	47	13	94	147	42	0	3	1	191	379	312	1.215
1946	127	91	44	174	316	80	0	5	1	400	748	604	1.238
1947	74	71	25	120	192	104	4	0	0	300	540	510	1.059
Career	1,276	1,051	331	1,996	3,142	852	16	58	26	4,042	8,034	6,096	1.318

Ken Griffey Jr.

Year	RBI	R	HR	NR	TB	BB	HBP	SB	CS	CB	PTS	PA	P/E
1989	61	61	16	106	191	44	2	16	7	246	458	506	.905
1990	80	91	22	149	287	63	2	16	11	357	655	666	.983
1991	100	76	22	154	289	71	1	18	6	373	681	633	1.076
1992	103	83	27	159	302	44	5	10	5	356	674	617	1.092
1993	109	113	45	177	359	96	6	17	9	469	823	691	1.191
1994	90	94	40	144	292	56	2	11	3	358	646	493	1.310
1995	42	52	17	77	125	52	0	4	2	179	333	314	1.061
1996	140	125	49	216	342	78	7	16	1	442	874	638	1.370
1997	147	125	56	216	393	76	8	15	4	488	920	704	1.307
1998	146	120	56	210	387	76	7	20	5	485	905	720	1.257
1999	134	123	48	209	349	91	7	24	7	464	882	706	1.249
2000	118	100	40	178	289	94	9	6	4	394	750	631	1.189
2001	65	57	22	100	194	44	4	2	0	244	444	417	1.065
2002	23	17	8	32	84	28	3	1	2	114	178	232	.767
2003	26	34	13	47	94	27	6	1	0	128	222	201	1.104
2004	60	49	20	89	154	44	2	1	0	201	379	348	1.089
2005	92	85	35	142	283	54	3	0	1	339	623	555	1.123
2006	72	62	27	107	208	39	2	0	0	249	463	472	.981
2007	93	78	30	141	262	85	1	6	1	353	635	623	1.019
Career	1,701	1,545	593	2,653	4,884	1,162	77	184	68	6,239	11,545	10,167	1.136

Rickey Henderson

Year	RBI	R	HR	NR	TB	BB	HBP	SB	CS	CB	PTS	PA	P/E
1979	26	49	1	74	118	34	2	33	11	176	324	398	.814
1980	53	111	9	155	236	117	5	100	26	432	742	722	1.028
1981	35	89	6	118	185	64	2	56	22	285	521	493	1.057
1982	51	119	10	160	205	116	2	130	42	411	731	656	1.114
1983	48	105	9	144	216	103	4	108	19	412	700	622	1.125
1984	58	113	16	155	230	86	5	66	18	369	679	597	1.137
1985	72	146	24	194	282	99	3	80	10	454	842	654	1.287
1986	74	130	28	176	285	89	2	87	18	445	797	701	1.137
1987	37	78	17	98	178	80	2	41	8	293	489	440	1.111
1988	50	118	6	162	221	82	3	93	13	386	710	647	1.097
1989	57	113	12	158	216	126	3	77	14	408	724	674	1.074
1990	61	119	28	152	282	97	4	65	10	438	742	594	1.249
1991	57	105	18	144	199	98	7	58	18	344	632	578	1.093
1992	46	77	15	108	181	95	6	48	11	319	535	500	1.070
1993	59	114	21	152	228	120	4	53	8	397	701	610	1.149
1994	20	66	6	80	108	72	5	22	7	200	360	376	.957
1995	54	67	9	112	182	72	4	32	10	280	504	487	1.035
1996	29	110	9	130	160	125	10	37	15	317	577	602	.958
1997	34	84	8	110	138	97	6	45	8	278	498	509	.978
1998	57	101	14	144	188	118	5	66	13	364	652	670	.973
1999	42	89	12	119	204	82	2	37	14	311	549	526	1.044
2000	32	75	4	103	128	88	4	36	11	245	451	519	.869
2001	42	70	8	104	133	81	3	25	7	235	443	465	.953
2002	16	40	5	51	63	38	4	8	2	111	213	222	.959
2003	5	7	2	10	22	11	1	3	0	37	57	84	.679
Career	1,115	2,295	297	3,113	4,588	2,190	98	1,406	335	7,947	14,173	13,346	1.062

Rogers Hornsby

Year	RBI	R	HR	NR	TB	BB	HBP	SB	CS	CB	PTS	PA	P/E
1915	4	5	0	9	16	2	0	0	2	16	34	61	.557
1916	65	63	6	122	220	40	4	17	19*	262	506	550	.920
1917	66	86	8	144	253	45	4	17	19*	300	588	589	.998
1918	60	51	5	106	173	40	3	8	9*	215	427	466	.916
1919	71	68	8	131	220	48	7	17	19*	273	535	577	.927
1920	94	96	9	181	329	60	3	12	15	389	751	660	1.138
1921	126	131	21	236	378	60	7	13	13	445	917	674	1.361
1922	152	141	42	251	450	65	1	17	12	521	1,023	704	1.453
1923	83	89	17	155	266	55	3	3	7	320	630	487	1.294
1924	94	121	25	190	373	89	2	5	12	457	837	640	1.308
1925	143	133	39	237	381	83	2	5	3	468	942	605	1.557
1926	93	96	11	178	244	61	0	3	4*	304	660	604	1.093
1927	125	133	26	232	333	86	4	9	10*	422	886	684	1.295
1928	94	99	21	172	307	107	1	5	6*	414	758	619	1.225
1929	149	156	39	266	409	87	1	2	2*	497	1,029	712	1.445
1930	18	15	2	31	45	12	1	0	0*	58	120	120	1.000
1931	90	64	16	138	205	56	0	1	1*	261	537	418	1.285
1932	7	10	1	16	18	10	2	0	0*	30	62	70	.886
1933	23	11	3	31	46	14	2	1	1*	62	124	108	1.148
1934	11	2	1	12	12	7	1	0	0	20	44	31	1.419
1935	3	1	0	4	8	3	0	0	0	11	19	27	.704
1936	2	1	0	3	2	1	0	0	0	3	9	6	1.500
1937	11	7	1	17	24	7	0	0	0	31	65	63	1.032
Career	1,584	1,579	301	2,862	4,712	1,038	48	135	154*	5,779	11,503	9,475	1.214

* CS totals estimated based on known statistics

Reggie Jackson

Year	RBI	R	HR	NR	TB	BB	HBP	SB	CS	CB	PTS	PA	P/E
1967	6	13	1	18	36	10	5	1	1	51	87	135	.644
1968	74	82	29	127	250	50	5	14	4	315	569	614	.927
1969	118	123	47	194	334	114	12	13	5	468	856	677	1.264
1970	66	57	23	100	195	75	8	26	17	287	487	514	.947
1971	80	87	32	135	288	63	6	16	10	363	633	642	.986
1972	75	72	25	122	236	59	8	9	8	304	548	572	.958
1973	117	99	32	184	286	76	7	22	8	383	751	629	1.194
1974	93	90	29	154	260	86	4	25	5	370	678	604	1.123
1975	104	91	36	159	303	67	3	17	8	382	700	669	1.046
1976	91	84	27	148	250	54	4	28	7	329	625	558	1.120
1977	110	93	32	171	289	74	3	17	3	380	722	606	1.191
1978	97	82	27	152	244	58	9	14	11	314	618	581	1.064
1979	89	78	29	138	253	65	2	9	8	321	597	537	1.112
1980	111	94	41	164	307	83	2	1	2	391	719	601	1.196
1981	54	33	15	72	143	46	1	0	3	187	331	382	.866
1982	101	92	39	154	282	85	2	4	5	368	676	621	1.089
1983	49	43	14	78	135	52	4	0	2	189	345	458	.753
1984	81	67	25	123	213	55	3	8	4	275	521	584	.892
1985	85	64	27	122	224	78	1	1	2	302	546	541	1.009
1986	58	65	18	105	171	92	3	1	1	266	476	517	.921
1987	43	42	15	70	135	33	4	2	1	173	313	374	.837
Career	1,702	1,551	563	2,690	4,834	1,375	96	228	115	6,418	11,798	11,416	1.033

Derek Jeter

Year	RBI	R	HR	NR	TB	BB	HBP	SB	CS	CB	PTS	PA	P/E
1995	7	5	0	12	18	3	0	0	0	21	45	51	.882
1996	78	104	10	172	250	48	9	14	7	314	658	654	1.006
1997	70	116	10	176	265	74	10	23	12	360	712	748	.952
1998	84	127	19	192	301	57	5	30	6	387	771	694	1.111
1999	102	134	24	212	346	91	12	19	8	460	884	739	1.196
2000	73	119	15	177	285	68	12	22	4	383	737	679	1.085
2001	74	110	21	163	295	56	10	27	3	385	711	686	1.036
2002	75	124	18	181	271	73	7	32	3	380	742	730	1.016
2003	52	87	10	129	217	43	13	11	5	279	537	542	.991
2004	78	111	23	166	303	46	14	23	4	382	714	721	.990
2005	70	122	19	173	294	77	11	14	5	391	737	752	.980
2006	97	118	14	201	301	69	12	34	5	411	813	715	1.137
2007	73	102	12	163	289	56	14	15	8	366	692	714	.969
Career	933	1,379	195	2,117	3,435	761	129	264	70	4,519	8,753	8,425	1.039

Harmon Killebrew

Year	RBI	R	HR	NR	TB	BB	HBP	SB	CS	CB	PTS	PA	P/E
1954	3	1	0	4	5	2	0	0	0	7	15	15	1.000
1955	7	12	4	15	29	9	0	0	0	38	68	89	.764
1956	13	10	5	18	39	10	0	0	0	49	85	110	.773
1957	5	4	2	7	17	2	0	0	0	19	33	33	1.000
1958	2	2	0	4	6	0	1	0	0	7	15	33	.455
1959	105	98	42	161	282	90	7	3	2	380	702	647	1.085
1960	80	84	31	133	236	71	1	1	0	309	575	517	1.112
1961	122	94	46	170	328	107	3	1	2	437	777	656	1.184
1962	126	85	48	163	301	106	4	1	2	410	736	666	1.105
1963	96	88	45	139	286	72	3	0	0	361	639	596	1.072
1964	111	95	49	157	316	93	8	0	0	417	731	682	1.072
1965	75	78	25	128	201	72	4	0	0	277	533	479	1.113
1966	110	89	39	160	306	103	2	0	2	409	729	677	1.077
1967	113	105	44	174	305	131	3	1	0	440	788	689	1.144
1968	40	40	17	63	124	70	2	0	0	196	322	371	.868
1969	140	106	49	197	324	145	5	8	2	480	874	709	1.233
1970	113	96	41	168	288	128	2	0	3	415	751	665	1.129
1971	119	61	28	152	232	114	0	3	2	347	651	624	1.043
1972	74	53	26	101	195	94	1	0	1	289	491	532	.923
1973	32	29	5	56	86	41	1	0	0	128	240	290	.828
1974	54	28	13	69	120	45	0	0	0	165	303	382	.793
1975	44	25	14	55	117	54	1	1	2	171	281	369	.762
Career	1,584	1,283	573	2,294	4,143	1,559	48	19	18	5,751	10,339	9,831	1.052

Mickey Mantle

Year	RBI	R	HR	NR	TB	BB	HBP	SB	CS	CB	PTS	PA	P/E
1951	65	61	13	113	151	43	0	8	7	195	421	386	1.091
1952	87	94	23	158	291	75	0	4	1	369	685	626	1.094
1953	92	105	21	176	229	79	0	8	4	312	664	540	1.230
1954	102	129	27	204	285	102	0	5	2	390	798	651	1.226
1955	99	121	37	183	316	113	3	8	1	439	805	638	1.262
1956	130	132	52	210	376	112	2	10	1	499	919	652	1.410
1957	94	121	34	181	315	146	0	16	3	474	836	623	1.342
1958	97	127	42	182	307	129	2	18	3	453	817	654	1.249
1959	75	104	31	148	278	93	2	21	3	391	687	639	1.075
1960	94	119	40	173	294	111	1	14	3	417	763	644	1.185
1961	128	132	54	206	353	126	0	12	1	490	902	646	1.396
1962	89	96	30	155	228	122	1	9	0	360	670	502	1.335
1963	35	40	15	60	107	40	0	2	1	148	268	213	1.258
1964	111	92	35	168	275	99	0	6	3	377	713	567	1.257
1965	46	44	19	71	163	73	0	4	1	239	381	435	.876
1966	56	40	23	73	179	57	0	1	1	236	382	393	.972
1967	55	63	22	96	191	107	1	1	1	299	491	553	.888
1968	54	57	18	93	173	106	1	6	2	284	470	547	.859
Career	1,509	1,677	536	2,650	4,511	1,733	13	153	38	6,372	11,672	9,909	1.178

Eddie Mathews

Year	RBI	R	HR	NR	TB	BB	HBP	SB	CS	CB	PTS	PA	P/E
1952	58	80	25	113	236	59	1	6	4	298	524	593	.884
1953	135	110	47	198	363	99	2	1	3	462	858	681	1.260
1954	103	96	40	159	287	113	2	10	3	409	727	601	1.210
1955	101	108	41	168	300	109	1	3	4	409	745	616	1.209
1956	95	103	37	161	286	91	1	6	0	384	706	651	1.084
1957	94	109	32	171	309	90	0	3	1	401	743	666	1.116
1958	77	97	31	143	250	85	2	5	0	342	628	649	.968
1959	114	118	46	186	352	80	3	2	1	436	808	682	1.185
1960	124	108	39	193	302	111	2	7	3	419	805	671	1.200
1961	91	103	32	162	306	93	2	12	7	406	730	672	1.086
1962	90	106	29	167	266	101	2	4	2	371	705	643	1.096
1963	84	82	23	143	248	124	1	3	4	372	658	675	.975
1964	74	83	23	134	207	85	1	2	2	293	561	590	.951
1965	95	77	32	140	256	73	3	1	0	333	613	626	.979
1966	53	72	16	109	190	63	0	1	1	253	471	517	.911
1967	57	53	16	94	171	63	3	2	4	235	423	511	.828
1968	8	4	3	9	20	5	0	0	0	25	43	57	.754
Career	1,453	1,509	512	2,450	4,349	1,444	26	68	39	5,848	10,748	10,101	1.064

Willie Mays

Year	RBI	R	HR	NR	TB	BB	HBP	SB	CS	CB	PTS	PA	P/E
1951	68	59	20	107	219	57	2	7	4	281	495	524	.945
1952	23	17	4	36	52	16	1	4	1	72	144	144	1.000
1954	110	119	41	188	377	66	2	8	5	448	824	640	1.288
1955	127	123	51	199	382	79	4	24	4	485	883	670	1.318
1956	84	101	36	149	322	68	1	40	10	421	719	650	1.106
1957	97	112	35	174	366	76	1	38	19	462	810	668	1.213
1958	96	121	29	188	350	78	1	31	6	454	830	685	1.212
1959	104	125	34	195	335	65	2	27	4	425	815	648	1.258
1960	103	107	29	181	330	61	4	25	10	410	772	669	1.154
1961	123	129	40	212	334	81	2	18	9	426	850	659	1.290
1962	141	130	49	222	382	78	4	18	2	480	924	706	1.309
1963	103	115	38	180	347	66	2	8	3	420	780	671	1.162
1964	111	121	47	185	351	82	1	19	5	448	818	665	1.230
1965	112	118	52	178	360	76	0	9	4	441	797	638	1.249
1966	103	99	37	165	307	70	2	5	1	383	713	629	1.134
1967	70	83	22	131	220	51	2	6	0	279	541	544	.994
1968	79	84	23	140	243	67	2	12	6	318	598	573	1.044
1969	58	64	13	109	176	49	3	6	2	232	450	459	.980
1970	83	94	28	149	242	79	3	5	0	329	627	566	1.108
1971	61	82	18	125	201	112	3	23	3	336	586	537	1.091
1972	22	35	8	49	98	60	1	4	5	158	256	309	.828
1973	25	24	6	43	72	27	1	1	0	101	187	239	.782
Career	1,903	2,062	660	3,305	6,066	1,464	44	338	103	7,809	14,419	12,493	1.154

Mark McGwire

Year	RBI	R	HR	NR	TB	BB	HBP	SB	CS	CB	PTS	PA	P/E
1986	9	10	3	16	20	4	1	0	1	24	56	58	.966
1987	118	97	49	166	344	71	5	1	1	420	752	641	1.173
1988	99	87	32	154	263	76	4	0	0	343	651	635	1.025
1989	95	74	33	136	229	83	3	1	1	315	587	587	1.000
1990	108	87	39	156	256	110	7	2	1	374	686	650	1.055
1991	75	62	22	115	185	93	3	2	1	282	512	585	.875
1992	104	87	42	149	273	90	5	0	1	367	665	571	1.165
1993	24	16	9	31	61	21	1	0	1	82	144	107	1.346
1994	25	26	9	42	64	37	0	0	0	101	185	172	1.076
1995	90	75	39	126	217	88	11	1	1	316	568	422	1.346
1996	113	104	52	165	309	116	8	0	0	433	763	548	1.392
1997	123	86	58	151	349	101	9	3	0	462	764	657	1.163
1998	147	130	70	207	383	162	6	1	0	552	966	681	1.419
1999	147	118	65	200	363	133	2	0	0	498	898	661	1.359
2000	73	60	32	101	176	76	7	1	0	260	462	321	1.439
2001	64	48	29	83	147	56	3	0	0	206	372	364	1.022
Career	1,414	1,167	583	1,998	3,639	1,317	75	12	8	5,035	9,031	7,660	1.179

Joe Morgan

Year	RBI	R	HR	NR	TB	BB	HBP	SB	CS	CB	PTS	PA	P/E
1963	3	5	0	8	8	5	0	1	0	14	30	30	1.000
1964	0	4	0	4	7	6	0	0	1	12	20	43	.465
1965	40	100	14	126	251	97	3	20	9	362	488	708	.689
1966	42	60	5	97	166	89	3	11	8	261	455	528	.862
1967	42	73	6	109	203	81	2	29	5	310	528	580	.910
1968	0	6	0	6	7	7	0	3	0	17	29	27	1.074
1969	43	94	15	122	199	110	1	49	14	345	589	657	.896
1970	52	102	8	146	217	102	1	42	13	349	641	658	.974
1971	56	87	13	130	237	88	1	40	8	358	618	689	.897
1972	73	122	16	179	240	115	6	58	17	402	760	680	1.118
1973	82	116	26	172	284	111	4	67	15	451	795	698	1.139
1974	67	107	22	152	253	120	3	58	12	422	726	641	1.133
1975	94	107	17	184	253	132	3	67	10	445	813	639	1.272
1976	111	113	27	197	272	114	1	60	9	438	832	599	1.389
1977	78	113	22	169	249	117	2	49	10	407	745	645	1.155
1978	75	68	13	130	170	79	2	19	5	265	525	533	.985
1979	32	70	9	93	164	93	1	28	6	280	466	538	.866
1980	49	66	11	104	172	93	0	24	6	283	491	562	.874
1981	31	47	8	70	116	66	0	14	5	191	331	378	.876
1982	61	68	14	115	203	85	2	24	4	310	540	554	.975
1983	59	72	16	115	163	89	4	18	2	272	502	504	.996
1984	43	50	6	87	128	66	1	8	3	200	374	438	.854
Career	1,133	1,650	268	2,515	3,962	1,865	40	689	162	6,394	11,424	11,329	1.008

Stan Musial

Year	RBI	R	HR	NR	TB	BB	HBP	SB	CS	CB	PTS	PA	P/E
1941	7	8	1	14	27	2	0	1	1*	29	57	49	1.163
1942	72	87	10	149	229	62	2	6	6*	293	591	536	1.103
1943	81	108	13	176	347	72	2	9	10*	420	772	701	1.101
1944	94	112	12	194	312	90	5	7	8*	406	794	667	1.190
1946	103	124	16	211	366	73	3	7	8*	441	863	702	1.229
1947	95	113	19	189	296	80	4	4	4*	380	758	677	1.120
1948	131	135	39	227	429	79	3	7	7*	511	965	694	1.390
1949	123	128	36	215	382	107	2	3	3*	491	921	721	1.277
1950	109	105	28	186	331	87	3	5	5*	421	793	645	1.229
1951	108	124	32	200	355	98	1	4	5	453	853	678	1.258
1952	91	105	21	175	311	96	2	7	7	409	759	676	1.123
1953	113	127	30	210	361	105	0	3	4	465	885	698	1.268
1954	126	120	35	211	359	103	4	1	7	460	882	705	1.251
1955	108	97	33	172	318	80	8	5	4	407	751	656	1.145
1956	109	87	27	169	310	75	3	2	0	390	728	682	1.067
1957	102	82	29	155	307	66	2	1	1	375	685	579	1.183
1958	62	64	17	109	249	72	1	0	0	322	540	549	.984
1959	44	37	14	67	146	60	0	0	2	204	338	404	.837
1960	63	49	17	95	161	41	2	1	1	204	394	378	1.042
1961	70	46	15	101	182	52	1	0	0	235	437	431	1.014
1962	82	57	19	120	220	64	3	3	0	290	530	505	1.050
1963	58	34	12	80	136	35	2	2	0	175	335	379	.884
Career	1,951	1,949	475	3,425	6,134	1,599	53	78	83*	7,781	14,631	12,712	1.151

* CS totals estimated based on known statistics

Mel Ott

Year	RBI	R	HR	NR	TB	BB	HBP	SB	CS	CB	PTS	PA	P/E
1926	4	7	0	11	25	1	0	1	0*	27	49	61	.803
1927	19	23	1	41	62	13	0	2	1*	76	158	180	.878
1928	77	69	18	128	228	52	2	3	2*	283	539	499	1.080
1929	151	138	42	247	346	113	6	6	3*	468	962	674	1.427
1930	119	122	25	216	301	103	2	9	4*	411	843	646	1.305
1931	115	104	29	190	271	80	2	10	5*	358	738	580	1.272
1932	123	119	38	204	340	100	4	6	3*	447	855	673	1.270
1933	103	98	23	178	271	75	2	1	1*	348	704	661	1.065
1934	135	119	35	219	344	85	3	0	0*	432	870	671	1.297
1935	114	113	31	196	329	82	3	7	3*	418	810	683	1.186
1936	135	120	33	222	314	111	5	6	3*	433	877	660	1.329
1937	95	99	31	163	285	102	3	7	4*	393	719	654	1.099
1938	116	116	36	196	307	118	5	2	1*	431	823	652	1.262
1939	80	85	27	138	230	100	1	2	1*	332	608	508	1.197
1940	79	89	19	149	245	100	6	6	3*	354	652	647	1.008
1941	90	89	27	152	260	100	3	5	2*	366	670	634	1.057
1942	93	118	30	181	273	109	3	6	3*	388	750	664	1.130
1943	47	65	18	94	159	95	3	7	4*	260	448	482	.929
1944	82	91	26	147	217	90	3	2	1*	311	605	494	1.225
1945	79	73	21	131	225	71	8	1	0*	305	567	532	1.066
1946	4	2	1	5	9	8	0	0	0*	17	27	78	.346
1947	0	0	0	0	0	0	0	0	0*	0	0	4	.000
Career	1,860	1,859	511	3,208	5,041	1,708	64	89	44*	6,858	13,274	11,337	1.171

* CS totals estimated based on 2:1 success ratio

Albert Pujols

Year	RBI	R	HR	NR	TB	BB	HBP	SB	CS	CB	PTS	PA	P/E
2001	130	112	37	205	360	69	9	1	3	436	846	676	1.251
2002	127	118	34	211	331	72	9	2	4	410	832	675	1.233
2003	124	137	43	218	394	79	10	5	1	487	923	685	1.347
2004	123	133	46	210	389	84	7	5	5	480	900	692	1.301
2005	117	129	41	205	360	97	9	16	2	480	890	700	1.271
2006	137	119	49	207	359	92	4	7	2	460	874	634	1.379
2007	103	99	32	170	321	99	7	2	6	423	763	679	1.124
Career	861	847	282	1,426	2,514	592	55	38	23	3,176	6,028	4,741	1.271

Manny Ramirez

Year	RBI	R	HR	NR	TB	BB	HBP	SB	CS	CB	PTS	PA	P/E
1993	5	5	2	8	16	2	0	0	0	18	34	55	.618
1994	60	51	17	94	151	42	0	4	2	195	383	336	1.140
1995	107	85	31	161	270	75	5	6	6	350	672	571	1.177
1996	112	94	33	173	320	85	3	8	5	411	757	647	1.170
1997	88	99	26	161	302	79	7	2	3	387	709	651	1.089
1998	145	108	45	208	342	76	6	5	3	426	842	663	1.270
1999	165	131	44	252	346	96	13	2	4	453	957	640	1.495
2000	122	92	38	176	306	86	3	1	1	395	747	532	1.404
2001	125	93	41	177	322	81	8	0	1	410	764	620	1.232
2002	107	84	33	158	282	73	8	0	0	363	679	518	1.311
2003	104	117	37	184	334	97	8	3	1	441	809	679	1.191
2004	130	108	43	195	348	82	6	2	4	434	824	663	1.243
2005	144	112	45	211	329	80	10	1	0	420	842	650	1.295
2006	102	79	35	146	278	100	1	0	1	378	670	558	1.201
2007	88	84	20	152	238	71	7	0	0	316	620	569	1.090
Career	1,604	1,342	490	2,456	4,184	1,125	85	34	31	5,397	10,309	8,352	1.234

Cal Ripken Jr.

Year	RBI	R	HR	NR	TB	BB	HBP	SB	CS	CB	PTS	PA	P/E
1981	0	1	0	1	5	1	0	0	0	6	8	40	.200
1982	93	90	28	155	284	46	3	3	3	333	643	655	.982
1983	102	121	27	196	343	58	0	0	4	397	789	726	1.087
1984	86	103	27	162	327	71	2	2	1	401	725	716	1.013
1985	110	116	26	200	301	67	1	2	3	368	768	718	1.070
1986	81	98	25	154	289	70	4	4	2	365	673	707	.952
1987	98	97	27	168	272	81	1	3	5	352	688	717	.960
1988	81	87	23	145	248	102	2	2	2	352	642	689	.932
1989	93	80	21	152	259	57	3	3	2	320	624	712	.876
1990	84	78	21	141	249	82	5	3	1	338	620	695	.892
1991	114	99	34	179	368	53	5	6	1	431	789	717	1.100
1992	72	73	14	131	233	64	7	4	3	305	567	715	.793
1993	90	87	24	153	269	65	6	1	4	337	643	718	.896
1994	75	71	13	133	204	32	4	1	0	241	507	484	1.048
1995	88	71	17	142	232	52	2	0	1	285	569	613	.928
1996	102	94	26	170	298	59	4	1	2	360	700	707	.990
1997	84	79	17	146	247	56	5	1	0	309	601	686	.876
1998	61	65	14	112	234	51	4	0	2	287	511	659	.775
1999	57	51	18	90	194	13	3	0	1	209	389	354	1.099
2000	56	43	15	84	140	23	3	0	0	166	334	339	.985
2001	68	43	14	97	172	26	2	0	2	198	392	516	.760
Career	1,695	1,647	431	2,911	5,168	1,129	66	36	39	6,360	12,182	12,883	.946

Brooks Robinson

Year	RBI	R	HR	NR	TB	BB	HBP	SB	CS	CB	PTS	PA	P/E
1955	1	0	0	1	2	0	0	0	0	2	4	22	.182
1956	1	5	1	5	17	1	0	0	0	18	28	45	.622
1957	14	13	2	25	42	7	1	1	0	51	101	126	.802
1958	32	31	3	60	141	31	5	1	2	176	296	507	.584
1959	24	29	4	49	120	17	2	2	2	139	237	333	.712
1960	88	74	14	148	262	35	0	2	2	297	593	651	.911
1961	61	89	7	143	265	47	4	1	3	314	600	736	.815
1962	86	77	23	140	308	42	1	3	1	353	633	697	.908
1963	67	67	11	123	215	46	1	2	3	261	507	648	.782
1964	118	82	28	172	319	51	4	1	0	375	719	685	1.050
1965	80	81	18	143	249	47	2	3	0	301	587	616	.953
1966	100	91	23	168	275	56	5	2	3	335	671	686	.978
1967	77	88	22	143	265	54	4	1	3	321	607	681	.891
1968	75	65	17	123	253	44	4	1	1	301	547	667	.820
1969	84	73	23	134	236	56	3	2	1	296	564	670	.842
1970	94	84	18	160	261	53	4	1	1	318	638	673	.948
1971	92	67	20	139	243	63	3	0	0	309	587	663	.885
1972	64	48	8	104	190	43	2	1	0	236	444	612	.725
1973	72	53	9	116	189	55	3	2	0	249	481	619	.777
1974	59	46	7	98	207	56	3	2	0	268	464	622	.746
1975	53	50	6	97	132	44	1	0	0	177	371	539	.688
1976	11	16	3	24	67	8	1	0	0	76	124	232	.534
1977	4	3	1	6	12	4	0	0	0	16	28	52	.538
Career	1,357	1,232	268	2,321	4,270	860	53	28	22	5,189	9,831	11,782	.834

Frank Robinson

Year	RBI	R	HR	NR	TB	BB	HBP	SB	CS	CB	PTS	PA	P/E
1956	83	122	38	167	319	64	20	8	4	407	741	668	1.109
1957	75	97	29	143	323	44	12	10	2	387	673	677	.994
1958	83	90	31	142	279	62	7	10	1	357	641	623	1.029
1959	125	106	36	195	315	69	8	18	8	402	792	626	1.265
1960	83	86	31	138	276	82	9	13	6	374	650	562	1.157
1961	124	117	37	204	333	71	10	22	3	433	841	636	1.322
1962	136	134	39	231	380	76	11	18	9	476	938	701	1.338
1963	91	79	21	149	213	81	14	26	10	324	622	580	1.072
1964	96	103	29	170	311	79	9	23	5	417	757	662	1.144
1965	113	109	33	189	314	70	18	13	9	406	784	674	1.163
1966	122	122	49	195	367	87	10	8	5	467	857	680	1.260
1967	94	83	30	147	276	71	7	2	3	353	647	563	1.149
1968	52	69	15	106	187	73	12	11	2	281	493	508	.970
1969	100	111	32	179	291	88	13	9	3	398	756	643	1.176
1970	78	88	25	141	245	69	7	2	1	322	604	553	1.092
1971	99	82	28	153	232	72	9	3	0	316	622	545	1.141
1972	59	41	19	81	151	55	2	2	3	207	369	405	.911
1973	97	85	30	152	261	82	10	1	1	353	657	630	1.043
1974	68	81	22	127	216	85	10	5	2	314	568	579	.981
1975	24	19	9	34	60	29	0	0	0	89	157	149	1.054
1976	10	5	3	12	24	11	0	0	0	35	59	79	.747
Career	1,812	1,829	586	3,055	5,373	1,420	198	204	77	7,118	13,228	11,743	1.126

Alex Rodriguez

Year	RBI	R	HR	NR	TB	BB	HBP	SB	CS	CB	PTS	PA	P/E
1994	2	4	0	6	11	3	0	3	0	17	29	59	.492
1995	19	15	5	29	58	6	0	4	2	66	124	149	.832
1996	123	141	36	228	379	59	4	15	4	453	909	677	1.343
1997	84	100	23	161	291	41	5	29	6	360	682	638	1.069
1998	124	123	42	205	384	45	10	46	13	472	882	748	1.179
1999	111	110	42	179	294	56	5	21	7	369	727	572	1.271
2000	132	134	41	225	336	100	7	15	4	454	904	672	1.345
2001	135	133	52	216	393	75	16	18	3	499	931	732	1.272
2002	142	125	57	210	389	87	10	9	4	491	911	725	1.257
2003	118	124	47	195	364	87	15	17	3	480	870	715	1.217
2004	106	112	36	182	308	80	10	28	4	422	786	698	1.126
2005	130	124	48	206	369	91	16	21	6	491	903	715	1.263
2006	121	113	35	199	299	90	8	15	4	408	806	674	1.196
2007	156	143	54	245	376	95	21	24	4	512	1,002	708	1.415
Career	1,503	1,501	518	2,486	4,251	915	127	265	64	5,494	10,466	8,482	1.234

Ivan Rodriguez

Year	RBI	R	HR	NR	TB	BB	HBP	SB	CS	CB	PTS	PA	P/E
1991	27	24	3	48	99	5	0	0	1	103	199	288	.691
1992	37	39	8	68	151	24	1	0	0	176	312	454	.687
1993	66	56	10	112	195	29	4	8	7	229	453	519	.873
1994	57	56	16	97	177	31	7	6	3	218	412	405	1.017
1995	67	56	12	111	221	16	4	0	2	239	461	517	.892
1996	86	116	19	183	302	38	4	5	0	349	715	685	1.044
1997	77	98	20	155	289	38	8	7	3	339	649	648	1.002
1998	91	88	21	158	297	32	3	9	0	341	657	617	1.065
1999	113	116	35	194	335	24	1	25	12	373	761	630	1.208
2000	83	66	27	122	242	19	1	5	5	262	506	389	1.301
2001	65	70	25	110	239	23	4	10	3	273	493	470	1.049
2002	60	67	19	108	221	25	2	5	4	249	465	440	1.057
2003	85	90	16	159	242	55	6	10	6	307	625	578	1.081
2004	86	72	19	139	269	41	3	7	4	316	594	575	1.033
2005	50	71	14	107	224	11	2	7	3	241	455	525	.867
2006	69	74	13	130	239	26	1	8	3	271	531	580	.916
2007	63	50	11	102	211	9	1	2	2	221	425	515	.825
Career	1,182	1,209	288	2,103	3,953	446	52	114	58	4,507	8,713	8,835	.986

Pete Rose

Year	RBI	R	HR	NR	TB	BB	HBP	SB	CS	CB	PTS	PA	P/E
1963	41	101	6	136	231	55	5	13	15	289	561	695	.807
1964	34	64	4	94	168	36	2	4	10	200	388	558	.695
1965	81	117	11	187	299	69	8	8	3	381	755	757	.997
1966	70	97	16	151	301	37	1	4	9	334	636	700	.909
1967	76	86	12	150	260	56	3	11	6	324	624	647	.964
1968	49	94	10	133	294	56	4	3	7	350	616	692	.890
1969	82	120	16	186	321	88	5	7	10	411	783	728	1.076
1970	52	120	15	157	305	73	2	12	7	385	699	728	.960
1971	44	86	13	117	266	68	3	13	9	341	575	707	.813
1972	57	107	6	158	269	73	7	10	3	356	672	729	.922
1973	64	115	5	174	297	65	6	10	7	371	719	752	.956
1974	51	110	3	158	253	106	5	2	4	362	678	770	.881
1975	74	112	7	179	286	89	11	0	1	385	743	764	.973
1976	63	130	10	183	299	86	6	9	5	395	761	759	1.003
1977	64	95	9	150	283	66	5	16	4	366	666	731	.911
1978	52	103	7	148	276	62	3	13	9	345	641	729	.879
1979	59	90	4	145	270	95	2	20	11	376	666	730	.912
1980	64	95	1	158	232	66	6	12	8	308	624	735	.849
1981	33	73	0	106	168	46	3	4	4	217	429	484	.886
1982	54	80	3	131	214	66	7	8	8	287	549	718	.765
1983	45	52	0	97	141	52	2	7	7	195	389	555	.701
1984	34	43	0	77	126	40	3	1	1	169	323	421	.767
1985	46	60	2	104	129	86	4	8	1	226	434	500	.868
1986	25	15	0	40	64	30	4	3	0	101	181	272	.665
Career	1,314	2,165	160	3,319	5,752	1,566	107	198	149	7,474	14,112	15,861	.890

Babe Ruth

Year	RBI	R	HR	NR	TB	BB	HBP	SB	CS	CB	PTS	PA	P/E
1914	2	1	0	3	3	0	0	0	0*	3	9	10	.900
1915	21	16	4	33	53	9	0	0	0*	62	128	103	1.243
1916	15	18	3	30	57	10	0	0	0*	67	127	150	.847
1917	12	14	2	24	58	12	0	0	0*	70	118	142	.831
1918	66	50	11	105	176	58	2	6	6*	236	446	380	1.174
1919	114	103	29	188	284	101	6	7	8*	390	766	542	1.413
1920	137	158	54	241	388	150	3	14	14	541	1,023	615	1.663
1921	171	177	59	289	457	145	4	17	13	610	1,188	693	1.714
1922	99	94	35	158	273	84	1	2	5	355	671	495	1.356
1923	131	151	41	241	399	170	4	17	21	569	1,051	699	1.504
1924	121	143	46	218	391	142	4	9	13	533	969	681	1.423
1925	66	61	25	102	195	59	2	2	4	254	458	426	1.075
1926	150	139	47	242	365	144	3	11	9	514	998	652	1.531
1927	164	158	60	262	417	137	0	7	6	555	1,079	691	1.562
1928	142	163	54	251	380	137	3	4	5	519	1,021	684	1.493
1929	154	121	46	229	348	72	3	5	3	425	883	587	1.504
1930	153	150	49	254	379	136	1	10	10	516	1,024	676	1.515
1931	163	149	46	266	374	128	1	5	4	504	1,036	663	1.563
1932	137	120	41	216	302	130	2	2	2	434	866	589	1.470
1933	103	97	34	166	267	114	2	4	5	382	714	575	1.242
1934	84	78	22	140	196	104	2	1	3	300	580	471	1.231
1935	12	13	6	19	31	20	0	0	0*	51	89	92	.967
Career	2,217	2,174	714	3,677	5,793	2,062	43	123	131*	7,890	15,244	10,616	1.436

* CS totals estimated based on known statistics

Ryne Sandberg

Year	RBI	R	HR	NR	TB	BB	HBP	SB	CS	CB	PTS	PA	P/E
1981	0	2	0	2	1	0	0	0	0	1	5	6	.833
1982	54	103	7	150	236	36	4	32	12	296	596	687	.868
1983	48	94	8	134	222	51	3	37	11	302	570	699	.815
1984	84	114	19	179	331	52	3	32	7	411	769	700	1.099
1985	83	113	26	170	307	57	1	54	11	408	748	673	1.111
1986	76	68	14	130	258	46	0	34	11	327	587	682	.861
1987	59	81	16	124	231	59	2	21	2	311	559	587	.952
1988	69	77	19	127	259	54	1	25	10	329	583	679	.859
1989	76	104	30	150	301	59	4	15	5	374	674	672	1.003
1990	100	116	40	176	344	50	1	25	7	413	765	675	1.133
1991	100	104	26	178	284	87	2	22	8	387	743	684	1.086
1992	87	100	26	161	312	68	1	17	6	392	714	687	1.039
1993	45	67	9	103	188	37	2	9	2	234	440	503	.875
1994	24	36	5	55	87	23	1	2	3	110	220	247	.891
1996	92	85	25	152	246	54	7	12	8	311	615	621	.990
1997	64	54	12	106	180	28	2	7	4	213	425	480	.885
Career	1,061	1,318	282	2,097	3,787	761	34	344	107	4,819	9,013	9,282	.971

Mike Schmidt

Year	RBI	R	HR	NR	TB	BB	HBP	SB	CS	CB	PTS	PA	P/E
1972	3	2	1	4	10	5	1	0	0	16	24	40	.600
1973	52	43	18	77	137	62	9	8	2	214	368	443	.831
1974	116	108	36	188	310	106	4	23	12	455	831	686	1.211
1975	95	93	38	150	294	101	4	29	12	416	716	674	1.062
1976	107	112	38	181	306	100	11	14	9	422	784	705	1.112
1977	101	114	38	177	312	104	9	15	8	432	786	667	1.178
1978	78	93	21	150	223	91	4	19	6	331	631	616	1.024
1979	114	109	45	178	305	120	3	9	5	432	788	675	1.167
1980	121	104	48	177	342	89	2	12	5	440	794	652	1.218
1981	91	78	31	138	228	73	4	12	4	313	589	434	1.357
1982	87	108	35	160	281	107	3	14	7	398	718	631	1.138
1983	109	104	40	173	280	128	3	7	8	410	756	669	1.130
1984	106	93	36	163	283	92	4	5	7	377	703	632	1.112
1985	93	89	33	149	292	87	3	1	3	380	678	645	1.051
1986	119	97	37	179	302	89	7	1	2	397	755	657	1.149
1987	113	88	35	166	286	83	2	2	1	372	704	613	1.148
1988	62	52	12	102	158	49	6	3	0	216	420	451	.931
1989	28	19	6	41	55	21	0	0	1	75	157	172	.913
Career	1,595	1,506	548	2,553	4,404	1,507	79	174	92	6,072	11,178	10,062	1.111

Al Simmons

Year	RBI	R	HR	NR	TB	BB	HBP	SB	CS	CB	PTS	PA	P/E
1924	102	69	8	163	256	30	2	16	15	289	615	644	.955
1925	129	122	24	227	392	35	1	7	14	421	875	696	1.257
1926	109	90	19	180	329	48	1	11	3	386	746	642	1.162
1927	108	86	15	179	262	31	1	10	2	302	660	458	1.441
1928	107	78	15	170	259	31	3	1	4	290	630	509	1.238
1929	157	114	34	237	373	31	1	4	2	407	881	629	1.401
1930	165	152	36	281	392	39	1	9	2	439	1,001	611	1.638
1931	128	105	22	211	329	47	3	3	3	379	801	563	1.423
1932	151	144	35	260	367	47	1	4	2	417	937	718	1.305
1933	119	85	14	190	291	39	2	5	1	336	716	648	1.105
1934	104	102	18	188	296	53	2	3	2	352	728	613	1.188
1935	79	68	16	131	224	33	2	4	6	257	519	561	.925
1936	112	96	13	195	275	49	2	6	4	328	718	620	1.158
1937	84	60	8	136	182	27	4	3	2	214	486	453	1.073
1938	95	79	21	153	240	38	2	2	1	281	587	512	1.146
1939	44	39	7	76	144	24	2	0	0*	170	322	381	.845
1940	19	7	1	25	32	4	0	0	0	36	86	85	1.012
1941	1	1	0	2	4	1	0	0	0	5	9	25	.360
1943	12	9	1	20	35	8	0	0	1	42	82	141	.582
1944	2	1	0	3	3	0	0	0	0	3	9	6	1.500
Career	1,827	1,507	307	3,027	4,685	615	30	88	64*	5,354	11,408	9,515	1.199

* CS totals estimated based on known statistics

Sammy Sosa

Year	RBI	R	HR	NR	TB	BB	HBP	SB	CS	CB	PTS	PA	P/E
1989	13	27	4	36	67	11	2	7	5	82	154	203	.759
1990	70	72	15	127	215	33	6	32	16	270	524	579	.905
1991	33	39	10	62	106	14	2	13	6	129	253	338	.749
1992	25	41	8	58	103	19	4	15	7	134	250	291	.859
1993	93	92	33	152	290	38	4	36	11	357	661	641	1.031
1994	70	59	25	104	232	25	2	22	13	268	476	458	1.039
1995	119	89	36	172	282	58	5	34	7	372	716	629	1.138
1996	100	84	40	144	281	34	5	18	5	333	621	541	1.148
1997	119	90	36	173	308	45	2	22	12	365	711	694	1.024
1998	158	134	66	226	416	73	1	18	9	499	951	722	1.317
1999	141	114	63	192	397	78	3	7	8	477	861	712	1.209
2000	138	106	50	194	383	91	2	7	4	479	867	705	1.230
2001	160	146	64	242	425	116	6	0	2	545	1,029	711	1.447
2002	108	122	49	181	330	103	3	2	0	438	800	666	1.201
2003	103	99	40	162	286	62	5	0	1	352	676	589	1.148
2004	80	69	35	114	247	56	2	0	0	305	533	539	.989
2005	45	39	14	70	143	39	2	1	1	184	324	424	.764
2007	92	53	21	124	193	34	3	0	0	230	478	454	1.053
Career	1,667	1,475	609	2,533	4,704	929	59	234	107	5,819	10,885	9,896	1.100

Tris Speaker

Year	RBI	R	HR	NR	TB	BB	HBP	SB	CS	CB	PTS	PA	P/E
1907	1	0	0	1	3	1	0	0	0*	4	6	20	.300
1908	9	12	0	21	32	4	2	3	2*	39	81	125	.648
1909	77	73	7	143	241	38	7	35	28*	293	579	606	.955
1910	65	92	7	150	252	52	6	35	27*	318	618	608	1.016
1911	70	88	8	150	251	59	13	25	20*	328	628	589	1.066
1912	90	136	10	216	329	82	6	52	41*	428	860	675	1.274
1913	71	94	3	162	277	65	7	46	36*	359	683	608	1.123
1914	90	101	4	187	287	77	7	42	29	384	758	668	1.135
1915	69	108	0	177	225	81	7	29	25	317	671	652	1.029
1916	79	102	2	179	274	82	4	35	27	368	726	647	1.122
1917	60	90	2	148	254	67	7	30	24*	334	630	612	1.029
1918	61	73	0	134	205	64	3	27	21*	278	546	549	.995
1919	63	83	2	144	214	73	8	15	12*	298	586	595	.985
1920	107	137	8	236	310	97	5	10	13	409	881	674	1.307
1921	75	107	3	179	272	68	2	2	4	340	698	588	1.187
1922	71	85	11	145	258	77	1	8	3	341	631	516	1.223
1923	130	133	17	246	350	93	4	8	9	446	938	693	1.354
1924	65	94	9	150	248	72	4	5	7	322	622	575	1.082
1925	87	79	12	154	248	70	4	5	2	325	633	518	1.222
1926	86	96	7	175	253	94	0	6	1	352	702	661	1.062
1927	73	71	2	142	232	55	4	9	8	292	576	597	.965
1928	30	28	3	55	86	10	2	5	1	102	212	212	1.000
Career	1,529	1,882	117	3,294	5,101	1,381	103	432	340*	6,677	13,265	11,988	1.107

* CS totals estimated based on known statistics

Frank Thomas

Year	RBI	R	HR	NR	TB	BB	HBP	SB	CS	CB	PTS	PA	P/E
1990	31	39	7	63	101	44	2	0	1	146	272	240	1.133
1991	109	104	32	181	309	138	1	1	2	447	809	700	1.156
1992	115	108	24	199	307	122	5	6	3	437	835	711	1.174
1993	128	106	41	193	333	112	2	4	2	449	835	676	1.235
1994	101	106	38	169	291	109	2	2	3	401	739	517	1.429
1995	111	102	40	173	299	136	6	3	2	442	788	647	1.218
1996	134	110	40	204	330	109	5	1	1	444	852	649	1.313
1997	125	110	35	200	324	109	3	1	1	436	836	649	1.288
1998	109	109	29	189	281	110	6	7	0	404	782	712	1.098
1999	77	74	15	136	229	87	9	3	3	325	597	590	1.012
2000	143	115	43	215	364	112	5	1	3	479	909	707	1.286
2001	10	8	4	14	30	10	0	0	0	40	68	79	.861
2002	92	77	28	141	247	88	7	3	0	345	627	628	.998
2003	105	87	42	150	307	100	12	0	0	419	719	662	1.086
2004	49	53	18	84	135	64	6	0	2	203	371	311	1.193
2005	26	19	12	33	62	16	0	0	0	78	144	124	1.161
2006	114	77	39	152	254	81	6	0	0	341	645	559	1.154
2007	95	63	26	132	255	81	7	0	0	343	607	624	.973
Career	1,674	1,467	513	2,628	4,458	1,628	84	32	23	6,179	11,435	9,785	1.169

Honus Wagner

Year	RBI	R	HR	NR	TB	BB	HBP	SB	CS	CB	PTS	PA	P/E
1897	39	37	2	74	111	15	1	19	13*	133	281	258	1.089
1898	105	80	10	175	241	31	6	27	18*	287	637	635	1.003
1899	113	98	7	204	282	40	11	37	25*	345	753	626	1.203
1900	100	107	4	203	302	41	8	38	26*	363	769	580	1.326
1901	126	101	6	221	271	53	7	49	33*	347	789	619	1.275
1902	91	105	3	193	247	43	14	42	29*	317	703	599	1.174
1903	101	97	5	193	265	44	7	46	31*	331	717	571	1.256
1904	75	97	4	168	255	59	4	53	36*	335	671	558	1.203
1905	101	114	6	209	277	54	7	57	39*	356	774	616	1.256
1906	71	103	2	172	237	58	10	53	36*	322	666	590	1.129
1907	82	98	6	174	264	46	5	61	42*	334	682	580	1.176
1908	109	100	10	199	308	54	5	53	36*	384	782	641	1.220
1909	100	92	5	187	242	66	3	35	24*	322	696	591	1.178
1910	81	90	4	167	240	59	5	24	16*	312	646	640	1.009
1911	89	87	9	167	240	67	6	20	14*	319	653	558	1.170
1912	102	91	7	186	277	59	6	26	18*	350	722	634	1.139
1913	56	51	3	104	159	26	5	21	14*	197	405	454	.892
1914	50	60	1	109	175	51	2	23	16*	235	453	616	.735
1915	78	68	6	140	239	39	4	22	15	289	569	625	.910
1916	39	45	1	83	160	34	8	11	7*	206	372	484	.769
1917	24	15	0	39	70	24	1	5	3*	97	175	264	.663
Career	1,732	1,736	101	3,367	4,862	963	125	722	491*	6,181	12,915	11,739	1.100

* CS totals estimated based on known statistics

Ted Williams

Year	RBI	R	HR	NR	TB	BB	HBP	SB	CS	CB	PTS	PA	P/E
1939	145	131	31	245	344	107	2	2	1	454	944	677	1.394
1940	113	134	23	224	333	96	3	4	4	432	880	661	1.331
1941	120	135	37	218	335	147	3	2	4	483	919	606	1.517
1942	137	141	36	242	338	145	4	3	2	488	972	671	1.449
1946	123	142	38	227	343	156	2	0	0	501	955	672	1.421
1947	114	125	32	207	335	162	2	0	1	498	912	693	1.316
1948	127	124	25	226	313	126	3	4	0	446	898	638	1.408
1949	159	150	43	266	368	162	2	1	1	532	1,064	730	1.458
1950	97	82	28	151	216	82	0	3	0	301	603	416	1.450
1951	126	109	30	205	295	144	0	1	1	439	849	675	1.258
1952	3	2	1	4	9	2	0	0	0	11	19	12	1.583
1953	34	17	13	38	82	19	0	0	1	100	176	110	1.600
1954	89	93	29	153	245	136	1	0	0	382	688	526	1.308
1955	83	77	28	132	225	91	2	2	0	320	584	417	1.400
1956	82	71	24	129	242	102	1	0	0	345	603	503	1.199
1957	87	96	38	145	307	119	5	0	1	430	720	546	1.319
1958	85	81	26	140	240	98	4	1	0	343	623	517	1.205
1959	43	32	10	65	114	52	2	0	0	168	298	331	.900
1960	72	56	29	99	200	75	3	1	1	278	476	390	1.221
Career	1,839	1,798	521	3,116	4,884	2,021	39	24	17	6,951	13,183	9,791	1.346

Carl Yastrzemski

Year	RBI	R	HR	NR	TB	BB	HBP	SB	CS	CB	PTS	PA	P/E
1961	80	71	11	140	231	50	3	6	5	285	565	643	.879
1962	94	99	19	174	303	66	3	7	4	375	723	719	1.006
1963	68	91	14	145	271	95	1	8	5	370	660	668	.988
1964	67	77	15	129	256	75	2	6	5	334	592	646	.916
1965	72	78	20	130	265	70	1	7	6	337	597	571	1.046
1966	80	81	16	145	256	84	1	8	9	340	630	680	.926
1967	121	112	44	189	360	91	4	10	8	457	835	680	1.228
1968	74	90	23	141	267	119	2	13	6	395	677	664	1.020
1969	111	96	40	167	306	101	1	15	7	416	750	707	1.061
1970	102	125	40	187	335	128	1	23	13	474	848	697	1.217
1971	70	75	15	130	199	106	1	8	7	307	567	620	.915
1972	68	70	12	126	178	67	4	5	4	250	502	535	.938
1973	95	82	19	158	250	105	0	9	7	357	673	652	1.032
1974	79	93	15	157	229	104	3	12	7	341	655	633	1.035
1975	60	91	14	137	220	87	2	8	4	313	587	634	.926
1976	102	71	21	152	236	80	1	5	6	316	620	636	.975
1977	102	99	28	173	282	73	1	11	1	366	712	643	1.107
1978	81	70	17	134	221	76	3	4	5	299	567	611	.928
1979	87	69	21	135	233	62	2	3	3	297	567	590	.961
1980	50	49	15	84	168	44	0	0	2	210	378	412	.917
1981	53	36	7	82	120	49	0	0	1	168	332	390	.851
1982	72	53	16	109	198	59	2	0	1	258	476	523	.910
1983	56	38	10	84	155	54	2	0	0	211	379	437	.867
Career	1,844	1,816	452	3,208	5,539	1,845	40	168	116	7,476	13,892	13,991	.993

Index

Aaron, Hank, 198, 247–48, 254, 267–68, 285–87, 289, 358, 371, 375
Abreu, Bobby, 248
Adcock, Joe, 50
Agee, Tommie, 216, 217
Allen, Richie, 292
Alley, Gene, 148
Alomar, Roberto, 87, 88, 93, 100–101, 113, 346, 376
Amoros, Sandy, 180, 181
Anderson, Garret, 180
Anderson, Sparky, 88, 89
Anson, Cap, 314
Aparicio, Luis, 148, 153, 154, 171, 178, 331
Appling, Luke, 148, 153, 155, 178
Ashburn, Richie, 216
Averill, Earl, 216, 222, 239, 340, 368
Avila, Bobby, 88

Babb, Charlie, 148, 149
Babe, Loren, 122, 123
Baerga, Carlos, 88–90
Bagwell, Jeff, 50, 55, 66–67, 80, 348, 368, 369, 377
Baines, Harold, 292, 293
Baker, Dusty, 180
Baker, Home Run, 122
Bancroft, Dave, 148
Banks, Ernie, 291, 292, 297, 303–4, 311, 350–51, 378
Bannister, Alan, 298

Battey, Earl, 18
Beckley, Jake, 315
Belanger, Mark, 148, 178
Bell, Buddy, 122
Bell, Cool Papa, 322
Belle, Albert, 180, 185, 186, 206, 339, 368
Beltran, Carlos, 216
Bench, Johnny, 17, 18, 23, 29–30, 33, 38, 39, 43–45, 356, 379
Berra, Yogi, 17, 18, 23, 31–33, 38, 43–44, 46, 181, 356, 372, 380
Bichette, Dante, 180
Biggio, Craig, 88, 93, 94, 112, 333
The Bill James Historical Baseball Abstract (James), 80
Blair, Paul, 216
Boggs, Wade, 122, 127, 128, 130, 140, 333
Bonds, Barry, 3, 13, 179, 180, 185, 194–95, 208–10, 359, 367, 371, 381
Bonds, Bobby, 248
Boone, Bob, 18, 48
Bottomley, Jim, 50, 55, 56, 78, 339
Boudreau, Lou, 148, 153, 156, 173, 178, 343
Bowa, Larry, 148, 178
Boyer, Clete, 122–24
Boyer, Ken, 122, 124–25, 140
Bresnahan, Roger, 18, 19, 47
Brett, George, 121, 122, 127, 130–32, 141–43, 351, 382
Brock, Lou, 152, 180, 185, 187, 338
Brooks, Hubie, 292–94

Brouthers, Dan, 315
Brown, Willard, 323
Buckner, Bill, 50
Burkett, Jesse, 315
Butler, Brett, 216

Caminiti, Ken, 122
Campanella, Roy, 18, 23, 33–34,
    38, 43, 349, 383
Canseco, Jose, 292
Career P/E Averages
    catchers, 18
    center fielders, 216
    first basemen, 50
    left fielders, 180
    multiposition players, 292
    right fielders, 248
    second basemen, 88
    shortstops, 148
    third basemen, 122
    top 25 players, 367–68
Carew, Rod, 292, 297, 298, 311,
    342
Carey, Max, 216
Carter, Gary, 18, 22–24, 42, 340
Cash, Norm, 50
Castilla, Vinny, 122
Catchers, 17–18
    best 162-game averages, 23
    career P/E averages, 18
    Categories 1–3, 19–23
    Category 4, 24–28
    Category 5, 29–40
    resemblances between, 47–48
    Top 10, 41–46
Categories of players, 9, 11–12
Category 1 players, 12
    catchers, 22–23
    center fielders, 217–18
    first basemen, 54–55
    left fielders, 181

multiposition players, 295
right fielders, 253
second basemen, 89
shortstops, 149
third basemen, 123
Category 2 players, 11–12
    catchers, 20–22
    center fielders, 217, 220
    first basemen, 53–54
    left fielders, 181–83
    multiposition players, 293–94,
        297
    right fielders, 249, 251
    second basemen, 89–90, 92
    shortstops, 152
    third basemen, 123–25
Category 3 players, 11
    catchers, 19–21
    center fielders, 218–21
    first basemen, 51–52
    left fielders, 183–85
    multiposition players, 293–96
    right fielders, 249–52
    second basemen, 90–93
    shortstops, 149–52
    third basemen, 124–27
Category 4 players, 11
    catchers, 24–28
    center fielders, 222–25
    first basemen, 56–65
    left fielders, 186–93
    multiposition players, 298–302
    right fielders, 255–66
    second basemen, 94–99
    shortstops, 154–62
    third basemen, 128–30
Category 5 players, 11
    calculating P/E Averages,
        373–424
    catchers, 29–40
    center fielders, 226–37

first basemen, 66–77
left fielders, 194–205
multiposition players, 303–10
right fielders, 267–82
second basemen, 100–111
shortstops, 163–70
third basemen, 131–38
Caught-stealing totals, 6–7
Center fielders, 215–16
  best 162-game averages, 221
  career P/E Averages, 216
  Categories 1–3, 217–21
  Category 4, 222–25
  Category 5, 226–37
  Top 10, 238–43
Cepeda, Orlando, 8, 50, 55, 57,
  335–36
Cerv, Bob, 180–82
Cey, Ron, 122
Chance, Frank, 50
Charleston, Oscar, 323
Chavez, Eric, 121, 122
Clark, Jack, 292
Clark, Will, 50, 84
Clarke, Fred, 315–16
Clemente, Roberto, 247, 248, 254,
  269–70, 284, 347, 384
Clift, Harlond, 122
Cobb, Ty, 6–7, 170, 216, 226–27,
  240–42, 307, 359, 367, 370,
  385
Cochrane, Mickey, 17, 18, 23, 30,
  35–36, 38, 43–45, 352, 386
Colavito, Rocky, 248
Coleman, Vince, 152, 180, 182–83
Collins, Eddie, 88, 93, 102–3, 114,
  118, 351–52, 387
Collins, Jimmy, 122
Combs, Earle, 215, 216, 223, 238,
  338–39
Complete bases, 5–7

Concepcion, Dave, 148–50, 178
Connor, Roger, 316
Cooper, Cecil, 50
Cramer, Doc, 216
Crandall, Del, 18
Crawford, Sam, 248, 254, 255
Cronin, Joe, 148, 153, 157, 172,
  178, 339
Cuyler, Kiki, 248

Damon, Johnny, 216
Dandridge, Ray, 323
Davis, George, 316
Dawson, Andre, 184, 248, 254, 256,
  333
Delahanty, Ed, 316–17
Delgado, Carlos, 50
Dent, Bucky, 192
Dickey, Bill, 18, 23, 37–38, 42, 347,
  388
DiMaggio, Dom, 216
DiMaggio, Joe, 215, 216, 228–29,
  240–41, 243, 360, 362, 367,
  371, 389
Doby, Larry, 216
Doerr, Bobby, 88, 93, 95
Doubtful Hall of Fame players,
  12
Doyle, Larry, 88, 118
Duffy, Hugh, 317
Durocher, Leo, 161

Edmonds, Jim, 216
Effectiveness, 1. *See also*
  Production
Efficiency, 1–3
  complete bases, 5–7
  defined, 2
  measures of, *xii*, 3–4
Elliott, Bob, 122
Evans, Darrell, 145, 292

Evers, Johnny, 88, 118
Ewing, Buck, 317

Fernandez, Tony, 148
Ferrell, Rick, 18, 47
Fielder, Cecil, 50
First basemen, 49–50
  best 162-game averages, 55
  best postseason series, 84–85
  career P/E averages, 50
  Categories 1–3, 51–55
  Category 4, 56–65
  Category 5, 66–77
  Top 10, 78–83
Fisk, Carlton, 18, 23, 25, 41
Flick, Elmer, 248
Flood, Curt, 216
Foster, George, 180, 183
Fox, Nellie, 88, 119
Foxx, Jimmie, 9, 49, 50, 55, 68–69,
    80–82, 201, 358, 367, 369–71,
    390
Francesa, Mike, 126
Freehan, Bill, 18–20
Frisch, Frankie, 88, 93, 96, 113,
    118, 340
Furillo, Carl, 248

Gaetti, Gary, 122
Galarraga, Andres, 50
Garciaparra, Nomar, 148
Gardner, Larry, 122
Garvey, Steve, 50, 51
Gehrig, Lou, 9, 49, 50, 55, 70–71,
    80–81, 83, 261, 360, 362–63,
    367, 369–71, 391
  best postseason series, 84–85
  Murderer's Row, 99
  and Wally Pipp, 53
Gehringer, Charlie, 88, 93, 104–5,
    115, 117, 119, 355, 392

Giambi, Jason, 50
Giambi, Jeremy, 163
Gibson, Bob, 204
Gibson, Josh, 323–24
Gonzalez, Juan, 248, 254, 257, 335
Gordon, Joe, 88, 90–91, 119
Goslin, Goose, 180, 185, 188, 335
Grace, Mark, 50, 84
Grant, Frank, 324
Greenberg, Hank, 49, 50, 55,
    72–73, 80–82, 354, 367, 370,
    393
  and Willie McCovey, 58
  missed playing time, 60
Grich, Bobby, 88
Griffey, Ken, Jr., 216, 230–31, 240,
    354, 394
Griffey, Ken, Sr., 248
Grissom, Marquis, 216
Groat, Dick, 148
Groh, Heinie, 122
Guerrero, Vladimir, 248–50, 368
Gwynn, Tony, 3, 247, 248, 254, 258,
    283, 342

Hack, Stan, 122
Hafey, Chick, 180
Hall of Fame status, system for
    specifying, 12–13
Hamilton, Billy, 317–18
Hartnett, Gabby, 18, 23, 26, 41, 335
Heilmann, Harry, 248, 254, 259,
    283, 343–44
Heist, Al, 216–18
Helton, Todd, 50, 367
Henderson, Rickey, 6, 152, 180,
    185, 196–97, 208, 354, 395
Herman, Billy, 88
Hernandez, Keith, 50, 301
Herr, Tommy, 88
Hill, Pete, 324

Hirschbeck, John, 101
Hit-by-pitch totals, 6
Hodges, Gil, 50–52
Home runs, 5
Hooper, Harry, 248
Hornsby, Rogers, 87, 88, 93, 106–7,
    115, 116, 118, 355, 367, 369,
    396
Howard, Elston, 18
Hrbek, Kent, 50

Imminent Hall of Fame players,
    12
Intentional walks, 6
Irvin, Monte, 324–25

Jackson, Joe, 180, 183–84
Jackson, Reggie, 248, 254, 271–72,
    284, 346, 397
Jackson, Travis, 148
James, Bill, 80
Jennings, Hughie, 318
Jeter, Derek, 148, 153, 163–64, 168,
    173, 178, 348, 398
Johnson, Bob, 180
Johnson, Davey, 88
Johnson, Howard, 122, 125
Johnson, Judy, 325
Johnson, Walter, 170
Jones, Andruw, 216
Jones, Chipper, 67, 121–22, 127,
    129, 141, 337
Judge, Joe, 50

Kaat, Jim, 135
Kalas, Harry, 219
Kaline, Al, 248, 254, 260, 341–42
Keeler, Willie, 318
Kell, George, 122
Kelley, Joe, 318
Kelly, George, 50

Kelly, King, 319
Kent, Jeff, 87, 88, 93, 97, 112, 119,
    336
Killebrew, Harmon, 145, 292, 297,
    305–6, 311, 347, 399
Kiner, Ralph, 180, 185, 189, 207,
    219, 341
Klein, Chuck, 248, 254, 261, 331,
    370
Kluszewski, Ted, 50
Knight, Ray, 122
Knoblauch, Chuck, 88
Knoop, Bobby, 88

Lajoie, Nap, 88, 93, 98, 113, 341,
    369
Landis, Kenesaw Mountain, 206
Lansford, Carney, 122
Larkin, Barry, 148, 153, 158, 171,
    178, 331
Larsen, Don, 31
Lazzeri, Tony, 88, 93, 99, 330
Left fielders, 179–80
    best 162-game averages, 185
    career P/E Averages, 180
    Categories 1–3, 181–85
    Category 4, 186–93
    Category 5, 194–205
    Top 10, 206–11
Leonard, Buck, 325
Lindstrom, Freddie, 292
Lloyd, Pop, 325
Lofton, Kenny, 216
Lollar, Sherm, 18
Lombardi, Ernie, 18
Long, Terrence, 163
Lopes, Davey, 88, 91
Lopez, Al, 18, 20–21
Lopez, Javy, 18
Luzinski, Greg, 180
Lynn, Fred, 216, 218–19

Mackey, Biz, 326
Maddox, Garry, 216, 219
Maddux, Greg, 135
Madlock, Bill, 122
Magee, Sherry, 180
Malzone, Frank, 122
Mantle, Mickey, 13–14, 135–36,
    215, 216, 232–33, 240, 244,
    358, 368, 371, 400
Manush, Heinie, 180, 185, 190
Maranville, Rabbit, 148
Marion, Marty, 148
Maris, Roger, 248, 250–51, 257
Martinez, Edgar, 292, 294–95
Martinez, Tino, 50
Mathews, Eddie, 121, 122, 127,
    133–34, 141, 345–46, 401
Mathewson, Christy, 19, 149,
    170
Mattingly, Don, 50, 52
May, Lee, 50, 84
Mays, Willie, 5, 198, 216, 234–35,
    240–42, 244, 359, 371, 402
Mazeroski, Bill, 87, 88
McCarthy, Tommy, 319
McCovey, Willie, 50, 55, 58, 337
McEwing, Joe, 292, 295
McGee, Willie, 216
McGinnity, Joe, 149
McGriff, Fred, 50, 55, 59
McGwire, Mark, 50, 55, 74–75, 79,
    281, 345, 368, 403
McMillan, Roy, 148
McPhee, Bid, 319
McReynolds, Kevin, 180
Medwick, Joe, 180, 185, 191, 206,
    338
Meusel, Bob, 99, 180
Military service, 212
Minoso, Minnie, 180
Mitchell, Kevin, 180

Mize, Johnny, 50, 55, 60, 79, 344,
    367
Molitor, Paul, 146, 292, 297, 299,
    311, 336–37
Monroe, Marilyn, 229
Morgan, Joe, 88, 93, 108–9,
    115–16, 119, 353, 404
Most Valuable Players. *See* MVP
    shares
Multiposition players, 291–92
   best 162-game averages, 297
   career P/E Averages, 292
   Categories 1–3, 293–97
   Category 4, 298–302
   Category 5, 303–10
Munson, Thurman, 18, 21
Murcer, Bobby, 216
Murphy, Dale, 216, 257
Murray, Eddie, 50, 55, 61, 79, 343
Musial, Stan, 179, 180, 185, 186,
    198–99, 208–10, 357, 371, 405
MVP shares, 13–14
   career, 371–72
   for New York Yankees, 17
   second basemen, 118–19

Negro League stars, 321–28
Net runs, 5, 8
Nettles, Graig, 122
Nineteenth-century stars, 313–20
No chance for Hall of Fame
    players, 12

Offensive Production and
    Efficiency Average (P/E
    Average), *xii*, 4–9
   career. *See* Career P/E Averages
   complete bases in, 5–7
   components of, 4–7
   formulation of, 7–9
   levels of, 14–15

measures incorporated in, 4
net runs in, 5
single-season, 369–70
Oglivie, Ben, 180
Olerud, John, 50
Oliva, Tony, 248
Oliver, Al, 292
162-game averages, 14
  catchers, 23
  center fielders, 221
  first basemen, 55
  left fielders, 185
  multiposition players, 297
  right fielders, 254
  second basemen, 93
  shortstops, 153
  third basemen, 127
O'Neill, Buck, 326
O'Neill, Paul, 248
Ordonez, Rey, 148
O'Rourke, Jim, 319–20
Ortiz, David, 292, 368
Otis, Amos, 216
Ott, Mel, 248, 254, 273–74, 285, 349, 368, 406

Palmeiro, Rafael, 50, 55, 62
Palmer, Jim, 217
Parker, Dave, 51, 248, 254, 262, 332
Parker, Wes, 50
Parrish, Lance, 18, 22
P/E Average. *See* Offensive Production and Efficiency Average
Peckinpaugh, Roger, 148
Pena, Tony, 18, 22
Pendleton, Terry, 122
Pepitone, Joe, 50
Perez, Tony, 8, 50, 55, 58, 63
Piazza, Mike, 18, 23, 27, 42, 335

Pinson, Vada, 216
Pipp, Wally, 50, 53
Porter, Darrell, 18
Posada, Jorge, 18, 163
Possible Hall of Fame players, 12
Post, Wally, 248, 251
Powell, Boog, 50
Power, Vic, 50
Probable Hall of Fame players, 12
Production
  measures of, *xii*, 1–3
  net runs, 5
  as ultimate goal of players, 2
Puckett, Kirby, 216, 224, 238, 340
Pujols, Albert, 50, 55, 76–77, 80, 352, 367, 372, 407

Rader, Doug, 122
Raines, Tim, 180, 184–85
Ramirez, Manny, 248, 254, 273–74, 285, 351, 367, 408
Randolph, Willie, 88
Reese, Pee Wee, 148
Reynolds, Harold, 88
Rice, Jim, 180, 185, 192, 207, 344
Rice, Sam, 248, 254, 263
Richardson, Bobby, 88
Right fielders, 247–48
  best 162-game averages, 254
  career P/E Averages, 248
  Categories 1–3, 249–53
  Category 4, 255–66
  Category 5, 267–82
  Top 10, 283–88
Ripken, Cal, Jr., 148, 153, 165–66, 174, 175, 178, 350, 409

Rivers, Mickey, 216, 220
Rizzuto, Phil, 32, 148

Robinson, Brooks, 121, 122, 127, 130, 135–36, 141–43, 350, 410

Robinson, Frank, 247–48, 254, 277–78, 285–87, 289, 355, 371, 411

Robinson, Jackie, 32, 119, 292, 297, 300, 312, 344

Rodriguez, Alex, 148, 153, 167–68, 174, 175, 178, 349, 356, 367, 372, 412

Rodriguez, Ivan, 18, 23, 39–40, 43, 413

Rolen, Scott, 121, 122

Rose, Pete, 146, 292, 297, 307–8, 312, 345, 414

Rosen, Al, 122

Roush, Edd, 216

Rudi, Joe, 180

Runs batted in, 5

Runs scored, 5

Ruth, Babe, 170, 200, 247–48, 254, 279–80, 285, 286, 288, 289, 360, 363, 367, 369, 370, 415
  home runs, 53
  Murderer's Row, 99

Samuel, Juan, 88

Sandberg, Ryne, 87, 88, 93, 110–11, 114, 119, 346, 416

Santiago, Benito, 18, 48

Santo, Ron, 122, 126, 139

Santop, Louis, 326

Sax, Steve, 88, 92

Schalk, Ray, 18

Schang, Wally, 18

Schmidt, Mike, 121, 122, 127, 137–38, 141–42, 144, 357, 371, 417

Schoendienst, Red, 88

Scott, George, 50

Scully, Vin, 269

Second basemen, 87–88
  best 162-game averages, 93
  career P/E Averages, 88
  Categories 1–3, 89–93
  Category 4, 94–99
  Category 5, 100–111
  MVPs, 118–19
  Top 10, 112–17

Sewell, Joe, 148, 153, 159, 178

Sheffield, Gary, 248

Shortstops, 147–48
  best 162-game averages, 153
  career P/E Averages, 148
  Categories 1–3, 149–53
  Category 4, 154–62
  Category 5, 163–70
  defensive analysis, 177–78
  Top 10, 171–76

Simmons, Al, 180, 185, 200–201, 208, 353, 367, 369, 418

Simmons, Ted, 18, 23, 28

Single-season P/E Averages, 369–70

Sisler, George, 50, 55, 64, 338

Skowron, Moose, 50, 53–54

Slaughter, Enos, 248, 254, 264, 331

Smith, Ozzie, 135, 148, 153, 154, 160, 172, 178, 336

Snider, Duke, 216, 225, 239, 244, 341

Snyder, Cory, 248, 249

Soriano, Alfonso, 87, 88

Sosa, Sammy, 248, 254, 281–82, 284, 348, 419

Speaker, Tris, 216, 236–37, 239, 353, 420

Stargell, Willie, 292, 297, 301, 312, 342

Statistics. *See also* Offensive Production and Efficiency Average
  efficiency, 2–3
  limitations of, 1–4
  production, 2
Stearnes, Turkey, 326–27
Stengel, Casey, 54
Steroid controversy, 13
Stolen bases, 6–7, 152
Strawberry, Darryl, 248, 252
Sundberg, Jim, 18
Suttle, Mule, 327
Suzuki, Ichiro, 248

Taylor, Ben, 327
Tejada, Miguel, 148
Templeton, Garry, 148
Terry, Bill, 8, 50, 55, 65, 78, 343
Third basemen, 121–22
  best 162-game averages, 127
  career P/E Averages, 122
  Categories 1–3, 123–27
  Category 4, 128–30
  Category 5, 131–38
  honorable mentions, 145–46
  Top 10, 139–44
Thomas, Frank, 292, 297, 309–10, 312, 352, 368, 371, 421
Thome, Jim, 292, 368
Thompson, Sam, 320
Throneberry, Marv, 50, 54–55
Tinker, Joe, 148
Top 3 players
  Joe DiMaggio, 362
  Lou Gehrig, 362–63
  Babe Ruth, 363

Top 10 players
  Hank Aaron, 358
  Barry Bonds, 359
  catchers, 41–46
  center fielders, 238–43
  Ty Cobb, 359
  Joe DiMaggio, 362
  first basemen, 78–83
  Jimmie Foxx, 358
  Lou Gehrig, 362–63
  left fielders, 206–11
  Mickey Mantle, 358
  Willie Mays, 359
  right fielders, 283–88
  Babe Ruth, 363
  second basemen, 112–17
  shortstops, 171–76
  third basemen, 139–44
  Ted Williams, 360
Top 100 players, 329–63
  factors in arriving at, 329–30
  list of, 330–63
Torre, Joe, 146, 292, 296
Torriente, Cristobal, 327
Total bases, 6
Trammell, Alan, 148, 150–51
Traynor, Pie, 122, 127, 130, 140, 332
Troskey, Hal, 50

Uecker, Bob, 18, 22–23

Vail, Mike, 248, 253
Van Slyke, Andy, 216
Vaughan, Arky, 148, 153, 161, 178
Ventura, Robin, 122
Vernon, Mickey, 50
Versalles, Zoilo, 148, 151

Vidro, Jose, 88
Vizquel, Omar, 148, 153, 154, 162, 172, 178, 336

Wagner, Honus, 147, 148, 153, 169–70, 174, 176, 178, 356, 422
Walks, 6
Wallace, Bobby, 148
Wallach, Tim, 122
Waner, Lloyd, 216
Waner, Paul, 248, 254, 265, 335
Ward, Monte, 320
Washington, U. L., 148, 150, 152
Wells, Willie, 328
Wheat, Zack, 180
Whitaker, Lou, 88, 92–93, 151
White, Bill, 50
White, Frank, 87, 88
Williams, Bernie, 216

Williams, Billy, 180, 185, 193, 335
Williams, Ken, 180
Williams, Matt, 122, 126–27, 139
Williams, Ted, 179, 180, 185, 202–3, 208, 209, 211–13, 360, 367, 370, 371, 423
Wills, Maury, 148, 152–53
Wilson, Hack, 216, 220–21, 367, 369
Wilson, Jud, 328
Winfield, Dave, 248, 254, 266, 332

Yastrzemski, Carl, 180, 185, 204–5, 207, 345, 424
York, Rudy, 50
Youngblood, Joel, 292, 297
Youngs, Ross, 248
Yount, Robin, 292, 297, 302, 312, 337